INVISIBLE NOW: BOB DYLAN IN THE 1960s

Bob Dylan's stuff in dressing room, Buffalo,
New York State, 1964. Photo © Daniel Kramer

Invisible Now:
Bob Dylan in the 1960s

JOHN HUGHES
University of Gloucestershire, UK

LONDON AND NEW YORK

First published 2013 by Ashgate Publisher

Published 2016 by Routledge
2 Park Square, Milton Park, Abingdon, Oxfordshire OX14 4RN
711 Third Avenue, New York, NY 10017, USA

First issued in paperback 2016

Routledge is an imprint of the Taylor & Francis Group, an informa business

Copyright © John Hughes 2013

John Hughes has asserted his right under the Copyright, Designs and Patents Act, 1988, to be identified as the author of this work.

All rights reserved. No part of this book may be reprinted or reproduced or utilised in any form or by any electronic, mechanical, or other means, now known or hereafter invented, including photocopying and recording, or in any information storage or retrieval system, without permission in writing from the publishers.

Notice:
Product or corporate names may be trademarks or registered trademarks, and are used only for identification and explanation without intent to infringe.

British Library Cataloguing in Publication Data
Hughes, John.
  Invisible now : Bob Dylan in the 1960s. – (Ashgate popular and folk music series)
  1. Dylan, Bob, 1941– Influence. 2. Popular culture – United States – History – 20th century. 3. Nineteen sixties.
  I. Title II. Series
  782.4'2166'092–dc23

The Library of Congress has cataloged the printed edition as follows:
Hughes, John, 1957–
  Invisible now : Bob Dylan in the 1960s / by John Hughes.
    pages cm. – (Ashgate popular and folk music series)
  Includes bibliographical references and index.
  ISBN 978–1–4094–3002–5 (hardcover : alk. paper)
  1. Dylan, Bob, 1941– Criticism and interpretation. 2. Popular music – United States – 1961–1970 – History and criticism.
  I. Title.
  ML420.D98H77 2013
  782.42164092–dc23   2012042529

ISBN 13: 978-1-138-26876-0 (pbk)
ISBN 13: 978-1-4094-3002-5 (hbk)

For David, Joanna, and Mark

Contents

List of Figures ix
Preface xi

PART ONE: THEMES

I	'Continual Becoming'	3
II	Humour	7
III	Photographs	15
IV	Voice	25
V	Leave Taking	35
VI	Aversiveness	43
VII	Inspiration	51

PART TWO: THE 1960S

1	'Mind Like a Trap': *Bob Dylan, The Freewheelin' Bob Dylan, The Times They Are A-Changin'*	59
2	'Weird Monkey': *Another Side of Bob Dylan* and *Bringing It All Back Home*	85
3	'There is No Eye': *Highway 61 Revisited*	111
4	'Trapeze Artist': *Blonde on Blonde*	133
5	'Ghosts Passing Through on Their Way to Tangiers': *The Basement Tapes*	155

6 'Not Too Far But Just Far Enough So's We Can Say That We've
   Been There': *John Wesley Harding* and *Nashville Skyline* 175

Notes *195*
Select Bibliography *217*
Index *227*

List of Figures

	Frontispiece: Bob Dylan's stuff in dressing room, Buffalo, New York State, 1964. Photo © Daniel Kramer	ii
1	Dylan with Victor Maymudes in tree, Woodstock, New York State, 1964. Photo © Daniel Kramer	106
2	Dylan in dark glasses, New York City, 1964. Photo © Daniel Kramer	107
3	Dylan and John Sebastian at 'BRINGING IT ALL BACK HOME' session, New York City, 1965. Photo © Daniel Kramer	108
4	Forest Hills Stadium sound check, New York City, 1965. Photo © Daniel Kramer	109
5	Dylan backlit on stage, Forest Hills Stadium, New York City, 1965. Photo © Daniel Kramer	110
6	Dylan on stage, England, 1966. Photo © Barry Feinstein Photography	130
7	Dylan with children, Liverpool, 1966. Photo © Barry Feinstein Photography	131
8	Dylan and The Band (Robbie Robertson, Richard Manuel, Rick Danko, Garth Hudson, Levon Helm), Woodie Guthrie Memorial Concert, Carnegie Hall, New York City, 1968. Photo © Elliott Landy, LandyVision Inc.	151
9	Dylan with son Jesse Dylan outside his Byrdcliffe home, Woodstock, NY, 1968. Photo © Elliott Landy, LandyVision Inc.	152
10	Dylan and Sara Dylan on the porch of Byrdcliffe home, Woodstock, NY, 1968. Photo © Elliott Landy, LandyVision Inc.	152
11	Dylan in his living room, Byrdcliffe home, Woodstock, NY, 1968. Photo © Elliott Landy, LandyVision Inc.	153
12	Dylan outside his Byrdcliffe home, Saturday Evening Post session, Woodstock, NY, 1968. Photo © Elliott Landy, LandyVision Inc.	153
13	Dylan outside Elliott Landy's home, Nashville Skyline photo sessions, Woodstock, NY, 1969. Photo by © Elliott Landy, LandyVision Inc.	173
14	Dylan at his Byrdcliffe home, Nashville Skyline photo sessions, Woodstock, NY, 1969. Photo by © Elliott Landy, LandyVision Inc	174

Preface

Bob Dylan's televised press conference in the studios of KQED in San Francisco on 3 December 1965 is a genial *tour de force*, as well as a mid-60s comedy of manners. Jazz critic Ralph J. Gleason introduces Dylan as 'one of America's leading poets' to an audience including beat luminaries Michael McClure, Allen Ginsberg, and Lawrence Ferlinghetti, as well as sundry journalists, news anchors, promoters, aspiring writers, students, activists, musicians and comedians.[1] The questioning is opened by a disturbingly fixated photographer who would in later life claim (not implausibly it seems) to be San Francisco's infamous Zodiac killer.[2] Dylan wears a sharply tailored wool jacket and a twenties-style collar pin. He variously fidgets in his chair, purses his mouth, chews his lip, lights cigarettes, and intermittently supports his face with his hand. His demeanour is breezy and ebullient, and he often mimes comic embarrassment or desperation at the overblown claims or miscomprehension directed his way. Some moments he stalls, appearing vacant, apathetic or at a loss. At others, he is ignited, retaliating sardonically or with inimitable, drawling responses that appear nonsensical or blithely dismissive. When asked if he would rather be thought of as a 'singer or a poet', he replies that he thinks of himself as 'more as a song and dance man'. Nor can his work be described as 'folk-rock': 'I like to think of it more in terms of vision music … it's mathematical music … The words are just as important as the music' (Artur, 235). And when the words come to him, he can hear the music at the same time. When asked what his 'new book' is about, he answers 'just about all kinds of different things – rats, balloons' (Artur, 240).

Benjamin Hedin takes Dylan's KQED 'performance' as a master class in hip, in the put-on and put-down. The singer is careless of meaning and '[c]learly ad-libbing in search of the most absurd answers to each query'.[3] However, from another aspect Dylan's responses are characteristically suggestive – as if he is cryptically saying more than he knows. When asked which poets he admires, he includes W.C. Fields and 'the trapeze family from the circus' (alongside Rimbaud and Allen Ginsberg), and it can be said that Dylan's performance here incorporates much of Fields's stock-in-trade – elements of vaudeville, repartee, and juggling – as well the trapeze artist's elating sense of flight (Artur, 236). Pursuing this last metaphor, Dylan answers are those of someone launching himself, as if across a void, and riskily dependent on his intuitive skill in making verbal connections, catching hold of meaning. Words and images for Dylan, after all (as he often complained in the 1960s), do not communicate a definite message.[4] Rather they are vehicles of response, means of transport or 'vision', their incidental flaws and failings inseparable from their dynamic occasions.

Certainly, in the KQED conference Dylan's answers are all the more intriguing because they appear in this way to come out of thin air. In general terms, his art at this time works by way of a creative commerce with the unseen, its forward impetus inseparable from surrender to what comes *ex nihilo*. Three days earlier, on 30 November 1965, very newly married, he had recorded two versions of 'Visions of Johanna' backed by The Hawks, and at the Community Theatre Berkeley on 4 December he will debut the song. A lyric of visions and of the night, it is often taken as one of those songs that signal a turning point: here a new departure into the world of *Blonde on Blonde*, with its transfixing art of subjective dislocation. However, to listen to these experimental early versions (provisionally entitled "Freeze Out") one can detect Dylan still taking blind steps across the threshold that separates the music of 1965 and 1966. This electrified, acerbic lover's plaint has yet to enter the rapt, dissociative, hypnotic dimension that the song will soon occupy and which will be ever more expansively unfurled in the concert halls of 1966.

My main focus in this book is on describing such effects of emergence in Dylan's work in the 1960s, and in tracing the galvanic, qualitative shifts of his artistic sensibility. In 2004 he said that '[i]n the early years everything had been like a magic carpet ride for me' and it is this sense of inspiration as a magic vehicle, deployed in ways that are thrilling, open, and often unaccountable that I pursue.[5] Always an artist in transit, Dylan's originality with words and phrasing at this time dealt essentially in irresistible disjunctions, surges, and adaptations, displaying what Eric Von Schmidt called the capacity of his mind for 'strange jumps, like electricity'.[6] The heedless, risky momentariness of Dylan's art – the sense that it was discovering itself in what it discovers, and that it was riding near to a fall – was internal to its effect. Its careering quality brings to mind John Ashbery's observations that 'recklessness is what makes experimental art beautiful', and that such beauty is heightened by the impression that it may be 'founded on nothing'.[7] Unsurprisingly, Dylan would often deny that his 1960s achievement had anything to do with premeditation or any career plan: 'I did that accidentally [...] I was doing something, you don't know what it is, you're just doing it ... .'[8] Always resistant to attempts to explain or define what he does, in the studios of KQED he disowned the separate roles of poet, pop star, prophet or youth leader, and refused to decode his recent work such as *Highway 61 Revisited* – with its division between its bleak view of social conformity ('rats') and its euphoric sense of uplift and escape ('balloons').

Nonetheless, at least one question from 3 December remains to this day a pressing one. Broadcaster Claude Mann asks Dylan 'Can you explain your attraction?' and he rebuffs the question, answering 'My attraction to *what*?'[9] Any genuine answer would need to acknowledge the feedback loop between Dylan's inspiration in this period and the contexts that amplified and incorporated it – all the massive socio-historic convulsions and tectonic cultural shifts that granted popular song such a heady, exponential increase in significance, power, and resonance. Greil Marcus testified to the euphoric combination of critique and possibility in the air at the Berkeley concert of the same night as the San Francisco conference.[10] Marcus found the aesthetic, subjective, and political to be utterly fused on stage, as if all were simultaneously at stake within the whole mysterious and spell-binding theatre of gesture, speech, dress that Dylan manifested: 'There was a way in which he would throw an arm out, and you'd feel as if you'd been grabbed, as if someone was questioning all the basic assumptions by which you lived your life' (Marcus, *Bob Dylan*, 188). For Marcus the concert was a sort of forest-fire, consuming all the social paraphernalia of proscription, legitimacy, institution: 'And by the end – and this could be five minutes later, five days, five months – you're questioning the meaning of life. That's what happened in that performance' (Greil Marcus, *Bob Dylan*, 189). Marcus's response can seem extravagant, but it is by no means unrepresentative, and it pointedly raises the central issue of Dylan's cultural status in the mid-60s as an exemplary avatar of emancipation, an artist whose powers of self-projection appear inseparable from the social cruxes, and the ever-widening, ramifying circles of political, artistic and social contestation that spread out from his career.[11]

For Marcus indeed, Dylan at this time resembled some demiurge, conjuring an unknown future out of chaos, or a magus who conducted an often exhilarating, privileged sense of possibility. By the same token, the excitement and freedom Marcus describes in December 1965 was inseparable from a prior sense of cancellation and negation. Dylan's creativity begins with a riposte, his expansive powers inseparable from combustible elements of remonstration, provocation, defiance or protest. This raises a conviction at the heart of this book: self-truth for Dylan is a matter primarily not of message but of process, a function of a turning away, and an overturning, that involve also a self-dividing motion, an inner creative imperative of self-displacement.[12] A corollary is that both he and his listener are in essential ways always still unknown, and that what he turns towards is still indefinite.[13] To be oneself in a yet unknown way, after all, is at the heart of what the songs describe, and at the heart of Dylan's values as a writer and performer. But, equally importantly, it is at the heart of the response they produce in the listener. It follows that beyond theme and enactment, any attempt to account for Dylan's 'attraction' involves one respecting the enthusiasm and shifts in sensibility that his work bring about in his audience.[14]

The dynamics of subjectivity within Dylan's work accordingly are displayed simultaneously in the content, performances, and effects of the songs. The drama of expression in his work is all at once a matter of representation, enactment and transmission. To be schematic for a moment, one might say that his creativity obeys a sort of fractal principle of endlessly variable constitution, his inspiration subject to the intermissions of a generative power of self-difference. And when the magic takes place, its productions can unaccountably appear wholly resistant to precedent, singular and spontaneously self-organising. Subjectively speaking, the effect is to convert the self into a kind of vacuum, 'invisible now', its lack of availability indistinguishable not only from refusal, but from the exhilarating, inrushing, sense of possibility that it relays to the listener. To take a tiny, rather random example, this dynamic is manifest in a telling moment in Martin Scorsese's *No Direction Home*, when Dylan rounds on his French interviewer who accuses him of insincerity: 'I'm not sincere at all … I'm not any more sincere than you are …'[15] Sincerity is disowned through this reply as an instrument of conformity. As a moral category it is a kind of guard-rail necessary for the social rat-run or, perhaps, a trap that pins us to precedent and prevents us getting carried away. In any case it keeps our feet on the ground, reminds us who we are ... Yet the further implication of Dylan's words is that rejecting what others call sincerity is the best way of renewing it, by reclaiming it as yet to be discovered.[16] In such small exchanges, there typically floats free a tiny, ballooning, possibility of transcendence, based on this refusal of socially underwritten forms of subjectivity.[17]

Because my book asks what Dylan's art does, and how it works and works on his audience, it follows that it is not primarily about one or other of his politics, his life, his spirituality, his cultural impact, his image, his musicological debts or influence, the 1960s, or even his words as such – though it continually touches on all these. Rather, I am concerned with the internal workings of Dylan's inspiration as it disarticulates verbal art, song, and cultural identity from within, and over and again challenges itself to fashion new creative passages between them. In so doing, it recreates song as a genuinely popular and profound form of art while also confronting his listener to recreate himself, herself. The French thinker Gilles Deleuze touched on the transformative and creative features of Dylan's work, describing him as 'an astonishing producer rather than an author ... with his clown's mask, with a technique of contriving and yet improvising each detail'.[18] Clearly the notions of improvising, becoming, and producing that Deleuze associates with Dylan's creativity can usefully be identified with his work, and they highlight also its essentially temporal, emergent, *eventual* character. At San Francisco someone asks: 'What's more important to you: The way that your music and words sound, or the content, the message?' He answers:

> The whole thing while it's happening. The whole total sound of the words, what's really going down is – it either happens or it doesn't happen, you know. That's what I feel is ... just the thing that is happening there at that time. (Artur, 246)

Of course, the further challenge is to describe the significance and quality of what is 'happening' on stage at Newport in 1964, or 1965, in the basement in 1967, or in the spiralling, fulminating climax of the Free Trade Hall concert in 1966. Performances of this kind can be said to be dynamic in themselves and dynamos for various kinds of cultural change, as well as sources of huge, emancipating elation for the listener. My attempt in what follows at times will be to trace some passages between such performances and their larger conditions, circumstances, or effects. An important part of such occasions is their singularity and Dylan's way of tapping into kinetic powers that marshal the unfolding potentials of an unknown self, and that transform a stage into an event. Reviewing the two Berkeley shows of December 1965 (where Dylan appeared with all the members of The Hawks, except Levon Helm) Gleason, a recent convert, concluded that the show afforded perhaps 'a glimpse of the future' and that 'it is a very special and highly emotional happening every time he comes alive on the stage'.[19] Sam Shepard's *Rolling Thunder Logbook* is a meditation on such matters:

> This is Dylan's true magic. Leave aside his lyrical genius for a second and just watch this transformation of energy which he carries ... He's infused the room with a high feeling of life-giving excitement. It's not the kind of energy that drives people off the deep end but the kind that brings courage and hope and above all brings life pounding into the foreground.[20]

The following pages pursue such interlocking aspects of Dylan's vital inspiration as a singer, performer, and enigmatic cultural figure throughout the 1960s. I have chosen to concentrate on this decade because it offers such an obvious narrative arc and displays Dylan's gifts so forcibly. Because Dylan's impact and relation to his audience are so multiform and mobile, I will interwork discussions of the work with references not only to larger political or biographical contexts, but also to press conferences, photographs, and particular performances. Part One that follows unfolds my main argument. However, it can usefully be emphasised here that the book holds to a simple focus through what is obviously confounding, singular, diverse, or complex in all this material. Following Dylan's own words, I take the idea of becoming as my main topic. It can be easily described: Dylan's art is essentially temporal and conflictual in its configurations. It projects a sensibility in motion between a discarded past and an unresolved future. I take this ethical and existential drama of an ungrounded, transformative subjectivity as bound up with the most minute, as well as the most large-scale contexts, manifestations and qualities of his work, and with the shifts in attitude, response, feeling, that Dylan makes available to his listeners through his songs.[21] Freedom for Dylan is inseparable from an emancipating attitude of rejection in which the self is deducted from its social conditions. Autonomy is felt on the pulse and through the veins, as the self is introduced, now without prescriptions, into its innate capacity to renew itself, and to join itself, potentially, to different possibilities of truth and expression. To this day, if Dylan's world tour is never-ending, it is because it must begin again, every night.

Within the ever-burgeoning field of Dylan writing, one finds that many of the essential contexts have been given expert and nuanced treatment already. Clinton Heylin and Michael Gray in particular were the pioneers, in the first land-rush of writing on Dylan, who staked out so much of the broad territory. Heylin's meticulous industry will remain for a long time the first port of call for anyone interested in pursuing the facts about Dylan's life, the where-and-when of his compositions, the dates and detail of his recordings, even the micro-facts of the man's day-to-day existence.[22] Michael Gray was the first critic to write in a sustained way of the literary and imaginative dimensions of Dylan's art, and further to connect his work (through successive revisions of *Song and Dance Man*) to the musical and literary traditions that underpinned Dylan's imagination.[23] After this first generation of magisterial writers, encyclopaedic in ambition, studies have clearly become more specific, but the standard of writing, insight, and research remains equally high, as more narrowly circumscribed topics have lent themselves to cultivated study.

Confining myself to the period of this study, it is impossible not to mention my appreciation of Mike Marqusee's very fine account of the intersecting political and aesthetic dimensions of Dylan's sixties writing,[24] Mark Polizzotti's scintillating book on *Highway 61 Revisited*, Stephen Scobie's searching *Alias Bob Dylan Revisited*, and Christopher Ricks's brilliant, painstaking demonstration of how far Dylan's words can sustain literary examination in *Dylan's Visions of Sin*.[25] Again, there are biographies, from Anthony Scaduto's vivacious *Bob Dylan*, to Daniel Mark Epstein's poised *The Ballad of Bob Dylan*,[26] and Robert Shelton's inward memoir and biography, *No Direction Home*.[27] The two books that are possibly closest to my account in topic and approach are Paul Williams's accounts of Dylan as performer in *Bob Dylan: Performing Artist* and *Watching The River Flow*.[28] Further, one has to mention the stylish work and deep research of David Hajdu's *Positively 4th Street* and Sean Wilentz's *Bob Dylan in America*, as well as the original, regional perspective offered by David Pichaske in his *Song of the North Country*.[29] C.P. Lee's *Like the Night* and Toby Thompson's *Positively Main Street* are marvellous, indispensable memoirs.[30] And all the time, there is Greil Marcus, whose haunting evocations of Dylan's work and his imaginative world, remain utterly inimitable, a kind of verbal auxiliary to the music they celebrate.[31] Further, new titles appear almost on a daily basis, dealing with Dylan's politics, his life, particular phases and albums, his religion, and so on. Last of all, as I came to the end of writing this book, I found its themes (with a predictable mixture of pleasure and chagrin) explicitly anticipated by Perry Meisel in a review of Ricks and Marcus. Meisel is someone who has emphasised the intractable generic and imaginative disjunctions of Dylan's work:

> ... Dylan is as distant from himself as the rest of us are.
> Dylan's work both is and is about this dislocation within the self, especially as he grows older. Dislocation is not inhibitive; it is enabling and productive. Temporal movement or deferred action is Dylan's active principle both poetically and musically, the very nature of his labor.[32]

From there it was a short step for me to Meisel's book, *The Myth of Popular Culture*, which reflects on these issues of critical and cultural reception, and touches on many preoccupations in what follows, not least the central question for me: how can one begin to describe, to do justice to 'the full effect' of Dylan's art?[33] Inevitably also, there are many personal debts that I need to acknowledge. Alan Brown, Rob Chapple, David Hughes, Roy Kelly, C.P. Lee, Ian Thackray, Jill Terry and Neil Wynn all offered valuable feedback on early versions of the material included here. Mark Ford and Paul Rosenbloom read late drafts of the book very closely and made many suggestions that I have incorporated with gratitude. I am grateful also to the University of Mississippi Press for allowing me to reproduce and rework material from a piece on Dylan and Britain ("'It's Not British Music,

It's American Music": Bob Dylan and Britain') that was published in their 2012 volume, *Transatlantic Roots Music: Folk, Blues, and National Identities*, edited by Jill Terry and Neil A. Wynn. Further, I would like to acknowledge John Wraith, editor of *The Bridge*, who has allowed me to reproduce material from three pieces (for which fuller details are supplied in the bibliography): one, also entitled 'Invisible Now', was a dry-run for many of the ideas that run through this book; while another 'Through the Looking Glass', was a version of the discussion of photographic images of Dylan in the 1960s that follows in Part One; and a third, "There Was No In-Between' was the discussion of the voice that similarly follows there.[34] I am grateful also to the University of Gloucestershire for funding the photographs and index for the book. At Ashgate, Heidi Bishop and Celia Barlow have provided expert assistance in bringing this project through the different publication stages and eventually to press. Finally, I would like to thank photographers Daniel Kramer and Elliott Landy for being so generous with their time and their work. In a similar spirit, Dave Brolan oversaw the inclusion here of two photographs by the late Barry Feinstein.

PART ONE
Themes

I
'Continual Becoming'

In Scorsese's *No Direction Home*, Bob Dylan gives voice to the belief that the artist should remain in a 'continual state of becoming'. As everyone knows, the idea of self-transformation is familiar and indispensable in all kinds of respects in discussing Dylan's work and career. However, I think it is important to distinguish it from another, superficially similar, idea that recurrently attaches to it. This is the notion that self-change for Dylan has to do with him being a 'protean' or 'chameleon' figure. On this view, it is as if the dynamic or drama of selfhood involved were a matter of successively assuming identities, like taking off and putting on (or hiding behind) one mask after another. Speaking of the Hibbing days, Richard Williams writes that '[i]t was at this time that he began to try on other identities',[1] while Greil Marcus puts it memorably: 'few performers have made their way onto the stage of the twentieth century with a greater collection of masks' (Marcus, *The Old Weird America*, xviii).[2] Stephen Scobie's book places the idea at its centre: 'What Dylan has always presented to us is a succession of "shifting masks"' ... Identity for Dylan is always hidden ... mask or disguise' (Scobie, 35). Michael J. Gilmour writes that 'Bob Dylan has spent nearly fifty years as a pubic figure hiding behind masks'.[3] Mark Polizzotti suggests that *Highway 61 Revisited* is an exception to the general rule that Dylan's is an art of self-dissimulation:

> Dylan has always presented a persona, which is to say (following the etymology of the word) that he has always worn masks – whether the clean-cheeked innocence of his folksinger days, the jawline scrub of his country period, or the more overt whiteface of the Rolling Thunder Revue. *Highway 61* is perhaps the only moment where he shows us, and himself, what it looks and sounds like to be Bob Zimmerman, the rock n' roll kid with the dark imagination and truckloads of attitude, not to mention crateloads of insecurity; the only time he challenged us to know just how it feels. (Polizzotti, 21)

Nicholas Roe lucidly makes a similar point, but in terms of vocal mimicry, a kind of ventriloquism:

> Unlike nearly every other writer, for whom 'finding a voice' or unique verbal identity may be an imperative, Bob Dylan is apparently most himself as a sublimely capable alias, merged into a babel of others' voices.[4]

Are we to take from this, though, that Dylan is a cipher whose face or voice is always changing as he rushes to imitate or merge with this one or another? As

Roe says, Dylan has 'no stable identity', and indeed he can be seen as someone perpetually and calculatedly 'recasting his image and music', switching as 'Guthriesque folk-protester' becomes 'electric rocker to ballad-preacher', and so on.[5] But, how are we to think of this impulse to self-change? Is Dylan a master of disguises, the mass-culture version of the men from the carnival who fascinated him as a boy, Napoleon or George Washington in blackface, and whom he discusses at the beginning of *No Direction Home*?

Broadly, my view is that the idea of a career made up of an imitative kind of identity-play is deeply misleading, though so prevalent as to constitute one of the most dominant clichés around. It is both the ready-to-hand shorthand passed on by every journalist as well as something of an orthodoxy among knowledgeable writers on Dylan. This is not to deny though some important truths wrapped in the idea: no-one doubts Dylan modelled himself on Guthrie, and his current persona cannily references something like the 'Old, Weird America' of which Marcus first spoke in *Invisible Republic*.[6] Again, as Roe suggests, a virtue of the idea of disguise is that it highlights Dylan's elusiveness. This apparent non-availability at any moment of his career is, after all, a key part of his abiding fascination, the sense that he is, like the girl in "Like a Rolling Stone", somehow both 'invisible now', and with 'no direction home'.[7] Above all, it importantly highlights the fact that much of Dylan's work has to do with a drama of identity – a process that is not only perpetually intriguing, mysterious, and surprising, but also unique in popular music, not least for the relations between the songs and the life.

The central problem with the trope of the mask, though, is that it reduces Dylan to a one-man Noh theatre (or one-man repertory troupe, perhaps), as if his creativity involved merely a kind of virtuosity in imitation, in rehearsing a series of static *dramatis personae*. Most importantly, the ideas of a mask or ventriloquism themselves distort and obscure the ways in which self-renewal works in Dylan's songs and throughout his career. Against this, I would say that Dylan's creativity obeys not a desire to hide behind impersonations, but an essential and recurrent temporal dynamic that leaves him always in motion between two incarnations of the self, past and future. There is the one to which he cannot return, and the one he has not yet reached.[8] So, to begin with, one can admit that Dylan has clearly cultivated people's fascination with his selfhood in many ways, as in the liner notes, for instance, to 'Up to Me' on *Biograph*, where he makes the link to Rimbaud's famous dictum, '*Je est un autre*': 'I don't think of myself as Bob Dylan. It's like Rimbaud said, "I is another".'[9] As suggested, though, if the self who sings Dylan's songs is always partly 'not there', this is not because he is pretending to be someone else, but because the self is always divided, strung out, in time. Dylan's best work always has this theatre and tension of a self who is illegible, caught between a discarded, rejected, or superseded version of who he has been, and a future self that he has not yet become. Indefiniteness and obscurity are internal to this transitional subjectivity, in motion between the *no longer* and the *not yet*. As Roe points out, the Latin meaning of alias was, originally, '"at another time"' (Corcoran, ed., 88), and Dylan, one can say, is one who, like Hamlet, finds always that the 'time is out of joint'.[10]

II
Humour

Many of Dylan's comments in interview or press conferences – witty, barbed, enigmatic, fleet-footed, retaliatory, gnomic, unfathomable – are certainly reminiscent of Hamlet, as in the memorable remark in the February 1966 *Playboy* interview that 'People have one great blessing – obscurity – and not really too many people are thankful for it.'[1] It would not be an overstatement to say that Dylan's career and work perpetually cultivate, in the face of world fame, this need for remaining, as it were, imperceptible in plain view. The need is to be not who you had been thought to be, to be an alias to the self, refusing to allow people to play on you like an instrument, as Hamlet puts it, or pluck the heart out of the mystery. So, the irrepressible, mercurial, laconic figure of the San Francisco press conference is mostly inviting and charming, as we have seen, though incapable of fitting himself to his audience's lumbering, off-beam questions. Humour, wit, and personal openness weave momentary intimacies with the audience, but the point is the inverse ratio between these revelations of self, on the one hand, and the content of what he says, on the other. The aim of this teasing play is always a purposeful inaccessibility, a refusal to be identified or pinned down, to play the game of access, of comprehensibility. Often noted, this is neatly described by Polizzotti as Dylan's 'psychic tug-of-war with the press and the public', his way of 'pushing them away while doing his best to keep them coming back for more' (Polizzotti, 14).

Indeed, Dylan's quicksilver humour in its mid-60s heyday is so rich, so varied, so far-reaching and inventive a resource, that it could provide a study in its own right. Usually delivered straightfaced and deadpan, Dylan is like a matador deftly side-stepping the antagonist who wishes to impale him, before retaliating unseen. It is usually an expectation embedded in the question that is exposed by Dylan's fugitive wit, and the laughter carries an exhilarating dividend, as the terms of the discussion are turned over and assumptions are laid belly-up. Often, the humour is further compounded by the confusion, pomposity, or obtuseness of the questioner who ploughs on, seemingly oblivious, but reduced now to coming across as merely condescending, or else desperately intent on ignoring the emptiness of his own words. This kind of verbal confrontation is clear in these exchanges from the opening minutes of the Los Angeles press conference of 16 December 1965.[2] Dylan is noticeably less personable, and his humour more barbed, than in San Francisco not two weeks previously:

> *Interviewer 1*: … I wonder if you could tell me, that among folk singers, or if you are properly characterised as a folk singer, how many, would you say, could be characterised as protest singers today?

Dylan: Hmmm ... I don't understand. Could you ask the question again?
Interviewer 1 (pedantically): Yeah. How many people who labour in the same musical vineyard in which you toil, how many are protest singers? (patronisingly) That is, people who use their music, use the songs, to protest the social state in which we live today – the matter of war, or the matter of crime, or whatever it might be.
Dylan: How many?
Interviewer 1: Yes, are there many?
Dylan: Yeah, I think there's about a hundred and thirty six. [Laughter]
Interviewer 1: You mean exactly a hundred and thirty six?
Dylan: Uhhh – either a hundred thirty six or a hundred and forty two.
[…]

Interviewer 2: ... Is it true that you've changed your name, and if so, what was your real name?
Dylan: My real name was Kunezevitch, and I changed it to ... uh ... to avoid obvious ... uh ... relatives that come up to you in different parts of the country, and ... uh ... want tickets for, tickets to the concerts and stuff like that.
Interviewer 2: It was Kunezevitch?
Dylan: Kunezevitch, yes.
Interviewer 1: That was the first or the last name?
Dylan: That was the first name. [Laughter and applause] I don't really want to tell you what the last name was.
[…]

Interviewer 3: Bob? Do you have any movie plans coming up in the near future?
Dylan: Yeah.
Interviewer3: What would you like to do?
Dylan: (aside) Uh, she's very excited! Uh, it ... uh ... just make a movie.
Interviewer3: Would you play yourself or would you actually act, do something different than you are?
Dylan: No, I'm gonna play my mother [Laughter ...]
Interviewer 3: What would you call the movie – any idea?
Dylan: Uh, No ... Oh ... *Mother Revisited*.

Dylan's gift for straight-face repartee reveals what is socially determined in the question through an excess of definition or weirdness that blows the questioners' circuits. He divests the interviewer's words of their conventional supports, and reveals how coercive the questions actually are. In so doing, he both lays bare how desperate is the journalist's blind need for definition and fact, while also showing how far this is bound up with paranoid fantasy and normative pressure. The interviewer is left like a cartoon character, panicking in mid-air as the ground disappears beneath his feet. Certainly, he is unable to emulate Dylan's own virtuosity or agility in improvising, as the singer jumps stag-like from remark to remark, often capping himself in the process ('No, I'm gonna play my mother').

Undoubtedly the answers can be taken merely as trivial word-play bent on dismantling the generic apparatus of the interview, but there is also more going on. Dylan's answers betray a mind intuitively working beneath the surface, often registering like sonar some hitherto undisclosed aspect while radically and secretly diverting the course of the discussion. Like Hamlet's words or the free associative improvisations of Lenny Bruce, his rejoinders often carry a mysterious arsenal of implication. Nat Hentoff in March 1966 asks him how he gets his kicks these days, and Dylan replies: 'I hire people to look into my eyes, and then I have them kick me' (a fair enough account of his predicament, when one thinks of it). 'And that's the way you get your kicks?' continues Hentoff, to which Dylan replies 'No. Then I forgive them. That's where my kicks come in' (a fair enough parody of the middle-American Judeo-Christian ethic for the interviewer to chew on, when one thinks of it) (Artur, 321). Again in Los Angeles he is asked:

> *Interviewer 1*: What does the word protest mean to you?
> *Dylan*: To me? It means – uh – uh – singing, you know, when you don't really want to sing.

Dylan gives the interviewer a more literal answer than he can handle: a protest singer is someone who sings under protest, under constraint ... But though the facetious absurdity of the answer does its business on the surface, it is again true that there is a paradoxical underlying truth here, should the interviewer be capable of hearing it. After all, Dylan could be said to have spent so much of 1964 and 1965 cuffed to his former material. He was indeed someone singing what and when 'you don't really want to sing'. Such answers involve an abrupt shift of direction, a rapid change of co-ordinates. The exchanges resemble a card game in which Dylan backs himself to deal words and turn them over, trumping his opponent.

At times, though, Dylan's attitude can be more openly exasperated or dismissive. Visibly weary, his answers at Los Angeles are much more astringent:

> *Interviewer 4*: Do you really feel the things that you write and sing?
> *Dylan* (riled): What is there to feel? Name me some thing [...]
> *Interviewer 1*: We are talking about standard emotions – we are talking about pain, or remorse, or love ... do you experience those?
> *Dylan*: I have none of those feelings at all.
> *Interviewer*: What sort of feelings do you have when you write a song? [...]
> *Dylan*: I don't have to explain my feelings. I'm not on trial.
> [...]
>
> *Interviewer 5*: Why are you putting us, and the rest of the world on so?

> *Dylan*: I'm not, I'm just trying to answer your questions – you know – as good as you can ask them.

Dylan is still conducting an anti-interview, but is now needled into direct confrontation. His hostility is directed against the interview game itself. His answers target the set-up whereby he is supposed to owe an answer to questions that are stupid, intrusive, unanswerable, or badly framed. What appeared breezily zany and surreal now seems bitingly appropriate to a situation where genuine questions are not being asked – where journalists who have never heard the songs meaninglessly quiz him over and again about his methods, his intentions, his sincerity, his background, his politics, his earnings, his spending, his taste in cars, his haircut, his appearance, his drug use, the draft, the war, other singers, his thoughts on folk-rock and protest and other musical genres, his opinions on Danish girls and the Green Berets ('I was thinking of joining them if they want me' [Artur, 358]), on his possible status as a leader of the youth or of 'Singers With A Message', and whether he feels the songs, or means them.

In this context, Dylan is intriguing because he appears all at the same time unprotected and in control, highly sensitised yet wholly impervious. He is constructed as a monster of fame, to be poked, prodded, and locked up within the sort of cultural clichés that his work essentially unpicks. His answers imply that the only sane recourse is not to mime dialogue or offer 'opinion', so much as to put the skids under the whole process. Ironic side-spin, more or less concealed, is one element in his armoury in 1965, as when he imitates the nice young man with the High Sheriff's lady in *Don't Look Back* while her sons ('David and Steven' who have left their 'terribly important' exam revision) writhe in eviscerating embarrassment. In the encounter with the unimpressed *Time* magazine reporter in the same film, Dylan is openly confrontational. But in both kinds of case, he might be said to resemble one of the *Gunsmoke* cowboys or the anti-heroes that fuelled his adolescent imagination, and our investment is often to will his triumphant escape. He eludes a bum rap by using his wits to evade his captors and leave them tied up in their own ropes.

In the early days, though, humour had been a fundamental way of claiming attention rather than deflecting it (although it has always been integral to the songs). In the Greenwich Village coffee houses, it was a key resource in winning over his audience. Dave Van Ronk memorably described Dylan on stage:

> Back then, he always seemed to be winging it, free-associating, and he was one of the funniest people I have ever seen onstage ... He had a stage persona that I can only compare to Charlie Chaplin's 'Little Fellow'. He was a very kinetic performer, he never stood still, and he had all these nervous mannerisms and gestures. He was obviously quaking in his boots a lot of the time, but he made that part of the show. There would be a one-liner, a mutter, a mumble, another one-liner, a slam at the guitar. Above all, his sense of timing was uncanny: he would get all of these pseudoclumsy bits of business going, fiddling with

harmonica rack and things like that, and he could put an audience in stitches without saying a word.[3]

Until the mid-60s, improvised humour was artfully employed to link the viewer to someone who cultivated the sense of being unguardedly at stake on stage, whose intensity and authenticity as a performer were inseparable from a certain vulnerability, riskiness, and clownishness. In possibly his first interview, with Billy James in October 1961, Dylan claimed that on stage 'the biggest idol goin'' all through my head all the time is Charlie Chaplin'.[4] The effect one gleans from anecdotes or recordings of Dylan's humorous stage improvisations in the early days is a little like watching a star of the silent screen walking through a collapsing building, or a juggler or high-wire walker: someone who wins you over by injecting apparent peril and spontaneity into the performance, to make the eventual achievement of grace or balance all the more affecting. The capo-fiddling, witty routine with Joan Baez at Newport in 1963 still retains elements of this early pantomime, before he sings a compelling 'North Country Blues'.

A more celebrated example of humour, delivered with a typical artful hesitancy, would be the famous remark at the Philharmonic Hall in 1964 that it was Halloween, and 'I've got my Bob Dylan mask on ... I'm masq-uer-ading' ...[5] In 1965 he more than once provoked laughter by introducing 'It's alright Ma' with the words 'This is called ... "It's alright Ma, I'm only Bleeding: Ho, Ho, Ho"', or adding, with comic redundancy, after 'The Gates of Eden'. 'That was called "The Gates of Eden".' The performances of 'If You Gotta Go, Go Now' similarly brought welcome humour to the set in 1965. It is worth saying that humour in such contexts clearly brings about a tiny change of aspect, and a small but important temporal shift. In so doing it can leaven what might seem determinedly pious, ritualistic, or self-serious in the performances, jolting the audience out of their gravity, and preserving the values of surprise and instability that are integral to the songs themselves. An interestingly different, because more inadvertent, case is the very early performance of 'Desolation Row' at Forest Hills in 1965 (a few days before the release of *Highway 61 Revisited*). The outbreaks of audience laughter that punctuate the song throughout actually allow us to hear it in a totally new and valid way, turning the song's parade of the lost into something mordant and biting, a dark carnival. Marcus remembers:

> people would laugh out loud, and he would grin. His music wasn't a burden his audience was expected to shoulder; it was an adventure its audience was free to join and free to reject. (Marcus, *Bob Dylan*, 123)

By the mid-60s the knowing interviewer, as Nat Hentoff said of the celebrated *Playboy* interview of March 1966, had no recourse but to play 'straight man in our questions, believing that to do otherwise would have stemmed the freewheeling flow of Dylan's responses'.[6] The encounters had become a *ju-jitsu* that flips question and questioner alike. However, what needs emphasising is that this humour is *intra*personal as much as interpersonal: a matter of Dylan endlessly surprising himself as much as his interlocutor by each turn of the kaleidoscope, or throw of the dice. As obvious versions of this, there are various concocted interviews of March 1965 that made it into the pages of *Village Voice* or *Cavalier* in 1965 (Artur, 102–5), or the spoof-sequence at Sydney Airport in April 1966 where he takes advantage of a pause in proceedings, switching seats to interview himself:

> *How long is it since you saw your mother?*
>   About three months.
> *Why don't you see her more often? Doesn't she approve of your music?*
>   Well my mother doesn't approve of it but my grandmother does.
> *I see you've got about twelve people there with you: What's that, a band? Don't you play pure music any longer?*
>   No, man, that's not a band with me. They're all friends of my grandmother.
> (Artur, 340)

This slapstick clearly obeys the essential rhythms of Dylan's imagination in the 1960s as it oscillates between an everyday and a surreal self. It straddles different worlds, like the 'vision music' (as Dylan called his work in San Francisco) that shifts endlessly back and forth between the mundane, and its phantasmatic or transfigured other.

Similarly, in interviews or on stage Dylan will endlessly depart from this mundane self in comic flights. Examples of this are the series of hapless losers he will impersonate phrase by phrase in *Tarantula* or in the celebrated verbal pyrotechnics of his delirious, fast-cut, mid-60s songs or narratives. The following answer to Hentoff for *Playboy* is surely the most quoted reply ever:

> *Hentoff*: ... what made you decide to go the rock-and-roll route?
> *Dylan*: Carelessness. I lost my one true love. I started drinking. The first thing I know I'm in a card game. Then I'm in a crap game. I wake up in a pool hall. Then this big Mexican lady drags me off the table, takes me to Philadelphia. She leaves me alone in her house, and it burns down. I wind up in Phoenix, I get a job as a Chinaman. I start working in a dime store, and move in with a thirteen-year-old girl. Then this big Mexican lady from Philadelphia comes in and burns the house down. I go down to Dallas. I get a job as a 'before' in a Charles Atlas 'before and after' ad. I move in with a delivery boy who can cook fantastic chilli and hot dogs. Then this thirteen-year-old girl from Phoenix comes and burns the house down. The delivery boy – he ain't so mild: he gives her the knife, and the next thing I know, I'm in Omaha. It's so cold there, by this time I'm robbing my own bicycles and frying my own fish. I stumble onto some luck and get a job as a carburettor out at the hot-rod races every Thursday night. I move in with a high school teacher who also does a little plumbing on the side, who ain't much to look at, but who's built a special kind of refrigerator that can turn newspaper

into lettuce. Everything's going good until that delivery boy shown up and tries to knife me. Needless to say, he burned the house down, and I hit the road. The first guy that picked me up asked me if I wanted to be a star. What could I say?
Hentoff: And that's how you became a rock-and-roll singer?
Dylan: No, that's how I got tuberculosis. (Artur, 314–15)

Absurdity and hyperbolic exaggeration intensify the impression of life as a matter of anxious and inventive adaptation: whether answering an interviewer's questions or eluding knifes and fire. Life is all game-playing and ad-libbing, and one just does find oneself in new places and having to make it up on the spot ('I wind up in Phoenix ... The next thing I know I'm in Ohama'). Survival is attempting activities that one dimly understands and which turn out to be self-defeating ('by this time I'm robbing my own bicycles and frying my own fish'). The humour and invention enact the sheer vitality and capacity of this self that weaves itself anew out of the warp of happenstance, circumstance, and loss. He is always *en route*, on his mettle, and at stake, caught in this discombobulating mix of the absurd, the fanciful, the life-threatening, and the humiliating. Selfhood is not about premeditated imitation, but about improvising. It is an ongoing drama of self-fabulation with endless daily episodes. Dylan both describes this and *does* it here, fashioning such scenarios on the spot and extemporising about the self's extemporisations: getting hired as a Chinaman or a puny 'before' model in a Charles Atlas ad, or 'building a special kind of refrigerator that can turn newspaper into lettuce'... In both the absurd odyssey of their content and the endlessly paratactic sequence of their form, Dylan's answers revel in the instability and forward-pressing resourcefulness of the self, while figuring and tipping over what is intolerable and repressive in social prescriptions of identity. Within the little scenes, as with Chaplin's little tramp, Dylan precipitates a sense of the arbitrariness of social norms through a deadpan comedy that reveals how dysfunctional they are, and through a laughter that prises a certain opening to the indefinite.

III
Photographs

Dave Van Ronk perceived that the young Dylan was 'always thinking of the effect that he [was] having' (Van Ronk, 159). However, although Dylan always seems aware of his photogenic power over the camera, he never appears straightforwardly to invite its attentions. Right from the start of his career, in fact, his magnetic way with a camera lens is inseparable from a deep wariness in face of it. By the mid-60s this wariness is a more or less restrained hostility, a bristling desire to reject the camera's claims and its voracious desire to hold, package, represent. If Dylan in the 1960s is such a compelling photographic subject, it is because he is a divided and profoundly reluctant one. As he put it himself: 'It rubs me the wrong way, a camera. It's a frightening feeling. Cameras make ghosts out of people.'[1] One suspects that it is the adversarial tension that produces the magic, and that it unfolds from the deepest values of Dylan's artistic sensibility and their incompatibility with the camera's intrusive ambition.

This, to begin with, is to raise two related issues. Firstly, photographs reveal the same principles of creative morphogenesis as do the songs. Pictures convey a sense of a self that can multiply itself into innumerable eloquent and photogenic images. Each picture summons a different scenario, tells a different story, reveals a different aspect. Further, on another level, Dylan's self-hood seems subject to qualitative alteration, as if taking on different allotropic states: there is the Dylan of New York in 1963, of the road trip of 1964, of the world tour of 1966, and of Woodstock in 1968. Secondly, though, it is not simply because Dylan is an inexhaustible or changeable subject that he resists the camera's grip. Rather, there is also the further quality of temporal self-division, a dynamic of duration, a tension of futurity that is fundamental to his creativity, and that means that any image also trails the sense that Dylan is in significant ways always invisible here and now, eluding its grasp, or already in motion.

So even when he is looking the other way or past the camera, Dylan often gives the impression that he is both aware and instinctively dismissive of it, impatient of its capacity to confine him. Clearly, it can seem an irony of Dylan's iconoclastic career during the sixties that it should itself have generated so many iconic photographic images, in spite (or because) of this distrustful and ambivalent attitude. Characteristically, he ignores or refuses to engage directly with the lens. His attitude conveys avoidance or, at best, a wry tolerance. As with an interviewer's questions, Dylan intuitively responds to the camera as a challenge, even as he overthrows its interruptive designs. And over and again, in this spirit of retaliation, he is delighted to wield the camera himself, disdainfully turning it on his pursuers in *No Direction Home*, or more playfully brandishing it against Daniel Kramer,[2] D.A. Pennebaker,[3] or Elliott Landy. The paradox, though, is that however dismissive he is, he absorbs our interest. He instinctively or unconsciously takes over the frame like a cockerel commanding a barnyard, but while holding himself in reserve, and discounting the image's capacity to detain him.

My first set of examples is from the CBS Whitmark Tapes booklet, which accompanies the CDs and offers a representative dossier of excellent, early black-and-white pictures.[4] One finds even in the shots of 1962 or 1963, a sense that Dylan is already operating with a wily and agile awareness beyond that of the culture that pursues him. He is on the cusp of mass fame, and we detect the future opening up (as well as detecting, rather poignantly, a rapidly vanishing aura of access, spontaneity, intimacy around him). There is a perceptible eagerness in the photos, a youthful sense of buoyant readiness. He is evidently aware of the interest he can generate, and of the camera's ability to help impart momentum to his career. There is a colour publicity shot of Dylan in the corduroy cap for the first album, for instance, his face plump, his mouth set. The photo questions the seeming disparity between his youth and the assurance of his talent, projected in the self-possession of his level gaze. Meanwhile, the claims of tradition appear to be signalled in the huge-seeming, old-seeming, Gibson that he clutches, as if it were an embodiment of the anachronistic values of his art, its power to resist the closures of chronology.

After all, this is the boy, we might remind ourselves, who can sing 'Moonshiner' in the 'Gaslight' so that the performance seems like a visitation, as compelling as a Shakespearean tragedy in miniature.[5] The young Dylan unlocks the voice in the song so that the sentiments of a despairing, lifelong drunk reveal a secret, causative, condition of irrepressible, romantic, yearning. In such early interpretations, we find Dylan's inspiration manifesting itself in this dramatic and deeply characteristic capacity for being possessed by a song, rather than being in possession of it. Summoned by the song, Dylan summons the listener, revealing an instinctive and determining principle of self-annulment, an anonymous power of becoming that extends to us and anticipates so many features of his later work. More particularly, it shows that Dylan's genius as an interpreter was there from the beginning, a matter of his finding an axis of self-division in the song on to which he can expressively transpose his own complications, and lack of a fixed self. Like so many traditional songs then and since Dylan treats 'Moonshiner' as if it were a vessel for the spirit – all the more as it is a song of someone so confounded and imprisoned, deprived of his spirit, by alcoholism. In contrast, the camera, as a vehicle of finitude, the fixed present, and of appearance might be said to confine and turn one into a ghost, as Dylan said.

It is unsurprising then, given that his gifts manifested themselves in this way in the early years, that Dylan should turn away from the camera's attempts to possess him. His art is a matter of his not being in possession of himself, so that its creator will essentially elude the camera that fronts him. Again, in temporal terms, one can tease out the logic of Dylan's resistance a little perhaps. Given that Dylan creatively steps away from a former self into a kind of invisibility, he is caught between the ghost of his former self, and the virtual, indefinite self his work pursues. In this situation, the camera can only be intrusive in its attempt to wrest stabilising imagery from the present, and necessarily interruptive and mistaken in its aim to convert becoming into being. Hence there is Dylan's attitude of defensive self-possession as he faces the camera down, and his resistance to its attempts to make a ghost of him, to make him 'visible now'. Even in the early photos this recalcitrance is of a redoubtable kind, and as we detect that this very young man is a worthy adversary, as well as subject, for the packaging designs of the camera. Typically he stands out in an image, but also apart from it. In many photos, however podgy, doughy, and unlined the face, the eyes and pursed mouth suggest that he is intent on taking the measure of his world.

In the Whitmark booklet, there are many further celebrated pictures that bear out such points. There is a cropped version of a famous image of Dylan in sheepskin and cap performing at *The Singer's Club* in London on 22 December 1962. He is clearly caught up in his power to cast a spell over his audience who themselves appear as if from a different age from Dylan himself, and yet to make the transition from post-war austerity and the folk boom to anything recognisable as 1960s London. In the photo the sense of transition and futurity clearly have larger and powerful historical significances, and it is a moving document of the changing times. In other photos in the booklet, he is abstracted, reading a paper or privately engrossed with downcast eyes. Perhaps he is determinedly ignoring the camera because, as Victor Maymudes was to recall, he was always so ruminative, 'always *processing*' (Hajdu, 158). In other images, too, he is unaware in the camera, because so clearly consumed in actual production. There are shots of Dylan in the Columbia studios pensively waiting his cue before the microphone, or singing into it, his lips faintly curled in enjoyment. In another, he muses with John Hammond listening to a playback. He is wearing clip-on sunglasses and work-shirt, Hammond has a buzz-cut and suit. However, their body-language mirror each other exactly. Both are engrossed, their heads tilted slightly.

In these early photographs for all the lack of availability there is often the impression of an animating vividness, engagement, and responsiveness that reciprocally transmit themselves to the viewer. The facial expressions vary from determination to impressionability, from passivity to vigilance. At times the set of the mouth seems pouting or petulant, like a child's, while at others, the mouth that breaks out into an infectious smile, baring his teeth, is that of the sardonic adolescent. And other faces pass through the photos too: the fiery beat-poet; the familiar Jewish scholar or student; the young, boyish, farmhand in the plain work shirt; the troubadour with the furrowed brow, reading the signs of the times; the impassive, exquisite, starlet. As 1963 gives way to 1964, though, the attitude in these photos from the Whitmark booklet tends to become more clearly avoidant or disdainful of the camera, and one is aware of a more marked steely and artful manipulation. In jeans and holding a cigarette, Dylan sits languidly astride a folding chair, arms folded across its top, radiating a certain *ennui*. In another shot, he is poetically lighting a cigarette over a bohemian meal in polo-neck sweater, his hair now thick and wavy. The Guthriesque figure has yielded to someone whose imagery is closer to the beats, a person who simultaneously masters the camera and evinces disengagement, even contempt, for its bourgeois mechanics of appropriation. He is now also decisively a new prototype of cool and rebellion.

Hence even Daniel Kramer's photographic memoir of Dylan is a record of endless wrangling, as Dylan's politeness and amiability continually runs aground on his instinctive resistance to being photographed. On their first meeting in Woodstock in 1964 Dylan would refuse to be shot with his guitar or doing everyday things, preferring to move from a rocking chair to a swing outside:

> His mood changed when he stood up and pumped the swing higher and higher. He smiled – a rare thing, I learned, for Dylan to do for the camera. (Kramer, 14)

Kramer's instinct was that 'I was being challenged and decided to meet it by not forcing the situation' (Kramer, 14), evolving the method of anticipation that serves his images so well, as he waited for the moment that fuses Dylan's individuality with a situation. Accordingly, Kramer's best photographs always have the dynamism of a segment of time, accentuated by his poetic uses of contrasts and focus: Dylan taking hold of a zip-wire; sitting aloft in a huge tree; laughing and stamping his blurred foot facing John Sebastian in the studios of the *Bringing It All Back Home* sessions; restringing his guitar, oblivious to the camera; turning the blurred pages of a newspaper; ironing Joan Baez's hair; lining up a pool shot; his face tilted and antagonistic on the cover of *Highway 61 Revisited*; or exhaling smoke while he ponders the Forest Hills set list with a bespectacled Robbie Robertson.

But as the decade unfolds, the relation to the camera comes to seem like a fatal pact or curse. What might have seemed in part necessary, even desired at first, has become all but intolerable. The camera is an instrument of tortuous intrusion, demanding in Dylan a massive forbearance or evasion, or at best an assumed indifference. Publicity and fame are hydra-headed or petrifying monsters, needing to be constantly contested. So one can gauge the difference between the increasing sense of Dylan's retreat into a coterie existence, on the one hand, and the spontaneous sociability that is captured in early photos, on the other. Some early well-known Greenwich Village photos have him in his apartment, laughing out loud with a cigarette, or caught with Suze mid-romp on the bed, or mid-banter with Van Ronk and his wife Terri Thal walking the snowy Manhattan streets. Perhaps what is most revealing about such photos is that they display an unguardedness, a self-forgetfulness (call it availability), that then appears almost wholly absent afterwards. By the mid-60s, his disengagement appears much more to suggest outright refusal, alienation, and an inalienable and troubled sense of privacy. He has lost the possibility of passing anonymously in the world, and is fenced in by the perpetual gaze of others. Increasingly, his face comports itself with a studied blandness. As he was to say in 1966: 'It is always lonely where I am' (Artur, 657).

In the mid-60s, this paradox appears to shape itself as a form of existential fate, as if Dylan had found himself a latter-day King Midas, cursed by his gift of transmutation. He is unable to tear himself free from his capacity to spread himself everywhere, to change irrevocably everything he miraculously touches. Under this aspect, his gift recoils upon itself, with an endless, surreal, irony that converts dream into nightmare. Socially, his rejection of mid-60s America as it is has ironically left every gesture impossibly and absurdly subject to scrutiny, as if every glance or smile were imbued with social import and encoded a message about what society might become. Personally, his art projects emancipation and expression, but it has boxed him in, inevitably leaving him feeling haunted, hunted, the one person on the outside of the collective fantasy, the mass imagining of Bob Dylan. Culturally, his power and influence are unlimited, but this is in fact a predicament, ironically indistinguishable from powerlessness, precisely because the expectations are so exorbitant, so impossible. Dylan in the 1960s can thus appear consumed by the ironies of his own magic, coiled in the tentacles and exponential insanities of mass fame, subject to unimaginable torsions. Above all, he is divided from his uncomprehending audience who do not see that the price of their continual desire that Dylan be present to them is that he becomes ever more absent from himself. Perhaps this ironic compounding of Dylan's creative division into a personal predicament by 1966 is close to the feeling of twenty or so years later, that at times he felt that there was 'a missing person inside of myself' (Dylan, *Chronicles*, Vol. 1, 147).

Looking at Barry Feinstein's black and white shots of Dylan's 1966 world tour, one gets such a sense of alienation. Dylan appears as both the incarnation of the times, and yet someone totally outside and beyond the world he inhabits. Wired, remote in some private and incommunicable way, and increasingly wasted and emaciated, his aspect is often extra-terrestrial. At the same time, he is this endless target of runaway fame, an enviably and alluringly cool *fashinista* in the suede jacket with epaulettes, the Carnaby Street striped trousers, the pointed, Cuban-heeled boots – an epicene figure with nicotine-stained graceful long figures, diaphanous eye-lids, milk-white skin, pursed mouth. It is a point of honour not to give anything away, to maintain the determinedly fixed, apathetic, unimpressible expression of one retreating behind the Ray Bans. Only at moments is this attitude of transcendent disdain broken by mundane and fleeting moments of self-forgetfulness – throwing rocks or interacting with children outside a derelict warehouse near Liverpool's Dock Road, putting his head down on a tablecloth flat-out with exhaustion, talking animatedly with two female poets, or pulling on a boot in a boutique, cigarette in mouth.

But his main respite, it seems, is when abandoned to his gift on stage. In Feinstein's photographs, or listening to the concerts, one is aware of how triumphantly Dylan's sense of dislocation is raised to a new creative power, night by night. Above all, Feinstein wonderfully captures this contrary freedom, the sense that here Dylan is overwhelmingly affected by the unbridled dynamism and euphoria of the surging music of the 1966 tour. The images are famous and, as they say, iconic – the aureole of the thousand-corkscrew pompadour in the spotlight, the lizard-lidded expression from the front, or the curved nose in profile. The ratios of the utterly inexpressive and the utterly, infinitely, expressive emerge again in the contrast between the lack of affect in the other photos, and the flat-out intensity of performance. Front on close-ups from below can show the hexagonal, alabaster face taking on an unearthly quality of sublime supplication, almost of ecstatic immolation, with hands crossed. Other full-length, side-on shots catch the mouth pursed over the telecaster, in the attitude of someone with a cocked gun, out to settle every old score. In more dynamic photographs, his body is twisted, and an arm might be expansively thrown aloft or outstretched, as if he were singing in the eye of a hurricane, or riding a witch's broom. At such ecstatic moments, the body language and facial expressions convey someone rapt or elated, consumed and uplifted by the transporting power and energy that is being conducted through the magnificent, tempestuous music that Dylan and The Hawks are discovering on stage.

Perhaps, though, this is another way of saying that what Feinstein's performance pictures convey is Dylan's need in 1966 to lose himself, to escape his world. This is evident in the dualities of those shows that provided them with their internal dynamic, common to the two halves. Both sets in different ways generate an inspiring sense of infinite possibility out of a besetting sense of finitude. The acoustic sets conjure an unerring beauty from sounding out and inhabiting our deepest privacies and interiority. They revive our capacity for longing and expression while registering our spiritual condition as one of constraint and self-opacity. And the electric sets convey a sense of exhilarating power, a sublime and ravishing potentiality to find the energy to live outside and beyond what the world and other people would make us be. Every night Hudson's diabolic, Gothic organ hubbles and bubbles while Dylan tears up our life scripts, thrillingly confronting the Mr Jones within us all with the bracing freedom to respond to a world that is not what we thought, and that is happening without us.

By about 1965 or 1966, certainly, Dylan's attitude towards the camera had becomes contemptuous, as if conveying a sense that photographic portraiture is a genre of lies. The photographic image could never capture a self whose internal tensions generate such a powerful impetus towards self-cancellation, whose self-presentation is so evidently and paradoxically a matter of refusal. Characteristically, as the decade develops his expression – rueful, amused, impassive, guarded, sardonic, avoidant, ruminative – expresses an increasing and genuine antipathy because the visual image is now so bound up with a whole host of new ways in which he cannot be understood, ways bound up with the iconography of fame, the pressures of his audience, the conflicts of his career. With ever-increasing sharpness, photos of this time make us feel that a thousand photos might express him in a thousand different ways, but that no picture could ever really reveal him. One might say that there are at least two interconnected ways in which this impossibility is true: *De facto*, his attitude is determined, cussed, hostile: you can never see me (in fact) because I will resist your every attempt. *De jure*, his self-division resists the camera's emphasis on the here and now: you could never see me (in principle), since I am always in transit, never wholly here.

Thus, by the mid-1960s an instinctive distrust or impatient indifference towards the camera has become a desire to confront and outlast it, a James Dean anti-pose that sets out to confront the camera with its intrusiveness, to accuse it of falsity. His eyes – unfathomable – often screw down as if taking stock or aim, as if confronting what he sees from a far-off vantage. His mouth purses slightly, suggesting that there is something in the whole process he can't swallow. In one sense, this refusal of the viewer indicates a deeply genuine and instinctive personal attitude, close to that identified by Albert Greenhill as the difference between Dylan and Richard Fariña:

> So Richard made me a little uncomfortable. Dylan was offensive in that he would really be rude to people, and Dick wouldn't really be rude to people. But Dick was like 'Look at me – here I am. Dig me!' Dylan was like, 'Look all you want. You'll never see me.' (Hajdu, 229)

On the world tour of 1966, this attitude has intensified, as in D.A. Pennebaker's remark that Dylan was a:

> Byronesque pop figure, a guy who was inventing a whole new kind of mood in popular music. Here's this middle-class kid who goes out on the road, hangs out with people, and he becomes or decides to become a kind of hobo-type character, and with all the romance that carries – the music, the freedom, everything that gets lost in the movement towards the middle class – and once he's made it, he looks out at everybody and says, 'Fuck you!' (Hajdu, 249)

One may feel that Pennebaker's note of triumph, however engaging, is crudely simplifying and off-beam. It misses how far, in fact, Dylan reins in his feelings, often comically, while always refusing to make them hostage to the camera.

Nonetheless, Pennebaker's emphasis has a broad truth, and one thinks of the out-take of *Eat The Document* where Dylan's uncompromising barbed-wire and bayonet play of wit and cool reduces even John Lennon to flailing impotence as the two indulge in horrendous, lowering verbal jousting in the back of a car on the day of Dylan's Royal Albert Hall concert.[6] His comments chime also with how far Dylan at this time generated a whole thrilling and ironic iconographic style that replicated the emotional world of *Highway 61* or *Blonde on Blonde* – now projecting attitudes of resentment, hostility, now an acerbic irony, now a sense of mysteriously captivated subjectivity. These images of Dylan, all sharp clothes and gestures, his eyes now wholly obscured by Ray Bans, are so potent and mysterious because of the sheer vitality and drama of the self-predicament they convey. They signal a mind caught up by an intolerable present, and bound by the necessity of getting free, away. And in this context, one must not underestimate the exhaustion of touring, and the depredations of his lifestyle and drug-use, the sense that he was burning the candle at both ends and in the middle ... It is the furthest reach of the irony that Dylan's refusal of fame – genuine and instinctive – should result in images that should be so utterly compelling. Their glamour, and the singular and changeable fascinations of his facial expressions, are inseparable from an uncompromising attitude that looks past the camera, or stares back and through it, as if to annihilate it, abolishing in a moment the generic rules of fame, the star's craven need.

Probing this a little further, one can say that the unleashing of resentment that provides a primary focus of Dylan's work in 1965 is evident in this kind of retributive relation to the camera. His eyes, vigilant and narrowing, cultivate their own vanishing point, as if he reciprocally can find a spot outside the field of representation, and so by a counter-magic can make the world of the photograph, the photographer, and the viewer disappear. While it is all too true, ironically enough, that this visual style of non-compliance would come to be much imitated, it is also true that it is inimitable. The instability of selfhood, the sense of self-in-motion, that are so vitally present in these images is a power of self-absence wholly integral to Dylan's gifts. Hence the difference between Dylan and, say, the career narcissism of a Mick Jagger who assumes a disdain that conceals endless resources of self-admiration.

At times, the greatest irony is that it is as if Dylan in the mid-60s appears to be about the only person on the planet uninterested in anything about Dylan, uninterested in *being* Dylan. Soon, he will even be bent on dismantling, as far as he can, the whole apparatus and iconography of his own myth, offering the bewilderingly different persona of *Self Portrait* or *Nashville Skyline*. The attitude can appear essentially one whereby emancipation *of* the self involves emancipation *from* the self, even at times a wholescale self-rejection. He will not become his own ghost, caught by his past, confined and defined. Suze Rotolo said that 'He just won't accept any one's point of view about himself', and this is perhaps because no-one else can get beyond the image, but also because the image is never who he is (Heylin, *Behind the Shades*, xvi). And how various and unstable the images can be. Like Wittgenstein's duck-rabbit, disjunctive aspects shuffle and exchange, the imagery circulating back and forth between the abrasive cool of a street-smart rock punk, or the lyrical refinement of a latter-day Rimbaud. Sometimes the mystery involves a certain destabilising of gender itself, the charismatic aspects of facial beauty and the *hauteur* and *froideur* of Dylan's attitudes conveying the fascination and glamour of a screen goddess.

Later, in Elliott Landy's famous photos of Dylan in Woodstock, Dylan has decisively cultivated the refusal to be any longer the telecaster-toting renegade, or hipster, of those very 1966 shows.[7] By the late sixties he will mime the beatific, hat-tipping, backwoods patriarch of Landy's *Nashville Skyline* cover photo. Landy's photos seemingly identify a brief truce in Dylan's attitude towards the camera. Alongside Feinstein and Daniel Kramer, Landy is Dylan's other great poet-photographer in the 1960s, and like Feinstein, he uses contrast to create a dynamic opposition between darkness and illumination. Even so, his images of Dylan's Byrdcliffe home in 1968, for instance, eloquently convey a wholly different dynamic.[8] The photographs spiritually mythologise Dylan's post-crash life as something like the rebirth of a character in a late Shakespearean romance, as if in a world now given over to miraculous, pastoral regeneration. Or (to take a literary reference closer to home), one might say that the iconography of bucolic retreat in the photos recalls the Romantic element in the New England of David Henry Thoreau and Ralph Waldo Emerson. He has withdrawn from the world, but so that he might no longer feel that the world has been withdrawn from him. In such a retirement Thoreau felt his art could encounter, as if at a turning point in the woods, the still eventual truth of America, converting its origins and history into its future:

> In any weather, at any hour of the day or night, I have been anxious to improve the nick of time, and notch it on my stick too; to stand on the meeting of two eternities, the past and the future, which is precisely the present moment; to toe that line. [9]

Certainly, then, Landy's images are a world apart from Feinstein's work, and outwardly communicate a wholly new accommodation with the camera on the part of their subject, introducing the viewer into the intimacies and spaciousness of this Woodstock world. Landy's images foreground the stray, obdurate, everyday detail of the Dylans' laid-back domestic arrangements – the cans at the dishevelled dining table, the huge old truck, the piles of logs, the children in nappies, the round-eyed, round-mouthed, toddler Jesse, Sara in headscarf holding a baby, the improvised tire-seat leant against an old saw-bench, the thrown cushions and rugs, the huge ornamented piano, the unswept yard ... At the same time, everything in the photos take the surrounding, immemorial, woodland as their informing and glorious out-of-field, as when Landy arranges his images of Dylan at the piano around the dual aspect of the living room. These pictures use focus and contrast to accentuate the dynamic opposition between the sonorous deep massed black of the interior, and the two huge windows luminescent with the flaring green and yellow world outside.

In such ways, the trees and trails of the Woodstock woods – ancient, endless, breathtaking – provide the perpetual back-drop and pastoral context for someone whose revivification has taken the oldest, newest, form of wife and children, nature, retreat. Throughout, Dylan unconcernedly and casually poses for the camera, though typically he avoids looking directly at it. In all these photos, though, his demeanour is temperate, acquiescent, as he sits astride on old tire, or on a disintegrating slatted bench, dressed in white shirts and pressed trousers, broad-brimmed hat, and sandals, while desultorily fingering a gold-toned, well-seasoned, acoustic with tortoiseshell scratch-plate. Through such effects of light and composition Landy conveys his sense of the mysterious, idealised, entwinements of the everyday and the paradisal in this domestic, and aboreal, world. In shots taken of Dylan and Sara on their balcony, for instance, the blurring of focus again irradiates the background tones of gold and green so that they become dynamic indices of renewal, of an imminent *natura naturans*. In another celebrated shot, Dylan in white hat leans back, against a huge, square, shiny black car. His arms are folded atop his guitar, his trousers are sharply creased, while the infrared shot blazes with an unworldly, crimson foliage. Nonetheless, a year or so later, in September 1969, he would be living again in New York, restless for a different kind of renewal, and sick of the crazed interlopers who perpetually stalked him in Woodstock.

IV
Voice

From the early days, Dylan's singing (like his harmonica playing) polarised listeners: 'I'd either drive people away or they'd come in closer to see what it was all about. There was no in-between' (Dylan, *Chronicles*, Vol. 1, 18). For his admirers the voice in the recordings of the 1960s is a uniquely vital and inspiring medium, the essential vehicle for putting his work across. Bono (a singer with the group U2) claims it as the marker of Dylan's artistic authenticity, his way of busting 'through the fourth wall' of popular song to make singing about 'telling the truth'.[1] It is undoubtedly a voice that has always put pundits on their mettle, from Robert Shelton's early review:

> Mr. Dylan's voice is anything but pretty. He is consciously trying to recapture the rude beauty of a Southern field hand musing in melody on his back porch. All the 'husk and bark' are left on his notes, and a searing intensity pervades his songs.[2]

Time magazine in May 1963 described his voice as sounding 'as if it was drifting over the walls of a tuberculosis sanatorium', while Andrea Svedburg prefaced her notorious *Newsweek exposé* by writing that his 'singing voice scratches and shouts so jarringly that his success, at first, seems incredible' (Artur, 62, 71). Greil Marcus noted how this early voice, 'like a cat stuck in barbed wire' was yet effectively 'supple', the flexible and 'captivating' resource of someone who can emphasise a word so that it can 'come across in so many different ways'.[3] Joyce Carol Oates writes of the 'dramatic and electrifying' effect of first hearing 'this raw, very young, and seemingly untrained voice, frankly nasal, as if sandpaper could sing'.[4] Betsy Bowden describes how mothers and fathers throughout the land in the 1960s clutched their ears while hearing this 'whining, grating, snarling voice'.[5] Tim Riley multiplies epithets in pursuit of Dylan's own gift for self-multiplication, eloquently describing how Dylan's 'coyote yowl and scurry-to-catch-up phrasing scatter furious accusation, self-mocking glee, postromantic loathing, self-directed bile, lost chances, fleeting regrets, earned cynicism, and contempt for falsity with biting, unsentimental candour'.[6] As Bono put it, 'there is a voice for every Dylan you can meet', but Mike Masterson is more ambitious still. He claims that Dylan is a congregation. Like Whitman the singer contains multitudes within his voice. He is '[s]inging the sounds of a culture':

> That's what I hear in Bob Dylan's voice – the multiple pitches of many possible interpretations. It's as if a gathering of people were also singing the song, each using their own slightly different set of pitches and rhythms.[7]

For Dylan's detractors, such claims appear crazily zealous and outlandish, compounding the irritation they feel when confronted by a voice that sounds variously charmless, whiney, adenoidal, mannered, complaining, insinuating, wheedling, adolescent, sneering, gravelly, unpleasant, unmusical. For them, Dylan's attitude as a singer carries with it unforgiveable presumption, with its bracing, brazen, hectoring, demandingness, trailing its pretentious, first-draft high school poetry. Consequently, they react with their own different kinds of repelled fervour: one person retreats, throwing up his hands in mystification as if he has happened on an incomprehensible cult; another opines that the emperor has no clothes; another claims that Dylan's gift dissolves away without residue into its influences and debts; another plays the dog-eared, patronising trump card that the songs are so much better sung by someone else.[8]

What is at issue to both sides though is the distinctively unyielding nature of the voice – with its insistent tone and urgent, inimitable phrasing. This is a voice that clearly refuses to please. It does not mimic an interpersonal intimacy – as might Paul Simon, for instance – offering a kind of virtual friendship, the flattering solace of identifying as a beautiful soul, and the enjoyments of a music whose attractions everyone can understand. Rather, the voice is abrasive, and the effect of the singing is interruptive, uncompromising. It is the voice of one who identifies as a hammer rather than a nail, and who sings (like Nietzsche philosophises), with a hammer. Indeed, the voice nails you. It can be cutting, but it always cuts into your attention, makes you stop, joltingly compels you to listen. It arrestingly lays claim to your freedom and responsiveness, and all the more effectively for its air of utter indifference to you. As Aidan Day put it, the singing 'at once solicits and rebuffs'.[9] Above all, through the 1960s, it distinctively manages to retain a compelling aura of introducing you into a changing world, paradoxically preserving an inaugural, even imperious quality and authority precisely because so utterly careless of itself and regardless of its listeners. Its spell depends on its refusal of social or personal co-ordinates, while Dylan's lack of a definite personality means that his songs are devoid of the usual pit-falls of sentimentality, piety, self-preoccupation or self-aggrandisement. The voice addresses its listeners by going past them, as if speaking to something anonymous, common, and concealed within their subjectivity, and drawing them into the new reality that it is entering, even constituting.

What are the stakes of this voice? One might say, to begin with, that it offers an aural image of selfhood as forward-pressing contingency, as the refusal of pathos. It asks for no confirmation or sympathy. Instead, the singing obeys a principle of instability, intent not on reproducing the song so much as on gambling on discovering it anew through intonation, rhythm, and timing. As the songs' dramas often turn on the comings and goings of self-hood, so too vocally the songs are animated by an expressiveness that is a function of passing connections, dynamic adaptations. The voice is bent on forging expressive self-truth in the moment, and extricating the self from its incidental flaws and failings, its residual and defunct elements. Anecdotally, Dylan's recording career and life as a performer bear out how invested Dylan is in such a driving open-endedness, in seeking out a situation in which context and precedent are suspended. Riley describes how the musicians in Nashville for the *Blonde on Blonde* sessions, would find themselves 'basically ... learning his songs as they played' (Riley, 97). Subjected to the never-ending, unrehearsed accumulations of 'Sad-Eyed Lady of the Lowlands', recorded in the middle of the night, Kevin Buttery confessed that he feared for Dylan's sanity ('I thought the guy had blown a gasket and we were basically humouring him' [Riley, 129]). In Riley's words, this was 'gut-charged music-making without a net' (Riley, 97).

In general, one can say that Dylan's voice in the 1960s makes a *call* in addressing the listener and demanding a response to its own clamouring responsiveness. This changes in marked ways during the decade, corresponding to the mutations and reconfigurations in his sensibility, and the different voices that he uses. In the early songs, it is less a matter of addressing us as recognisable subjects than of calling out about something, calling us forth, calling out to something inside of us, about something outside and beyond us. The address is impersonal in effective ways, yet it draws out possibilities of selfhood and collectivity that have been too long covered over by social habits of personality and identity. Dylan implicitly calls on the listener to intervene against a world that is itself also called out in the same moment: confronted as accursed and blackened, perhaps irredeemably, by its own inhumanity, injustice, indifference, exploitation. We are enjoined implicitly to participate in changing the world by listening, but then – by a contagion of transformative possibility – by acting, speaking, or taking a stand. The Dylan of 1963 has his eye fixed beyond the times he inhabits. He implicitly projects himself as a vessel of political changes, and demands that his audience reciprocally remake themselves as a new dissentient, expansive political collective.

By *Highway 61 Revisited*, though, the calling is of a different, more aggressive, kind. Dylan is now calling someone out or calling society down, soliciting change as a function of a corrosive vision directed against others who would specifically restrict the self and separate it from its powers. He is pulling off masks, and attempting to call off relations with intimates or a society who have become burdensome, or invasive. The impersonal, collective dimension of this lies in our covert sense that socialisation always masks our buried resentments. In this respect, anger has a fluent power in its blind, aggressive, disregard for how self and other are normally composed. However unappealing or destructive, it harbours this impulse to authenticity, this jubilant sense of possibility. In a different way again, the Dylan of *Blonde on Blonde* inhabits a space of sublime inwardness, bent on the self-consuming intensities of an art that founds its intimacy in calling forth our most solipsistic, dispossessed, obscure sense of ourselves, and in fashioning a baroque vocal style to furnish unapologetically the furthest, hidden recesses of our interiority.

It is a further feature of the prodigality of Dylan's art in the 1960s that one can passingly hear in tapes from hotel rooms in Denver or Glasgow in March or May 1966, for example, the emergence of another singular voice again, as Dylan and Robertson work up songs, melodies and structures that have an eloquent, tender, unguarded yet durable lyricism of their own. Again, by the time of *John Wesley Harding*, Dylan's voice has become fluent, flexible and lean, invigoratingly bound up with implacably delivering the cryptic ballads of finitude, spiritual aspiration, mendacity, or ruin. This voice appears to belong to no particular place or time, indeed to no particular self. Its enigmatic declarations are an expressive correlate of the way the contingencies and opacities of the song's scenarios ultimately figure self-hood as a redoubtable vagrancy, bent on a perpetual self-dedication to following one's lights in a treacherous world. In *Nashville Skyline*, though, the voice no longer seems to be openly calling in these invocatory, ethical, ways. Instead, Dylan's self-erasure now appears to be more about calling on the stabilising resources of the country tradition.

In such ways Dylan's voice in the 1960s is essentially a means of his confronting the existing, repressive, state of society, and claiming our attention. It forces itself on us with the urgency of the present continuous, representing itself as a catalyst for self-difference. If Dylan is essentially forgetful of self and audience in the moments of singing, one might say it is to make them revisit and remember themselves, to surprise them into taking possession of their own experience. In this sense, he draws comparison with Emerson's poet or artist, who is 'representative of man, in virtue of being the largest power to receive and impart' (Emerson, 241). Creativity is a matter of conductive and transmissive power, of conveying to his audience a liberating vision, and transporting them in turn through their participation. Emerson's metaphors are of electricity, fire, 'divine energy', and a vitality that creates form. The following well-known formulation usefully identifies creativity with these qualities of emergence:

> For it is not metres, but a metre-making argument that make a poem, – a thought so passionate and alive that like the spirit of a plant or an animal it has an architecture of its own ... The thought and the form are equal in the order of time, but in the order of genesis the thought is prior to the form ... (Emerson, 245)

Because the function of this voice is individuation, it addresses what is restless and searching within the freedom of its listeners, while retaining its own independence from them. As Mark Polizzotti put it, 'the real attraction of Dylan's voice is that it exists on its own terms, [without] pandering to audience expectations ... that [it] invites you in even while holding you at a safe distance' (Polizzotti, 89).

More specifically, though, what are the changing qualities of this voice itself? If one listens to performances from the early 1960s, one gets a sense of old and new entwined, in a voice that mixes accents, attitudes, timbres and tones. In David Yaffe's words, it 'sounded like it wanted to be older than it was' in contrast to Dylan's own 'scruffish, boyish appeal'.[10] These antimonies are evident though in the voice itself too, which sounds croaky, rusty and weather-beaten, yet which is also alternately lined with youthful tenderness, even vulnerability.[11] Often described as both old and young at the same time, it moves between sounding fatalistic, unillusioned, on the one hand, and knowing and hopeful, even innocent, on the other. So, the delivery alternates between being weary, unheeding, wary, or indignant one moment, and imploring, humorous, tender, or reflective, the next. In timbre or tone, it is often predominantly torn, husky, cracked, raspy, ancient, ragged, but it can also sound, by effective contrast, plaintive, tender, adolescent, poignant. In a very early song like 'Rambler, Gambler', for instance, we hear how the singing effectively divides itself between a voicing of the lessons of experience and the unchanging sense that 'There's changes in my true love / Ain't no change in me'.[12]

Such complex passages between retrospection and youthful persistence are part of the constitutive, temporal tensions in the songs themselves, as they enact the division between past and future, and create their singular, forward-moving, openness of texture. By the time Dylan has got to New York, under the aegis of Guthrie, Van Ronk, and the folk revival, the voice outwardly sounds like a sort of world-weary shell, though always enclosing the fugitive seeds of emergent emotion and of living, naked, youthful potentiality. Often this means that Dylan's skill is evident in how he manages without histrionics the moments where the self appears at stake in the singing, where the voice catches or cracks open – on a version of 'Worried Blues', 'Cocaine, Cocaine', or 'He Was A Friend of Mine', for instance. Indeed, one can feel that an important underlying motive of the performance is to find the moments where it can manage these transitions, or open itself to influxes of a romantic, tragic, heartrending, or comic kind, and discover a turning point around which the song can move.

Dylan's singing is often importantly both a matter of timing and of taking himself by surprise in these respects. The tools for doing this are often a kind of understatement – an artful hesitancy, small shifts in dynamics and phrasing – that works alongside the guitar work whose insistent, often pounding rhythms often sound like someone banging in nails, as if knocking together in song a sensibility for all weathers. When Dylan sings 'This Land is Your Land' in an early recording, the strumming provides an effective counterpoint, underpinning a restrained voice that lingers behind the beat, at once youthful, unillusioned, and hesitant, yet determinedly laying claim to the singer's lost, alienated country. This contrasts with the vanishing future of the singer in 'I Was Young When I Left Home'. The singer is living out his boyhood fantasy of being 'out in the winds' or on a train, but is now ironically powerless to return to the home that endlessly inhabits his thoughts. Dylan's foot emphatically thuds the rhythm, while the guitar picks, hammers, and slides, creating transitory effects of fugitive beauty. This tension in the accompaniment expressively frames the singer's bleak, divided sense of the remorseless blows of fate or circumstance, and the ineradicable incursions of hopeless longing. The voice conveys a singer who can never go home, whose only home now is the song itself.

'A Hard Rain's A-Gonna Fall' is a very different, and much more important song. Hearing it, Dave Van Ronk felt so affected that he had to leave the venue:

> I heard him sing that for the first time during one of the hoot nights at the Gaslight, and I could not even talk about it; I just had to leave the club and walk around for a while. It was unlike anything that had come before it, and it was clearly the beginning of a revolution. (Van Ronk, 206)

And certainly, Dylan's is a voice on the Gaslight recording that knows where his song is going. His tentativeness holds the reins of a deeper conviction that drives the song on beneath the husky accents, the farmhand's drone. It is a voice, like so many of the folk revival, that cultivates its impression of unworldliness. However, as Van Ronk suggests, it is genuinely revolutionary because it appears not to belong to the folk scene, or even to the singer who is singing it. Indeed, an effect of timelessness and other-worldliness is of its essence. At times the recording sounds as if Dylan might be singing from a scroll, so hypnotically dispassionate, impersonal, insistent, is the delivery. Yet such features of the singing contribute to the song's conviction and power, as if he can only confront his times by spurning them, by singing to them from a point outside them. This is evident in the mesmerising, inexorable intensity of the voice, as it moves again towards the apocalyptic reckoning of the chorus. Alex Ross observed that the verses conspire with the effect of visionary transcendence, in that they are longer each time, so the listener feels both that the resolution of the chorus is always moving 'a little further out of reach', and that '[c]oming down the mountain of the song, [Dylan] starts to sound like a prophet'.[13] But one can note too how Dylan's zero-degree, insistent, rough and ready guitar style – with its dropped D tuning, hammered motifs, open strings and sliding chord shapes – helps to give both rhythmic impetus and tonal tension to the way the song moves us into its intensified visionary space.

In such ways the guitar work on these early songs plays off against the voice, often evoking the anonymity of an early field recording while the vocal is prone to the more involuntary and instinctive operations of Dylan's vigilant sensitivity. The main resource of the guitar (rudimentary Carter family echoes notwithstanding) is often merely unadorned rhythm and Dylan can sound at times as if he were playing a washboard, or sawing a piece of wood. ('He's just a strummer', said Richard Manuel when Dylan first approached the Hawks.[14]) However, this reduced musicality just intensifies the song's unremitting focus on the possibilities of change and loss. The voice does not seem to address its listeners so much as to provoke and invoke them, to force them through its own unapologetic example to take ownership of their own authentic, unvarnished, voices. By the second and third albums, clearly, the sense of a voice addressing its times from a revolutionary turning point has become powerfully politicised. Now the rejection of a disappointing past and the affirmation of a certain inevitable renewal become decisively translated into the political vision that expands beyond critique and announces the inevitability of changing times.

But how far the pendulum swings from this world to the sardonic inflections of *Highway 61 Revisited* ... Hostile intonations here shape a survivor's soured knowingness of fate as a social condition, and distil a retaliatory sense of its imprisoning illusions. Listen to out-takes from 1965 (including some from the earliest *Blonde on Blonde* sessions), and one can hear how the music exuberantly whips up an ominous atmosphere, through snarling and relentless arrangements on 'I Wanna Be Your Partner', 'Medicine Sunday', 'Jet Pilot', 'Lunatic Princess Revisited', or early versions of 'It Takes a Lot to Laugh'. The voice glides, or yammers and hollers. Refusing to be ignored, it deals in shocks, its whip-cracking, vitriolic intonations both scourging society and goading us into response. Declaiming over the machinic potency of the accompaniment on studio versions of 'Phantom Engineer' or 'Barbed Wire Fence', the singing directs itself against the ways our culture makes automatons of us all, the hostile or sardonic tones (and uses of paradox and the surreal), up-ending our customary docility.

As Yaffe put it this 'mid-60s voice sounded like a college kid on amphetamines arguing about ontology' (Yaffe, 19). It is button holing and raw, and cuts through to provoke our residual autonomy as itself automatic. The voice is so visceral it forces a response, from habitual conformity into anger, pleasure, humour. The aim of the songs is certainly to 'needle', as Dylan said of 'Positively 4th Street' and 'Like a Rolling Stone' in the KQED studios, but beyond provocation there is the pulsating recognition that our liberation within this society must involve angry rejection of its disintegrative mystifications, its powers of relaying lifelessness (Artur, 236). Hence one can take the sound on the album as a kind of counter-punching: the organ is purgative, the guitar transportingly aggressive, the harmonica wailing, yelling, or lyrical, the voice at stake in the bonds of a subjection that it is excitedly seeking to convert to triumph, insight, declamation. If the songs punch us, one might say, it is to make us stop being punch-bags, and this provocation – this sense of life reclaimed – is the key to the exhilaration of the music and the voice, the fairground sense of surging abandonment that coexists with all its derision and fatalism. In fact, the voice is still exploring social estrangement, political alienation, but now as internal to the mind itself whose optic is exposed as utterly distorted by social conditions and myths. The voice stretches and snaps back like a piece of elastic, or jerks and whips like an eel – full of lithe, contorted, nervous energy and electricity. Its uncompromising and urgent dedication is to ride out or sinuously evade the claims of others, or else to sting us alive. Dylan's voice on *Highway 61* – defiant, rebarbative, lined with the abjection he turns on to others – is that of someone urgently inspired to separate himself from the surreal carnival world of distorting mirrors in which he is holed up, the door knob broke. By the 1966 tour, it is a voice that seems to be tearing itself apart, but all the more intent on going for broke, transmuting subjection into an expressive onslaught on his audience. As Jim Miller puts it of famous versions of 'Like a Rolling Stone' from that tour: 'Dylan's singing is demonic ... his voice rising and falling, almost without pitch, before homing in on a note with a dive-bomb drone' (Miller, 29).

In *Blonde on Blonde* the voice takes as it were triumphant possession of the self's dispossession. The metaphors that spring to mind for Dylan's entrancing intonations on this record are hydraulic. It is as if freedom for this voice were a function of its capacity mesmerisingly to inundate our minds, expressively placing in circulation the paradoxical contortions and mysterious fluctuations of confusion, private pain and desire. This is a voice indifferent to custom and precedent. It emancipates by abolishing the distinction between the singer's subjectivity and our own. Through its hypnotic, majestic sway it enacts the truth that 'anybody can be just like me, obviously' (*Lyrics*, 206). In the world of *Blonde on Blonde* subjectivity is amazement, and our awareness is endlessly swept away or engulfed by the obscure courses of affectivity. Emancipation here involves facing the shortfalls of what we take as knowledge, and expressively inhabiting, lyrically transfiguring, the loops of our customary self-estrangement. The songs reveal the self as an alienated structure divided between the storm-surges of feeling, and society's words. All the time, the singer turns words against their social uses, to cultivate a sublime, incantatory, and inspiring opacity. On 'Visions of Johanna', for instance, the singing quietly infiltrates our consciousness with expressions of our confused, benighted selves. Or else, the voice can bear us down then aloft, as on a song like 'One of Us Must Know' that produces its own vocal or aural image of desire. The music on this song heaves, rolls, and swells, while the singer rides waves and billows in arrangements that themselves can indeed sound 'oceanic', in Michael Gray's formulation (Gray, *The Bob Dylan Encyclopedia*, 59).

In such ways, the songs on *Blonde on Blonde* can be described as sounding the inescapable excess, and occluded human dignity and beauty, of desire. On the Basement Tapes the songs proceed from the gulf between the secular and the spiritual, so that the wonderful 'Goin' to Acapulco' (for example) may read like the banalities of a bar-room deadbeat, but it sounds as if it is being sung by St John of the Cross. By *Nashville Skyline* and *Self Portrait*, though, Dylan's is a voice that inhabits structure, melody, and genre rather than departing from them, serving a singer whose emphasis is on the values and complexities of location. This voice is no longer intent on ambushing, arresting, or dislocating our consciousness through its own incidental spontaneity or tonal self-divisions. By *Nashville Skyline*, the key value is a kind of beguiling modulation, so that the singer appears hospitable to the listener. Everything here is about rapport. It is as if the values of huskiness and smoothness in the voice were themselves on neighbourly terms, blended together. In a similar way, the arrangements bring together bluesiness and sweetness, and the album itself balances songs of celebration and songs of loss. Self-division is now ironically a matter of the elided figure of the Dylan of *Highway 61 Revisited* or *Blonde on Blonde* who is now himself invisible, past, and absent. The mid-60s Dylan is now unrecognisable, as if covered over like the old suede jacket beneath another coat in John Cohen's photo on the cover of *Self-Portrait*. The voice of *Nashville Skyline* becomes surprising for being so different in tone and register, while the singing surprises for being so unlike Dylan – so confoundingly out to please, so apparently generic, so bent on dying falls and languorous modulations ... In *Rolling Stone*, Country Joe McDonald wrote 'he's like a ghost of his former self, and it drives me up the wall. I don't know where the real Bob Dylan went, but I don't believe this one. He don't fool me, man.'[15] At the same time, as Echo Helstrom remarked of the voice of *Nashville Skyline*:

> Bob's voice has always been good, he could sing like he's singing now years ago, back when he was a teenager. But no, he had to make it sound rough, that was going to be his gimmick, how he would be different. The same for the long hair, he was the first. And now look! So he's cut his off ... He's for ever the

individual; always had to do it his way, and by himself. (Thompson, *Positively Main Street*, 159)

Hitherto identifiable as a force of self-alteration and surprise, Dylan surprises on this record with a voice and singing style that so enigmatically and wilfully conveys a different kind of self-deletion – his refusal any longer openly to enact self-division.[16]

V
Leave Taking

Within the art of emancipating rejection that I have been tracing, the explicit activity of leave-taking is an important and primary type of gesture or trope. It would be easy to fill pages quoting lines and songs that are organised around moments of leaving, as in 'Song to Bonny', 'I Was Young When I Left Home', 'Liverpool Gal', 'It Ain't Me, Babe', 'Restless Farewell', 'It's All Over Now, Baby Blue', 'Most Likely You Go Your Way (and I'll Go Mine)', and so on throughout his career. Broadly, Dylan's songs predominantly treat love not as a present fact but as something that is over or yet to happen. The following examples are respectively from 'Long Time Gone', 'Don't Think Twice, It's Alright', and 'Farewell':

> Just give to me my gravestone
> With it clearly carved upon: 'I's a long time a-comin'
> An' I'll be a long time gone' (*Lyrics*, 29)

> I'm walkin' down that long, lonesome road, babe
> Where I'm bound, I can't tell
> But goodbye's too good a word, gal
> So I'll just say fare thee well (*Lyrics*, 61)

> So it's fare thee well my own true love,
> We'll meet another day, another time. (*Lyrics*, 48)

In other, often major, songs, the leaving is – on the face of it – more involuntary, and the song proceeds from the pain of loss and rejection that the singer suffers: 'I Don't Believe You', 'She's Your Lover Now', 'Boots of Spanish Leather', 'Ballad in Plain D', 'If you see Her Say, Hello', 'You're a Big Girl Now', 'Highlands', 'Tangled Up in Blue', 'Where Are You Tonight', 'I'll Remember You', and so many others.

However, the distinction between the two types of songs is perhaps less important than the ways in which both register the imbrication of painful dislocation with a certain excitement and uncertainty. This combination places the song at its turning point, in a time between times, as in 'Tangled Up in Blue', and 'It's Alright Ma (I'm Only Bleeding)':

> But me I'm still on the road
> Headin' for another joint (*Lyrics*, 333)

> … he not busy being born is busy dying (*Lyrics*, 156)

Artistically, what is common to all of them is a secret kind of ecstasy, in the original sense of the word, of an inspiring moment in which the self stands outside itself and time, looking ahead. Even a much later song like 'Mississippi' shows this. It projects a state of hopelessness, of being 'boxed in' by the city, by other people's games, age, longing, and memory, even by clothes tight on the skin. However, there is the intermitted sense that 'I know that fortune is waitin' to be kind', and that things can start to become interesting 'right about now' (*Lyrics*, 562). However variously the songs register pain, they often figure in their closing scenarios, moments of illumination or re-orientation that bear out a dedication to (albeit painful) renewal, the lure of futurity, as well as an intensified and animated sense of life, out there, in the open moment.

This pattern of intermittence and anticipation – of keeping on keeping on, of blowin' in the wind, and all the rest of it – is related also to Dylan's own larger sense of vocation, the feeling that 'destiny ... was looking right at me and nobody else' (Dylan, *Chronicles*, Vol. 1, 22). The Dylan who stepped away first from being Robert Zimmerman, and Hibbing, and who moved to New York, displayed always the courage of someone prepared to go off the high board, sustained by the readiness for the occasions that his powers could answer. Acknowledgement of that youthful courage and self-trust is something that Dylan's admirers always feel, even if they more rarely verbalise it. The need to break attachments, the iconoclast's need to break idols, corresponds also, clearly, to how Dylan is an artist who has always thrived on confounding the audience's wishes. Overturning expectations, even provocation, needle and the risks of a certain self-destructiveness, have always seemed part of his stock in trade, of his need to move away. Hence he was often seen as waspish in the 60s, or taciturn, or cussed, or protective of his mystique in the 80s and 90s. At times in his youth Dylan's deeply instinctive refusal to 'be what [you] wanted me to be' took the form of something closer to outright provocation, or antagonism. Beyond the coruscating press conferences, there was the vicious court presided over by Dylan and Neuwirth in *The Kettle of Fish* or *Max's Kansas City* in the mid-60s, where the put on and the put down were entwined in the notorious 'truth attacks' visited upon more or less hapless victims. Mike Bloomfield inimitably described to Larry Sloman what one could call Dylan's barbed-wire fence demeanour (or his wired barb-fencing perhaps), when he got to know Dylan, just prior to *Highway 61 Revisited*:

> I started seeing that this guy Dylan was a very famous guy. I mean he was invited to all the Baby Jane Holzer parties, and all these people would be walking around with him, and the Ronettes would come up to him and Phil Spector would be talking to him and I noticed that he and Albert and Neuwirth had this game that they would play and it was the beginning of the character armor, I think, it was intense put-downs of almost every human being that existed but the very few people in their aura that they didn't do this to. It was Bob, Albert, and Neuwirth, they had a whole way of talking ... It's just like this very intense put-down.[1]

Pennebaker has described this theatre of cruelty as a defence against the invasive effects of fame, but it is also possible to see it as self-excoriation, even a cauterising training in the inhuman discipline of living with fame. On this view it is a moral razed-earth policy that consigns old associations to the flames, even old friends like Phil Ochs and Dave Van Ronk.[2] Dylan's stock-in-trade in 1965 on this description is to trample his vulnerability underfoot by extinguishing sympathy, and projecting weakness on to another.

Artistically, the need to cut ties has meant repeatedly he would invite or require situations where he would betray the wishes of his audience. In a lesser talent, this might be a matter of perversity, or unreconstructed hostility, but in Dylan's case these things appear functions of a deeper artistic need and vision, of someone whose powers of creativity and response require the impetus offered by refusal – the adrenalin of a certain theatre of betrayal, the exhilaration of a moment where disaster and renewal hang in the balance ... Risk puts him on his mettle, anxiety is externalised, traded for a thrill. The black-jacketed, orange-shirted, raid of Newport 1965 with Butterfield and Kooper, for instance, was preluded by an afternoon rehearsal whose volume was – like the groovy, billowing, green and white polka dotted shirt – designed to prime the confusion and rage of the audience for the brief evening set. The impulse behind this, and the sheer rending din and wail of the evening concert, was surely to whip up conflict, to widen and intensify the division by which he would be able to encounter or control his destiny, and leave his former self in the hands of the raucous, inchoate Newport crowd as surely as a snake leaves its skin.[3]

So what is it, for instance, that primes the gladiatorial intensity, the exhilarating hostility of the 1966 tour and gives it its whiff of sulphur? Greil Marcus has memorably written that the source of the audience anger is the underlying suggestion that the whole folk movement had been a pose, and that his standing on stage tricked out in Carnaby Street motley and drainpipes, Cuban heels and the rest, bobbing and bopping, gyrating and tripping across the stage, was the final straw. It signified the deflation of the collective political hope and aspiration, not to say the *armour propre*, of his folk audience, who felt that The Hawks were taking a wrecking ball to their moral self-projections.[4] In the 1965 San Francisco conference, Dylan quips, 'they must have a lot of money, to be able to go some place and boo', but what better index of their connection to him than the belief that they could win him back by protest?[5] Similarly, Dylan has intimated more recently that the whole of his late sixties career was importantly predicated not on contentment, family, the big Bible in his study, and the beautiful New York State woods, so much as the desire to repel the expectations and fantasies of the Woodstock generation.

Of course, if the Newport electric set was not the last such confrontation, nor was it the first, being itself prefigured in the performance at Hibbing High School on 6 February 1958 where Dylan, a cherubic agitator fronting *The Golden Chords*, was tricked out with 'extra mikes for his piano and vocals' (Gray, *Bob Dylan Encyclopaedia*, 314). The performance, rambunctious and deafening, was a callow anticipation of the shape-shifting and power-play of the mid-60s, of the bombardments of Newport or Forest Hills. During the second number (one less than Newport), he wrecked the pedal on the Baldwin Grand and his English teacher (according to Michael Gray's version) succeeded where Pete Seeger was to fail, and 'cut the power to the house mikes' (Gray, *Bob Dylan Encyclopaedia*, 314).[6] What seems necessary and instinctive in all these cases is the desire to reject, to express a counter-reaction to the perceived forces of entrapment, to all compulsory attitudes – even those of the listener, the protest movement, or the counter-culture itself.[7] To take another example outside the 1960s, Marcus described Dylan's singing on the 1974 tour, as a shaking up of his audience, a 'reaching for an equivalent, though nothing like a copy, of his original sound, something very rough, disturbing, disorientating, not easy to like' (Marcus, *Bob Dylan*, 48).

Though the nature of the conflict has changed, his live performances – from the Free Trade Hall in 1966 to the Isle of Wight in 1969, from Fox Warfield in 1979 to Live Aid to the Grammys in 1991 – have nearly always more or less openly and consciously sought in part to refuse or confound audience expectation. The Dylan who in 'Desolation Row' (and elsewhere) mocked those who chorused 'Which Side are You On' is one, nonetheless, whose concerts always ask his audience this question in one form or other. At Newport the choice was stark, and driven home to the audience: were you a protective, protesting, moralising, custodian of a past artist, or an excited respondent, welcoming whatever it was, this 'something' that 'is happening here' (as he was to put it in August, 1965) (*Lyrics*, 174)? Divisive as the responses are, there would have been few in the Newport audience who would not have felt at that time the choice. At the same time, though, for many, if not all, probably, excitement and anger – the desire to look back, and the imperative not to – would have been entwined, or have alternated to some degree. ('Nostalgia is death' Dylan has said.[8]) More recently, though, there have been times, and shows on the 'Never Ending Tour', particularly in the 90s, where nostalgia, and lowered expectations, have seemed the only recourse when faced by a singer searching – often fruitlessly – for his renovating gift on stage, his scabrous persona and perfunctory performances dispiriting, as if self renewal has no recourse but self-destruction.

Dylan in 1965 or 1966, of course, was a singer whose inspiration was huge, and whose artistic gifts and opportunity appeared unprecedented, as he turned away from the folk arena to ride an artistic wave. Dylan as an artist always trusted, as well as believed, in the inspiration of the present, and the presence of inspiration. As he told Ed Bradley, in the '60 Minutes' interview in 2004, he believed a sense of dislocation, even of destiny and dedication, overhung his Hibbing childhood,

> I really didn't consider myself happy or unhappy. I always knew there was something out there that I needed to get to. It wasn't where I was at that particular moment.[9]

One could reflect, also, on the connection between this sense of selection, and the way in which, in that interview as elsewhere, Dylan talked about the 'magic' of the process by which the songs would arrive through him. The surrender to inspiration is a trust in the recreational power of the moment, and inseparable from the responses the songs create in those listeners who are attuned to them, and who take from them not only effects of meaning, but changes in attitude, rushes of energy, and shifts of feeling. Dylan creates, as Springsteen also memorably said about 'Like a Rolling Stone', out of a sense of displacement, the sense of a new innocence, of spontaneity and everything being now up for grabs. The present and future are obscure, but this is an art propelled by invigorating effects of openness. Again, as Roe puts it, 'Dylan thrives by creating a sense of enthralling absence' (Corcoran, ed., 84).

So, one can say that the first released version of 'Like a Rolling Stone' does not seem to begin so much as to have already begun, to be underway. Disregard of the audience here is a revitalising dismissiveness, evident in the famous opening double-snap of snare and bass-drum that propels us into the thrilling slipstream of this jeering, disdainful voice, one no longer bound by social nicety, social masks, schooling. The song is a roller-coaster, and we must feel at stake within this dynamic world, where everything appears divided between degradation or aggression, life reduced to its inmost possibilities of loss or forced renewal. The bracing-then-exhilarating mode of the song positively demands of its audience that it recreates itself, that the listener finds a response to all this visceral, untrammelled, majesty. It is a song that threatens otherwise to leave us behind, rolling down hill to obscurity, as it leaves behind the girl and the contemporaneous genres of rock music. Mark Polizzotti has written of Kramer's cover photo of *Highway 61* in terms of this kind of recalcitrance that draws on hostility to make new. It is the 45rpm version of a Nietzschean 'active destruction' that brings about uplifting possibilities of originality, a transvaluation of values, the overcoming of nihilism:

> The record grabs your attention even before the wrap comes off the sleeve. It's in the gaze. No one else was making that kind of immediate challenge from an album cover ... somewhere between defiance and annoyance ... he's gearing up for a fight. (Polizzotti, 5–6)

In its live versions over the following year, this song ever more intensified the sense that the song was both inside and outside the listener, the ever-more zooming, scorching music propelling him or her into some interim zone where he or she feels the provocative challenge of Dylan's voice.

Throughout the 1960s, of course, Dylan's gifts for antagonism and non-conformity, for leave-taking, were always seeking new forms, so that ironically enough the crowds that braved the cold, and the insanitary conditions of the Isle of Wight festival on 1 September 1969, for instance, waiting for hours into the night, were waiting for the satin shirted iconoclast of the *Highway 61 Revisited* cover, or the acme of cool and defiance that they had booed three and a half years earlier at Liverpool, Manchester, Newcastle, Dublin, or Edinburgh. In the event they were repaid by a brief set by a Dylan and The Band, and by a confounding, dismissive, emollience. The opening words, 'It's nice to be here, sure is' were so uncharacteristic as to seem rehearsed, wilfully perverse, an index of how the performance would resist the audience's wishes by its weird old New England courtesies, and its very mellifluousness. It included throwaway, busker versions of 'Highway 61 Revisited', 'Quinn the Eskimo' and 'Like a Rolling Stone'. In the latter song Dylan, the only person in the world apparently uncertain of the words, mumbles, stumbles or weirdly whoops his way through the verses at points, seemingly as careless of the song as an eccentric millionaire making a bonfire of dollar bills. The Band, on 1 September 1969, were at the apex of their powers. A couple of weeks before they had triumphed at Woodstock, and three weeks later would release *The Band*. Yet for once in all their association with Dylan, their accompaniment appears lackadaisical, perfunctory, overblown, and the sound badly mixed, and afflicted by feedback to boot. The looseness of the performance, at worst disabling and careless, lends itself nonetheless to moments of beguiling lyricism on the high spots of the set, in 'To Ramona', the obscure 'Minstrel Boy' (never performed again or elsewhere it seems), the Scottish song, 'Wild Mountain Thyme', and – appropriately enough – 'I Threw it All Away'. In these songs, looseness becomes a relaxed openness, and Dylan's patriarchal persona – white-suited, strumming beautiful large Gibson or Martin acoustics – appeared to find his new appetite for languor sustained by melody, rhythm, cadence.

It would not be until the best of the Christian shows of 1979, 1980 and 1981, not least those at Fox Warfield and Earls Court, that Dylan would find his aesthetic of rejection elevated again in sustained fashion to a concerted intensity of focus, comparable to that which surfaced in the folk clubs of 1962–63 or the theatres of 1966. So far as that antagonism is an artistic and cultural matter, however, one might recognise its American provenance again in Ralph Waldo Emerson's account of the poet, the one who is more ourselves than we are, because he anticipates what we want to say, yet are too afraid, too oblivious, or inarticulate to express. The poet, for Emerson, is, as this might imply, the enemy of convention. Turning away from those who censure him, '[h]e unlocks our chains, and admits us to a new scene'.[10] Mark Ford has written of Emerson as a strange precursor of Dylan, less a direct influence than someone whose superficial differences belie deep and abiding parallels and affinities, and whose influential articulation of the American mind makes him of particular use for illuminating the cultural, philosophical and poetic features of Dylan's work.[11] In terms of the specifics of becoming in Dylan's case, for instance, Emerson offers a useful rubric:

> The soul's advances are not made by gradation, such as can be represented in a straight line, such as can be represented by motion in a straight line, but rather by ascension of state, such as can be represented by metamorphosis – from the egg to the worm, from the worm to the fly. The growths of genius are of a certain *total* character ...[12]

A central aspect of the Emersonian aspect of Dylan's imagination is the way in which his art exemplifies a particularly American vision of the poet, caught up in his own private war of independence and self-change. Emerson's non-conformist, self-reliant, poet is one who kicks over the traces, by mining in his art truths we are too hidebound, too cowardly to own. We are hitherto only half-ourselves, because unexpressed, while the poet speaks our common secrets on our behalf, and reaps the reward of public acknowledgement. In 'The Poet', Emerson writes: 'the experience of a new age requires a new confession', and '[t]he young man reveres men of genius, because, to speak truly, they are more himself than he is' (Emerson, 245, 242). This view of the poet as the revealer of suppressed or unarticulated truths also allows one to connect up one or two threads here, since Dylan's way of speaking the truth in fact involves a fundamental refusal (however inaccessible he might be) to do what his Masters of War (and lesser artists) do, and hide behind masks. Clearly that song, like many of the earlier songs, had represented the kind of digging out of buried truths that Emerson talks about, a song that identified what needed saying at a particular time, and that brought about the kind of liberating effects that he identified with his poet. Such an art (about changing times, and in large part inaugurating them) is then, clearly, an art of enfranchisement both in theme and effect. This effective politics – creating a mass audience galvanised by their shared acknowledgment of glaring injustice, corruption and greed – was clearly how Dylan's early protest songs worked.

In such underlying or specific ways leave-taking – leaving oneself and one's culture behind, or transforming it through new affiliations – can thus be taken as an important motif to describe Dylan's engagements with the American cultural imagination. David Pichaske has suggested further nuances and inflections. In his regional study, *Song of the North Country*, he discusses the theme of journeying and departing in Dylan's songs, and traces the American mythology of the road, back past Fenimore Cooper, Melville, Twain, Steinbeck, Whitman, Kerouac to 'the adventures of Aeneas, Odysseus, Christ, Dante, Chaucer's Canterbury pilgrims', as well as Bunyan and Fielding... Prefacing a discussion of medieval epic, Pichaske further cites Joseph Campbell's idea of the journey as archetype:

> The usual hero adventure begins with someone from whom something has been taken, or who feels there's something lacking in the normal experience available or permitted to the members of society ... This person then takes off on a series of adventures beyond the ordinary, either to recover what has been lost or to discover some life-giving elixir. It's usually a cycle, a going and a returning. (Pichaske, 146)

What most distinguishes Pichaske's work, though, is that it construes Dylan's imagination as one perpetually steeped in the Midwest, as if – with its idioms, geography, culture, and narrative – it was the place he always and never leaves behind, inflecting every thing he does, and discernible in his jeremiads, his pastoralism, and his prophetic strain.[13] Clearly, this identifying of leave-taking with return might even be linked to the trope of a creative 'Odyssey' that Dylan referred to in the interview on *No Direction Home*, when he spoke of trying to return to some home he had left behind 'a while back'.

VI
Aversiveness

Dylan in the 1960s, we have seen, always appears to gain traction by setting himself against his society, his past, his family, his former associates, and his former self. Creatively, this corresponds to an imperative whereby, like Emerson's poet, he draws impetus from contesting socially invested prescriptions of subjectivity. In this section, I want to probe this further, taking up the idea of aversiveness from Stanley Cavell's use of the term in an account of traits in Emerson's thinking that have to do with rejecting conformity.[1] In doing so I will move from a philosophical preamble towards biographical uses of the idea. It might be as well to stress that my motive in doing so is not to take a philosophical detour for its own sake, but to use the idea of the aversive attitude to bring out useful and fundamental connections between the aesthetic, the political, and the existential aspects of Dylan's subjectivity, as well as between different facets, dimensions and stages of Dylan's career.

Philosophically, aversiveness can be identified with a metaphysics of ungrounded subjectivity in Dylan's work, in so far as his artistry unpicks philosophical fabrications of subject and object. Emerson writes in 'Experience' that 'Dream delivers us to dream' (Emerson, 269), that '[t]emperament' is a 'prison of glass', and that '[t]he secret of the illusoriness [of our experience] is in the necessity of a succession of moods or objects' (Emerson, 272). With this in mind, we can think of the truant, phantasmagoric world of *Highway 61 Revisited* which thrillingly divides us between anguish or exultation and leaves us always *en route*, caught in a mesh of myth, fantasy and fact, and revisiting again the routes of our endless displacements from ourselves and our culture. Ephemerality in mood and mode – a registration of radical contingency and a torching of society's mythological projections of identity – are key to the wildly careering, joyous sense of artistic possibility in the work of the mid-60s. Again, one might cite how Emerson follows the statement just quoted with sentences that seem appropriate to the abyssal sense of self in *Blonde on Blonde*, or the fugitive selves of *John Wesley Harding*: 'Gladly we would anchor, but the anchorage is quicksand. This onward trick of nature is too strong for us' (Emerson, 272). Dylan's work constantly turns not only on a lived sense of futurity and successiveness (of leave-taking as it were), but on this transitional sense of reality itself, configured now as *departure*. As Cavell says of this passage: '[t]his very evanescence of the world proves its existence to me; it *is* what vanishes from me' (Cavell, *Emerson's Transcendental Etudes*, 13).[2] Reality is what departs from me as I also take leave, stepping away and forward towards my unknown alias, what Emerson terms in 'History' 'the unattained, but attainable self' (Emerson, 117). Though this book does not offer a theorised account, then, one can digress philosophically for a moment to say that it might be possible to redescribe the subjective dynamic that concerns me in terms of such a transcendental form of experience and relatedness in Dylan's work: he endlessly returns to his sense of a world experienced as left behind or disappearing, including his former selves, while he must set his face against it, so as to depart from and pursue himself over and again.[3]

More broadly there are important ethical and social components of this that will allow us to loop back from the epistemological to the American context and Dylan's 60s career. In terms of American philosophy, Cavell describes how Emerson responds to the modern European philosophical sense of metaphysical disjunction, of the mind as caught between the knowable world of the senses, and the moral world of ideas, choices, will. In 'Experience' Emerson writes that 'I know that the world I converse with in the cities and the farms is not the world I *think*' (Emerson, 289). Emerson's decisive American act is to recast this Kantian division in terms of a single temporal drama of social estrangement and ethical imagination. Writes Cavell:

> The very conception of a divided self and a doubled world, providing a perspective of judgment upon the world as it is, measured against the world as it may be, tends to express disappointment with the world as it is, as the scene of human activity and prospects, and perhaps to lodge the demand or desire for a reform or transfiguration of the world. [4]

The divisions of European philosophy are absorbed into an American drama of subjective eventuality that importantly opens the world we know to the philosophical and spiritual. The human is bound up with 'a sense of the world as cursed, perhaps as a kind of punishment for being human' (Cavell, *Cities of Words*, 3). Constitutively riven by the bondage of socially prescribed consciousness, we are in turn driven on restively to express our Emersonian sense of recoil, our need for freedom, resistance, self-change, self-reliance. For Dylan self-division is compounded with an openness that involves living perpetually in uncertain transition from former modes of being, in rejection of what Emerson called our 'secret melancholy', or Thoreau 'quiet desperation', in therapeutic pursuit of a world that will come alive again, and me with it.[5]

Politically and culturally, this temporal dynamic of aversion and provisional renewal, of disillusion and hope, of dejection and reanimation, can be seen as importantly and deeply American, since what is more American than the impulse to non-conformity, the rededication to the future, the original act of dissent? The counter-culture spawned by Dylan clearly spoke to that perennial American dedication in the 1960s whereby the country's political survival is predicated on renewing its ideals, in the face of lowering reality. Andrew Gamble has identified Dylan with the circulations of the apocalyptic and the edenic in the American religious mythology of the polis:

> What Dylan almost never offers is a straightforward accommodation to the world as it is, certainly not the political world. Instead, his starting point is always a 'world gone wrong', a world which fails to live up or match its ideal ... this is the ideal of America, and Dylan belongs in an American romantic tradition which was inaugurated by Emerson, and includes Thoreau, Whitman and Melville, but which also has deep roots in American Protestantism. The idea of the American people as God's Chosen People, in the same way that the Israelites had been, became closely allied to the sense of America as a new beginning, a break with the past, particularly the old European past, and the birth of a nation that was forever young and forever capable of renewing itself.[6]

As Gamble describes, the political, ethical, and spiritual are inevitably enmeshed, and '[t]his possibility of renewal' is 'never a matter of cautious, incremental reform but a moral revolution, a cleansing of the nation's soul, stripping away the pretences, corruption and lies, casting down the false idols and returning to a life of simple purity and goodness' (Boucher and Browning, 26). In the broadest terms, America is always to be (re)discovered. Thus, Sally Bayley identifies the Basement Tapes with an American literary imagination predicated on the immensity of the country, conditioned by the excess of space over specific places and interiors, and resulting in an 'America ... always on the point of becoming.'[7]

Drawing together some of these threads in relation to the biographical context, one can describe the young Dylan, like Emerson's figure of self-reliance, as one indeed who felt compelled to 'shun father and mother and wife and brother when my genius calls me' (Emerson, 142). Aversiveness, rejection, departure, and instability are from the first the values of Dylan's sense of self-reality. Writers on the very youthful Dylan have understandably highlighted the undeflectable, steely ambition that underlay the lies, the put-ons, the evasions, the chancing, the sheer impatient verve and ruthlessness of his self-fabrication. However, as John Gibbens points out, the young Dylan's endless, sometimes ludicrous, concoctions were motivated perhaps not so much by the desire to be believed, but by the aversive necessity not to be known, not to be identified with where he had come from:

> the dead parents, the circus he ran away with, the teenage years of hoboing, the spells under the wings of bluesmen and folksingers – did not really amount to an alternative, fictitious biography so much as an *evasion* of biography. The important thing was ... that he should be from nowhere in particular.[8]

If the self is always yet to be attained, then it follows that its truth is always entwined with imagining itself differently, with clearing the decks, and holding to the possibility that one can identify, like Odysseus, as No-One, from nowhere. This remains the necessary kernel of truth in the self-mythology of rootlessness that he propagated in the early days, with tales about his vagabond and orphaned youth, accompanying a black street singer on spoons aged ten, hopping freight trains and working the ferris wheel with the carnival. Becoming as a transformative process is common to both the life and the work, compounded out of an artifice that is internal to the reality of the self and manifest through time.[9] The self necessarily turns away from a past whose attachments no longer fit, or are not available anymore. Aversiveness to one's past, like the rejection of other's images of you, is integral to self-becoming because the past stands for a certain exhausted falsehood, and because the future essentially identifies the truth of a self with a certain romance.

Clearly in the early days, though, this determination to evacuate the past and recreate oneself was inseparable from fabrications that were, in a literal way, extreme and discomfiting. Suze Rotolo wrote of the besetting paranoia and perpetual strain that surrounded his denials, and his discomfort when she found his draft card with 'Zimmerman' on it.[10] As Scobie put it, the name '"Bob Dylan" ... sealed him off definitively from Hibbing, from Robert Zimmerman' (Scobie, 41). Hence, Dylan's huge anger and embarrassment when Andrea Svedburg uncovered for *Newsweek* the presence of his parents at an early Carneige Hall concert (Heylin, *Behind the Shades*, 129–30). Yet for the most part people appeared to conspire not to expose him. If one listens to the radio interview with Cynthia Gooding from March 1962 where Dylan haws and hums and flounders under the most gentle questions, or with Studs Terkel when he claims to have seen Woody as a youngster, the embarrassment is borderline excruciating.[11] Indeed, the discomfort appears to work in Dylan's favour, making the interlocutor hold off, or even feel protective (if only so that the interview will not stall).

Certainly for whatever motive, it seems the case that most people in the New York folk scene understood, relished the story-telling, screened out the hogwash, or were up to it themselves. Dave Van Ronk described Dylan as incapacitated by laughter by the revelation that Ramblin' Jack Elliott, Guthrie's great torch-bearer and acolyte, was a doctor's son from Ocean Parkway, named Elliott Adnopoz:

> Bobby literally fell off his chair; he was rolling around on the floor, and it took him a couple of minutes to pull himself together and get up again. Then Barry [Kornfield], who can be diabolical in things like this, leaned over to him and just whispered the word 'Adnopoz', and back he went under the table. (Van Ronk, 1962)

Van Ronk also describes Dylan's own inventions at the time:

> He had that Guthriesque persona, both on and off stage, and we all bought it. Not that we necessarily believed he was really a Sioux Indian from New Mexico or whatever cocakamamy variation he was pedalling that day, but we believed the gist of his story, and even what we didn't believe was often entertaining ... It was an old showbiz tradition – everyone changed their names and invented stories about themselves. So we kidded him some, but nobody held it against him, I don't think Bobby ever understood that. He never really got the fact that nobody cared who you had been before you hit town. We were all inventing characters for ourselves. (Van Ronk, 162)

Van Ronk seems to acknowledge that people would conspire with Dylan's process of self-remaking because it theatrically played out the deeper truth, that the self is integrally a matter of artifice: of imagining and enacting oneself otherwise. Contrarily, the danger of exposure is that the project of expression can seem reducible to mere lies. Certainly, the important issue was as Robert Shelton generously put it in the *New York Times* piece that propelled Dylan's career and CBS contract: 'Mr. Dylan is vague about his antecedents and birthplace, but it matters less where he has been than where he is going, and that would seem to be straight up'.[12]

As this suggests, Dylan's success is surely inseparable from his audience's underlying perception that he was embodying in exemplary fashion the twin necessities of aversion and invention. The fictiveness that Dylan was demonstrating was thus a saving resource, integral to the self as it projects itself beyond itself. Caspar Llewellyn-Smith described Andrew Loog Oldham's early encounter with Dylan on the first London visit at the turn of 1962–63:

> At some point in this period, Dylan briefly met a young Andrew Loog Oldham, shortly to become the manager of The Rolling Stones. He had heard of Grossman's reputation, and inveigled an introduction at the Mayfair, taking from him the job of Dylan's 'press representative' for a week for the fee of a fiver. He took Dylan shopping to Dobells on the Charing Cross Road (like Collets, a nexus of the folk scene) and remembers him 'looking like a busker: grey face, eyes both dead and knowing. Neutral colours, neutral army and Greenwich Village clobber. Dylan was Bob Dylan already, just as he's Bob Dylan now. It wasn't an act, even if it was.'[13]

As Oldham says, *Bob Dylan*, both *was* an act, and *wasn't* an act, since in terms of the American ethic of subjectivity described here we must all first imagine ourselves again, if we are to convert the provisional virtualities of self-hood into actuality. Dylan's audience, one might say, wouldn't care what his real name was, to the extent that they understood that his work was enacting and inviting new opportunities of individual and collective self-exploration. At the same time, the self as an on-going project demands an iron will and nerve, in holding to the refusal to be bound by what one has been or by what others might think.

In more down to earth terms, as the press conferences or Pennebaker's films demonstrate, this corresponds to the characteristic ways Dylan steps away from the usual social desire to protect or project oneself as an available, accountable, personality. George Harrison memorably identified a total lack of interest in what others thought of him as key to Dylan's forward-pressing appeal:

> I like his whole attitude. The way he dresses, the way he doesn't give a damn. The way he sings and plays discords. The way he sends up everything. (Shelton, *No Direction Home*, 203)

Dave Van Ronk similarly identified his early 'gung-ho, unrelenting quality, a take-no-prisoners approach that was really very effective' (Marqusee, 44). Undoubtedly, this combines a conviction about self-truth with a certain temperamental spikiness, as Dylan refuses the designs of others upon the self, their demands that identity must be understood, defined, contained:

> When people believe that I am *this* or *that*, already there is a misunderstanding, a barrier between them and me. (Shelton, *No Direction Home*, 15)

> Who cares about tomorrow and yesterday? People don't live there, they live now.[14]

> Greed and lust I can understand, but I can't understand the values of definition and confinement. Definition destroys. Besides, there's nothing definite in this world.[15]

Hence, for instance, Dylan comes to recoil as if instinctively from the simplistic identifications of subjective freedom associated with 1960s American counter-culture. Emancipation for him is always a matter of an on-going resistance to the culture that claims us: more a case of escapology – an obscure grappling with social chains and restraints in an underwater sack – than easy riding or the sunny nirvana of Haight-Ashbury fantasy.[16]

In terms of thinking of Dylan's aversiveness within its larger socio-historical contexts, it is worth contemplating a little further the vortical cultural pressures on Dylan in this tumultuous period. Geoff Dyer wrote, in a parallel way, of how the currents of racial and political violence of 1960s American met in John Coltrane, and demanded a spiritual and aesthetic response from the saxophonist:

> As the civil rights movement gave way to Black Power and America's ghettos erupted in riots, so all the energy, violence, and hope of the historical moment seemed to find their way into the music. Simultaneously the music became less a test of musicianship or as in bebop, of experience and more a test of the soul, of the saxophone's ability to tear out the soul within. Commenting on the new addition to his band, Pharoah Sanders, Coltrane emphasized not his playing but his 'huge spiritual reservoir. He's always trying to reach out to truth. He's trying to allow his spiritual self to be his guide.'[17]

Clearly Dylan, like Coltrane (or Miles Davis who is so similar to Dylan), throughout this decade breathes in, and must vocalise a workable response to, the volcanic and divisive atmosphere of his times: Cold War paranoia, the Bomb threat, the military-industrial complex, the Bay of Pigs, assassinations, the Civil Rights movement, the Vietnam war, the emergent counter-culture, the tumultuous politics of race, gender and sexuality, the tensions and conflicts of the American Left, the trial of Abbie Hoffman, the Black Panthers, Malcolm X, student unrest ...

And like Davis or Coltrane, Dylan was confronting these outer changes within an art-form that he also felt charged with successively breaking and remaking. In the leading edge of Dylan's voice throughout the 1960s, one might imagine oneself hearing how his profound unsettledness of sensibility is continually seeking out, through phrasing or imagery, an accommodation with the turbulent forces of musical and social change that converge on him, and pass through him, as if a lightening rod. As this image suggests, the access of power was potentially destructive as well as transformative, and it is unlikely that anyone without an eventual instinct for self-insulation, as well as an innate capacity for self-alteration or even self-evacuation, would have been able so well to survive and conduct these currents. Dyer suggests that in jazz the early self-destruction of its major creators was perhaps a function of an art that, like Dylan's work, was furiously remaking itself in the eye of social and cultural storms. Dyer's words could equally apply to Dylan's music of the 1960s:

> How could an art form have developed so rapidly and at such a pitch of excitement without exacting a huge human toll? If jazz has a vital connection with 'the universal struggle of modern man' how could the men who create it not bear the scars of that struggle? (Dyer, *But Beautiful*, 198)

VII
Inspiration

In turning to the idea of inspiration, it is important to emphasise the links and divergences between the aesthetic imperatives of Dylan's art in the 1960s, his changing self-presentation, and his ambition, his making a name for himself. In the first place, his personality and temperament were wired, reactive, assimilative and sensitised to an extraordinary degree, and he was voraciously, even ruthlessly, intent on self-advancement as well as creative innovation. Van Ronk has described how fiercely competitive and driven was the early New York scene, yet Eric Anderson, a Greenwich Village contemporary, seemed to single out Dylan's particular kind of drive as both a creative and personal trait, not wholly identifiable as mere ambition: 'The earmark or hallmark of Bob Dylan is his curiosity, and that kind of restlessness would make anyone nervous. And he can't stop. I mean, he is a driven maniac' (Epstein, 155). Dylan's inability to settle was clearly evident in small gestures (like the relentless, jack-hammer leg movement that everyone noted in the early days), and the whole kinetic gamut of intonation, grimace, movement, gesticulation, comedy, mouth-chewing, aggression, and shifting gazes that he brought to public settings in the mid-1960s.

Anderson's identification of restless curiosity and bristling nervous energy suggests how inseparable are the breakthroughs of Dylan's ambition from the outbreaks of his inspiration. This inspiration is also not merely personal and artistic, but something that he transmits to his audience, as Marcus described at Berkeley, where the singer's every movement or word on stage appeared to emit provocative signals, as if every throwaway nuance of speech, dress, and performance were invested with a singular import and portent, were manifestations of a contagious originality, signs of the times issuing from some creative vanguard, incitements to be different. Watching Dylan on *Eat The Document*, for instance, is to be aware of someone whose unpredictability and magnetism tends to draw the viewer's attention to himself, like a whirlpool, every aspect of his demeanour seeming mysteriously eloquent. The viewer might variously latch on to the way Dylan walks or stands; the glances or turns of wit; the moments of sharpness, gentleness, forbearance or civility; his hounds-tooth suit; the wry, weary, affectless, dismissive, sardonic, merciless, or mischievous tones of his voice. As Marcus observed at Berkeley it can even seem as if there is almost no trivial aspect of his behaviour that does not seem as if it might appear obscurely come to trail with it a flash of genius, or encode some new way of being. Marcus quotes Paul Nelson:

> In the mid-sixties Dylan's talent evoked such an intense degree of personal participation from both his admirers and detractors that he could not be permitted

so much as a random action ... Hungry for a sign, the world used to follow him around, just waiting for him to drop a cigarette butt. When he did they'd sift through the remains, looking for significance. The scary part is they'd find it – and it really would be significant. (Marcus, *Bob Dylan*, 348)

Indeed, so hyperbolic can this investment threaten to become at times that the Dylan enthusiast can soon feel him/herself uncomfortably akin to A.J. Weberman, whose bespectacled eyes loom over Dylan studies in the way that Dr T.J. Eckleberg's eyes stare out of the ubiquitous hoardings over the landscape of Fitzgerald's *The Great Gatsby*. For Weberman, Leader of the Dylan Liberation Front, Dylanology and garbology (rummaging through Dylan's MacDougal Street garbage for esoteric fragments and portents) were inseparable practices:

One night I went over Ds garbage just for old time's sake and in an envelope separate from the rest of the trash there were five toothbrushes of various sizes and an unused tube of toothpaste wrapped in a plastic bag. 'Tooth' means 'electric guitar' in D's symbology.[1]

Weberman's zeal for his garbological archive was undimmed by soiled children's nappies, and by Dylan placing extra dog feces in the trash and ensuring for good measure that it was smeared all over the bags and their twist ties. Indeed, to corroborate his findings that the lyrics of *Nashville Skyline* were code for Dylan's heroin addiction, Weberman was prompted by the rigorous protocols of his discipline to advertise in the *East Village Other* for a bottle of Dylan's urine.[2] Unsurprisingly, garbage of one kind of another seems the outcome as well as method of Weberman's researches. Weberman had a genius for turning everything inside-out and upside down, for emptying out what was expansive in Dylan's art and substituting his own kingdom of trash: whether he was constructing his *Dylan to English Dictionary*; or playing the songs backwards; or inducting his class in the hermeneutical niceties of garbology; or leading a mob, megaphone in hand, to mass in the street on Dylan's 30th birthday (having decorated a cake with hypodermic needles for candles). Beyond the demented black comedy though, as Weberman's admiration for Dylan soured to paranoid accusation, he constructed a deranged, nightmare world: Dylan was a long-time (government controlled) heroin addict and AIDS sufferer; he was a racist who wrote 'Blowin' in the Wind' in approval of lynched bodies swaying in trees; he was a holocaust denier who identified Israel with Nazi Germany. Eventually Weberman was to abandon his field research in the bins of 94 MacDougal Street after Dylan jumped off a bicycle in Greenwich Village to punch him and bash his head against the pavement. Predictably perhaps, A.J. even took some disquieting solace from this encounter, asking: 'I mean how many people can say they've had Bob Dylan on top of them, apart from his wife?'[3]

If Weberman is a cautionary figure, then, it is as an embodiment of the fanatical tendency that lurks in the popular imagining of Bob Dylan. Importantly though, he is someone who reveals by his wrong-headed mania for litter(y) criticism how far Dylan's songs essentially both invite and elude interpretation.[4] His aggressive, invasive reading indicates how Dylan's creative sensibility and inspiration thrive on withdrawal and provisionality, on the sense that he is never quite *there*. If what defines garbage is that we need to find some other place for it, what identifies a star like Dylan (or Garbo, one is tempted to say) is that they seem already somehow to belong to some other place, however much we might want to detain them or bring them down to earth (or to the gutter). Creatively and culturally this means that Dylan appears able to recreate his times and his audience all the more by seeming utterly divorced from them, even indifferent to them. According to some Archimedean principle of leverage, Dylan appears able to exert his kind of exorbitant influence, to move the world a little, because he belongs intensively, forcefully, to a point outside it. Like all genuine inspiration, Dylan's is a function of an inimitable kind of displacement, and an essential futurity. It is as if he can surprise and command his audience because, like a comet that blazes a trail across our firmament, he appears not to belong wholly to our system or our time.

Thus, one can say that Dylan fascinates the viewer in *Eat The Document* (flawed and frustrating as the film can be in other respects) because he comes across as untimely, so cool as to be other-worldly, different in kind from everyone else on the film. He resembles an *über*-freak, who has wandered into mid-60s Europe as if from some different plane of being, with no interest in the attention he attracts. When he haltingly says 'I think I'll go get a ... cup of ... *tea*' on the train in *Eat The Document* the viewer could be forgiven for expressing surprise that a Martian is familiar with the beverage. Even this casual remark is comic and magnetic, and it reverberates in our minds in a way that reveals the tendency of *amour fou* in Dylan's admirers, the impression that his relation to words is in itself somehow unaccountable and compelling, that the significance of *how* he speaks, of his speaking *at all*, transcend the significances of what he actually says. Such annunciatory effects of Dylan's presence are singular, incongruous, and dislocating, and the basis of the endless social comedy of the film. His inspiration appears implicit in his physical appearance, in the enigmatic restless vitality, and the wilful obduracy or weariness that betrays a contrary sensitivity, even refinement. His eyes are watchful, ruminative, and intense, indices of a creative and personal reserve yet to be expended, while his mouth is most characteristically set, as we have noted in photographs, as if in a kind of defiant distrust and disappointment with existence.

Further, in both of Pennebaker's films Dylan's position at the zenith of his culture appears ironically indistinguishable from massive, confining forces of compression and expectation. His inspiration appears both threatened and heightened by the consuming forces of fame. Pre-eminence means in fact that he is perpetually reacting, responding, retaliating, or retreating in the films, and all the time visibly animated, excited, or exhausted. Often apparently dependent on external stimulants and Neuwirth's zippy wit to raise him, he cannot avoid having in some way to protect his territory and his creative energy: from Donovan, journalists, or his audience. The fascinations of the films are inseparable from our detecting how the liberations of his position – taken by millions as their 'vagabond god' – actually entail this sense also that he is embattled, on top of the world yet also in a corner, and needing to fight his way out of it.[5]

Inspiration emerges also in the musical scenes where Dylan is often visibly taken outside himself. At one point in *Eat The Document*, during 'One Too Mornings', Garth Hudson punctuates Robertson's note-twisting, contorted blues instrumental by extemporising a brief organ passage. What has been a purling, eddying accompaniment now becomes imperious as Hudson's organ whooshes into the foreground, piling up a glorious chord whose downward intervals and gathering volume work – for one or two seconds at the most – to irradiate the whole song like a waterfall. The momentary choral effect is so transfiguring that Dylan's mask of concentration slips for a micro-second, and his face betrays surprise then delight, that these musicians could return and augment his inspiration. The film's great virtue in fact is that it catches how Dylan's inspired expressiveness on the electric music of the tour is a matter of the animating passages between The Hawks' punishing, ear-splitting, jet-powered accompaniment, and the transporting or tormented voice. In these concerts the inherent loneliness and abjection of the blues is lifted to new heights, shot through with the nightly inspiration channelled by Dylan on stage – like some rapt enchanter in the acoustic set, or whirling dervish in the electric. As Robertson put it with no small understatement: 'We played some jobs with Bob where the music was sailing – and he was sailing' (Lee, *Just Like The Night*, 65).

In comparison, the Dylan of the Johnny Cash show in June 1969 is studiedly self-composed, his air of restraint heightened by his short hair, plain black suit, acoustic guitar and the blacked-out stage on two of the songs. One can still, though, feel the kind of surprise that the audience might have felt by the time of the Cash show and *Nashville Skyline*, as Dylan's characteristically dislocated and dislocating kind of inspiration here appears itself largely to be held in reserve. Up to this point, the music of the 1960s has appeared itself always to be arriving, visiting Dylan and moving through him. On the stage at the Cash show, the refusal to unleash this kind of inspiration appears evident, even to be exploited as part of the effect. His face is now handsome rather than androgynous, while his myopic but penetrating eyes cultivate an indefinite middle distance. He moves and conducts himself for the first time as someone now taking possession of his own myth. He projects himself as someone who has come through, his songs of heartbreak knowingly registering a dialogue between self-composure and losses of all kinds: 'Girl From The North Country', 'I Threw It All Away', 'Living the Blues.' The Dylan who is visibly carried away in 1966 like some human cannonball is now intent on carrying himself, and in singing in a way that now itself artfully contains loneliness and beauty, as in the way the voice curls and falls itself around the phrase 'when the snow-flakes fall' in the first song.

And in later years, as Dylan developed his craft as a songwriter, the aleatory component in his inspiration has tended to diminish, to become an incidental quality of his work rather than the air it breathed. Indeed, certain songs have arguably tended to become vehicles for him, rather than taking him as their vehicle.

They have become ways of renewing his inspiration and his influence, of making artistic statements, reclaiming the territory, climbing the peak. In the process, songs like 'Changing of the Guards', 'Journey Through Dark Heat', 'Caribbean Wind', 'Blind Willie McTell', 'Brownsville Girl' (written with Sam Shepard), 'Dignity', 'Series of Dreams', 'Mississippi', 'Red River Shore', or ''Cross The Green Mountain' might be said plausibly to be the greatest, most achieved, songs he has ever written, and each certainly reveals a monumental quality, scope, and architecture all of its own. However, what is lacking within them are the prevalent features of his improvisational, unfinished, inspirational, qualities as an artist in the 1960s where he appeared to stand at the cross-roads of his culture (as Marcus said in an image we shall return to), with his gifts forced into the open in all their youthful, ebullient invention by the concentric pressures of fame, and the delirious, dangerous, swirling uncertainties of the period.

Unsettledness and intensity are certainly the features that particularly distinguish Dylan's improvisational qualities during the 1960s. As a writer, from the early days he often worked up sounds and words together, more or less hypnotically allowing lines and the song to unfold. Throughout his career, though, Dylan never reveals his gifts more openly than when he is given over to the song in its process of turning into itself, and perhaps no experience is as engrossing to the listener. If this sense of transformation in performance and improvisation is essential to Dylan, it is also often necessarily evident in obscure places, and most potent where the explorations are unfinished. There is probably more of the essential Dylan, for instance, in the exquisite versions of 'I Can't Leave Her Behind' or 'On a Rainy Afternoon' recorded in a Glasgow hotel room in 1966,[6] or in 'Pattie's Gone to Laredo' on *Renaldo and Clara*,[7] or in the different all-consuming, versions of 'Ain't Gonna Go to Hell for Anybody' sung at Los Angeles, Portland, and Seattle in November and December 1980,[8] or in the back stage piano humming, stamping, and strumming in *Don't Look Back*,[9] than in many of the studio albums. And books and anecdotes about Dylan abound with songs thrown out in the moment or in rehearsal, and never recorded and recovered. In this connection, the Basement Tapes take on a particular status, as providing an intimate and sustained portrait of Dylan's creativity at its most unpressured, expansive, and exploratory.

Such cases display again the inwardness of the serendipitous and ephemeral with Dylan's inspiration. Like the genie from the bottle it shapes itself in air – instantaneous, powerful, enriching, and transformative – before vanishing, only to renew itself again. As Dylan put it in conversation with Hubert Saal in 1968: '[I]t's the difference between the words on paper and the song. The song disappears into the air, the paper stays' (Artur, 402). In 1960s press conferences and interviews, when pressed about where the songs come from, he would have only the banality of the literal to fall back on, asserting just that the songs came to him, or that he could hear the music with the words when they did, or that occasionally he would hear the music first, etcetera. Often, he would offer bland, quietly exasperated, responses when pressed about the relative importance of words and music, or his processes of composition, as at San Francisco (as we have seen) when he says that '[t]he words are just as important as the music. There would be no words without the music', or 'I'll be just sitting around playing so I can write up some words. I don't get any ideas though [...] of what I want to, you know, or what's really going to happen here' (Artur, 235, 244). Like a jazz musician, Dylan emphasises the eventual, unaccountable, nature of his genius, the fact that the magic may not always happen, and is certainly not simply controlled. And when it does, the words and music similarly surprise and transform the listener's consciousness, introducing him or her for an indefinite interval into an enveloping imaginative world. In 1978 Dylan would confide to Matt Damsker that suddenly sometime around the world tour it was 'like I had amnesia all of a sudden ... I couldn't learn what I had been able to do naturally – like *Highway 61 Revisited*. I mean you can't sit down and write that consciously because it has to do with the break-up of time' (Artur, 666). For this reason, Scobie understandably calls the 1960s Dylan's 'Years of Creation'.[10]

More broadly, the inwardness of these values of the evanescent and the eventual with Dylan's creativity was always evident as spectacle in the 1960s, almost as a power of transfiguration, intensive and collective in its effects. The concerts caught in *Don't Look Back*, in those echoing, lofty, shabby British theatres, exemplify in a clear way how the audience enters into a collective sense of rapt expectancy, their attentiveness bound to how the singer shapes air into words. For Allen Ginsberg on Scorsese's *No Direction Home*, Dylan around 1965 or 1966 was a shamanistic presence, 'a column of air', channelling cultural change (or conducting it, in an Emersonian metaphor). It is clear that there is a strong connection between what I am exploring here and Ginsberg's sense that these performances were about animation and transformation, and the speaker's presence, call it incarnation on the stage, as much as about mere intelligibility. Responding to these performances is inseparable from being mesmerised by the play of gesture and facial expression, the turning on the point of a heel, the flickers of humour or intimacy; all the imagery of the concert hall – the gilded tiers, the glitter of metal, and the theatre of the singer picked out by the spot in the dark. The sense of risk, of potential conflict and troubled connection, of an adventitious event, of inspiration, marks the performances. It is a matter of delivery, of timing, and of the ways Dylan often in the acoustic sets of 1965 and 1966 increasingly rejects known songs, or known ways of singing known songs like 'She Belongs to Me' or 'It's All Over Now, Baby Blue' in terms of a performance dominated by shifts in timbre and phrasing. Certainly, if one listens to the acoustic sets from the 1966 tour the transfixing intensity of Dylan's possession of the unfolding moments of his performances can almost seem to challenge time itself to stand still. The listener is spellbound by a singer who is obviously creatively fashioning his material on stage and remaking it in the moment, along with himself and his audience.

PART TWO
The 1960s

Chapter 1
'Mind Like a Trap'

Bob Dylan, The Freewheelin' Bob Dylan,
The Times They Are A-Changin'

Suze Rotolo, in her memoir of the early days in Greenwich Village, wrote that 'Bob was charismatic; he was a beacon, a lighthouse. He was also a black hole' (Rotolo, 273). And in the early New York days Dylan's inspiration does flash forth most authentically against a background of darkness, vacancy, or obscurity. What is evident from 1961 or 1962, fully-fledged when so much else about his artistic sensibility is in development, is Dylan's lifelong capacity as an interpreter to dissolve himself within the often tragic situations and voices of traditional songs.[1] His gift resembles a Keatsian 'negative capability', his subjectivity accepting of mystery, and invisible in what it brings to expression.[2] In particular, it allows the twenty-year-old to sound out, as if by some occult correspondence, deep subtractive realities of experience within a song's own scenario. As he leaves himself behind, so Dylan's strange sixth sense dramatically registers someone who is fatefully lost to him or herself, whose powers of expression have become captive to addiction, homelessness, affliction, prostitution, alcoholism, guilt, or heartbreak. In song after song the burden is an irrevocable predicament of consuming loneliness and silence. So, he will intuitively create moving effects out of voicing the fractured self-hood of a cocaine addict (in 'Cocaine, Cocaine'), a blind man ('It's Hard to Be Blind'), the girl in 'House of the Rising Sun', a vagrant ('I Ain't Got No Home'), an abandoned woman (in 'Dink's Song'), a grieving friend (in 'He Was a Friend of Mine'), and many others. In third-person ballads also the voice will turn on its inwardness with murdered victims in 'Omie Wise', 'Hezekiah Jones/Black Cross', 'Railroad Boy', '1913 Massacre', or 'Poor Lazarus'.

More specifically, one can surmise that Dylan creatively draws in these songs (and often in his own earliest compositions) on a besetting fantasy: the anxiety of disappearing unexpressed – the fear of anonymity, of not being seen, of vanishing with no-one knowing … Further, if Dylan's gift, as I am arguing, is one that works *ex nihilo*, as an expressive emancipation of the self from prior conditions, then it is unsurprising if in these early days his imagination was caught by a fear of inexpression, of not being heard, a dread of being locked up in anonymity, unvoiced.[3] Hence the haunted fascination with those whom life and society have carelessly discarded and who remain unknown, like the nameless vagrant in 'Man on the Street', or those who are happy to die underground in 'Let Me Die In My

Footsteps' or who disappear while 'you never even know', in 'Hard Times in New York Town'.[4] More generally, as the songs describe such dramas of expression and inexpression, so also a corresponding tension grips and divides the performances themselves, as memories or possibilities of lyricism, vision, and relatedness break through in singing that otherwise is bound by the imagined fate of loss or isolation. The first half of the chapter explores how the theme or fantasy of an unexpressed life recurrently possessed Dylan's best early performances and compositions, up to the end of 1962 with *The Freewheelin' Bob Dylan* part-written.

Broadly speaking, Dylan's indignation in these early songs is directed against the all-too-human capacity for inhumanity, indifference: the man who will rob you with a fountain pen in 'Talkin' New York' (in a line robbed from Guthrie) or the man who will turn his head in 'Blowin' in the Wind', pretending that he just doesn't see. As these songs bear out, Guthrie's influence allows Dylan as a writer to construe issues of expression and inexpression in terms of political struggle, and the fight against alienation, prejudice, corruption, and oppression. Self-becoming involves an implicitly collective refusal of the current state of things and a commitment, however indefinite, to freedom and progress, to being heard. 'The trail is dusty/ And my road it might be rough', he sings in 'Paths of Victory':

> But the better roads are waiting
> And boys it ain't far off ('Paths of Victory', *Lyrics,* 100)

Human dignity involves standing up, walking forward, keeping going, and hopefully recognising and even joining with fellow travellers, perhaps in seeking the paths of victory. Travelling and walking, upstanding and forward motion – these are key tropes for self-emancipation, taken from Guthrie, and disseminated by Dylan, would-be Okie hobo troubadour, in song after song from this time. If Dylan's rhythmical, rasping voice projected both hardship undergone and hope, in terms of purely musical values too, Wilfred Mellers describes Dylan as having imbibed from Guthrie ways of constructing and phrasing melody that entwined internal progressive movements of their own, as from the drab and the dejected to the uplifting and inspiriting:

> Guthrie's own numbers stem from the monody of deprivation in their flat, deadpan vocal production and in the self-enclosed, usually stepwise moving tunes or mumbles ... [and] from the white euphoria in their chattering, major diatonic banjo or guitar accompaniments, and in the use of harmonica or fiddle as a blissful evocation of Eden ... 'Pastures of Plenty' is a dust-bowl trudge, melodically deprived but rhythmically and tonally euphoric, offering escape and pie in the sky by and by.[5]

In the second half of the chapter, the London visit at the turn of 1962–63 is taken as a watershed in Dylan's song-writing. Throughout 1963 there is evident a stabilising of mode – the self-modelling identification with Woody Guthrie, on the one hand, is blended with a more conscious incorporation of British and traditional folk influences and structures, on the other. From the early talking blues, or hard drivin' sounds that tended to prevail under the influence of Guthrie, there comes a shift, with a more thoroughgoing absorption and tranformation of the time-honoured tropes and modes of traditional (especially British and Irish) songs. Though this process in part pre-dated the London visit, the use of such songs as models became more marked afterwards. They lent an aura of abiding truth and anonymity that counterbalanced the individuating ethic first identifiable with Guthrie's influence. Questions of influence are complex, but many of the songs of 1962–63 are evidently indebted, as shall be shown, in musical structure and unsparing tragic focus, to British folk songs, such as those English and Scottish ballads collected, numbered and published by Francis James Child during the late nineteenth century. Throughout 1963, Dylan melded this more anonymous tone with the more native influences of Woody Guthrie, or Harry Smith's 1952 *Anthology of American Folk Music*.[6] This combination allowed Dylan in 1963 to be identified with an exemplary, ethical viewpoint transmitted through the song, and to make the songs seem at once timeless and wholly of their time, while also both universal and American.

Ever a figure more prone to visceral critique or apocalyptic visions than to ideological affiliation or constructive political projects, though, it can be further argued that Dylan found in the encounter with British folk music assistance in avoiding what seemed factitious or pious in the programmatic aspects of American folk culture. For all his admiration for Guthrie, Dylan was never one to subscribe unreservedly to the idea that 'There's a Better World a'-Coming', or to promulgate any of the diverse narratives of progress identified by the often competing and overlapping liberal, radical, nostalgic, or anarchic elements in the American folk revival of the late 1950s and early 1960s. Dylan's canny assimilation of British idioms seemingly allowed him productively to channel political indignation into impersonal, balladic modes during most of 1963 – when British models held sway – while allowing him to avoid being boxed in as a spokesman pedaling specific pedagogical or political prescriptions bearing on a time to come, beyond current conflicts.

Nonetheless, Dylan's temperamental aversion to offering salving visions for the future did not prevent him tapping, with undeviating directness, into the one unifying cause that galvanised him, along with everyone in the U.S. folk revival at the time, whether of a Nationalist or Internationalist persuasion: the Civil Rights Struggle. Racial injustice was to be the abiding theme of so many of the songs written in the year following the visit to England. It was here that the British influence was vital, if short lived, allowing the songs, as we shall see, to sound at once contemporarily engaged – narrowly focused on situation – yet also of the ages. During 1963 Dylan's own values of rejection and change become clearly identified with these larger political themes and contexts, yet the distinctiveness of the songs is also in how far they themselves reject simplicity and obviousness.

And as 1963 comes to a close, Dylan himself is decisively moving away from identification with larger causes.

I

Prior to the London visit, Dylan's career took an equally crucial turn in mid- to late-December 1960, as he set off via Chicago for New York, intent among other things on visiting Guthrie. Nonetheless, his arrival in New York in January 1961 nearly did not happen. After sleeping on floors in Chicago for two weeks or so, he decided to abandon the trip, and to return to Minnesota.[7] He hitchhiked to Madison, Wisconsin on the way 'to check out the local folk scene' in David Hajdu's words (Hajdu, 71). Once there, though, he ran into a young politico and folk artist, Fred Underhill, and the two became fellow-passengers on the 24-hour car trip to New York.[8] Dylan himself described the arrival in the city on 24 January 1961:

> The big car came to a full stop on the other side, and let me out. I slammed the door shut behind me, waved good-bye, stepped out onto the hard snow. (Dylan, *Chronicles*, Vol. 1, 9)

The rest, one might say, is history, were it not also part-myth. Hajdu's account (like Dylan's in Scorsese's film) more prosaically has Underhill accompanying Dylan into Greenwich Village on that first night:

> The weather was as cold as the North Country – fourteen degrees Farenheit, twelve degrees below normal for the day, with nine inches of snow in the streets; undeterred, Bob and Underhill trudged to the coffeehouses. At the *Cafe Wha?* each of them was allowed to sing a few songs. (Hajdu, 71)

On the first night, having played at the *Café Wha?* on MacDougall Street, Dylan was put up by Manny Roth, the club's owner.[9] The next day, he set out for the Greystone Hospital in New Jersey, to visit Woody Guthrie, whose autobiography, *Bound for Glory*, he had been consuming with an addict's fervour since the previous September.

The folk scene Dylan encountered in New York must have bracingly presented to him how far his career was a gamble. The survivors in Greenwich Village appeared to be those who proceeded on the basis of a certain artistic capital, who held the tenure of a certain defined gift or *persona*, and who had paid their dues. In contrast, Dylan was in no way the finished article in the early days, and was sustained, Dave Van Ronk suggested, primarily by his love of the music, and his dedication to Guthrie. Initially 'he was just a kid with an abrasive voice':

> Sam Hood, who took over the Gaslight around that time, insists that he would use Bobby only on crowded nights when he wanted to clear the house. So Bobby's

> experience and his memories of that time would be quite different from mine, because I was at least making a living. Bobby was doing guest sets whenever he could and backing people up on harmonicas and suchlike, but there was no real work for him. He was cadging meals and sleeping on couches, pretty frequently mine. (Van Ronk, 159)

Dependent as the nineteen-year-old Dylan may have been just on sheer chutzpah, presumption and self-belief in 1961, he fairly soon established himself in New York, and eked out a changing network of contacts, venues and overnight hospitality, as he moved up from the basket houses to supporting John Lee Hooker at Gerde's Folk City in April, and to the solo spot at the Carnegie Recital Hall in November 1961. Indeed, by the very first weekend in January, Dylan had made contact with Bob and Sid Gleason (a New Jersey electrician and his wife who hosted weekend gatherings for Guthrie), Alan Lomax, Pete Seeger and others. Dylan's mixture of Huck Finn charm, wit, talent, and brazen hucksterism, are evident too in the uneven East Orange tape recorded at their house a few weeks later. His eye for the opportunities of New York depended on a gambler's intuitiveness, nerve, and sharp selectivity ('a city like a web too intricate to understand and I wasn't going to try' [Dylan, *Chronicles*, Vol. I, 9]). The passages in *Chronicles* that deal with this time are extraordinary in their evocative descriptions of the people – Suze Rotolo, Fred Neill, Izzy Young, Dave Van Ronk – and the apartments, the cafés, the performers, and the music industry men. Though the factual is always blended with the fictive, the writing bears out the truth of the statement that: 'My mind was strong like a trap, and I didn't need any guarantee of validity' (Dylan, *Chronicles*, I, 9):

> It was a freezing winter with a snap and a sparkle in the air; nights full of blue haze [...] Walking down 7th Avenue in Manhattan in the early hours, you'd sometimes see people sleeping in the back-seats of cars. I was lucky I had places to stay – even people who lived in New York sometimes didn't have one. There's a lot of things that I didn't have, didn't have too much of a concrete identity either. 'I'm a rambler – I'm a gambler. I'm a long way from home.' That pretty much summed it up. (Dylan, *Chronicles*, Vol. 1, 55)

There is certainly 'a snap and sparkle' about this syntax that evokes how contingencies impressed themselves on the mind of this unsponsored young man without 'too much of a concrete identity'.

In this context, it is important to emphasise how indispensable were Dylan's humour, verve, and fabled charisma for his survival. Mark Spoelstra remembers of the earliest times in New York, that 'Bob loved to perform, and he had a magnetism and a strength up there that would sometimes just make me laugh', and Happy Traum said 'We just thought he was the greatest thing ... The audience wasn't so sure because he was pretty rough and raw ... But he was very animated. He was very funny.'[10] In accounts of Dylan's enticing, exuberant, stage routines in 1961 what emerges is how much it was a high-wire act that elevated risk-taking and self-improvisation, even the absence of content and a self, into a performative mode:

> *Jack Nissenson*: He was always an incredible story-teller ... he could do these long, long monologues, with no point, and no punchline – except they kept you in hysterics.
>
> *Arthur Kretchmer*: Onstage he was essentially a funny character ... I recall him standing up there looking behind the curtains for the words of his next song, or cracking up at something he was mumbling to himself. He was natural and loose, a real country character, and that is what everybody loved about him ... Sometimes he would play piano, or tell a funny story, or just clown around for a few minutes. (Heylin, *Behind the Shades*, 67–8)

Dave Van Ronk described another such moment:

> I saw him one time onstage, with just his guitar and harmonica, and he was playing a harmonica chorus that consisted of one note. He kept strumming the guitar, and every now and again he would blow this one note, and after a few measures you were completely caught up in trying to figure out where the next note was coming. And you were always wrong. By the end of two choruses, he had us all doubled over laughing, with one note on the harmonica. (Van Ronk, 161)

Van Ronk said that '[h]e had the same kind of unique timing when he sang, though in that context you would call it phrasing' (Van Ronk, 161). As an example, one thinks of the kind of *joie de vivre* and comic timing that punctuate live performances of 'Talkin' Bear Mountain Picnic Massacre' when Dylan incorporates, variously each time, his own improvisations into the changing catalogue of personal injury that follows the boat going down ('...I was bald...').

What is clear from very early recordings, is how far Dylan was able to turn an artistic profit from instability. As throughout his career, his voice functions as a revealing agent for the selfhood he detects within the song. Greil Marcus makes the point in a typically vivid way, writing about Dylan's 1962 Gaslight performance of 'Handsome Molly'. He imagines a sceptical listener to the concert overcome by the way in which Dylan's rendition of broken-heartedness in the song can by a kind of hypnotic transference, deprive the listener of his own sense of selfhood:

> You were about to say it again – anyone can do that strum – but your mind isn't quite your own anymore. Your memories are not your own. Your memories are now replaced by those of a lovesick man who died before your parents were born. He's travelling the world, to get away from his memories of Handsome Molly, knowing that the further he goes, the more indelible her face will be.

You see it; right now, in this moment, it beckons you towards everything you've ever lost.

You leave. This isn't folk music, not as Mark Spoelstra or Tommy Maken or Joan Baez or Pete Seeger or Martin Carthy make folk music. This is not a gesture. This is not respect. This is not for good or evil. You realize you have the rest of your life to catch up ... (Marcus, *Bob Dylan*, 297)

Certainly, in 'Handsome Molly' Dylan's own lack of a fixed persona means that he is able to enter into its tale of displacement. The old song tells of a man who sails the world round, unable to escape the memory of handsome Molly. If Dylan's version can possess the listener, as Marcus suggests, it is perhaps because Dylan is himself so utterly possessed by this man, now himself a ghost in his own life, his present endlessly consumed by his past ('Don't you remember, Molly, you gave me your right hand?').[11] What Dylan's performance movingly brings out is how compellingly the lover's lost self – passionate, vigorous, ebullient, searching, gentle, forlorn – is still tragically evident within the now fateful circuits of his loss and pain. Now jaunty and loud, now tender and quiet, the strummed accompaniment and singing convey a mind rising and falling on the tides of memory, gripped by losses it can never accept. Often Dylan will fadingly stretch out the last syllable of a word ('London', 'round', 'town', 'ocean', 'sea', river', 'Sunday'), as if to express an ardour that has now nowhere to go, and that can only set out to exhaust itself by unceasingly and rendingly revisiting the terms of loss ('But you broke your promise / With whom you please'...).

From the first, Dylan's versions of traditional songs betray this extraordinary clairvoyance for inhabiting the voice of someone tragically divided from their former self, for registering the expressive impasse, the fate of self-loss. In early versions of 'Worried Blues', 'Man of Constant Sorrow', 'Barbara Allen', 'Remember Me (When the Candlelights are Gleaming)', 'Corrina, Corrina', 'Buffalo Skinners', as well as often in songs by Woody Guthrie, Dylan is compellingly transported by the destitute subjectivity that he intuits within the song. As mentioned above, this is powerfully evident in early performances of 'Moonshiner', another song inhabited by a passionate, yet captive and lost, voice. Marcus eloquently describes the CBS Bootleg series version of this 'Appalachian ballad' as 'five minutes of suspension, single notes from the singer's throat and harmonica held in the air as if to come down would be to bring death with them'.[12] Tension is again a matter of the braided attitudes – pathos, painful regret, remorse, shame, rueful self-awareness – that circulate in the alcoholic's mind and in the different inflections of Dylan's voice – now abrasive, hesitant, or yearning. Dylan creates a mysterious and consuming intimacy with the voice in the song, as if ventriloquising someone captive within the closed world of his addiction. If the voice in 'Handsome Molly' imagines circling the whole globe, though compassed by his own memory, the moonshiner's soul is caught inside a bottle. And yet here too the singer divines within the song a lost residual self, the yearning romantic trapped for seventeen long years in the rounds and routines of alcoholism:

> God bless them, pretty women
> I wish they were mine,
> Their breath is as sweet as
> The dew on the vine ...[13]

The bottle has a beauty of its own – suggested by the liquidity of the gentle, rippling, finger-picked accompaniment – and it continues to betray him with the unattainable promise of a transfigured world. Alcohol fatally draws him on, but leaves him contemplating the double bind of an existence whereby drinking is the only place where he can relive any sense of the self that he has abandoned to it and relieve his gnawing sense of the lost years.

One can imagine that it was Dylan's capacity for being taken over by a song that sustained him when much of the earliest work can sound at times uneven, imitative, flat, technically flawed, merely chancy, or marked by a kind of youthful effrontery. Some of it can occasionally set your teeth on edge, and appear as an extension of those callow moments where his self-mythologising on the fly threatens to fail. Even by the time of the first CBS album, *Bob Dylan*, songs like 'See That My Grave is Kept Clean', 'Fixin' to Die', or 'In My Time of Dying' appear failed gambles, at best the occupational hazards of someone who was merely young, and who is striving for range, undertaking exercises in his craft. In these songs, the failure to sound the depths of the song makes itself evident in a forcing of effect, in attempts to camouflage and compensate for what is lacking by crass, mannered, experiments in the tragic idiom of Bukka White, Robert Johnson, or Blind Lemon Jefferson. These songs are often described as betraying Dylan's famous early fixation with death. However, this fixation might not be about mere survival so much as a function of the young artist's fear, expressed by Keats: that he may die before he has reaped his artistic harvest. This anxiety would have clearly been accentuated also by the fact that Dylan as an artist was one whose gifts depended on the incalculable ratios of what is formerly inexpressive and what is currently unexpressed, so that he might presumably feel at any moment as if he was inhabiting a void between discarded and still unrealised selves, and so as if a kind of death was intrinsic to his creativity.[14] Dylan confided to Shelton in 1966 'I was actually most afraid of death in those first years around New York' and he goes on to make the point, surely related, that he knew all the time that he 'hadn't written what I wanted to' (Shelton, *No Direction Home*, 60).

Certainly, when Dylan's performances flounder, the self-assurance that elsewhere allows him subtly to register expressive tension is lacking, and one wonders at his refusal to do multiple takes while ploughing on, miming attitudes that he cannot bring off. 'Gospel Plow', 'Sally Gal', or 'Quit Your Low Down Ways' set off in a hectic pursuit of a driving emotion or *joie de vivre*, with strings buzzing, hack-strumming, harmonica flying, the voice veering between whooping, snarling, gnarling and yelping. In such songs, Dylan's high-wire talent for finding an expressive point of interpretive balance and complexity in a song is absent and he appears merely to over-reach himself. What results is close to a forced mimicry, a desperate brazenness, as if the song is trapping Dylan rather than releasing him, so that he appears to be displaying mere relentless ambition, overdoing everything. Often such songs tend also to highlight failings of technique – in finger-picking, bottle-neck, blues licks, or uses of alternate tunings – that might otherwise be submerged, or effective, as part of the song's expressive texture. If inspiration is (as its etymology has it), a matter of the creative air that the artist breathes, these songs appear audibly deflated, hollowed-out from within by the absence of Dylan's creative spirit. 'Fixin' to Die', for example, appears a strained, breathless, and presumptuous assault on White's grooved, movingly self-possessed meditation on death and family. However, with the following song on *Bob Dylan*, 'Man of Constant Sorrow', the listener hangs on every nuance of Dylan's singing. Alternately clinging to long extended notes, then scurrying to make up for lost time, Dylan's weather-beaten, worn, voice conveys a man divided between his inner world of regret, sorrow and loss, and the outer world that he must encounter every day, with the 'morning railroad'.

II

Dylan possibly wrote 'Song to Woody' in mid-February 1961, after he had been in New York only a few weeks.[15] He was, indeed, in the words of the song 'a thousand miles from home', and it is a tactful, even reticent tribute. Equally, much of the song is obviously self-mythologising, as the nineteen-year-old Dylan – steeped in Guthrie's imagery and musical idiom – projects himself as a Guthrie heir, surveying from the open road a world divided 'between those who work and those who don't and … interested in the liberation of the human race and [the creation of] a world worth living in' (Dylan, *Chronicles*, Vol. 1, 245). As poverty is the measure of righteousness, so its paradigm is that of the outsider – the rambler, the gambler, the hobo, the drifter, Gypsy Davey, Pretty Boy Floyd and Jesus Christ, the deportee, the dust-bowl refugee, the prisoner. He is in the world but not of it, suffering, recording, and resisting social inequity as he passes through. The deeply congenial aspects of this romantic and political mythology of self-hood for the young Dylan are neatly summarised by David Hajdu:

> In Guthrie, Bob found more than a genre of music, a body of work, or a performance style: he found an image – the hard travellin' loner with a guitar and a way with words, the outsider the insiders envied, easy with women, and surely doomed. An amalgam of Bob's previous heroes, the Guthrie he found in *Bound for Glory* was Hank Williams, James Dean, and Buddy Holly – a literate folksinger with a rock and roll attitude. (Hajdu, 70)

Evidently, too, in these early days, Dylan's uses of Guthrie were partly a way of infiltrating the folk world of Minneapolis or New York, offering a protective colouring while he was rehearsing instincts and gifts that were yet to become decisively evident. In this context, 'Song to Woody' is an important achievement. Dylan is reluctant as usual to describe the process behind the song, beyond saying (also somewhat typically) that it was something that came to him very quickly ('in five minutes') when he thought about Guthrie. 'Song to Woody':

> was written in the 1960th winter ... in New York City in the drug store on 8th street. It was one of them freezing days that I came back from Sid and Bob Gleason's in East Orange, New Jersey ... Woody was there that day and it was a February Sunday night ... And I just thought about Woody, I wondered about him, thought harder and wondered harder ... I wrote this song in five minutes ... it's all I got to say ... (Heylin, *Revolution in the Air*, 37)

Nonetheless, Ricks has demonstrated the considerable formal art and linguistic craft of the song (Ricks, *Dylan's Visions of Sin*, 51–55). In the first place, as he suggests and as every listener has felt, this song dedicated to Woody is equally importantly a self-dedication, even an inaugural address of kinds, however much hedged round with youthful disclaimers ('I can't sing enough'...). While acknowledging Ricks's account, I would want to emphasise that a more improvisational dynamic, an enactment of expressivity, is inextricable from the effect. Here are the first four lines:

> I'm out here a thousand miles from my home
> Walkin' a road other men have gone down
> I'm seein' your world of people and things
> Your paupers and peasants and princes and kings (*Lyrics*, 5)

What appears at first hesitant, obscure or fumbling suddenly gives way to a more confident view. Initially, the lines appear to be marking time, to be indefinite, and uninspired. The song is underway, but it appears flat, desultory. The diction is lackadaisical ('other men', 'people and things') and the rhymes ('home', 'down') are failing. However, as always in Dylan's work, what is important are not the apparent dead spots, but the eventual incorporation of them. In the lines quoted above, for instance, the singer represents himself as away from home, but what we hear through the verse is someone who is at first tentative before a metrical and alliterative focus, establishes itself. Thus, the final line takes on (abetted by the reiterated 'and') a loose-limbed swing and control ('Your *pau*pers and *peas*ants and *prin*ces and *kings*'). The influx of energy evident in these features of sound and form (in the plosive impetus of the 'p' sounds for instance) is also of someone hitting his stride in other ways too. The words convey the attitude of someone who now surveys before him a whole world, suddenly arranged as in a viewfinder: as focused and ordered by title and position, by property and poverty. At the same time, as Ricks points out, there is also an important poise evident in the word 'Your' which shows both a tactful, accurate, mindfulness, that Guthrie's inheritance is not one that can be simply appropriated.

At this point one can usefully digress briefly to consider Clive James's salutary remarks in 1972 that Dylan's admirers tend to be undiscriminating, crucially refusing to countenance 'whether the good songs were really as good as they could be', and turning a blind eye to what he describes as their flaws: 'slipshod organization, missed opportunities, easy rhymes, unfocused images'.[16] This raises an important crux. Against it, I would wish to emphasise not only that Dylan's art is more than verbal, but that it is also essentially temporal, its innate and eventual drama of self-hood making it an art of *coming to expression*. And as such, it often works itself by inevitably risking and redeeming failure, because it works by gambling on producing something new. What is important is to recognise that meaning and expression are here often functions of process, of the movement through the verse and all the uses of intonation, surprise and rhythm – the devices of timing and time – that can make a line, a phrase, a verse turn on its axis, depart from itself, and conjure a new configuration of expression and meaning. Incidental lapses, flaws, blemishes, clichés and filler-phrases, even sheer badness and falling flat at times, can be swept up in the process. In fact they can even seem markers of the authenticity of Dylan's gift, as it creates this internal relationship between its own expressive intuition and the dramas of sensibility and conviction within the songs, dramas that turn on the loss or recovery of voice or perspective. It is this sense of a song on a knife-edge that keeps us listening.

Another example, seemingly unpremeditated, that turns what seems a dead spot to aesthetic gain can be noted in the first verse of 'Talkin' New York', when Dylan artfully mimes a country hick's wide-eyed description of a place where one can see 'People goin' down to the ground / Buildings goin' up to the sky' (*Lyrics*, 3). The phrase 'goin' down to the ground' is ungrammatical, and the verse seems to falter: shouldn't he be saying 'under the ground' if he is referring to the subway? If one were reading the lyrics one would be reaching for the red pen. However, when one hears the line 'Buildings goin' up to the sky', a new perspective hoves into view, as if the previous vagueness has generated something new. The contrast of 'down to/ up to' provokes a wider, compassing perception: that the corporate aspirations of the rising buildings are at the cost of the people who work in them, downtrodden or ground down as they would be … Dylan's apparent verbal carelessness (in part the kind of thing James accuses him of) is here fortunately redeemed by an art that surprises the listener with its expansions of voice and viewpoint, its rhythmical drive, and its passing and casual, yet powerful effects of visionary suggestion.

What needs emphasising, then, is how far the songs, like Dylan's often comic stage presence or his tales of Gallup, New Mexico at this time work by risking failure, and chancing obscurity, in pursuit of enacting expressive moments of illumination, vocation, evocation.[17] Rambling and gambling, such recurrent motifs in the songs Dylan was singing or writing at the time, seem the values of art that is in so many ways dynamically connected by courting contingencies, risk, chance, and improvisation. Hence the inwardness between Dylan and the gambler in

'Rambling, Gambling Willie', where the singer matches, verse by verse, Willie's own way of generating novelty and surprise out of a deck of cards. Dylan deals out the verses of Willie's life of fixed rules and uncertain chances, until each verse comes to its anticipated yet unforeseen end, the humour and wit turning up each time like a winning hand:

> When the game finally ended up, the whole damn boat was his
>
> The man he left a diamond flush, Willie didn't even have a pair
>
> When Willie's cards fell on the floor, they were aces backed with eights *(Lyrics*, 10–11)

Willie and Dylan alike find ways to surprise and keep a step ahead of the game. However, the reality of the risks involved becomes clear at the end of the song where Willie suffers a gambler's fate: 'He shot poor Willie through the head, which was a tragic fate.' Dylan's whooping delivery of the line lampoons the cliché, but there is a certain evident fatalism at the song's end, even more marked at the end of 'Gypsy Lou'. That 'ramblin' woman with a ramblin' mind', she finds tragedy closing in on her at the end of the song, 'She left one too many a boy behind / He committed suicide' (*Lyrics*, 27).

Such aesthetic features reveal the key imaginative motif of Dylan's early New York work: underlying his most effective interpretations and songs, was the fearful image of a self deprived of expression, enthralled by habit, or broken by fateful circumstance, failed gambles ... As Dylan's song-writing developed through 1962 and 1963, this deep fantasy might be said to continue to dominate his work, but it was now often politically configured – translated into songs of oppression and liberation. One might even say, ironically enough, that Dylan found his own voice through this politically diagnostic art that interrogated the lost possibilities of voice and association for those he wrote about. For instance, 'The Ballad of Donald White' written at the beginning of 1962, reveals Dylan's creative instincts in the effortless, unforced way in which he assumes White's voice. Certainly flawed, the song might not have the concerted power and intensity of focus of so many of the great balladic protest songs it prefigures – 'The Ballad of Hollis Brown', 'The Lonesome Death of Hattie Carroll', or 'Who Killed Davey Moore?' However, what is important is Dylan's unmistakeable imaginative investment in the song, and the way it reveals further how his song-writing craft was increasingly to be about refusing to be obvious, and about distinctively wresting oblique effects of angle and unforeseen twists of perspective.

In 'Donald White' Dylan voices White's sentiments as he faces death and reflects on an upbringing that has made him cleave, in an horrific parody of nurture, to the penal institutions within which he had become naturalised. Identified since his 'life begun' as a menace to society, he comes at the end of his life to a clarity that takes his whole life as its text. The clear shining moon in the first verse seems appropriate for the changed perspective of lucidity, the tone of quiescence, even tranquillity and transcendence, that illuminates 'these ... final words / That you will ever hear'. Though White's words are full of unsocialised awkwardness, error and redundancy ('kill me dead', 'the institution home', 'the old north woods of which I used to roam'), he can nonetheless find words to articulate his predicament politically. For the first and last time, he can call to account the society that has made its victim its enemy, and ironically silence it by asking, without bitterness, an unanswerable question 'concerning all the boys that / Walk a road just like me':

> Are they enemies or victims
> Of your society? (*Lyrics,* 33–4)

In comparison to the resonating ironies and complexities of 'The Ballad of Donald White', other protest songs from this time like 'John Brown' or 'The Death of Emmett Till' appear perfunctory or strident.

By the end of 1962, though, Dylan's gift for sustaining and enacting a drama of vision in his songs is driving his art in ever more inventive, expansive ways. 'A Hard Rain's A-Gonna Fall' takes a voice which intensively inhabits a turning point, a dark moment outside of time, as he unfolds the song's visionary pageant. The song brings to mind the rolling verses of a jeremiad from *Lamentations*, or the prophetic books of Blake, or the periods of Whitman or Ginsberg. Within it, a young voice in the song answers the questions of an older one, while telling of unearthly experiences that no hundred lifetimes could hold. Line by line, the singer's iterations draw the listener into its unfolding panorama. The images, the epic snippets, sound both ancient and outside time. The lines are instantly compelling yet impossible to place, as they expand in the mind, melding biblical, folk-song, poetic, fantasy, and oracular elements. The song scours and scourges the fallen world, revealing its apocalyptic sense of imminent reckoning for a world of corruption, violence, inhumanity. This is a world in which the few figures of renewal – the new-born baby, the girl with the rainbow, the singer himself – are abandoned within a predatory, nihilistic landscape. The singer and listener are thrown back on their own resources, and if the seeds of renewal exist then they would only be in the urgent activities of listening, responding, seeing, imagining, or singing that the song produces. Once again, the song's own expressive enactments and effects appear internally related to the drama it unfolds.

On the sleeve-notes to *The Freewheelin' Bob Dylan*, he described the writing of 'A Hard Rain's A-Gonna' Fall' as if he himself were summoned, by the missile crisis of October 1962 to a vision of the end times. A comparable kind of immediacy is found in his often repeated claim that 'Blowin' in the Wind' (like 'Song for Woody') was a song that came quickly: 'I wrote [it] in ten minutes' (Artur, 1343). Whatever element of self-mythologising there may be in all this, though, is secondary to the fact that in both songs, inspiration is a matter of the way that the song's meaning arrives within the song as a gathering, transformative, effect. None of this is to dispute that Dylan wrote 'Blowin' in the Wind' in a casual, off-the-cuff way, nor that much in the writing could be depicted as careless, indefinite, and hazy. But it is to reiterate that what counts in the song is its dynamic redemption of diffuseness. In this song this corresponds to a cumulative forceful, convergence of significances, as it progressively turns inwards to address the listener's own resistances to change and freedom.

The song begins with images that swim in and out of a kind of vagueness while bearing on the external realities of political subjugation, war, and nuclear destruction:

> How many roads must a man walk down
> Before you call him a man?
> Yes'n' how many seas must a white dove sail
> Before she sleeps in the sand? (*Lyrics*, 52)

A man walking down a single road is an image, but a man who *must* walk down many roads is also an idea, though is it one of subjection, or historical progress, or moral quest? Again, the white dove is highly visual in itself, yet the image is puzzling: how could a dove sail? Do doves sleep in the sand? What kind of imperative means that a dove *must* sail *many* seas? And is the song drawing on the biblical associations of white doves with the Flood and the Pentecost? One might again be tempted to dismiss this all as mere incompetent wooliness. However, in making the case for the song one would emphasise the way it uses uncertainty initially as a way of awakening our powers as questioning and responsive, politicised, beings, as it comes to produce its larger, eventual movement towards an answering resolution (in both the ethical and linguistic senses).

On this view, these questions imply what becomes explicit, as the song moves decisively from the outer world to the inner, confronting the listener with his own daily complicity with the *status quo*, and forcing him to question himself, focus on himself. Thus the song shifts its axis to target our docility, our self-blinding ignorance of obvious truths – our pretence not to see or hear the suffering of otherness, our willingness to turn away, to prevent acknowledging '[t]hat too many people have died'. The song brings the questions back home, and addresses our unquestioning, internalised habits of avoidance. In doing so, it offers a road to expression, but one that involves another turning away, from this habitual inexpressiveness, this demeaning tolerance of injustice, this cultivation of vagueness about others. Dylan himself described the song's genesis in '[t]he idea that you were betrayed by your silence. That all of us in America who didn't speak out were betrayed by our silence' (Scaduto, 118). The song's own unspoken question then becomes: how can we claim or desire or talk of freedom or expression when we are party to this refusal of others, to this avoidance that is also an avoidance of ourselves? Thus the song turns on the crux that there can be no social liberation without self-liberation. In this way the overcoming of indeterminacy and wilful vagueness, in the interests of new possibilities of relatedness and expression, becomes both what the song is about and what it enacts.

III

W.H. Auden is rarely identified as an influential figure in the turbulent world of popular music in the 1960s. However, in the autumn of 1962 the poet made what can seem a decisive intervention. In his New York apartment, he recommended to the British TV actor-turned-director, Philip Saville, that he visit Tony Pastor's club, a crucible of artistic creativity. There Saville was to see the 21-year-old Bob Dylan perform, and to negotiate with Al Grossman to bring him to England to act in the BBC play, *The Madhouse on Castle Street*, written by the Jamaican playwright, Evan Jones. The play, reputedly flawed but haunting, was set in a lodging house, its tension ratcheted up by the political despair of the unseen, central character who had retreated to his room, seemingly to die. Dylan's spoken participation in the play was to dwindle to one line. However, he was to sing 'Blowin' in the Wind', and a beautiful reworked version of 'Ballad of the Glidin' Swan', as well as reworked versions of songs from Harry Smith's *Anthology of American Folk Music*: 'Hang Me, O Hang Me', and 'The Cuckoo'. The play went out to mixed reviews on 13 January 1963. Dylan's performances were by all accounts memorable, though the BBC was to wipe the tape in 1968.[18]

This first visit to London, between December 1962 and January 1963 (punctuated by a short visit to Italy), brought Dylan into contact – and at times abrasive and comical conflict – with the British folk fraternity, and has attracted much interest in the years since.[19] Dylan reportedly spent some nights during his stay sleeping on Martin Carthy's sofa or floor in London, in a winter locked up by frost, and by snows that lasted in much of England until March 1963.[20] On the 18th, his second night in London, Dylan was introduced to Carthy (three days his senior) who remembers him playing at *The Troubadour*. On 29 December 1962, he played there again, before moving on to *The Roundhouse* with Carthy. This was the night before the first day of filming, and on the 29th and 30th a blizzard blew across the country, leaving – I quote from the Met Office – 'drifts six metres deep which blocked roads and rail routes, left villages cut off and brought down power lines'.[21] The story is that Dylan and Carthy kept warm by chopping up the house piano: 'when he came to London in 1962 he used a samurai sword to help me chop up a piano to keep us warm while we had a cup of tea after a gig'.[22] Whatever the precise truth, the story is a useful metaphor for Dylan's voracious, not to say ruthless, consumption and transmutation of English musical material at this point in his career.[23] And part of what he did was to consign Carthy's 'Scarborough Fair', and 'The Franklin' to his creative fires, whence they rose, Phoenix-like, as 'Girl from the North Country', 'Boots of Spanish Leather', and 'Bob Dylan's Dream'.

In London, Dylan met up with Eric Von Schmidt, illustrator and singer, and the two were to fly back together on 15 January 1963.[24] And when he was to sing 'Masters of War' at Gerde's in New York less than a week later, it was the distinctive melodic delivery of a version of 'Nottamun Town' by Jackie Washington – a close friend of Von Schmidt's – that Dylan adopted.[25] Though this performance has often been taken to be the premiere of the song, Carthy (not someone likely to get his facts wrong) remembers Dylan singing it at *The Troubadour* on the night they met.²⁶ Certainly, Anthea Joseph, manager of *The Troubadour*, claims he sang it, along with 'The Ballad of Hollis Brown', at *The Singers' Club* run by Ewan MacColl, just before Xmas – presumably 22 December. This club in High Holborn was steeped in a traditionalist ethos that harked back ten years to its earlier manifestation as *The Ballads and Blues Club*, where Alan Lomax, MacColl, Bert Lloyd, Peggy Seeger, and many others regularly performed.²⁷ The Club's code was strictly traditional music only, and so MacColl had looked askance at Dylan arriving with his guitar. In response to the crowd's mounting clamour for him to sing, Dylan, ever the provocateur, drank more beer during the interval before eventually succumbing, presumably with a maximum of exasperating pantomime. He went on to sing four times the allowed period of five minutes, which did two things: it brought the house down, and it fomented a lifetime of righteous resentment on the part of MacColl who was enraged at Dylan's trampling on the club's defining protocols.

If 'Masters of War' was performed in London, it seems likely it must have been still something of a work in progress, since Dylan was to claim that the first version was written in the city, at a time when the papers were still full of the Cuban crisis. Heylin refers to the singer's prefatory remarks to the song, on a recording made when he sung it to Alan Lomax on his return to New York:

> 'I wrote it in London [...] I kept seeing in the papers every day [them] putting down MacMillan, [saying] Kennedy's gonna screw him, on these missiles ... They got headlines in the papers, underneath MacMillan's face saying, "Don't mistrust me, don't mistrust me, how can you treat a poor maiden so?"' (Heylin, *Revolution in the Air*, 117)

In 1991, Carthy said, 'I've read a lot of books about him and not one talks in any detail about his time in England. As far as I can hear, by listening to his records, his time in England was actually crucial to his development.'²⁸ By now, the researches of writers like Matthew Zuckerman, Hajdu and Heylin have demonstrated the truth of Carthy's remarks, and it is possible to see clearly how far traditional British, as well as Irish, songs provided early Dylan with a considerable, even crucial, resource, as he raided their melodies, their anonymous, immemorial, modes of address, and deliberate, four square verses and structures, for his own songs.²⁹

Nonetheless, it is also true that up to this point, Dylan had written and recorded many of the songs that would feature on *Freewheelin'*, and had often adopted English models. Indeed, as *Chronicles* makes clear, the influence of English ballads upon his sensibility dated back at least as far as the compelling influence of Harry Webber in Minneapolis:

> Webber was an English literary professor, a tweed-wearing, old-fashioned intellectual. And he did know plenty of songs, mostly roving ballads – stern ballads, ones that meant cruel business [...] I loved all these ballads right away.

> They were romantic as all hell and high above all the popular love songs I'd ever heard. Lyrically they worked on some kind of supernatural level and they made their own sense [...] I was beginning to feel like a character from within these songs, even beginning to think like one.[30]

Again, though it is arguable that the visit to England, and exposure to English models, was crucial to his songwriting over the next year or so, it can also be said that it was merely a consolidation and extension of a dependence on British idioms and song modes that was evident at this time, as Dylan moved away from Guthrie's persona, intuitively in search of modes of address and perspective that offered a greater, more timeless, breadth of scope, and that unhitched the music from the political and personal contexts and imagery associated with Guthrie. 'Tomorrow is a Long Time', the song written for the absent Suze in August 1962, was based on the fifteenth-century anonymous lyric, 'Westron Wind', as Heylin indicates.[31] In September, Dylan was to perform 'A Hard Rain's A-Gonna Fall' in 'The Gaslight', a song that was itself a rewriting of Child Ballad No 12, 'Lord Randall'. Similarly, 'John Brown', written in early October, reworks the Irish song 'Mrs McGrath' (Heylin, *Revolution in the Air*, Vol. 1, 95, 87, 101).[32]

English musical models, a fundamental part of his songwriting for the next year or so, then, offered Dylan a way of side-stepping the compulsory identifications, pieties, and labels of American folk culture, as well as further transforming his uses of Guthrie. English folk models cannily allowed him both to intensify the force of his political critique and to avoid being assimilated as an advocate for one of the various political factions – anarchic, communist, liberal, nostalgic, Trotskyist, Stalinist – that still divided Greenwich Village. Artistically, this meant that it was possible through assimilating the impersonal modes, and tragic focus of English folk balladic idioms (as 'A Hard Rain's A-Gonna Fall' had already shown), to move outside the personal into a more powerful and inclusively impersonal vision. Dylan drew on tonal and constructive features that bound the songs to tradition, so that they sounded anonymous, and of the ages. Daniel Mark Epstein described his astonishment at realising that Dylan had written 'Boots of Spanish Leather' when he heard him sing it in Washington in December 1963:

> There was not a line in the lyric that marked it as contemporary; there were many lines that sounded timeless, like stones worn smooth in a riverbed from centuries of water coursing over them.[33]

Though 'A Hard Rain's a Gonna Fall' or 'Masters of War', for instance were both probably written before the British visit, it seems as if the use of English models became more consciously consolidated afterwards, integrated with Guthrie's influence, and creating a powerful effect of the temporally indefinite. Songs like these would now convey, in their artfully unadorned, rough-hewn, yet effective fabric, the authority of something that had survived, whose reference was seemingly universal. At the same time, the interpolation of a critical vision modeled on Guthrie gave the songs their political dynamism, their undeflectable drive towards change. The vision was from the mountaintops, but it scanned the horizon. In such ways, the anthemic and visionary elements in these songs, viewing their world and broaching an uncertain future, can be seen as a bringing together of British and American modes. Certainly, it was this particularly American element that Dylan took from Guthrie, an individual angle and pay-off that he increasingly combined with the time-honoured dimension common to American and English folk music. The themes of these songs might be predictable, sound timeless, but the precise topic of the songs, and angle of approach became evermore subtly unpredictable, as in 'A Pawn in their Game', 'The Ballad of Hollis Brown', or 'The Lonesome Death of Hattie Carroll'.

This use of British and Irish songs continued until the end of 1963, and marked Dylan's prolific writing throughout the period, to the end of 'The Times They Are A-Changin''. It is possible to list the extensive use of British and Irish models. 'Liverpool Gal' is a mysterious song that references the structure and *mise-en-scène* of 'The Lakes of Pontchartrain', a song of possibly Irish (or Appalachian) origin. 'Who Killed Cock Robin' underpins 'Who Killed Davey Moore', and Child Ballad No. 173, 'Mary Hamilton', provides the basis for 'The Lonesome Death of Hattie Carroll'. Child Ballad No. 10, 'The Twa Sisters', contributes the melody of 'Percy's Song'. Again, Heylin shows, elements of an anthologised folk song, 'The Everlasting Circle' provided inspiration for 'Eternal Circle' while a Scottish ballad – 'The Road and Miles to Dundee' – provided the melodic structure for 'Walls of Red Wing' (Heylin, *Revolution in the Air*, 147). Further, Dylan himself identified the source of 'Lay Down Your Weary Tune' as being an unnamed Scottish ballad.[34] Again, the strong narrative of 'Seven Curses' draws irresistible comparison with Shakespeare's *Measure for Measure*, as Christopher Ricks has notably explored (Ricks, *Dylan's Visions of Sin*, 237). Finally, it has long been well known that a particularly rich source from this period were many of the songs that he would have heard by the celebrated Irish band, The Clancy Brothers, who were close friends in New York: songs like 'The Leaving of Liverpool', 'The Patriot Game', and 'The Parting Glass'. Respectively, these became reworked as 'Farewell', 'With God on Our Side', and 'Restless Farewell'.

Of course, American songs were often themselves reworking of their British counterparts, as was the case with 'Gypsy Davey', sung by the young Dylan, and by Guthrie. English and Irish folk songs, and their American variants, granted Dylan the means to inhabit or narrate seemingly timeless themes, injustices, and yearnings. Their aim is to shock and shame you out of political apathy and torpor, and in the process create as well as project effects of community. This is where Guthrie's example seems so important, and the combination of anonymous folk framework and individuating viewpoint so crucial. After all, what is the main effect of these songs? They tell you something you already know, while also insisting on a change of optic, of viewpoint, similar to that enacted by the speaker whose approach to the material involves looking again, with new eyes. The aim is to jolt you out of your political torpor, and in the process summon, anticipate a new community, new interpersonal realities such as those modeled in the response and connection that the songs demand. Political and self-change are inseparable. Guthrie's songs too incorporated this crucial connectivity of viewpoint in their tone, their wit and intelligence, as much as in their content. Through it, they conveyed the sense of a speaker in the world but not of it. He is without a home, passing through, anticipating in hope a world to come, while describing, with an outsider's sharpness, a truth clouded by everyday custom, greed, and compromise. Dylan's knowingness in the use of this transformative persona shaded at times into mischievously affectionate parody, as when he sought to win the farmer's trust in the 1964 song, 'Motorpsycho Nitemare' ('Well, by the dirt 'neath my nails / I guess he knew I wouldn't lie' [*Lyrics,* 123]).

So the bracing, arresting, effect of Dylan's early songs, as with Guthrie's, is to refuse to allow you to say you were not told, that you had not seen. Political dedication and change, they insist, are a matter of vision, and seeing remains accordingly an important trope, as well as the ultimate means of critical power. When Dylan sings 'But I see through your eyes' in 'Masters of War' (*Lyrics,* 55), for example, the listener first wonders what he means. Is this just lazy cliché backfiring, creating the idea that Dylan sympathises with these profiteers, sees things their way? For an instant, the song courts aesthetic disaster, the listener's comprehension stalling. Then one realises that the line echoes the earlier line 'But I see through your masks' (*Lyrics,* 55), and that this later line implies a deeper psychological uncovering – of the deceits these men practise to themselves, as well as to the world. They wear a mask in public, but also in private: self-justification is necessarily both of the self (to others), but also to the self itself. It is a matter of the lies and distortions necessary to continue doing 'what you do'. Moreover, at the same time as the listener's mind is provoked into a subtler comprehension of the situation, so he or she comes to see through the eyes of the singer, the song invoking the politicised community it implies. Christopher Ricks made similar points in discussing the renovations of language in these lines, as part of his account of how Dylan remakes clichés. We are alerted to the cliché, and our vision of and through it is altered:

> The cliché has been alerted, and we are alerted to its clichéness, seeing the words from a new perspective, a different point of view, and seeing penetratingly through them.[35]

By such enactments, expansions, of vision, as well by content, Dylan's early songs offer themselves not merely as interpretations of the world, but as ways of interpreting it, 'road maps for the soul', perhaps, small verbal anticipations of other revolutions and revisions.[36] Like Guthrie's, the songs tap into humour or anger as the motors of personal as well as political change, bringing about shifts in sensibility, conversions in attitude. Response entails ethical change, and indissolubly links the personal and the political. The impetus towards change is here based not on the supposed perfections of the speaker, but on the very

American orientation towards perfectibility, a shared future yet to be made. This sense of honesty outside the law, of non-conformity and autonomy, again indicates the decisive, transformative element in Dylan's work, usefully comparable with Emerson's thought, and running throughout his career.

At the same time, typically, there are comic songs that playfully parody the anthems and attitudes of *Freewheelin'*. So the final line in this verse from 'Bob Dylan's Blues' can be said to squash the romantic image of the songs:

> Well, the wind keeps-a-blowin' me
> Up and down the street
> With my hat in my hand
> And my boots on my feet
> Watch out so you don't step on me (*Lyrics*, 98)

In 'I Shall Be Free', the visionary capacity for change – so that one can 'see better days' and 'do better things' – is due not to inspiration but to being 'drunk all the time', and it is this that makes his 'little lady' try to hide, 'pretendin' she don't know me' (one imagines an alternative album cover, with Suze Rotolo making for the cover of the blue and white Volkswagon campervan on the snowy West Village street). Again, even the idea of political commonalty or solidarity is made absurd in 'Talkin' World War III Blues', when the singer meets a man in the aftermath of the bomb by a hot-dog stand, 'I said, 'Howdy friend, I guess there's just us two', / He screamed and bit and away he flew / Thought I was a Communist' (*Lyrics*, 65). Again, the idea of a collective, all dreaming of a better future, is further deflated by the doctor who admits 'I've been havin' the same old dreams', only to add that 'I dreamt the only person left after the war was me / I didn't see you around.' The speaker similarly himself reduces such hopeful idealism to childish wrangling: 'I'll let you be in my dream if I can be in yours.'

IV

The Freewheelin' Bob Dylan is a very diverse album – mixing together blues songs, love songs, talking blues, comic monologues, political and visionary songs. Yet for all its disjointedness, it effectively hangs together as all of a piece, as a resonating, unfolding whole. It takes its tone from Dylan's youthful vigour, and the attitude it forcibly transmits – the singer's forward-pressing, rough-and-ready kind of autonomy highlighted against the bleak world it depicts. The album showcases Dylan's verve and range, its incidental blemishes and different tones appearing part and parcel of its unswerving, driving, claim on free expression. What is implicitly collective in Dylan's effects on *Freewheelin'*, though, has become more explicit, even programmatic, by *The Times They Are-A Changin'*. This is an album that takes its more settled tone from its title song, which emphatically assumes that the singer is at the vanguard of change now underway, that these songs are consciously influencing their politically transitional moment. As a measure of this, the songwriting appears more technically adept, the songs more deliberately constructed and shaped. However, perhaps because the songs seem more finished, the album itself can seem to lack something of the sense of movement, the dynamic of provisionality and the open dialogic circulation of repeating themes that marked out its predecessor.

This greater effect of determination – both verbal and political – can clearly be seen in the invocatory title song, 'The Times They Are A-Changin''. For all Dylan's later disavowals of the role of spokesman, this is a conscious, no-holds barred, anthem for a generation. It articulates the incalculable yet irresistible movement of the present into the future, condensing into five verses a political vision swept along on the currents of the times. Right from its first ringing strums, the song is inaugural, a performative act that does what it says: summoning, describing, and creating changed times. Dylan admitted to Cameron Crowe in the 1985 liner notes for *Biograph* that:

> 'This was definitely a song with a purpose. I knew exactly what I wanted to say and for whom I wanted to say it to. You know, it was influenced by the Irish and Scottish ballads ... *Come All Ye Bold Highway Men, Come All Ye Miners, Come All Ye Tender Hearted Maidens*. I wanted to write a big song, some kind of theme song, ya know, with short concise verses that piled up on each other in a hypnotic way ... the civil rights movement and the folk movement were pretty close and allied together for a while at that time'...[37]

It is this uncompromising assurance – declaiming vision as reality underway – that is exhilarating. The song does not contest existing hierarchies so much as sweepingly, declare that their day is past. In its new dispensation, there is a contrary order of precedence, evident in the song itself, which begins with 'people', moves to 'writers and critics', before coming to the law-makers and politicians, and mothers and fathers. Senators and congressmen are stripped of authority and power, relegated to being mere obstructions identified with the repudiated interests, hierarchies, and assumptions of the past ('Come senators, congressmen / Please heed the call / Don't stand in the doorway / Don't block up the hall' [*Lyrics,* 81]). Past ideologies and political structures will be shaken and rattled. They are like windows that no longer offer stable ways of seeing, or walls that no longer offer protection and stability. Useless and discredited by the song's verbal *fiat*, they no longer demarcate who is on the inside/outside of the social order.

At the same time, as Marqusee shrewdly points out, the song is no Marxist prophecy of revolution or violence:

> ... this is no Marxist determinism. The song's lyricism derives less from its assertion of collective invincibility than from the tender confidence of its enormous – but elementary ambitions. (Marqusee, 90–91)

Marqusee describes how the quasi-biblical tone and imagery of the song implies that change is inevitable, while its forcefulness of vision co-exists with a total lack of specification of the future. So we can note that waters are rising, walls are shaking, while these hints of cataclysm and conflict co-exist with images of waning, fading, ageing, as if change could also be seen as merely a quasi-natural temporal process: 'Your old road is rapidly agin'... The order is rapidly fadin'' (Dylan *Lyrics,* 82). Nonetheless, the magic of the song is in the assertive power that commands a new world into being. These features are evident too in 'When the Ship Comes In', which similarly figures the obstructive forces of reaction – disbelieving, deprived of their powers and words of mystification – as triumphantly overcome. The oppressors are swept away by a quasi-Biblical advent of freedom, drowned like 'Pharoah's tribe' and 'conquered' 'like Goliath'. Significantly, this song offers perhaps the only specific images of a redeemed future in the whole of Dylan's early output, and they are notably disastrous. The song envisages an emancipated world presided over by the 'ship's wise men'. It is a world in renewed accord with nature, wishfully (and feebly) imagined in terms of (somehow) laughing fish, smiling seagulls, and a sun that respects everyone coming in on the ship (*Lyrics,* 93–4).

More effective is 'The Ballad of Hollis Brown' which (though written as far back as the autumn of 1962 and figuring in the *Freewheelin'* sessions) fits in well alongside the other ballads on the third album. Deliberation is evident in the song's constricted musical and formal features, as it horrifyingly conveys how poverty brings about a nightmare inversion of family life. The savagely ironic nursery-rhyme idiom, the iterative drive of the wracking guitar figures, and even the impoverished chord sequence all intensify the song's view of Brown's reduced situation, 'on the outside of town'. His is a life wholly without change, and time for him is a nightmare of unrelieved, dehumanising, murderous privation. His mind is deranged by his inability to provide for his starving family, maddened as he is by the unceasing nature of his baby's crazed eyes and loudening cries. Yet living and dying as an outsider, with no opportunities of transformation, he becomes an unforgettable embodiment of the necessity of change that the album calls for. At the end he repeats the lines 'There's seven people dead / On a South Dakota farm', before ending:

> Somewhere else in the distance
> There's seven new people born.[38]

For the first time, the final verse looks away from Brown's haunted world, into a distance where seven new people are born. In doing so, the song skilfully equivocates between the dominant implication that the cycle of poverty is beginning again, and the remote possibility that 'new' might conceivably be associated with social regeneration. The implication of these songs is that social change resides in us, and the changes in understanding, attitude, mood, and sensibility they bring about. More concertedly than in *Freewheelin'* these songs conspire to produce such changes in attitude, implying more definitely that hope, and social and political renewal, are matters of indignation, sympathy, and imagination.

The sense of the self as inhabiting changing times occurs in personal terms too. 'One Too Many Mornings' is a song of displaced emotion like 'Mama, You've Been On My Mind', not to mention 'Don't Think Twice, It's Alright', and 'Girl From the North Country' from *Freewheelin'*. In each of these, the singer is not wholly in possession of what he feels, and the song is not so much a love song as a *communiqué* from someone uncertainly detained in an emotional no man's land. These are songs of crossroads, roads, travel, and border-lines. In 'Girl from the North Country', for instance, the singer appears caught up against himself in reminiscences and feelings and images that keep drawing him back to the girl of former times. Love and memory cross the demarcations of time and self-knowledge, surprising the singer's present with nostalgic visitations, images, from a time he thought he had outlived and left behind. In each song the reaction to emotional displacement appears to be to 'move on', while the besetting, underlying anxiety is of not feeling the right thing at the right time. The singer is caught within an unresolved past, so that he does not really know what it is he feels, and whether the failure of expression is past or present. In their melancholy, these songs of loss and belatedness are close also to 'Boots of Spanish Leather' or 'North Country Blues'.

The masterpiece of the album, 'The Lonesome Death of Hattie Carroll' works by the extraordinary way in which it expresses Dylan's intuitions about inexpression, making it the culmination of this phase of his work. It tells the story of servant Hattie's casual murder at the hands of young socialite William Zanzinger, in the Baltimore hotel where she waited on tables. As Phil Ochs observed in *Broadside* on 20 July 1964, an important feature of the song is its way of avoiding the obvious.[39] The choruses have a certain opacity, but they counsel restraint, telling us not to be too easily provoked by our mounting sympathy for Hattie, as if anger must not replicate Zanzinger's lashing out. Nor, unlike the judge, must we rush to judgement. The singer displays reserve and restraint through the slow measured verses with their shocking details. His rumination, and holding back, though, becomes an important crux in the song, and it is finally and expressively disturbed in the final verse where he tells finally of how the judge handed down to Zanzinger 'for penalty and repentance, a six month sentence'. At this point, the waltz rhythm stalls, and a fast-beating, chaotic rhythm threatens momentarily to break through, and overturn the song's meditative poise.

Far-reaching discussion of 'Hattie Carroll' by Marqusee, Ricks and Richard Brown have turned on its political and philosophical dimensions, and the questions it provokes.[40] Certainly, it is notable how the dialectic of the specific and the ideal is built into the song, as the narration of the verses gives way to the strangely cloudy, abstract queries of the chorus, and as the song progresses from description of the murder to descriptions of Zanzinger and Carroll's different stations in life, and onwards to the judge's pronouncement and issues of justice at the end. The facts and the awful sadness of Carroll's death are undisputed, but how are we to understand and respond to what the song tells us? Everything reverberates with the need for answers, as if Carroll's awful lonesome death demanded understanding before tears, though the singer is himself divided between the two responses. Syntactically, each verse is a single sentence, patterned internally by various nested repetitions – alliterative, rhythmical, semantic, and rhyming – that contribute to the sense of both intensity and meditative expansion. Double vision of a kind is notable in the song in the way Dylan recurrently says what is *nearly* the same thing twice: Zanzinger is 'doomed and determined'; his parents 'provide and protect him', and he reacts to his deed with 'swear words and sneering'; the blow that kills her 'sailed through the air and came down through the room'; the song's addressee is one prone to 'philosophise disgrace and criticise all fears'; the judge is 'deep and distinguished'; the strings of the law are(n't) 'pulled and persuaded', the ladder of law has 'no top and no bottom', and so on. Again, clearly, even the word 'poor' has a double meaning in Carroll's case, referring to a tragic personal fate, as well as to impoverishment.

Through these features the song can be taken to multiply aspects, as if weighing things in the balance, as if adjudicating different verbal versions, seeking a perspective. But multiplication raises questions, not least the one that governs this chapter: what issues of expression are being enacted and represented here? One might begin by saying that the patterns of the song's language evoke a corrupt world of wheels within wheels (as Zanzinger's family's influence ensures his acquittal). At the same time, though, the duplicating, ramifying, language might also show that his freedom is at best equivocal. Zanzinger's parents are said not to provide *for* him, but to 'provide [and protect] him', and we hear on his release that he 'on bail was out walking'. If these locutions are not as careless as they appear, it might be because Zanzinger is not as carefree as he appears. In fact, the phrases imply powerfully, along with everything else in the song, that Zanzinger has no autonomy, no separate existence apart from the family that controls him. He is their puppet, their possession, deprived of identity and freedom by the very wealth and influence that appears to wrest these things from the judge, and to protect him. Throughout the song, Dylan's words suggest this sense of someone whose whole existence is permeated, deprived, by money. When the long delayed main verb identifies him in the second verse the tense shifts joltingly to the present ('William Zanzinger who had twenty four years / *Owns* a tobacco farm of six hundred acres). We might have expected to hear that he *has* twenty four years and *owned* six hundred acres, implying he is in prison for that period, and no longer in possession of his property. Contrarily, the words 'owns' implies that he is free and still in possession, though it also suggests that his life is a perpetual present tense of inherited, imprisoning, ownership.

The song's strange power is inseparable from such searching, double-sided explorations in the song. Zanzinger's twirling cane and diamond-ringed finger suggest someone compassed by wealth, and striving to display an insouciance that masks his murderous self-frustration. When Dylan later says of the cane that it 'sailed through the air and came down through the room' he brings the associations of high-society leisure – sailing, flying – into horrifying conjunction with violence. And at the same time the clause moves us from outward indignation at the scene (seeing the cane moving) to imaginatively inhabiting Carroll's body, her final sense of this blow coming '*down* through the room', of her being beneath him. However, the magical complexity of the song's play with expectation goes even further. So, rather than singing 'down through the *air*' Dylan intensifies the sense of an oppressive, confined space. This person whose parents protect him, who walks on bail, who sails and socialises, is also someone who seems by the same token utterly dislocated from nature, to live in *rooms* – deprived of *air*.

In such ways Dylan's dialectical mind is at work in the song, and its refusal of expectation leads even to its harbouring a strange subterranean, telepathic under-current of understanding with Zanzinger. It is as if Dylan as an artist has involuntarily found his powers liberated by the challenge that Zanzinger presents to them. When Dylan sings that Zanzinger was '[d]oomed and determined to destroy all the gentle', for instance, one can take 'determined' to mean both 'willed' and its opposite: Zanzinger has the desire to kill, but he has also been determined, surrounded and ringed by his wealth, and this is also a kind of confining doom. Repellent as Zanzinger is in the song, its treatment of him gives the song this profound emancipating complexity as art, and makes the song perhaps the finest (and maybe culminating) example, the last word, in Dylan's early explorations of the pathos of lives determined or lost by inexpression. On the Oscar Brand Show in March 1963, Dylan had prefaced 'Only a Hobo' by saying that 'some people go out' and see 'their garage and ... their car' while others see 'lilac trees', and others 'see a hobo' (Artur, 49). In this song, Dylan's inspiration can appear to demonstrate a strange instinctive coalescence of his sublime perversity as an artist, with his capacity for detecting, intuitively inhabiting, human impoverishment. When Dylan looks at Zanzinger, one might say, he even sees a 'hobo' of kinds, someone utterly dispossessed of himself. The song might even accommodate the sense that Zanzinger killed Carroll out of a more or less unconscious envy – a resentment against a poor woman who is less hidebound, less trapped, less lonesome, less deprived of humanity, than him. The reciprocity conveyed in the final verse about her and her family might thus suggest why this Baltimore Cain was 'doomed and determined to destroy all the gentle', trammelled within the repetitions of an existence that is mimicked in the spiralling reiterations, the alliterative motions, the syntactical postponements and detentions of the song.

This desire for ramifying complexity, and this artistic, deeply instinctive and searching refusal of easy answers, is typical of what is best on the album, and more obviously evident (if less successfully so) in songs like 'Only a Pawn in Their Game' or 'With God On Our Side'. Certainly, this sense of an imagination that must go against the grain is evident in the incisive 'Who Killed Davey Moore?', which turns, finally, on the resonant irony that Cuba outlaws the boxing on which our markets and democracy thrive. It is evident too as the kind of instinctive cussedness in Dylan's notorious and unsuccessful attempt to tell the National Emergency Civil Liberties Committee that he could see something of himself in Lee Harvey Oswald (Shelton, *No Direction Home*, 142–5). Finally, although

'Hattie Carroll' was a song that mourned the absence of social change, the song that succeeded it spoke powerfully of Dylan's need for a personal and artistic change of direction. Ironically or fittingly, it was the conversion of a further Clancy Brothers song, 'The Parting Glass' into 'Restless Farewell', that was to mark the next turning point in Dylan's career, and a turning from English folk models. The song's title and restrained valedictory fervour indicate Dylan's desire to move away from what the third album represented, not least that dependence on English music that the song itself both exemplified and relinquished. The third verse indicates the ironic reversals whereby identification with political causes can itself constitute a trap, and forestall possibilities of self-exploration:

> Oh ev'ry foe that ever I faced
> The cause was there before we came
> And ev'ry cause that ever I fought
> I fought it full without regret or shame

The 'farewell' of the final line in the verse indicates a decisive value shift, from political vision, from the dedication to causes and new dawns, to a pursuit of more unknown personal dimensions:

> And if I see the day
> I'd only have to stay
> So I'll bid farewell in the night and be gone (*Lyrics,* 37)

Written at the end of October 1963, 'Restless Farewell' was seemingly the last song he would write until the new year, which would begin with 'Chimes of Freedom', and 'Mr Tambourine Man', songs that in their theme, idiom and sentiment were suddenly scoping a wholly different sort of visionary mode and inspiration, and new routes of personal freedom.[41] The next album, *Another Side of Bob Dylan*, is, in this respect, as much a renunciation of the old as a new direction. There is a nice kind of symmetry in the fact that when Dylan returned to London in May 1964 he was to debut 'Mr Tambourine Man' at the Royal Festival Hall (Heylin, *Revolution in the Air*, 184). As before, Carthy was to be the first to hear the new song:

> Almost as soon as he landed [...] he was on the phone to Martin Carthy. As Carthy recalls, "He came around. And he sang ... 'Mr Tambourine Man' and it was [like], 'Where [the hell] is this man going?'" (Heylin, *Revolution in the Air*, 184)

Whatever the places that Dylan had been coming from, what was to be important from now on, as Carthy suggests, was that he was now going somewhere else altogether.

Chapter 2
'Weird Monkey'

Another Side of Bob Dylan and
Bringing It All Back Home

Joe Boyd, the stage manager when Dylan went electric at the Newport Festival, wrote: 'Anyone wishing to portray the history of the sixties as a journey from idealism to hedonism could place the hinge at around 9.30 on the night of 25 July 1965' (Epstein, 160). Yet one might equally claim the same of the Newport performances of a year earlier, where hedonism and idealism appear strangely entangled. Murray Lerner's film, *The Other Side of the Mirror*, captures Dylan singing of 'Chimes of Freedom' towards the end of his main set on Friday 26 July 1964, before the capacity audience of 15,000.[1] John Hammond Sr, Pat Clancy, and others, were privately to lambast the performance as slipshod and careless, while Tony Glover felt Dylan backstage was tense, reluctant. Robert Shelton noted that:

> As he tuned between numbers, Dylan sometimes staggered onstage. Being stoned had rarely prevented his giving winning performances, but he was clearly out of control. (Shelton, *No Direction Home*, 181)

Lerner's clip begins with the singer in exuberant, joking mood, presumably primed by marijuana or amphetamines. He initially joshes with the audience and with voices off-stage, and goes through a whole insouciant rigmarole of banter, laughter, harmonica preparation, tuning, and shoulder-shrugging, before pantomimically picking up a cowboy hat on the stage ('What's this'?), hitching his guitar, and throwing his head back in an adolescent grin at some joke.

The song, when it comes, though, has intensity and attack, and reveals a more driven vocal delivery, and a fleeter guitar style than the previous year. The singing is markedly nasal, and borderline-caustic. Its new urgency is physically expressed in a swimmer's bobbing of the head, up and away from the microphone. Rhythm and pace are paramount, as Dylan drives the song's litany of images into the listener's ear, the intonation screwing home each stretched-out, stressed syllable. If it is a commonplace to describe *Another Side of Bob Dylan* as a rock album in search of a band, this Newport performance certainly catches much of the musical transition of Dylan in 1964, on the way to rock and roll rhythms and attitudes, and riding the rising tides of mass fame. The singing has the arresting, pacey delivery of the

English shows in 1965 caught in *Don't Look Back*, that were, in Epstein's words; 'dark, hypnotic, and intensely personal, a one-man *tour de force*' (Epstein, 152).

Heylin persuasively claims of the Newport performance of 'Chimes of Freedom' that '[a]udio evidence contradicts' Shelton's assessment that the set was 'lacklustre' (Heylin, *A Life in Stolen Moments*, 62). Yet Shelton's view does appear understandable, given his proximity to the stage where Dylan's commitment to the song appears to be visibly unravelling. The ambivalences of the time – between constraint and excess (or idealism and hedonism) – surface starkly in what is perhaps the most striking, purely visual, feature of Lerner's film: Dylan's failing struggle against corpsing as he sings. As with moments in the brilliant *Quest* TV show earlier in the year, his clamorous intonations become dogged by an involuntary smile. In fact, it is noticeable that the higher the moral stakes in the song, the more Dylan's composure appears to crumble (even as the performance itself remains riveting on audio). At Newport, this ambivalence and the encroaching sense of irresponsibility mount, until at the very climax of the song's pathos, it is all too much. As if struck by moralistic requirement that he strike the attitudes of preacher, saviour, prophet, or leader, Dylan is unable to stop grinning incongruously, over and again, while singing: 'For the countless confused, accused, misused, strung-out ones and worse, / An' for every hung-up person in the whole wide universe' (*Lyrics*, 117).

In this performance, one can say, Dylan appears graphically at a crossroads. On the one hand, the song is an apotheosis of his art of political sympathy, bearing out Lawrence Wilde's view that it offers 'an unashamed profession of solidarity with the powerless and oppressed'. For Wilde it 'constitute[s] the most powerful and enduring political art', along with other signature songs like 'A Hard Rain's A-Gonna Fall', 'Gates of Eden', 'It's Alright Ma', 'Ballad of a Thin Man', and 'Desolation Row':

> Casting away traditional narrative form and popular song conventions, they combine modernist poetic technique with withering social criticism, at the same time evoking a real alternative, a subversive ethical community, the 'underdog soldiers in the night' mentioned in 'Chimes of Freedom'.[2]

On the other hand, though, there are clear ways in which the event anticipates the giddy hilarity of 1965 or 1966, where Dylan operated a scorched earth-policy against being co-opted by other people's sense of his responsibilities, as in the press conferences and interviews of 1965, in 'Positively 4th Street', or in his hostilities against the *Time* reporter or science student in *Don't Look Back*.[3]

Lee has written that Newport 1964 'is not an amphetamined gig. Rather it suggests marijuana and Wild Turkey' (Lee, *Like the Night*, 54). Drugs and alcohol aside, though, it is worth momentarily asking what else might have made Dylan laugh at Newport. Probably there is his oft-expressed sense of the absurdity of the audience's investments in himself as teacher, preacher, poet, beautiful soul, when only twenty-three-years old; perhaps his sudden sense, too, that the song's rhetorical pathos and vast political canvas, appear themselves suddenly exorbitant or outlandish. Here and now he cannot take himself as seriously as his audience does. What is unmistakeable is the impression that Dylan is visibly peeling away from his audience as he sings. Now 'surrounded by his mind guard and handlers' ... (Epstein, 159), the humour also has a coterie feel, as if the performance is rebounding on the audience while he secedes from them.[4] For Irwin Silber, who picked up on so much of this and articulated it in his famous letter to *Sing Out* in November 1964, Dylan's work at this time was moving fatally inwards, away from his audience and political issues. On top of the world, in terms of his gathering influence, he was also now fenced in by accomplices, drugs, and by Grossman (however crucial a support the latter was in many ways):

> I saw at Newport how you had somehow lost contact with people. It seemed to me that some of the paraphernalia of fame were getting in the way. You travel with an entourage now -- buddies who are going to laugh when you need laughing, and drink wine with you and insure your privacy – and never challenge you to face everyone else's reality again ...[5]

One can also see similar disjunctions in Lerner's film of the Newport version of 'All I Really Want to Do' in the 1965 workshop version. It begins ebulliently, though the abrupt edit brings out how it ends by becoming weirdly hostile and sneering, as if Dylan was refusing himself to be brought down or chained down by the song's sweet reasonableness.

What of 'Chimes of Freedom' itself though? In the previous chapter I suggested Dylan's imagination drew its dynamism from the tension between two possibilities – one an outward, collective, forward-stepping projection of subjectivity, and the other a more inward, solipsistic and fearful fantasy of inexpression. What seems to happen more by the turn of 1963–64 though, is that the tendencies towards hopeful expansion and vertiginous collapse have become more internalised as personal, subjective tension, and as artistic matters. Creatively speaking, it is as if a new, more conscious poetic ambition coexists with an opposite, threatened sense of self. 'Chimes of Freedom' is the one political song on *Another Side*, but even here emancipation is essentially to do with the mind's imaginative responses. Political change is no longer about *engagé* attitudes, but about experiencing a prophetic space, inhabiting a time out of time. Unlike 'The Times They Are A-Changin'', the song does not announce or demand social change, or construct an attitude of political responsibility. Rather, it relays visionary intimations, and identifies self-change with the accumulative *son et lumière* of the verses. What counts is the poeticising of the political, as we are induced into an unworldly starry-eyed altered state, through the long spooling verse paragraphs that echo the prophetic cadences of the Old Testament, or the strophic unfurlings of Blake, Whitman, Rimbaud, or Ginsberg.

So the song places the listener in a liminal space, along with the couple in their twilight, 'far between sundown's finish an' midnight's broken toll'. Daily reality is fractured, as darkness and illumination, visibility and obscurity, tempestuously succeed each other. Visionary, utopian intimations are in the air, but like the couple in the song, we are as yet mere hopeful spectators, refugees from our time. They hunker down in a doorway, transported yet subdued by all this incandescent, violent turbulence. For the listener too, the chimes of freedom flash, but the storm reveals visions only of a broken world. Like Shelley's 'The Triumph of Life' we are offered a huge parade of war, grief, cataclysm, injustice. Nonetheless, in this storm the uncertain future beckons through the rips in the fabric of the present. The synesthetic imagery - of flashing chimes of freedom, and 'bells' of lightning - fuse the apocalyptic, the historical, and the utopian, We are introduced into this strange interval in which we see sounds, hear sights, escape history, and trespass on the future.

In more general terms too, the compelling contradictoriness of the Newport performance points to Dylan's somewhat equivocal sense of creative opportunity at this time. Sean Wilentz emphasises how influential was the meeting with Allen Ginsberg at the end of 1963 that had Dylan returning to Rimbaud and the Beats for a poetic transfusion:

> Combined with a renewed attachment to Rimbaud, which he had affirmed to his friends … Dylan's dedication to writing from within – to capturing what Ginsberg had called, nearly twenty years earlier, 'the shadowy and heterogeneous experience of life through the conscious mind' – placed him within the orbit of the Beats' spontaneous bop prosody before he returned to playing with a band on electric guitar.[6]

Dylan's indebtedness to Ginsberg was surely never stronger than on the songs of this time – such as 'Chimes of Freedom' and the second side of *Bringing It All Back Home* (the earliest songs on that album). In lyrical terms, Dylan celebrated this experimentalism with the callow statement that 'Rimbaud's where it's at. That's the kind of stuff means something. That's the kind of writing I'm gonna do' (Heylin, *Behind the Shades*, 151). In effect, though, the willed search for new kinds of impetus can mean that the songs at times appear to falter, to be marking time or over-determined. Heylin's comment that 'the primary motivation' for the road trip of February 1964 'was to find enough inspiration to step beyond the folk-song form', catches this sense that Dylan had not yet arrived at what he was pursuing (Heylin, *Behind the Shades*, 147). Even Dylan's powerful performances cannot wholly disguise that 'Chimes of Freedom' is an uneven lyric, full of misfiring metaphors, confused high-flown imagery, and lines mercilessly abandoned on the high road to meaning. On the page, it is easy enough to dismiss it as an homage to Ginsberg or Rimbaud, or the image of a better song that flashed through his mind, or a song best listened to in a reverie, when the everyday world starts to loosen its bounds, and the senses and meanings start to bleed into one another.[7] Significantly, it was soon to be a song he would abandon in performance.

By a further irony, though, I have often wondered if 'Chimes of Freedom' can also be seen under another, more intimate aspect, as a covert love song for

Suze Rotolo, as imagined dedicatee of all its flashing images. As such, it might be a leave-taking, covertly a valedictory love song that imagines the two of them bound together in unifying political vision for the last time: they are on the side of the gentle, living in hope and idealism, surveying the signs of destitution, of a starkly abusive, rent, nihilistic, oppressive world. On this reading, the song offers a residual dream of intimacy while the gathering storm implies that radical, destructive change is inevitable, and external. Certainly such a reading, merging universal apocalypse and romantic break-up, might correspond to the strange undertow of pathos and poignancy in the song. Or again, one might take the song equally as one in which Dylan confronts his own need for freedom from the confines of his audience. After all, it is they who cast him as the figure of protest, while he intermittently eyes perhaps a more visionary aesthetic

However one takes it, the song itself clearly points backwards and forwards, indicating the transitional nature of Dylan's creativity at the time, as he moved from 'protest singer ... into someone determined to write songs that "speak for me"' (Heylin, *Behind the Shades*, 138). Its idioms clearly position it between the folk-revival audience of Dylan's earlier albums, and the emerging counter-culture of freaks for whom Dylan would be idol and catalyst. 'Chimes of Freedom' on this view seems less a song of the political vanguard, than a way-station between folk and rock, between 'Hard Rain' and 'Gates of Eden'. As Gray puts it, the song is as much 'blurry impressionism' as 'activist clarity' (Gray, *Bob Dylan Encyclopedia*, 21), and as Lee notes, the mid-60s audience that was emerging at this time was made up of many disparate, overlapping strands. For all its limitations, it is difficult to think of another song that would more have reached these different constituencies than 'Chimes of Freedom':

> The revival was a hybrid creature composed of disparate elements of the Old Left, union members, former Lincoln Brigade survivors, and so forth. Plus there was an input from the Jazz avant-garde, and the beatnick proto-hippies. People were beginning to experiment with marijuana and hallucinogenics, which were at that time still legal. This opening of the 'Doors of Perception' was leading to a dramatic realignment of visionary forces, heralding the dawn of a new era. (Lee, *Like the Night*, 41)

I

Another Side of Bob Dylan was famously recorded in a single session during the night of 9 June 1964, roughly eight months after the final session of the previous album. It was, Heylin notes, 'a transitional album' and it reflects Dylan's changes and self-uncertainty during the different, distracting, kinds of turmoil and ferment of the time (Heylin, *Behind the Shades*, 163). The road trip across the US in February 1964 had pursued an inspiring re-discovery of the country and invigorating reconnection with ordinary people. As such, it appeared an attempt both to escape and enjoy the celebrity accrued by *Freewheelin'* and *The Times They Are A-Changin'*, though it was also displaying a Dylan who was rapidly morphing into the heedless, aggressive figure of the rock and roll albums of the following year. For instance, in New Orleans during Mardi Gras, Dylan and friends recklessly courted antagonism by confronting segregationism in a succession of bars with a black companion. In the process, he appears simultaneously to recapitulate the political concerns of 1963 and anticipate the confrontational, theatrical and coterie modes of 1965.[8] Yet for all the abandon and the kicks, one effect of the trip was also reportedly to drive Dylan inwards, away from Suze Rotolo into a reclusive world whose tightening walls were ever more contradictorily bound by the drugs he depended on for a sense of imaginative freedom. Victor Maymudes recalled: 'Bob [was] a very internal being ... When we drove, I don't think he said much of anything to anybody. He was always *processing*' (Hajdu, 158). Encountering fans who veered between the vapid, the stupid, the paranoid, and the rabid, Dylan appeared someone for whom the outside world was fast becoming impossible to negotiate.

The road trip offers itself as a powerful fact and metaphor for thinking about the contradictions of the time, when an expansive sense of the possibilities of liberation and renewed vision, personal and artistic, coexisted with an uncertainty of direction, and a certain loosening of personal and political affiliations. In Douglas Gilbert and Dave Marsh's intimate photographic memoir of Dylan in June and July 1964, the singer certainly radiates a relaxed and accessible air, quietly buoyant and aware of his gathering fame. However, there is also the strong sense at this period – evident also in the personal vertigo of so many of the songs on *Another Side* – that the possibilities of free exploration and of being lost and isolated, can appear as twin sides of the same coin. Creatively and personally, life on the road and having nowhere to go or stay appear in danger of becoming inextricable. It is in terms of this background that Dylan's most sympathetic enthusiasms or moments of inspiration appear as fitful flashes of occasional, unsustainable freedom. One thinks of the tale in Shelton's book of the one-night, friendship with the schoolteacher in New Orleans (later referred to on the liner notes for *Another Side*), or the moment when he first heard The Beatles over the car radio. Reportedly, he stopped the car, got out and banged on the bonnet, shouting 'It's great!' Here was something that truly took him out of himself (Heylin, *Behind the Shades*, 148).

If Dylan was journeying towards rock and roll, he was a refugee too, not only from the expectations and fantasies of his audience, but also from protest songs, even song-writing itself. Over two days, as January becomes February 1964, he tells the *Toronto Telegram* and *Gargoyle* magazine that he is writing a novel and a play.[9] On the road trip he calls on Carl Sandberg and Lawrence Ferlinghetti. Creative instability surfaces in moments of enthusiasm but also uncertainty, and in the need for a succession of bolt-holes where he could escape to write, or escape from writing – Grossman's farmhouse or New York apartment, or the Café Espresso garret in Bearsville, or Joan Baez's cabin in Carmel, California. Clearly, there were also other kinds of personal and artistic dislocation at the time that heighten our sense of someone lacking clear direction, turned inwards or borne upwards by the thermals of the time, often elated but at times seemingly closer to a flat-spin than he wishes to acknowledge. The distressing and eviscerating end-game with Suze Rotolo and family had given way to the relationship with Joan Baez. Without doubt this relationship offered so much, but no-one has ever felt its imperatives were of the same spontaneous, open-ended, youthful kind that had driven him to Suze, and that had led him to write the beautiful 'Tomorrow is a Long Time':

> Right from the start I couldn't take my eyes off her. She was the most erotic thing I'd ever seen. She was fair skinned and golden haired, full-blooded Italian. The air was suddenly filled with banana leaves. We started talking and my head started to spin. Cupid's arrow has whistled by my ears before, but this time it hit me in the heart and the weight of it dragged me overboard. (Dylan, *Chronicles*, Vol. 1, 265)

What does distinguish *Another Side of Bob Dylan* is Dylan's bracing and unillusioned transformation of the love song. These push a new kind of sexual politics and clearly address issues of power and equality. But also they mine deeper, interrogating love itself, and revealing relationships as divided between socially conditioned, distorting fantasy and anxious need. Sometimes the swirling uncertainties are played out between two people, but at other times they consume the singer. The album is book-ended by two songs – 'All I Really Want To Do' and 'It Ain't Me Babe' whose iterations refuse the constraining social rhetoric of romance, and assault the coercive forces beneath. In the first, the singer benignly repudiates the chicanery of conventional roles in pursuit of a more unguarded openness between the sexes. In the second, he resists the girl's claims, refusing to pretend, and offering only a heart made stone in the face of her neediness, and fantasy. In the first song, the piled-up internal rhymes and yodelling are the means of eliciting intimacy, whereas in the second reiterated negation is the means of eclipsing any such possibility.

At times the emotional world of *Another Side*, with its refusal of romance and its reduction of passion to power-play, can be dismaying. Love is like snakes and ladders, a switchback of elation and loneliness with only one winner, like the double, manic, self in 'Black Crow Blues', who is sings that he is '[m]uch too high to fall', before singing that:

> Other times I'm thinking I'm
> So low I don't know
> If I can come up at all[10]

The vamped chords, turnaround twelve-bar structure and tin-tack doctored piano hammers on this great little song match the figure within it, who lives in the out of tune echo-chamber of his depressive desires. Weary, wasted, worn-out, wishful, standing, anxious, he looks out at the highway, not knowing if he is up or down, of if he can scare away the black crows that press in on him. The self-pleasing, hyper air and invention of 'All I Really Want to Do', gives way here to a see-sawing between depressive apathy and anxious intensity. Similarly, in 'I Don't Believe You', the persona in the song is discarded, tormented by vivid memories of a lost euphoria conveyed through the intensities of alliteration or rhyme: 'we kissed through the wild blazing night-time', 'Though the night ran swirling and whirling', 'Though her skirt it swayed as the guitar played / Her mouth was watery and wet' (*Lyrics*, 127–8).

In such ways on *Another Side of Bob Dylan* elation and emptiness circulate, to create a sense of someone caught in a rootlessness that is both creative and personal. He is singing a new kind of ur-love song (or anti-love song) in an ur-rock (or anti-folk) mode. As Heylin points out, Dylan's turn to rock and roll, fuelled by The Beatles, The Byrds, or The Animals, was far longer in the mix, less inevitable, than people have tended to assume.[11] And amidst all the heady ferment of the time there is the abiding sense that experiences with hallucinogenic and other drugs – reportedly intensifying about this time – exacerbated as much as overcame his sense of alienation, drawing him ever closer into a private orbit where the influence of Grossman (for all his gifts and genuine inwardness with his artists) and others can appear regrettable, even sinister or baleful on some accounts.[12] In retrospect, the whole period can appear like a long wait for the kind of singular mutations that were successively to occur with *Highway 61 Revisited*, *Blonde on Blonde*, the Basement Tapes, or *John Wesley Harding*. Even the frenetic creative burst of spring 1964 (writing most of *Another Side* on Mayfair Hotel notepaper as he travelled from Paris to Greece with Nico) can be seen as a forced reaction to a looming recording deadline. Certainly, the significant songs associated with the American road trip ('Chimes of Freedom' and 'Mr Tambourine Man') are often read as songs of emancipation. However, in fact they do not express power so much as solicit the need for renewed vision, while registering weariness, anxiety, or subjection.

Thus, dejection (and how to launch oneself beyond it) can appear the keynote of the best songs of the time. 'Spanish Harlem Incident' is rhetorically ambitious, and seeks to identify the mystery, wildness, and precariousness of sexual passion with the '[g]ypsy gal'. But what the song uncovers is a vertiginous sense of vulnerability in the face of the girl whose eyes can cast him down or make him feel he is drowning, lost, slayed, or swallowed up. Even his sense of his own reality appears held by her in the encounter ('So I can tell if I am really real' [*Lyrics*, 115]). Within this strange affective dimension though, what is outwardly lamentable in the writing, on the page, again often takes on a certain powerful tension in performance. For instance, the rhythmical insistence of the following line conveys the singer's feelings of desperation:

> Your pearly eyes, so fast an' slashing (*Lyrics*, 115)

'Slashing' here confuses the metaphor of the 'pearly' look of the eyes, but in fact it conveys the switch as he finds himself at stake in her gaze. From being objects of beauty, her eyes can turn to weapons that flash and wound, as she holds him in thrall:

On the cliffs of your wildcat charms I'm riding (*Lyrics*, 115)

He is up, and riding, both moved by her yet always precarious and close to falling.

Within this world of passion, as throughout the album itself, the contraries of being slayed, cast off, cast down, or being made, inspired, lifted up, are inseparable. Outside of social norms, desire is a psychic wild zone, and the effect is constantly of someone who is taken up by the bewildering courses of elation and dejection, and who never knows if he is riding his emotions or being ridden by them. The language too seems uncertainly compounded of power and powerlessness. On the page, the words can all too easily seem weak, pretentious, and sketchy. In listening, though, as at Newport, such disjunctions are often swept along by the expressive immediacies, the driving currents and rocking-and-rolling intonations of the performance. Accordingly, even so raw a song as 'Ballad in Plain D', regrettable in so many ways, captures – when performed – the turmoil of lived experience. It is a quarter-baked song and veers between tenderness, unbridled immaturity, raw self-pity, and vicious lashing-out. Nonetheless, although the song has so many atrocious lines and mangled metaphors, the performance has a certain spacious lyricism and gentleness, and a confessional quality that bear out David Hajdu's point that the 'another side' that 'the album showed was his inside' (Hajdu, 203).[13] Dylan himself gave credence to this idea when said to Nat Hentoff that '[t]here aren't any finger-pointing songs […] From now on, I want to write from inside me […] The way I like to write is for it to come out the way I walk or talk'.[14]

Another Side of Bob Dylan then expresses both a troubled, shifting interiority, and an artist caught between past and future modes. In retrospect, for instance, there is much on the album that suggests the disintegrative, interior world of *Blonde on Blonde*, though Dylan has yet to forge a lyrical and musical idiom to convey this with artistic conviction. One might say, for instance, that the emotional world of 'To Ramona' is condensed in a single high-octane image from 'Medicine Sunday', an outtake from the 1966 album: 'You smile so pretty, and nod to the prison guard.' Again, one might note how the song anticipates the theme of 'lifelessness' and the direct address of 1965, making it comparable to a song like 'Can You Please Crawl Out Your Window.' What is indisputable, though, is that 'To Ramona' again expresses the album's key emotions of need and insufficiency. The singer counsels Ramona to preserve her vivacity, autonomy and desire, in the face of the draining, vampiric, political fantasies of other people. And at the same time, he registers his own dejection, even abjection. He advises her that she is the one who beats and defeats herself by her own capacity for 'feeling bad' (*Lyrics*, 120), while also wearily acknowledging that he relapses into the errors he counsels against. So the song ends with lines anticipating his own vulnerability ('And someday maybe / Who knows, baby / I'll come and be crying to you' [*Lyrics*, 121]).

Within these songs, freedom and subjection are ironically inseparable. The self in the songs feels alternately boundless, euphoric, but also groundless and insubstantial. He is in control and declaiming independence, and yet also subject to the designs and images of others. The complex sense is of someone taking off yet not flying free so much as hanging, waiting to fall. This may account too for Dylan being so impressed, throughout his road trip, by the banal idea that surfaced in 'Ballad in Plain D'. This was the question, 'Are birds free from the chains of the skyway?' (*Lyrics*, 130), which was supposedly relayed 'most mysteriously' by him unto his friends in the prison:. If 'Ballad in Plain D' can be seen as a kind of flip-side of 'Chimes of Freedom', though, so also (in its strange way) can 'I Shall Be Free No 10':

> Well, I set my monkey on the log
> And ordered him to do the Dog
> He wagged his tail and shook his head
> And he went and did the Cat instead
> He's a weird monkey, very funky (*Lyrics*, 118)

For all its seeming artlessness and eccentricity, the song is a parable of its times and these issues of personal freedom. Social forces or other people, after all, may try to master the naughty monkey in all of us, and make us conform to their designs of obedient dog-hood. However, a monkey may decide, in a weird, freakish, defiance, to be something else altogether, even to be a Cat, as in beat idiom perhaps. Elsewhere in the song, the singer comically overthrows conformist, gullible attitudes by a certain paranoiac, idiotic excess that imbues them with elements of the visionary, as when he expresses horror that Russians might reach the gold streets of heaven first, or when he evinces a certain protectionism in expressing a liberal's horror of his daughter marrying Barry Goldwater. He breaks social codes not by design, but by the comically aberrant ways in which he embraces them. He wants to play tennis in high-heeled sneakers or in a wig-hat, or to play golf at the country club while carrying *The New York Times* (though on horseback, with his hair down to his feet). Dylan's subversive absurdity hollows out the conformist world from within. For all the unbridled weirdness of his self-portrayal, the song gloriously suggests the arbitrariness of convention and bears out the truth in the lines of the first verse ('It ain't no use a-talking to me / It's just the same as talking to you' [*Lyrics*, 118]).

'Motorpsycho Nitemare' is another song that rings comic changes on these themes. Its language is as vigilant, and deft as the singer has to be in manoeuvring his passage and escape in the song from Rita's crazy, paranoid, right-wing father. It contrasts in these features with 'My Back Pages' which is a much more important song (if a much more flawed one). The straightforward theme here – that freedom involves renouncing political moralising with all its swamping abstraction, fantasy, and self-delusion – is clear enough, though at odds with the often incomprehensible imagery:

Crimson flames tied through my ears
Rollin' high and mighty traps
Pounced with fire on flamin' roads
Using ideas as my maps (*Lyrics*, 125)

For Epstein, Dylan at this time is 'a poet in the state of becoming', which is another way of saying that these songs sound at times like pretentious drafts (Epstein, 156). Certainly Dylan is someone ambitiously seeking to conduct poetic forces and elements within an unstable cultural domain (even though the songs convey the sense of someone perilously close at times to going down an emotional plug-hole). 'My Back Pages' is a song that proclaims churning transitions, as 'Times They Are A-Changin'' or 'Restless Farewell' did. It is a signpost, pointing away from the past, and expressing a powerful ethical recoil from false temptations: to preach and pontificate ('A self-ordained professor's tongue'); to serve other people's agendas; and to mistake one's motives ('Girls' faces formed the forward path ...'). These images at least have a pithy resonance, however much they tend to become unstuck from the song itself. Again, when he refers to 'Lies that life is black and white', he appears to complicate even his self-identification with the civil rights movement. The line can be taken to suggest that such identification involved a moral fiction of self-purity uncomfortably similar to the kinds of prejudicial simplification, and racial fictions that it opposed. And the images signal forward too: a phrase like 'corpse evangelists' anticipates the very different forms of finger-pointing and imagery that will surface in the accusatory songs of 1965.

II

Throughout his career, Dylan's official output has been shadowed by an archive of unreleased songs, versions and live performances. In the early and mid-1960s this was a case of prodigious songwriting outstripping the opportunities of record production. Almost every album can be said to have a virtual twin, made up of songs passed over. For instance, the following songs could have made up an album arguably of equal quality to *The Times They Are A'Changin'*: 'Percy's Song', 'Only a Hobo', 'Who Killed Davey Moore', 'Ramblin' Down Thru the World', 'Dusty Old Fairgrounds', 'Eternal Circle', 'Gypsy Lou', 'Walls of Red Wing', 'Seven Curses', and 'Lay Down Your Weary Tune'.[15] By the time of *Another Side of Bob Dylan* and *Bringing It All Back Home*, however, there are less extra songs, and it is easy enough to see why Dylan would have passed over 'Guess I'm Doin' Fine', 'California', 'Love is Just a Four Letter Word', 'Playboys and Playboys' and 'Denise'. One might wonder at the side-lining of 'Farewell Angelina', 'If You Gotta Go, Go Now', 'Mama, You Been on My Mind', or 'I'll Keep it with Mine'.[16] However, a moment's reflection suggests how most of these songs would not conform to the two main principles which govern the new album: a more rhetorically ambitious, visionary strain on the acoustic side of the album; and a fast-cut, surreal, urban, mode on the electric side. In fact, they are closer to *Another Side of Bob Dylan*, as songs that complicate conventional attitudes to sex and romance. In contrast, there are only two songs about women on the later album – 'She Belongs to Me' and 'Love Minus Zero/No Limit' – and in both, the woman is gnomically evoked and idealised rather than addressed.

The album cover of *Bringing It All Back Home* introduces much of this changed world. The photo is of an interior, the ornate décor signalling elegant, moneyed privacy. The records and artefacts strewn around intimate a confident bohemian world of eclectic, singular inspirations. Daniel Kramer's framing effect, surrounding the main image with a blurred, refracting circle, suggests that we are peering through a key-hole or into an aesthete's burrow.[17] Sally Grossman lounges on a chaise longue, cigarette in hand, draped in red: a sibylline presence who invests the whole with allure and glamour. Her steady gaze threatens to deprive you of your ease, to reduce you to being a supplicant at the threshold. She is the tutelary spirit of the photograph, feline and mysterious like the cat which Dylan clutches (named 'Rolling Stone'). The cat is a familiar in this bewitching world, and uncannily radiates the same stare as Grossman herself. Though Grossman is the Suze Rotolo *de jour*, she has no desire to please, and Dylan himself transmits a certain wired aggression. His pinned shirt and elegant cufflinks associate him with this coterie exclusiveness, while his stare is combative, his posture coiled, his fist clenched. This is a world that constitutes itself, Kramer's image says, by resources of style, talent, beauty, and taste, but also by vigilance, energy, even aggression. It will outface you, is careless of you, and challenges you to respond in a suitable, immediate, stylish manner. There are no precedents, no prior contexts, only the moment there to be remade, and in which you remake yourself. Dylan, his gaze intent on rejecting you, doubts you can overcome his apathy.

This imagery embodies the values of nomadic urban self-reliance that the album conveys. Jean Tamarin has described the shift in these two years from 'earnest, eager-to-please folkie' to 'postmodern celebrity – scornful, superior … a kind of dark, mercurial god'.[18] It is tempting to date the final stage of this metamorphosis in the period between the end of November 1964 and the second week of January 1965. In a telling burst, Dylan wrote much of what is most distinctive and new on *Bringing It All Back Home*. As often, songs surfaced just before recording, including 'Subterranean Homesick Blues', 'Outlaw Blues', 'Love Minus Zero', 'She Belongs to Me', 'It's all Over Now, Baby Blue', 'Bob Dylan's 115th Dream', and 'Maggie's Farm'. According to Hajdu, most of these songs were actually written over a few days in January, when Dylan was 'holed up in a studio apartment above the Café Espresso in Bearsville', and by a method of composition in which he would work a song up from scraps, creating the song as a form of sung collage. His eyes closed, and sitting amidst 'dozens of photographs torn from newspapers and magazines in a montage on the floor', he would intone whatever phrases or lines were triggered by the images or texts:

Bob would start with a simple musical framework, a blues pattern he could repeat indefinitely, and he would close his eyes – he would not draw from the pictures literally but would use the impression the faces left as a visual model for kaleidoscopic language. He appeared to sing whatever came to him, disconnected phrases with a poetic feeling. When something came out that he liked, he scrawled it down hurriedly, so as to stay in the moment, and he would do this until there were enough words written for a song. (Hajdu, 233)

Having jotted down anything promising, he would transcribe and work up the songs on coffee, red wine, and marijuana, seeking to preserve the edge, intuitiveness, and spontaneity of the process. As the liner notes might suggest, the aim was to cultivate an effect of open-ended, uncertain immediacy:

Great books've been written. the Great sayings
have all been said/I am about t' sketch You
a picture of what goes on around here sometimes. though I don't understand too well
myself what's really happening (liner notes, *Bringing It All Back Home*)

With many of these songs, Dylan was assertively drawing on the American rock and roll structures of his youth, a move that would lead in 1965 to him increasingly overcoming much of the creative drift of the previous year. Notwithstanding the new sense of artistic direction though, it is easy to see why he didn't 'understand too well ... what was happening'. The ambivalences of his self-presentation were now powerful. The canny artfulness of the earlier self, fashioning an implicitly collective subjectivity, had given way to something more combative, private, recondite, and bohemian – closer to the Beats than to Guthrie. Yet, at the same time, the new music was propelling him to ever more stellar, public, and divisive levels of fame and notoriety. The self-mythologising of the very early days had now been transformed into a *noli me tangere* attitude that was in many respects easy enough to understand. In the KQED conference, Jean Gleason referred to Phil Ochs's view that 'it becomes increasingly dangerous for you to perform in public' (Artur, 238). Whether he liked it or not he had infiltrated people's minds ('twisted so many people's wigs' in Gleason's phrase), becoming a fully-fledged exemplar or introject in the collective psyche. The Dylan who had playfully sung 'I'll let you be in my dream, if I can be in yours', was now the target of unbridled and invasive fantasy (*Lyrics*, 65). Hence the detectable craving to move inwards and away, the desire not to be understood, or to be visible, or to please, to say what is expected, or engage on the level. In the liner notes, he is confronted by a 'middle-aged druggist up for district attorney' who blames him for riots in Vietnam and wants to electrocute him on the fourth of July. Unsurprisingly, we find him asking for help 'getting this wall on the plane'.

The ironies of this situation were noted by Carla Rotolo. The imperatives of Dylan's ambition and creativity had led to something that could not now be controlled: 'He knew exactly where he was going and how big he was going to be ... The only mistake he made was being caught up in the vortex of being "the messiah"' (Shelton, *No Direction Home*, 103). One can ponder these ironies in the evolution in *Bringing It All Back Home* towards a music that simultaneously expands his audience while emphasising alienation, even jet-set walled privacy. The songs display an enormous, self-differentiating drive and often a youthful, pumped-up jauntiness. However, the album predominantly shows solitary kinds of inspiration – songs of city angst, pell-mell surrealism, mysterious romance, or artistic vision. The songs on the acoustic side of the album were written first (with the exception of 'It's All Over Now, Baby Blue') and they reflect the aesthetic preoccupation that had been evident throughout 1964 as Dylan searched for a new direction and stimulus, through immersion in Blake, Rimbaud, Ginsberg, Dylan Thomas. His fervent eagerness to leave behind the world of protest song had led into experiments with 'poetry, prose-poems, at least one play, and a novel' (Hajdu, 193). This inspiration is evident on side two of *Bringing It All Back Home* with 'Mr Tambourine Man', 'Gates of Eden', and 'It's Alright, Ma (I'm Only Bleeding)'. Within them, the collective politics of *The Freewheelin' Bob Dylan* or *The Times They Are A-Changin'* is recast in terms of a visionary poetics that takes the freedom of the individual mind as its main site of conflict and creativity.

'Mr Tambourine Man' was reportedly written while staying up all night at the house of Al Aronwitz, though Judy Collins claims it was written at hers (Heylin, *Revolution in the Air*, 209). Whatever the truth, it is a song sung out of restlessness, weariness, sleeplessness, and numbness. The singer is waiting at dawn amidst a landscape figured as isolation, sorrow, fear, guilt, habit, and lifelessness. Nature and time are out of joint, and he is oppressed. The influences of the past weigh him down, threatening to draw him into this stricken world, like the ragged clown who chases shadows. Against this, his desire shapes itself as urgent forward-looking musical receptivity, from the song's invocatory, imperative opening ('Hey! Mr Tambourine Man, play a song for me' [*Lyrics*, 152]) and the determined, energetic, upswing of the strummed guitar. Music is a means of transmitting and pursuing an expressivity that might otherwise be lost. Within the song's *mise-en-scène*, it is the hopeful means of liberating vitality, of delivering the singer to a place beyond the 'frozen leaves', the foggy ruins of the past, 'the haunted, frightened trees', and 'the twisted reach of crazy sorrow' ... As in a romantic lyric, the words in the song reach for their vision of redemption and reconnection. The figure in the song projects through his words an animated but precariously conditional hope of a kind that can bind together art and nature, the social and natural, past, present and future, sound and meaning. He envisions dancing 'with one hand waving free' beneath a 'diamond sky'. However, such hopes remain as yet unachieved.

In this haunted landscape, then, art rather than politics is the primary means of restitution and expression. The song occupies a time of opposites and transmutation – of hope and sadness, transfiguration and loss, day and night. The collective inaugural summons of 'The Times They Are A-Changin'' is now transposed into a more personal, aesthetic key. While he waits, his words expressively signal beyond the forlorn landscape and mimic the uplifting relays he hopefully anticipates. The future infiltrates his words through their emergent musical qualities and patterns. The song's refrains and repetitions, its braidings of rhythm and rhyme ('sand ... hand ... stand ... sleeping ... feet ... meet ... dreaming ...'), and its echoic and alliterative effects ('reels of rhyme', 'circled ... circus sands', 'jingle-jangle morning') invigoratingly set out to convert what is flat and physical into what is musical and spiritual. Again, Bruce Langhorne (a figure plausibly identified by Dylan himself as the tambourine man because of his habit of carrying around a huge tambourine in the early New York days), reiterates on guitar a little modal counter-melody that helps transmit the stirring signs of reanimated feeling in this frozen, twisted, world.

Often taken to be a drug song (though Dylan repeatedly denied it), the composition of 'Mr Tambourine Man' reportedly pre-dates Dylan's use of amphetamines, and it is hard to imagine it being written under their influence. Anyhow, it is much more meaningfully a song about renewal, about a mind seeking to undo its own self-captivity and renounce the habitual and social forms that face and fence it. Gibbens concludes that the song is about overcoming the burdens of 'memory and fate' (*Lyrics*, 153), about 'the shedding of dead forms, and the possibility of a new beginning' (Gibbens, 133). 'Possibility' is the crucial emphasis, since the power of the song derives from the way that everything hangs in the balance at this uncertain dawn, Dylan's performance being searching rather than triumphant. Though the future is there to be reclaimed, the voice in the song cannot do it by himself, and in any case can only do so by leaving himself behind. As with 'The Chimes of Freedom', the desire for imaginative emancipation is what connects us to the singer, while again this connection happens through a visionary aesthetic internally related to the song's own effects of sound and imagery. Expressive renewal here, as with 'The Chimes of Freedom' is a matter of the song itself, not just its theme, as Gibbens again identifies:

> The joy of self-abandonment in 'Mr Tambourine Man' is that the artist had realised for the first time how his creative power could renew itself cyclically ... the discovery that he could follow music – and particularly rhythm – to new life, on a new morning. (Gibbens, 135)

In comparison, 'Gates of Eden' can seem a rather hit-and-miss affair, at once more ambitious and less successful than 'Mr Tambourine Man'. Heylin claims that it might have been a more chemically assisted song, being written in June or July 1964. It was recorded in a single take in Studio A on 15 January 1965 and received its first public performance at the famous Halloween Philharmonic Hall concert on 31 October 1964, where it was introduced as a 'sacrilegious lullaby in D Minor' (Heylin, *Revolution in the Air*, 208). Sean Wilentz, sadly too young to go off and smoke in the interval, nonetheless remembers leaving the concert feeling like everyone else:

exhilarated, entertained, and ratified in our self-assured enlightenment, but also confused about the snatches of lines we'd gleaned from the strange new songs. What was that weird lullaby in D minor? What in God's name is a perfumed gull (or did he sing, 'curfewed gal')? (Wilentz, *Dylan in America*, 91)

Whether or not Heylin is right about the song's medical pre-history, Wilentz is surely on strong ground when he claims that the song was written when Dylan was heavily under the mind-altering influences of Blake and Ginsberg.[19] The Blakean echoes in the song are perhaps most evident in the key lines, 'The kingdoms of Experience / In the precious winds they rot' (*Lyrics*, 155) where a Blakean wind (often associated in Blake's work with the physically conducted fluidities of desire, love, or Innocence) survives the dystopian 'Kingdoms of Experience.' Again, as Blake's songs and prophetic works have a powerful effect and radiate meaning without being reducible to paraphrase, so likewise 'The Gates of Eden", has a hypnotic suggestiveness, a cumulative visionary impact, that sustains in performance what on the page might otherwise collapse as sketchy, flawed, embarrassing, pretentious, uneven, overblown, rickety, or incomprehensible. Many listeners will understand Wilentz's memory of how much the initial impact of the song, for those exiting for the subway on 31 October 1964, was a matter of its atmosphere of unresolved, incantatory evocation. 'Gates of Eden' bears out the singer's lover's words in the final verse, as a dream or vision that resists interpretation.

However much the effect of the song is about the immersive possibilities of tone, mood, and imagery, its visionary panorama nonetheless has a powerful cumulative coherence, knitting together serial snapshots of the 'corrosive illusions' of political authority, religion, possessions, or education (Wilentz, *Dylan in America*, 100). Tamarin describes 'Gates of Eden' as a 'biblical, metaphysical, protest song', its 'epic, scary, slashing string of images', introducing us into a bleak and fallen world where 'there are no kings, no sins, no justice, no trials', where we have no lamp to light and welcome us, where gray flannel dwarfs scream, and where 'Nothing is what it seems' (Tamarin, 135). Similarly, Gabrielle Goodchild holds up Eden as the place outside '*this* world, a lying illusion of destructiveness, savagery, false promises, prophets and pimps, false security' (Shelton, *No Direction Home*, 194). In part a Beats-influenced *exposé* of the dark underside and inner delirium of American capitalism, the song also can be seen as something more far-reaching. Something like Dylan's equivalent to Nietzsche's *Genealogy of Morals*, it is a lyric that unpicks the repressive social forces that imprison the mind, distort the emotions, and shape consciousness through subtractive forces of guilt and shame. Dylan here is targeting an America that he was to recall in the 1985 *Biograph* interview with Cameron Crowe:

> America was still very 'straight', 'post-war' and sort of into a gray-flannel suit thing, McCarthy, commies, puritanical, very claustrophobic and what was happening of any real value was happening away from that and sort of hidden from view ... (Artur, 852)

In this world, everyone is captive, and 'from their fates' trying 'to resign'. The 'savage soldier' sticking his head in the sand and complaining, or the 'shoeless hunter' who's 'gone deaf / But still remains' are representative casualties of this conformist society which denatures instinct and vitality, and leaves them to live on in self-mutilating alienation or violence:

> Upon the beach where hound dogs bay
> At ships with tattooed sails
> Heading for the Gates of Eden (Lyrics, 154)

Without putting too much weight on lines that revel in dark, unspecifiable visionary portent, it is also worth teasing out some of their suggestion. The 'hound dogs' might be taken to figure the forces of instinct, while the tattooed ships could figure the piratical influences that are the true, if hidden, expression of social forces. They are bearing down on the Gates of Eden, to usurp this place identified with a Blakean or Nietzschean affirmation of existence as intrinsically innocent. So throughout the song, society unlawfully usurps and captures innate forces of power and joy, and makes its mark upon its citizens according to the designs of guilt and resentment, and the life-strangling fictions of ownership, kingship, priesthood, and hierarchy. We are deprived of ourselves, and impoverished because possessed by possessiveness and envy: 'paupers / Each one wishing for what the other has got' (*Lyrics*, 155). We are confined within the clanging closures of rational, moralising, consciousness. The 'gray flannel dwarf', with his 'breadcrumb sins', is a *petit-bourgeois* exemplar of the sado-masochism that locks him into his own guilt, subject to the torturing visitations of the 'motorcycle black madonna' and her phantasmal accomplice. Like him, we are powerless and mystified, passively subject and waiting 'for succeeding kings'. Yet even those who might appear to hold power – of reason or position – are as deluded as the rest, since rationality, knowledge, and hierarchy are illusions, as with the hollow philosophical exchanges of the prince and princess who discuss 'what's real and what is not'. In this culture, all hierarchies are false images of transcendence that disguise contaminated desire and fantasy, as with the image of 'Aladdin and his lamp', sitting alongside 'Utopian hermit monks' '[s]ide-saddle on the Golden Calf' (*Lyrics*, 155). For all its unevenness and indefiniteness, then, 'Gates of Eden', like 'Mr Tambourine Man', signals towards a renewal produced through aesthetic experience, and as enacted and produced by the song itself. It is a matter here of holding to one's precarious vision in the darkness. One must be outlaw and innocent, like the 'cowboy angel' holding his candle 'though its glow is waxed in black' (*Lyrics*, 154).

'It's Alright, Ma (I'm Only Bleeding)' exploits the forces of non-intelligibility and vision in different ways. The inhuman, reiterative velocity of the delivery purges the verses of any personal pathos or interpersonal dynamic. Instead the song acerbically identifies social corruption, intent on inspiring us to tear off the masks that society asks us to don in complicity to its craven designs.[20] Listening to Dylan singing the song on 27 March 1965 in Santa Monica, the day on which

Bringing it All Back Home was released, one detects the excitement and energy it whips up through its assault on our passive, unquestioning collusion with social forces. As with the early performances of 'Desolation Row', the sheer verve and audacity of the song's hostility provokes a kind of amazed laughter. What is missing in 'It's Alright, Ma' though is the sense of visionary expansion that was sought on the inspirational beach of 'Mr Tambourine Man', or that even suffuses the early morning prophetic dream world of 'Gates of Eden'. Instead, the song is all critique, summoning its counter-violence to the violence that society imparts and to our docility. Its relentless impetus and blues motifs drive home its points like a 1960s nail-gun, while suggesting how much of our suffering is a form of social crucifixion. This is a song of pain, but also of a spiritual struggle, albeit secular in nature, and directed against the socialising forces of education and religion:

> While preachers preach of evil fates
> Teachers teach that knowledge waits
> Can lead to hundred dollar plates ... (*Lyrics*, 157)

The song's unremitting urgency is created, then, not through mazy evocation but through rhythmical insistence, pace, and precision. Renewal here is identical with resistance to the suicidal forces and affects of 'society's pliers' (*Lyrics*, 158). Renewal is about an animating recognition of the current situation, and an on-going dedication, line by line, to be always 'busy being born', to the refusal of society's forms of death. Everything in the delivery and writing is about momentum and intensity, as if the singer were fighting his way clear of the dangers of being made to live in a 'vault', of occupying the 'hole' that someone else has dragged him down into, or of having to disguise the secretive 'thought-dreams' that would have him killed. Uneven as the song is, it expressively offers itself as a force of furious liberation: the resource of our having to meet the social forces of denial and negativity with this contrary, annihilating vigour and insight. Like the candle or the tambourine in the other songs, the song's images can be taken as tropes for its own specific means of illumination, critique and creativity. Like a 'handmade blade', one can say, the song is a bespoke tool for intervening surgically on successive points of the body politic with visionary critique; or like a 'child's balloon', it offers itself as a means of inspiring, but still nascent liberation. In its very singular way, the song becomes a privileged vehicle for a forceful targeting of political malaise, socio-economic disillusion. Its aphoristic powers of revelation and compression appear features of an artistic control that cuttingly targets the nihilistic influences of corruption, compliance, idolatory, 'propaganda'. Society threatens, tempts, mystifies, or seduces us into obedience or self-estrangement, recruiting all the forces of advertising, love, authority, fake morality, religious fantasy, to entrap us within 'fake morals' and 'people's games'. Within this world, even the ethics of non-violence appear as an illusion: 'others say don't hate nothing at all / Except hatred' (*Lyrics*, 156).

'It's All Over Now, Baby Blue' also expressively precipitates and advocates a forced necessity of self-change: old attachments, property, identifications must be left behind.[21] However, in this song illusion is also now personal matter, for someone who must struggle to face a cruel reality, counselled by this disillusioned voice. The singer's bitter candour is a dry run for 'Like a Rolling Stone', and similarly appears to be perhaps a displacement of losses undergone, of self-anxiety now turned on another. This is a world of nakedness, orphans, gamblers and uncertain saints, of sea-sick sailors, empty-handed and crazed painters, of thieving lovers and vagabonds: figures of an obscure world in which old systems of representation, clothing, calculation, love, property, and navigation are superseded, where even the carpet moves beneath your feet. As Pichaske puts it, the song's journey:

> liberates us from the dead we leave behind, but it's an act more of desperation than of exploration or inspiration, and Dylan's emphasis is as much on finding fragments of the past that he can hold on to as it is anticipation or starting anew. Seasick sailors, orphans, and vagabonds do not promise paths of glory; they are roadsick refugees tired of the journey and looking for a place to hole up. (Pichaske, *Song of the North Country*, 167)

In these terms, it is tempting to take 'It's All Over Now, Baby Blue' as a song that inaugurates the different kind of dynamic of songs written in 1965, where Dylan explores in personal terms the effects of social disorientation. Along with the rest of the songs on the album it dates from the early part of the year, and moves in the same kind of destabilising dimension as a song like 'Subterranean Homesick Blues' that shares its predatory urban world. This song was recorded in one take on 14 January, the first day that Dylan had recorded with a band since 'Mixed Up Confusion' on the *Freewheelin'* sessions (Heylin, *The Recording Sessions*, 35). On this clattering opening track, the singer counsels the disorientated kid to face up to the forces that threaten him, that keep him homesick, underground. The music is wired and wiry, full of nervous energy, its lean arrangement and accelerated tempo punctuated by a pealing electric guitar. As if ejected into the city, the song is a telegraphic rush of images and injunctions, its fast verbal cuts an analogue for the urban overloading and fragmenting of experience. The turbulent traffic of rhymes and cryptic vignettes puts us on our mettle, forcing us to wise up within this jungle of double-dealing where everyone is on the make, looking for angles, like '[t]he man in the trench coat / Badge out, laid off / Says he's got a bad cough / Wants to get it paid off' (*Lyrics*, 141).

In a discussion that identifies Dylan's development with his uses of the vignette, Mark Ford describes how by the mid-60s it was in Dylan's hand an instrument that was 'as keen and precise and remorseless and flexible and resonant and effective as the rhyming couplet was for Pope'.[22] In this song, the vignette is a means of allusively evoking 'a mini-Beat or underground or counterculture story in a few lines' (Ford, 'Bob Dylan and the Vignette', 4). What is distinctive about Dylan's use of the vignette in this period, Ford writes, is that unlike Ginsberg he avoids utopian pathos or uplift, the songs identifying Dylan as outside the scene he surveys, the 'king of the cats in New York' mercilessly surveying others in his 'triumphant pageant of knowing disaffection' (Ford, 'Bob Dylan and the Vignette', 5). What is clear is that no-one here is joining hands any longer in dedication to the signs of the times. Instead of incipient revolution, there is only alarming personal upheaval. Fellow-feeling amounts merely to counselling someone to keep his eye on the parking meter or the weather, or off the girl by the whirlpool. In these features, the song aligns itself with 'Maggie's Farm', 'Outlaw Blues', 'On the Road Again', and 'Bob Dylan's 115th Dream' where anxious confusion results in surreal narratives that bring together disillusion and exhilaration in a series of comic scenarios delivered with a frenetic electric accompaniment, of a kind characterised by Polizzotti as 'febrile rattling ... electrified folk' (Polizzotti, 19).

Because the vignette in Dylan's hands thrillingly alludes to contexts and narratives that elude us, it is an appropriate tool for these songs of 1965 as they confront social alienation and the disintegration of any constructive collective politics. The vignette summons its cutting edge out of its forceful brevity and makes the listener edgy, putting him in an uncertain spot. 'Maggie's Farm' vividly uses the vignette for its individualistic manifesto. We are on our own, are left to our own devices, searching for sustaining contexts and relations while addressing the simple difficulty of being 'just like I am', when so much rushes past and everyone 'wants you / To be just like them' (*Lyrics*, 144). Over and again in such ways, the surrealist condensations of the songs comically imitate the compressive, distorting effects of social living. 'On the Road Again' is a cousin to 'I Shall Be Free No 10', targeting daily repression and tyranny:

> Your mama, she's a-hidin'
> Inside the icebox
> Your daddy walks in wearin'
> A Napolean Bonaparte mask (*Lyrics*, 147)

In this world, one needs to step away from the accidents of circumstance ('Ain't it hard to stumble / And land in some funny lagoon'). Keeping one's footing means avoiding identification with any ideology and socialised self-image ('I ain't gonna hang no picture frame / Well, I might look like Robert Ford / But I feel just like a Jesse James ...' [*Lyrics*, 146]). All of this and more is played out in 'Bob Dylan's 115th Dream', a neglected song that scrambles the contemporary, the mythical and the historical, suggesting that life does not fit the narratives we buy into, and that society endlessly disrupts human connection. The idealism of discovery becomes simultaneous with rapacity, as Captain Arab sets out to colonise the new-found land by drawing up deeds and setting out to build a fort and start 'buying this place with beads' (*Lyrics*, 148). Later, the singer knocks on the door of a house with the American flag on display:

> The man says, 'Get out of here
> I'll tear you limb from limb'

I said, 'You know they refused Jesus too'
He said, 'You're not Him' (*Lyrics*, 149)

Throughout the song, like Jesse James he is on the run, a 'hobo sailor'. Running into a funeral parlour a man responds to his complaint about his jailed friends, by telling him to call him if they die.

Against this urban isolation and alienation, the two love songs 'She Belongs to Me' and 'Love Minus Zero / No Limit' offer the private worlds of art and love as implicit alternatives. Artistic vision can redeem and master contradiction, create alternative worlds: 'She can take the dark out of the night-time / And paint the day time black.' The artist is one who never loses her step: 'She never stumbles / She's got no place to fall' (*Lyrics*, 143). Her eye for the times consigns others to being merely walking antiques, and her influence can make others want to steal, to spy, to kneel. The idea of a private ethic rooted this time in love rather than art surfaces in 'Love Minus Zero / No Limit' where Dylan sings of someone whose speech is precisely not of 'ideals' or 'violence'. She is associated with silence, or laughing, and embodies values of fidelity and romance that others seek vainly to assert through futile words, promises, valentines, worldly striving, or family connections. The song opposes in its closing verse its uncertain, vulnerable, and reclusive romantic image ('My love she's like some raven / At my window with a broken wing' [*Lyrics*, 145]) to the failing connections of the external world: the designs of banker's nieces, the isolated humanity of the rambling country doctor, and the inhospitable hammering and blowing of the elements.

Any such tenderness was, of course, soon to be thrown aside in the rest of 1965. The dynamic drama of expression and inexpression that underpins Dylan's art of becoming now will find even sharper terms and values with Newport and *Highway 61 Revisited*. What is already clear is that the axis of critique and liberation in his work has shifted from the political scenario of 1963 to the more visionary aspirations of 1964, and on to a more urban, sociological canvas in *Bringing It All Back Home*. In the rest of 1965, it will shift again, as Dylan will confront from within the ways in which subjectivity is a social construct. Animating aggression and hostility will now be up-front as tools for fighting his culture's ways of configuring our subjectivity. No longer identifying himself as outside society, the songs of *Highway 61 Revisited* will rather explore how society is within the alienated self that it constructs. The consequence is that expression and self-truth inevitably become functions of an emancipating resentment. Tapping into these energies, Dylan will voice an expansive, driving vision of his society as a freak-show, a carnival where the compulsory lineaments of personality have frozen into masks that conceal the violence, poison, delirium, paranoia, and trapped desire beneath.

Figure 1   Dylan with Victor Maymudes in tree, Woodstock, New York State, 1964. Photo © Daniel Kramer

Figure 2   Dylan in dark glasses, New York City, 1964. Photo © Daniel Kramer

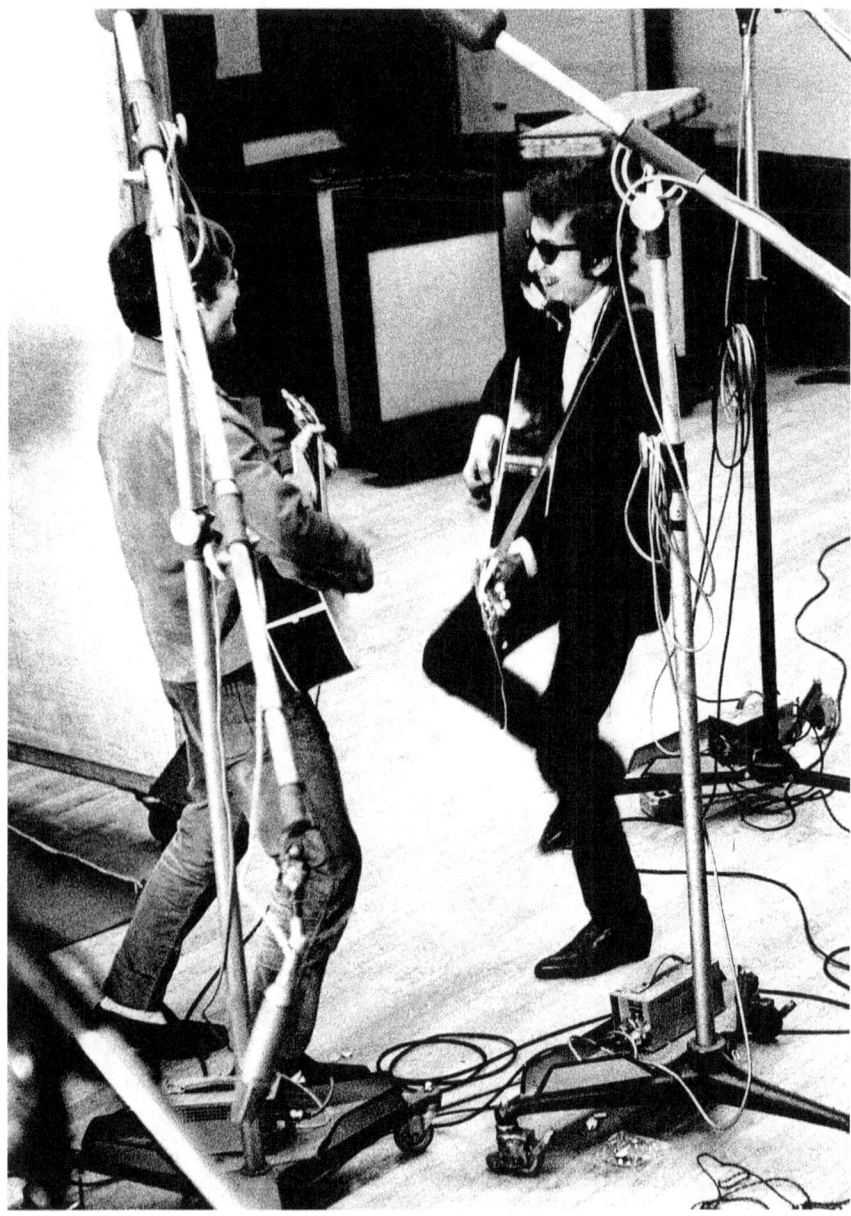

Figure 3 Dylan and John Sebastian at 'BRINGING IT ALL BACK HOME' session, New York City, 1965. Photo © Daniel Kramer

Figure 4 Forest Hills Stadium sound check, New York City, 1965. Photo © Daniel Kramer

Figure 5 Dylan backlit on stage, Forest Hills Stadium, New York City, 1965. Photo © Daniel Kramer

Chapter 3
'There is No Eye'

Highway 61 Revisited

As much of a *cause célèbre* as Dylan's first electric performance on Sunday 25 July 1965 at Newport has become, it is equally so that the final truth of the night has long passed into myth. Facts have long since been clouded by claim and counter-claim, the whole shrouded in cultural fantasy. Did Pete Seeger threaten to cut the cables with an axe? Were they microphone or power cables? How far did Dylan premeditate the performance? What proportions of the crowd were booing at his betrayal of his folk-singer mission, calling out for others to sit down or quiet down, or calling for a better sound, or a longer set? Were there tears on Dylan's cheeks when he returned to sing 'Mr Tambourine Man' and 'It's All Over Now, Baby Blue'? Why did he perform this encore, and was it prearranged? The footage of the raucous, three song set with Mike Bloomfield, Al Kooper et al., however, makes certain things appear undeniable: Dylan's air initially is one of willed cool and defiance, but it masks a certain initial apprehension. However, as the performance continues, he becomes visibly carried along, inspirited by the turbulent currents whipped up by the musicians.

He is clearly savouring, too, the gladiatorial intensity of the moment, his face and posture suggesting at points the fruition of a long-held adolescent fantasy of being a gunslinger or outsider – a Brando or Dean from the wrong side of the tracks. In even more direct ways, Dylan was definitely revisiting his adolescence on stage at Newport, the concert recalling the times when he had been booed by audiences in Hibbing and St Louis in the late 1950s while performing with an electrified band. Dylan's ex-girlfriend, Echo Helmstrom, told Toby Thompson of how around 1957–58 she 'used to get so upset, for days ahead of time when I knew he was going to sing in public':

> … in the big auditoriums people would laugh and hoot at Bob, and I'd just sit there embarrassed, almost crying.

Remembering the notorious incident when Dylan appeared in the school talent show, Echo recalled how loud the band was, and how Dylan afterwards seemed to be elated, as if thriving on the brickbats hurled by his audience: 'I guess he lived in his own world, 'cause apparently the audience's booing and laughter hadn't bothered him in the least' (Thompson, *Positively Main Street*, 69).

What is indisputable in the confrontational Newport performance is how far Dylan's music, like so much of the music of 1965 and 1966, was propelled to new, heady artistic heights by the visceral fuel of antagonism, resentment, and vituperation turned out against an imagined interlocutor (and here a resistant audience) who would otherwise trap him within their version of who he was. Mark Polizotti writes insightfully, even with understatement, of the album that Dylan was recording – both sides of the Newport performance that summer: 'What Dylan has abandoned in *Highway 61 Revisited* is not his sense of outrage or protest, but the illusion of community' (Polizzotti, 12). Indeed, it is possible to claim that at Newport itself there was a specific component of defiance or retaliation, and sheer happenstance, in this hastily rehearsed set. It seems likely that the decision to play an electric set was in fact only finally arrived at on the Saturday, probably in response to Alan Lomax's disparaging introduction of The Paul Butterfield Blues Band, another of Albert Grossman's stable of artists. Things turned physical, in a *contretemps* described by James Brewer. Lomax had:

> described their music as 'purely imitative' and basically asked for the forbearance of the audience. The pair of middle-aged men ended up rolling around in the dirt of the festival grounds.[1]

Whether Grossman's motivation was in defense of the artistic integrity of his clients or his royalties is not recorded. Greil Marcus actually has Lomax, as well as Seeger, both laying their hands on Seeger's famous axe during Dylan's electric set:

> Backstage [writes Marcus] Pete Seeger and the great ethnomusicologist Alan Lomax attempted to cut the band's power cables. Pete Yarrow and singer Theodore Bikel blocked them until a full guard could be rounded up. (Greil Marcus, *Invisible Republic*, 12)

One can only ponder what turn history might have taken if Lomax had managed to locate Seeger's axe for the earlier confrontation with Grossman. Certainly, this was all a shift from the on-stage communal linking of arms, between Dylan, Baez, Bikel, Yarrow, Seeger and the others in Newport two years earlier as they chanted 'We Shall Overcome'. By 1965, all that linked most of the stars was that they contributed 25 per cent to Albert Grossman.

As it was, the scratch ensemble had only the one night to rehearse before the Sunday afternoon sound-check, and, unsurprisingly the final performance (of 'Maggie's Farm', 'Phantom Engineer', and 'Like a Rolling Stone') is raw, frenetic, adrenalised. The band lacks togetherness and finesse, let alone the symphonic rapport that would develop between Dylan and The Hawks over the next twelve months. What is unmistakeable, though, is the huge energy – infernal, belligerent – of the music, and its effect on Dylan's voice that becomes increasingly driven by it. Afterwards, Dylan would gnomically opine to Maria Muldaur that he felt as if his hands were on fire, as if he had been himself physically conducting the power that surged through the amplifiers, louder than anyone could recall hearing ... The electric accompaniment sounds like a runaway train, all pistons pumping, and it emblematises a music that is now defiantly urban, machinic. Dylan's voice no longer reaches out to solicit or address its audience (collectively or intimately), its rough-and-readiness an ethical marker. Instead, it is now a vehicle for an untrammelled, alienated, hostile, sensibility, and Newport is its first public manifestation.

'[C]awing, derisive' is how poet Philip Larkin would memorably describe this voice, in a *Daily Telegraph* review of *Highway 61 Revisited*, in a formulation well-worth pondering.[2] Indeed, Dylan's voice in 1965 can often sound like some bird of bad omen ('The Titanic sails at dawn' [*Lyrics*, 183]), a triumphant feeder on carrion. He will not intone words, as in reasonable speech, so much as use his voice as a means of power, of marking territory, or of soaring in rebarbative songs of rejection, refusal, escape. Dylan's voice at this juncture is, assuredly, often intoxicating and exhilarating, but its core value is an emancipating aggression, driven by needful acts of self-erasure and disintrication. The voice of *Highway 61 Revisited*, of 'Like a Rolling Stone' (that had been released five days before Newport) and 'Positively 4th Street' (that would be written within the next three and a half days) soars, swoops, pecks and spits. The delivery no longer employs rhythm and rhyme as measures of thought, modes of intimacy, or signs of collectivity. Instead these formal means are hooks on which the singer seeks to hang his exhilarated, dismissive, crowing, vision. Intonation is astringent, sour, ironic, but also pulsating and self-delighting.

What is clear is that the music of Dylan's youth, would now assert itself more univocally in his work over the next year at least. As the album titles *Bringing it all Back Home*, and *Highway 61 Revisited* suggest, the returning and revisiting involved predominantly American sources, in particular rock and blues structures and arrangements. In the passage from *Chronicles* above, where Dylan references his assimilation of English folk songs (pp. 74–5), he indicates also how the transporting effects of this music could not elbow aside the rural and country blues music of his roots that shaped his musical imagination. The passage that refers to this reads less as description than as a homage to formative influences so deep that they demand evocation, as if the purpose of the prose were to summon the presiding spirits of self, past, place:

> But there was a lot more to it than that ... a lot more. Beneath it I was into the rural blues as well; it was a counterpart of myself. It was connected to early rock and roll and I liked it because it was older than Muddy and Wolf. Highway 61, the main thoroughfare of the country blues, begins where I came from ... Duluth to be exact. I always felt like I'd started on it, always been on it and could go anywhere from it, even down into the deep Delta country. It was the same road, full of the same contradictions, the same one-horse towns, the same spiritual ancestors. The Mississippi River, the bloodstream of the blues, also starts up from my neck of the woods. I was never too far away from any of it. It was my

place in the universe, always felt like it was in my blood. (Dylan, *Chronicles*, Vol. 1, 240–41)

If the turn to electricity at Newport indicated that Dylan was returning to his musical home, then in this important way this was the Hibbing of his youth, and pre-eminently the various rock and roll ensembles that practiced in his parents' garage and house – *The Jokers*, *The Shadow Blasters*, and *The Golden Chords*.[3] The names of these bands are intriguing, echoing DC comics as much as CBS records, so that for all the self-protective humour, they perhaps hint at the tie-in of music with identity changes and the taking on of new powers.[4] For Dylan in 1965, the route back to these times, Highway 61, was clearly not to be an accidental reference, as we have seen. It was the road that linked Duluth with the University of Minnesota, with the radio stations of his youth, and 'folk clubs of Minneapolis and St Paul'.[5] So too, it was the route that linked the Mississippi, the home of blues and jazz, with the North:

> It passes by the birthplaces and homes of Muddy Waters, Charley Patton, Son House, and Elvis Presley. The crossroads at which Robert Johnson made his supposed pact with the devil is said to have been the intersection of Highways 61 and 49, today his grave rests off Highway 61 in Greenwood, Mississippi […] The stretch of Highway 61 near Clarksdale, Mississippi, is the road on which Bessie Smith […] was fatally injured in 1937 […] (Polizzotti, 24–5)

What took place by 1965 was the rejection of a politically viable persona, of a self circumscribed by its responsibilities to others. Instead, on *Highway 61 Revisited* and *Blonde and Blonde*, Dylan's inspiration would take him – in ways both liberating and risky – into more intimate, opaque psychological and ethical areas. Dylan, who had seen Guthrie's influence as like that of a lightning conductor, becomes now an Emersonian poet in the sense of being a conductor of visions and unspoken truths, one whose words deny the constraints of social identity. As mentioned earlier, for Stanley Cavell, Emerson's work inaugurates American subjectivity as precisely 'aversive thinking', where self-reliance, one's private war of independence, depends on the vigorous turning away from the received script of social consciousness.[6] However, a further essential parallel between Emerson and Dylan, which Cavell's reading of the Emersonian schema allows us to see, is that the antagonism is always with the self. The coruscating singer and the victim of 'Like a Rolling Stone' can be seen as intimately connected, so that, indeed, appearances aside, the song can come to seem a soliloquy by other means. The song soars in celebration of the discarded presumptions of a defunct self. However, whether the self is identified as one's own or as that of one's scapegoat, is less interesting than the idea that the tension between the two can be identified with our own self-betrayals and self-blindness. Only by the uncertain transitions from former modes of being, can the American mind make progress to Emerson's 'unattained but attainable self' (Emerson, 117).

I

By the mid-60s, my argument runs, the values and truths of emancipation uncovered by Dylan were of a more purely subjective, interior, kind. Bruce Springsteen eloquently described the effect of the Dylan of *Highway 61 Revisited* in his speech inducting Dylan into the Hall of Fame in 1988.[7] He referred to Dylan as the artist who had freed the mind, as Elvis had freed the body. Emerson, ironically, had regretted that 'I look in vain for the poet I describe', but his essay on the Poet, as Ford has pointed out, is uncannily prescient of Dylan as an artist channelling new visions, even the Dylan of the Free Trade Hall in 1966:

> Doubt not, O poet, but persist. Say 'It is in me, and shall out.' Stand there, balked and dumb, stuttering and stammering, hissed and hooted, stand and strive, until at last rage draw out of thee that dream-power which every night shows thee is thine own; a power transcending all limit and privacy, and by virtue of which a man is the conductor of the whole river of electricity. (Emerson, 263)

Emerson associates the Poet with the liberating dynamism of the transformations he brings about and employs – intoxications, provocations, invigorations, as well as liberations, and his antagonistic sense that 'every word they say chagrins us' (Emerson, *The Portable Emerson*, 144).

In the unformed, inspirational, interval of time that I have identified with Dylan's artistic values, words can in Emerson's terms be vehicles – for the singer presumably, as much as his audience. Marcus describes Dylan emitting a 'long, high, wordless cry – a cry of delight' during 'Just Like Tom Thumb's Blues' at the Liverpool Odeon in May 1966:

> This is what it was for, that right to disappear, to be transfigured, to return an instant later as a being you no longer recognize.[8]

Being someone you no longer recognise, of course, though, is the predicament, and opportunity of the song's voice too, who takes stock of the endless betrayals that leave him at the end turning back to New York again, and away from Mexico – that site of both escape and destitution, as Polizzotti has elaborated:

> Mexico ... a symbol of escape from the strict regimentation of American society, and ... an index of how far down a person might have been forced to go ... 'Tom Thumb's Blues' paints a picture of bluffing and loss, of being in over your head, of fearing that you can never return home.[9]

Someone whose gravity has failed might even no longer know if he is high or if he is in free-fall. Mexico has compounded the singer's experience of dislocation, leaving him without even 'negativity' – the specific, gravitational, resentments of one's background, personality, and history – to help him through. The only gain in the song – but a real one – is that which can convert negativity to a positive: the fact the persona within the song is also, as Marcus says of the actual performer in Liverpool, someone now unrecognised by himself, and no longer taken in. The old gullible self, with its trust in rules and its routes of escape – Mexico, drink, drugs, women – must be left behind, as the song takes stock of punishments and betrayals undergone. The closing line, 'I do believe I've had enough' secretes, alongside exhaustion, an exhilarating recognition that the self-betrayals of former illusions are no longer possible, that a certain truth has broken in to lever an opening within the wired self, maybe an exit, from this cycle of double-dealing, treachery, dispossession and weakness (*Lyrics*, 180).

In these respects, 'Just Like Tom Thumb's Blues' is a song that anticipates the world of *Blonde on Blonde* where Dylan directly voices subjective destitution rather than ironically or aggressively externalising it and turning it onto another person, a cavalcade of freaks, or a nightmarish world inhabited by mythical figures. Unsurprisingly, then, as Marcus implies, it would be a song that would take on special resonances in Dylan's live performances of it in 1966. The more intensively Dylan ratcheted up his expression of disillusion or disorientation, the more powerful and liberating was the effect. In the famed performance of the song at the Liverpool Odeon on 14 May 1966 that Marcus refers to, the emotional stocktaking of the album recording has become something altogether more vortical, right from an opening in which the organ surges and swells, while the guitar is abrasive, nerve-shredding. Dylan's voice – seemingly hoarse and bleak – is less that of someone who is narrating his fall and looking back and beyond his current situation, than that of someone who is at stake, falling and failing, as he sings.

Mark Polizzotti has referred to the crepuscular Dylan of these concerts, strung out and expending himself in performance, as if he were a latter-day Prometheus, fated to destroy himself in coveting illumination and fire. Or perhaps he is a latter-day Robert Johnson (as he described his Greenwich Village self on *No Direction Home*): someone who has made a fatal move, a bargain with the devil, in order to create out of his own self-destruction music that is both ravishing and rending. Certainly at this time, he appears to be veering between exhaustion and inspiration, as for Jim Miller who vividly describes him as 'an artist flirting with death ... a spectral ... magician smashing and recombining images with manic energy and blinding brilliance'.[10] For Paul Williams the self-expenditure displayed in these concerts was inseparable from the open-ended musical symbiosis with The Hawks, as if they were also supplying the fuel for this consuming art:

> The concerts were incandescent because the singer was living for art, was literally burning himself out, not to please the audience and certainly not out of obligation but for the sheer joy of doing it, travelling with intrepid companions out into unknown aesthetic realms, shining lights into unexplored darkness. (Williams, *Bob Dylan: Performing Artist*, 214)

The impression of so many listeners to these live performances was of Dylan kindling inspiration out of dissolution in this way, and replicating in his own performance the dislocations of subjectivity encoded in the songs. To hear 'Just Like Tom Thumb's Blues' at Liverpool (or Manchester, or Melbourne or anywhere) is to hear Dylan and The Hawks screwing the song up in this way to a new expressive pitch, so that its precipitous scenario of flight and gravity, its travelogue of fantasy and failure, finds analogues in the soaring or abyssal values of Dylan's voice and the accompaniment. Robertson's urgent guitar offers by turns butting, bull-dozing, blues embellishments, and then wailing, nerve-stretching, high notes and phrases, while Hudson's organ is all-engulfing, a dissociative whirlwind of kinds.

However one conceives it, this ratio between a defunct and an emancipated self is both the predominant drama of the songs of *Highway 61 Revisited* and *Blonde and Blonde*, as well as what every responsive listener feels as the dynamic of the live shows of the period. And, as on 'Just Like Tom Thumb's Blues', disillusion, loosening the captivity to fantasy or habit, engenders (as inevitably as in mathematics) a self in transit, a new value for individuality. Many commentators, back to Paul Nelson's review in 1965, have touched on how a similar ambivalence can be found in 'Like a Rolling Stone', to take the most celebrated example. Euphoria is released by the song's diatribe. Ford writes:

> In the schizophrenic drama of the song [...] it is the addressee who is reduced to nothing, and becomes 'invisible', but it is this destitution, we are subliminally aware, that makes possible the expressive powers of vision of the singer. (Corcoran, ed., 133)

Watching someone going downhill in this song is grounds for celebration, as in Nelson's comment that the effect of the song was 'clearly optimistic and triumphant, a soaring of the spirit into a new and more productive present'.[11] And yet, as Ricks implies, this is also too straightforward, itself too much a case of 'Nelson's shining upward face', as he puts it (Ricks, *Dylan's Visions of Sin*, 186). As mentioned above, Ford's references to the 'schizophrenic' theatre of the song, and talk of the girl as 'alter-ego', imply that one can take the song's elation and critique as playing out as dialogue something that is also essentially a soliloquy. As Dylan later put it himself: 'when I used words like 'he' and 'it' and 'they', and talking about other people, I was really talking about nobody but me' (Heylin, *Revolution in the Air*, 241). The girl in the song is the self by other means, both the target and the vehicle for the song's breakthrough of vision, voice and idiom. She embodies the shortfalls of presuming to live according to great expectations. As such, she is a cautionary figure, and one who can only release the self so long as she is kept in mind as its 'other'. Like all figures of a certain contempt, she is also a surrogate, a scapegoat for the self, whose energies she releases because she embodies its fears, its potential for alarm and disintegration.

If the song is a breakthrough as Dylan described it, it is one, like 'Positively 4th Street', that taps into an acknowledgement of confusion, negativity, hatred, while trusting to his power to move beyond, make everything new, leaving his old self firmly behind. It was written, he told Nat Hentoff in March 1965, after he had quit songwriting, and it is inspired in many ways by an often-noted sense of inauguration: "Last spring, I guess, I was going to quit singing. I was very drained [...] But 'Like a Rolling Stone' changed it all ... it was something that I myself could dig" (Artur, 313). The joy of the song is released by an aggression both personal and artistic, a kicking down of the door in Springsteen's phrase, that is also a kicking open, and which led, as Ford puts it, to 'a kind of artistic exhilaration at the possibilities suddenly discovered within a seemingly exhausted genre' (Corcoran, ed., 133). After this song, everyone producing music was left behind, everyone was Miss Lonely, it can be said, reduced to stony inexpression. There is no returning, no 'direction home', though by the same token Dylan has decisively admitted his audience into what Emerson called a 'new scene' ... (Emerson, 259).

In these ways, the first version of 'Like a Rolling Stone' exemplifies such features of Dylan's unstable self-hood at this time, his desire, as it were, to eject himself into some obscure stratosphere by rejection. The song was always a step into the unknown, and Dylan did not recognise it himself to begin with, recording it over and again in the studio while the famous version was in the can after take four. Nonetheless, the song's famous opening double-shot has ever after been taken as an arresting trigger for what is less a song than a transformative event. Ethically, the world uncovered is one in which the self's most intimate entanglements and double binds are dynamically unravelled in the continuous present of the song, through a liberating expression in which self and other, hostility and pity, liberation and constriction, oscillate and exchange. As the phrasing bounces and weaves, struts and juts, so the song expansively searches out its own internal associations of internal rhyme, and rhythmical motifs. While the girl in the song is figured as having to make unseen accommodation with the 'mystery tramp', so words and phrases hook up, as if finding strange counterparts, unpredictably making momentary, chance deals and liaisons in some linguistic doorway or side-street away from the conventional, known, routes of syntax and communication.

The upshot is that Dylan, like the girl, finds himself through the song to be no longer well connected. He is tearing up his ties to his former audience when recording it on 16 June 1965, or singing it at Newport. He will never again be more invisible and cut off from any direction back, never more inspired yet obscure to himself. Through singing it, he becomes his own ghost, one might say, to use an image he later used for the uncanny, clairvoyant means by which the song came to him: 'It's like a ghost is writing a song like that. It gives you the song and it goes away. You don't *know* what it means' (Heylin, *Revolution in the Air*, 242). Dylan gives the song in the way he receives it: as a surprise, a shock, a bracing *communiqué* from someone self-divided by his new mercilessness, and addressed to someone who is themself self-estranged. Dylan places himself as it were, both outside and above society. The 'hippest of the hip' as Ford says, Dylan is now also a strange twin to himself: a Siamese cat perhaps (Ford, 'Bob Dylan and the Vignette', 5). He is without connections and history, yet also charting new territory. Though unknown to himself, he enters a new artistic empire as he gives vent to this iconoclastic voice that breaks up the idol of the self: 'Bonaparte in rags and the language that he used' indeed (*Lyrics*, 168).

Dylan's claim that the turn to electric music involved a renunciation of 'finger-pointin'' songs sounds extraordinarily mistaken when one considers how far every cadence – every crest and swell – of so much of this music was animated by rejuvenating aggression. A venomous fragment like 'Lunatic Princess Revisited', for instance, is a gloriously uplifting five-finger exercise in unbridled denunciation, opening with the spat-out lines: 'Why do you have to be so frantic/ You always said you wanted to live in the past ...' Closer to the truth is Dylan's remark to the press (captured in Scorsese's film) that: 'They're all protest songs. All I do is protest.' Dylan's description of 'Like a Rolling Stone' as emerging from a 20 page poem, 'this long piece of vomit' (Heylin, *Revolution in the Air*, 239) captures the sense that it, like 'Positively 4th Street' was both a projection and ejection of hatred, and as such part-liberating, part-painful, but unquestionably a relief. Artistically though, 'Like a Rolling Stone' is far less equivocal: Dylan described it as a 'completely free song', and it can be seen as an unalloyed triumph, a throwing off of the shackles (Heylin, *Revolution in The Air*, 237). Certainly, its power appeared to clear the way for *Highway 61 Revisited*, an album that was a watershed, both a breath-through and a recapitulation. Polizzotti wrote that Dylan for the first time 'sounds his real age' – as on 15 June, three weeks after his twenty-fourth birthday he entered Columbia's New York Studio A to start work on *Highway 61 Revisited*, an album that also displayed a Magpie eclecticism, as Robert Polito describes, since it:

> pieced together his divergent pasts: the early love of R&B and rock&roll ... his immersion in American traditional music, folk, blues, country, Woody Guthrie, Robert Johnson ... his reading of poetry and novels... *Highway 61 Revisited* is also the first occasion Dylan might be styled a modernist, the crazy quilt of folk process blasting into Dada collage.[12]

In the middle of these sessions, though, three and a half days after Newport on 29 July, Dylan was to record 'Positively 4th Street', a song directed against a resentful representative of his old milieu.[13] The singer's self-projection, above and ahead of the other person, appears figured in Kooper's teasing, mocking, fairground carousel organ as it swirls in the ether. Provocative in and of itself, this mercurial sound suggests the different universe in which Dylan is now moving. It traces a line of energy, as if it were a cloud-trail of the cyclonic forces that circulate in the singer's visceral intonations. Dylan throws out lines like a whip, the phrases rhythmically stretching, curling and snapping. The singer finds elation and freedom in this hostility, the phrasing transmuting mere resentment into something rich and strange. As with 'Like a Rolling Stone', the song's subjective drama is also ultimately self-reflexive, expressing someone whose brutality is purgative but also self-recoiling. Through denunciation, it is also his own sensitivity, regret, and weakness he is seeking to exorcise, as he seeks to break ties with his former self no less than the other person. In this aspect, he is in thrall to his gesture of rejection, the song resembling some endlessly contradictory primal scene of subjective constitution replayed endlessly by Dylan at this time, whereby he is driven endlessly to find himself anew through outfacing, rejecting another. The entrance into genuine expression, and the stepping clear of an inexpressive self, are clearly the stakes, the twin faces, of this internal drama of denigration.

'Can You Please Crawl Out Your Window', recorded in its best-known form with The Hawks in early October 1965, is the third in this triptych of songs of resentment.[14] Its significant difference is that hostility is not primarily expended against the addressee, the woman, but against the vampiric man who holds her in an abusive, dysfunctional relationship. The volcanic stop-start musical structure, the clattering arrangement, and the scatter-gun chain of images are designed to tear off masks, and to mimic the switch from lifelessness and torpor to activity that the song calls for, as it rallies and rails ('Come, crawl out your window, / Use your arms and legs it won't ruin you...'). The dreamlike imagery condenses the affective distortions of the relationship, and releases the singer's own complex counter-violence and desire. In so doing, the song exemplifies Dylan's depiction of his music at this time as 'vision music' (Polizzotti, 39) or his remark that 'My songs are pictures and the band makes the sound of the pictures' (Heylin, *Revolution in the Air*, 238):

> He sits in your room, his tomb, with a fist full of tacks
> Preoccupied with his vengeance
> Cursing the dead that can't answer him back. (*Lyrics*, 186)

The design and impetus of the song is to lever her away from the man's enervating powers, by exposing the contaminating undercurrents of the relationship:

> Why does he look so righteous while your face is so changed
> Are you frightened of the box you keep him in
> While his genocide fools and his friends rearrange
> Their religion of little tin women. (*Lyrics*, 186)

In the dangerous viciousness of its sentiments and delivery, the song is again exhilarating and youthful, as if the singer were venting out of the open window of a too-fast car.

The great discovery of this mid-60s music, then, was of the energy and joy that inhabit the expression of disillusion. Acknowledging one's illusions and confusion is the mainspring to stepping beyond fateful self-captivity, as – for Thoreau or Emerson – the American mind must acknowledge desperation or dejection. This is both what the mid-60s songs are about, in some form or other, and the hidden source of their own powers. If one focuses on the performance of 'Like a Rolling Stone', for instance, as opposed to its scenario, it is clear that the song's euphoric rush is inseparable from the vituperative dynamism of the singing, and the sense of renewal, of recreation it produces. Listen to the studio version, and the analogies that come to mind for the singing are physical, even athletic – a boxer weaving, ducking, and throwing jabs, seeking a knockout, carried away by his powers, like the newly renamed Muhammed Ali.[15] The live performances in 1966, too, are so enthralling because they are all – in Emerson's words – ways of conducting the song, nightly discoveries of how it can be different from itself. The comment in the *Highway 61* liner notes that the songs are exercises in breath control, conveys this, and brings to mind how much one's response involves holding one's breath, adjusting physiologically to the singer's intonation, reacting to the transporting surprises of the words. The song was always about the new beauty and the power (whether of dreams or rage, in Emerson's terms) that Dylan transmitted through it, and the way that it made invisibility both a predicament and an opportunity.

II

According to Dylan, most of the songs on *Highway 61 Revisited* were written in the six weeks prior to the album sessions, after he moved into the Woodstock house. Given the immediacy and freedom that sweep through *Highway 61 Revisited*, the notion of 'going electric' seems much more than a matter of amplification or an infusion of Chicago blues. Electricity is an inevitable trope for an album so jolting in its effects, where inspiration is a matter of a vision and new sources of creative power. The songs can be said to forge strange circuits and unforeseen connections of thought, new dynamics and exchanges of desire, new reversible poles of identity and feeling. As this suggests, although the songs offer no positive philosophy, their inspiration is evident in the extemporary connections of the cerebral and visceral. A song's content (its cascade of images and abrupt shifts of perspective) becomes inseparable from expression (its intonations, rhythms and 'rapid-fire vocal delivery' [Polizzotti, 19]) and its effects (the propulsive expansions and transformative energy of its performance). In the summer of 1965, at Newport, Forest Hills, or Studio A, Dylan resembles some mad scientific genius in a '50s comic or episode of 'The Twilight Zone' creating a vast electric forcefield or invisible shield. Through his art, bodily sensation and affectivity becomes the transmissive media of thought and imagination, registers of galvanising effects that endlessly overrun social controls and surprise the conscious mind. And add to this, of course, the effect of 'the sheer volume':

> Marlon Brando said the fucking loudest thing he'd heard in his life was Bob Dylan and The Hawks. (Scobie, 113)

> *Rick Sanders*: 'I never heard such a apocalyptic roar. It took your breath away, like a squadron of B-52s in a cathedral.' (Egan, 116)

On this description, physical, ethical and aesthetic transport – the different ways the songs affect us – are inseparable. Thrillingly disjunctive in form, tone, theme, and impact the songs are a white-knuckle ride in the phenomenology of repudiation and vision. Dylan can be said even to unleash the equivalent of a powerful socio-philosophical critique of subjectivity – transforming and liberating the captive energies bound up in the base, affective, material of human consciousness. Each line he sings can be a like a jump lead, working on us in the same way that Dylan's own mind works, in Eric Von Schmidt's suggestion, as if by electric jolts (Scaduto, *Bob Dylan*, 18). As Dylan said: 'The point is not understanding what I write, but *feeling* it' (Heylin, *Revolution in the Air*, 259), experiencing what Emerson had called in the passage cited earlier 'that dream-power which every night shows thee is thine own; a power transcending all limit and privacy, and by virtue of which a man is the conductor of the whole river of electricity'. On stage during the 1966 tour Dylan would thrive on his renovating dismissals of the audience that booed him, energised by the equal and opposite reaction that accompanied his rejection of his previous audience. As D.A. Pennebaker recalled:

> He was having such a fantastic time ... He was jumping around like a cricket out there. The whole scene had changed instantly. It was a different kind of music.
> (Sean Wilentz, *Bob Dylan in America*, 157)

From this vantage, Dylan creates a new art of the unknown self by setting out not only to refuse the past, but to overcome socialised melancholy, to release energies tied up with false consciousness and false conscience. He is an Orpheus or poet-philosopher with a Fender, his target identifiable with what Spinoza called the sad passions, Emerson dejection, or Neitzsche *ressentiment*. One might even compare the album's effects to a form of ethical electro-therapy that emancipates and expands by shocking the listener out of the false coherences and hierarchies, the phoney naturalism and moralism, of social ideology. After all, on the liner notes Dylan writes of 'some college kid who's read all about Nietzsche comes by & says "Nietzsche never wore an umpire's suit"', and the songs certainly resemble a Nietzschean raid on social moralism. Ranged against lifelessness, their aim is to incarnate inspiration, breath, vision, life itself: words are torn out of their customary circuits, and recombined, suddenly criss-crossing in new ways, according to an intuitive, on-going, process of inspiring re-connection. The songs on the record are 'not so much songs but exercises in tonal breath control' and their 'subject-matter – though meaningless as it is – has something to do with the beautiful strangers':

> you are right john cohen – quazimodo was right – mozart was right. ... I cannot say the word eye any more . ... when I speak this word eye, it is as if I am speaking of somebody's eye that I faintly remember . ... there is no eye -- there is only a series of mouths – long live the mouths – your rooftop – if you don't already know – has been demolished . ... eye is plasma & you are right about

that too – you are lucky – you don't have to think about such things as eye & rooftops & quazimodo.

Society's great ideological fable, he implies, its great lie, is that there exist commanding viewpoints ('rooftops'): that the single, inclusive view is possible, that the eye can oversee and transcend everything, not least its own material substance, 'plasma'. Instead, what the songs express is that there is no single over-arching way of seeing, merely a potentially endless number of radically disjoined ways and events of saying: 'there is no eye – there is only a series of mouths'.[16] Further, beauty and expressivity are irreducibly physical, ways of saying and feeling things, a matter even of 'tonal breath control'. And Dylan's intonation and writing specialise in ambushing the listener, confronting him with the dynamic and disconnective in language, using words as vehicles for the liberating, energising antagonism of the songs. In such ways, the songs combat the ideological limitations of the 'WIPE OUT GANG' and 'Lifelessness' by refusing the fiction of a stable, representable world, and by maximising an exuberance which intensively celebrates the innate potential of words to incarnate, moment by moment, wholly singular dimensions, unforeseen linkages and suggestions, new configurations and perspectives. Disjunction becomes the means of revealing the distortions of society as a carnival of malformed freaks ('quazimodo'). However, as an adventitious artistic principle, disjunction is also the means of a beautiful estrangement, of an unrestrained invention and exuberance ('Mosart').

Hence, these songs of 1965 depend for their inspiration on their gusto, on the life and breath, the abandon, anxiety, and thrill, that zip and race through them. They traffic in verbal pictures that dislocate ideology by creating an alternative world where culturally mythological figures from literature, history, science, or the bible are introduced into elliptical parables, surreal scenarios. The effect is to disclose the hidden desire, violence, and abuse beneath our necessary fictions, our phantasmatic repertoire of mythical figures and narratives. In 'Tombstone Blues', for instance, iconoclasm is delivered with accelerated menace. The beat is febrile and Bloomfield's feral guitar figures punctuate Dylan's voice, which successively unfolds a frantic, pointed, succession of paradoxical revelations:

> The geometry of innocent flesh on the bone
> Causes Galileo's mathbook to get thrown
> At Delilah who is sitting worthlessly alone
> Yet the tears on her cheeks are from laughter. (*Lyrics*, 170)

The world we think we recognise is a cover for violent forces and contaminated desires, and the song's dream-like distortions are the means by which it mirrors society's own distortions. Sexuality is so repressed that those like Delilah who delight in it are seen as worthless, capable of responding only with sardonic laughter. Indeed, diabolic black humour itself runs through these songs like a high-voltage current. Jack the Ripper is the song's tutelary figure. He wears a 'bald wig'. He is a figure of misogyny, secrecy, violence, sitting at the head of the Chamber of Commerce. The City Fathers, supposed custodians of freedom, see the 'reincarnation of Paul Revere's horse' merely as a financial opportunity (a dead horse to be flogged, one might say …). The old folk's home is in the college, and Brother Bill has eroticised religious servitude into sado-masochistic ritual.[17] Meanwhile, even John the Baptist has turned torturer. He hero-worships the Commander-in-Chief, who in turn identifies violence and power with right and mocks the Baptist's weakness. In its series of condensed, enigmatic episodes, the song displays the death-dealing, twisted, influences of its society, and nowhere more powerfully than in the lines that cryptically allude to the ideological blandishments, the murderous cynicism, the *realpolitik* that underpinned the Vietnam war:

> The king of the Philistines his soldiers to save
> Puts jawbones on their tombstones and flatters the graves
> Puts the pied pipers in prison and fattens the slaves
> Then sends them out to the jungle. (*Lyrics*, 170)

Freedom in 'Tombstone Blues' – no less than in 'Blowin' in the Wind' – is still a matter of social resistance, of the imperative for the self to reflect on how society abuses words, narratives, and myths to deprive us of meaningful experience or self-expression. We are left, like the singer in the choruses, as impoverished, hungry, deprived of life, alone with the 'tombstone blues'. The song maps the routes of the social or cultural unconscious, laying bare how illusion and myth pre-empt reality. Knowledge becomes 'pointless and useless' because so curbed by destructive ideological fantasy (*Lyrics*, 171). As Polizzotti put it, 'Tombstone Blues' reveals:

> A mix of historical, fictional, mythical, and musical figures, the protagonists of 'Tombstone Blues' intermingle to form a world at once recognizable and wholly alien, an out-sized American landscape, made up not only of our daily reality, but also of our myths, dreams, cultural archetypes, and barely formed nightmares – 'history recast as phantasmagoria'. The landscape traversed is an unholy alliance of the scientific and the spiritual (Gallileo throwing his math book at Delilah), the familiar and the uncanny (the city fathers and the ghost of Revere's horse), the sacred and the abject (John the Baptist torturing a thief), the modern and the classical (Ma Rainey and Beethoven in their bedroll; the same marriage that Dylan was attempting in his music) – a veritable 'cast of thousands' directed by Cecil B. DeMille himself. (Polizzotti, 74)

'Tombstone Blues', like other songs on *Highway 61*, does not offer (any more than the songs of 1963 did) any simple way of transforming our situation, or of moving beyond its negative insights of society as death-in-life. The songs joltingly confront us with our nihilistic mystification like Queen Jane, Miss Lonely, or Mr Jones, and goadingly tip us into a vertiginous new reality where we must shift as best we can. Yet the leverage the songs exert is again one that points towards a certain renewal, and opens up a sliver of freedom that is inspiring, as well as troubling. We are like the figure in 'Desolation Row', who moves back and forth between being observer and inhabitant of the bewildering world he surveys, holding to a certain truth before he finds himself alone again, enclosed and betrayed in a room with the doorknob broken.

Indeed, 'Desolation Row' offers the most comprehensive social panorama of the record, a Nietzschean nightmare world where faceless social forces, like malign umpires falsely coated in white, ensure that weakness triumphs over strength. Everyone is divided from their powers and desires, afflicted by murderous lifelessness. Social values and iconography are all-pervasive mirages, and even mythical or archetypal figures have come to be afflicted by violent self-suppression. The inner truth of society here is shown as hallucination, freak-show, an underworld or snake-pit of tormented and repressed energy. Because ideology mystifyingly separates desire from itself, Dylan's caustic and hilarious surrealism is the only mirror that can reflect social reality. As Marqusee notes:

> It's as if the historical specificity of topical song were turned on its head. The aim there was to tie the song to events in the real world; the aim here is to make an unreal world sound as it it's real and vice versa. This is the experience of history recast as phantasmagoria. (Marqusee, 141)

Accordingly, the residual hope in 'Desolation Row' lies in the way it offers a critical voice and imagery for disillusion, and in the sheer artistic exuberance and originality of the song's caustic, comic vision. Like other songs on the album, expressivity is a function of this voice, as its intonations produce a creativity and vitality, a drive for truth, that are lacking within the world it surveys. The song opens with postcards of a hanging (an image rooted in Dylan's family memory in Duluth), beauty parlours filled with sailors, a commissioner who is hypnotised, blind, tied to a tight-rope walker, with his hand in his pants … Ignorance, violence, venality, and distorted, repressed, desire, are thus unforgettably surveyed in the song's opening scene, before its various scenes of defeat, and impending disaster. The world of the song is epitomised in the line, 'The Titanic Sails at Dawn', as human ambition and industry set sail towards death, nihilism. Ophelia is divided from her own vitality. She has bargained her life away for religious dreams of renewal and transcendence, yet she cannot control her prurient fascination with the seamy underworld:

> And though her eyes are fixed upon
> Noah's great rainbow
> She spends her time peeking
> Into Desolation Row. (*Lyrics*, 182)

Conformity is figured as enforced through the sinister figures of Dr Filth and his nurse who keep their 'sexless patients' playing on their pennywhistles. Cinderella, Romeo and Casanova, in their different ways, pay the price of impossible romance, through world-weariness, heartbreak, and delusion. Similarly, the fortune-telling lady, Cain and Abel, the hunchback of Notre Dame, the Good Samaritan, are sketched in as figures caught up in impending disaster, in this world where making love and expecting rain are yoked together. Here even the arch-spirits of modernity, T.S. Eliot and Ezra Pound, are incapable of finding the beauty of life in their struggle for precedence and mastery, in false pursuit of the inclusive view, '[f]ighting in the captain's tower' (*Lyrics*, 183). No wonder Dylan appeared to Hunter S. Thompson at this time as the:

> voice of an anguished and half-desperate generation ... that saw itself as doomed and useless in terms of the business-as-usual kind of atmosphere that prevailed in this country as war in Vietnam went from bad to worse and the United States, in the eyes of the whole world's 'under thirties generation', seemed to be drifting towards a stance of vengeful, uncontrolled militarism.[18]

III

Disorientation appears as a privileged trope in the world of *Highway 61* in a comparable way as captivity does in *Blonde on Blonde*. The self has lost its bearings and sense of direction, become forced by catastrophe to sink or swim. Meisel likens it all to the Fall, a trope he identifies as at work in Dylan's imagination and his audience's perception of him, and paradigmatically evident in 1965: 'The fall from acoustic to electric at Newport in 1965 repeated the Biblical fall from innocence to sin', and its American variant 'from the garden to the machine' (Meisel, *The Myth of Popular Culture*, 156). Dylan, like Adam, now has the unredeemed world all before him like the ribbon of the highway. Although the various songs find different ways of figuring the situation, the common vision is of the life-denying, dysfunctional spiritual abjection of mid-60s America. Even love or intimacy appears as a kind of möbius strip within which life and death, love and loss, appear inextricable, as in the imagery of 'It Takes a Lot to Laugh (It Takes a Train to Cry)', or 'From a Buick 6'. Yet, as suggested, no less than in 1963, *Highway 61* involves the self in political critique, and entails an exhilarating shred of autonomy. The difference from 1963, though, is that there is no suggestion that the singer or listener can easily assume a position outside his or her murderously repressive world, linking arms on the road to the future. However, the supercharged linguistic dash and vigour on the album pass on a creative energy to the listener that inspires us to slip the bonds of ideological fantasy in a troubled and dangerous movement of freedom. Each of us is implicitly on our own, but the songs give the listener the means of seeing through mystification, hurtling the interstate between the daylight world and our cultural dreamscape.

Paraphrasing 'Ballad of a Thin Man', we can say that the songs place us where something is happening, but we don't yet know what it is. The choice is whether to deny the irreality of our situation, as Mr Jones appears bent on doing, or not. 'Ballad of a Thin Man' is a song that mocks Mr Jones not so much for his alienation, isolation, or belatedness, as for his wilful failure to respond to them. The song is a reworking of 'The Times They Are A-Changing" from communal anthem to blackly comic psychodrama, and it twists the knife in someone who is turned inside out by this world he no longer understands. The song confronts him with strange new configurations every instant, deepening his uncanny entrapment with every dismaying turn of the kaleidoscope. Adrift with a pencil, like an uncomprehending journalist trapped in a Dylan song, Mr Jones struggles to understand and reason. The malign, ironic mocking of the singer drives home to him the torturing impotence of his fate, but when he hears the word 'Now' shouted by the one-eyed midget, his disturbing alter-ego, he can only belatedly respond misguidedly: 'For what reason?' But the 'Something that is happening here' cannot be controlled. Instead, Mr Jones finds himself addressed as a freak by a geek, in a world that propels him, like the girl in 'Like a Rolling Stone' into evermore discomfiting intimacies. The high-heeled sword-swallower who kneels while dispossessing Mr Jones of his throat is someone who scrambles the codes of gender and sexuality, drawing him into a sexual vortex. Figured in the opening lines as someone with a pencil in his hand, Mr Jones is estranged there from the nakedness of a man who is also surely himself, so that what he confronts from the first here is his own alienated sexuality. Mr Jones's pencil is both a token of the uselessness of his schemes of representation, as well as obvious sub-Freudian code for sexual repression: for Mr Jones's desire to translate the penis into the pencil, as it were, to contain sexual energy within what is socially prescribed. At the end of the song, the humiliating irony of his predicament becomes complete, as the singer declaims: 'There ought to be a law / Against you comin' around' (*Lyrics*, 176).

Of course, the further irony is that such interpretations can bring out the Mr Jones within us all. We are armed only with our pencils and our Scott Fitzgerald references, trying to face down or surrendering to the giddy exaltation of the song, with its Hammer-horror dynamic and eviscerating vision. Interestingly, given the confrontational nature of the 1966 tour, this is the song that Marcus hears as being most labile on stage, a kind of a barometer of the actualities of cultural unmasking, as Dylan rounded on his pious antagonists. It is 'the most bitter, unstable song ... it is also the song that is somehow most alive to the particular ambience of any given night, the weather, the frame of the hall, the mood of the crowd, sucking it up and using it like a karate fighter turning an opponent's strength against him'. 'On some nights', he continues, the song is 'the biggest blues anyone has ever heard, with Garth Hudson's organ finding a mode so mocking, so sadistic, a whirlpool opening and then laughing at you as it closes, with Robbie Robertson's first guitar notes enormous, Godzilla notes, so big they throw the audience back'... (Marcus, *Invisible Republic*, 8–9).

In a similar vein, 'Queen Jane Approximately' is a song directed at someone estranged from her familiar world, no longer (or only approximately) monarch of what she once surveyed. She is rejected not only by those most intimately connected, but even by herself:

> When your mother sends back all your invitations
> And your father to your sister he explains
> That you're tired of yourself and all of your creations. (*Lyrics*, 177)

Queen Jane's destitution, stripped of her flowers, abandoned by her children, her clowns, her advisers, and even her bandits, contrasts with a singer who offers her nothing, except to be 'somebody you don't have to speak to'. The sense that all her attractions have become superfluous is conveyed by the piano that sardonically enacts its rinky-tinky embroidered prettiness as a mocking effect. Like Miss Lonely or Mr Jones, she is someone who needs to face that her life has become a game in which she goes down every snake, musically suggested when the third line of each verse shifts to the minor. Polizzotti's sense that the song might be addressed to Joan Baez is highly possible, a way of construing the song as an acidic truth attack foretelling that her audience will resent her, that she will become 'sick of all this repetition' (*Lyrics*, 177).

Nonetheless one recalls also here Dylan's half-throwaway remark to a *New York Post* reporter that 'Queen Jane is a man' (Shelton, *No Direction Home*, 199), and it is hard to deny Sean Egan's comment that 'there is a lot of homosexual allusion' in the lyric (Egan, 89). The Dylan who has left behind the overt politics of the Civil Rights movement is someone who appears to be engaging in passing with a different political target, since it is indisputable that notions of homosexuality and gender-shifting are prevalent motifs in his imagination at the time.[19] Dylan in 1965 and 1966 is in some imaginative free-zone where all norms and narratives – of family, society, bible, sexuality, and gender – are prone to being overturned and placed into the mix without misgiving. The result is elating and threatening, comic and disturbing in equal measure. Moment by moment he unlocks taboos without seeming to see he is doing it, sleep-walking into intimate private zones like Mr Jones's room, and ventilating barely registered aspects of subjectivity. Dylan's way with imagery, scenario, and language fashions in art the undisclosed truths of the psyche. With a tone and delivery that is almost comically authoritative, he resembles some Ali Baba commandingly calling out 'Open Sesame'. He passes into the cave of our collective unconscious, only to find it populated not only by thieves, naked strangers, alarming alter-egos, mythological figures, sexual outlaws, impresarios, politicians, and imposters. Ironically, in doing so, the effect is parallel to the emancipating effects of the songs of his earlier period. Where they summoned us to identify as our best selves with a larger, radical, counter-cultural, collective, Dylan again here speaks of the kinds of radical privacy and self-blindness that are functions of social fictions of identity, and shines a light on our unknown, disowned selves. Through his disjunctive, endlessly surprising art on this record he prises open and junks our socially invested self-fantasies, and forces us to confront ourselves again.

Highway 61 then, is not merely the graveyard of our illusions, it is the place where the inner social mechanics of repression, and the predatory powers of exploitation, lust, greed, and violence are nakedly displayed. Nowhere is this more true than on the title song where the lines between religion and violence, entertainment and mass conflict, are troublingly criss-crossed. 'Highway 61 Revisited' careers along, veering back and forth between euphoric hilarity and comically horrific visions of our all too human capacity to be dominated by inhuman impulses – rapacity, cupidity, mendacity, and betrayal – and all punctuated by the whooping alarms of the police whistle. Unsurprisingly, sexuality and love again are out of kilter in this predatory world. And in the penultimate verse of the song, the ultimate betrayal of incest is cryptically intimated – between daughter and father who talk of her physical changes, 'my complexion she said it is much too white':

> He said come here and step into the light he says hmm you're right
> Let me tell the second mother this has been done
> But the second mother was with the seventh son
> And they were both out on Highway 61. (*Lyrics*, 178)

As in the first verse, the Old Testament world, the world of 'Numbers' and complex structures of genealogy, has here been stripped of theological and cultural resonance and value. So too, humanity itself has been stripped out of these relationships. Human behaviour shows itself again as all-too-inhuman, and is unmasked as monstrous, perverse, taboo-ridden, power play. In this aspect, Dylan's *Highway 61 Revisited* can be described as driven by a vision of how we can only own ourselves (be junkyard angels, perhaps) by forcibly disowning the society that dehumanises us and forces us to wear its masks and mimic the simulacra of the mythologised human past that it parades before us.

Figure 6   Dylan on stage, England, 1966. Photo © Barry Feinstein Photography

Figure 7   Dylan with children, Liverpool, 1966. Photo © Barry Feinstein Photography

Chapter 4
'Trapeze Artist'

Blonde on Blonde

For many listeners *Blonde on Blonde* is the apex of Dylan's meteoric trajectory in the 1960s, the culmination of his achievement and influence. However, an important paradox is that this album of untrammelled verve and invention is dominated by scenarios of the self as captive, exploited, rejected, confused, betrayed, or lost. The blurred album cover photo is perfect for the urban, nocturnal, or amorous world within: a world of self-opacity, perplexity, desire, paralysis, and abandonment, even incarceration. But all the time the songs also release alluring resources of youth, invention, and escape encoded in music and singing that often seem the sound of desire and longing: ravishing, driven, languorous, clamorous, unappeased, abandoned … . As Michael Gray put it: '*Blonde on Blonde* offers a person awash inside the chaos and speaking to others who are acceptedly in the same boat and on the same ocean … [and yet] the feel and the music are on a grand scale, truly oceanic' (Gray, *The Bob Dylan Encyclopedia*, 59). At the heart of this chapter is this obscure generative ratio between the passive, oppressed self who the songs figure, and the provisional, exuberant self who is released through them. The first is lifeless, targeted, and caught within his nocturnal, subtractive world, and the circuits of his pain, mystification, reproach, or desire, whereas the second is secreted through enactment and performance to find new, aversive resources of movement, force, elation, élan, and beauty.

Thematically speaking, it is clear there has been a further twist of perspective inwards, away not only from the anthems, ballads and narratives of the early work, but also from the panoramic and accusatory songs of 1965. Whatever the differences between the songs of 1963 and 1965, in both Dylan had voiced opposition to an oppressive confusion located outside himself. The Dylan of 1963 had shaped our response through identifying with a political collective girded against the forces of cold war reaction, capital, militarism, and racial discrimination. For the Dylan of 1965, ethical and political diagnosis had involved drawing into the daylight the nightmarish figures of the cultural unconscious. The exhilarating sense of exposure and black comedy that charged these songs of 1965 was of a self invigoratingly tearing itself free from all the forces of lifelessness ranged against him. In contrast, the Dylan of 1966 offers no jeremiads. Instead, he sings in the first person, from within the disintegrative experience of this confounded interiority. He is caught up in a predatory world, betrayed by others, stuck and strung out. Perpetually, he finds his life structured as irony, double-cross, disappointment, longing, or confusion. He takes stock, realises that he doesn't fit in, has been let down, or is split between what he needs and what he wants. In *Blonde on Blonde*, Dylan brings home the fate of inexpression, amorous confusion, subjection and constraint that has always been a mainspring of his art, but now by inhabiting it from within. Suitably enough the album occupies still the landscape of the blues – its imagery, its twisting structures and torsions, its subjective idioms of betrayal, injustice, failure, repetition, complaint and disenchantment. As on *Highway 61*, the musical basis of the album is sinewy, agile, unflaggingly rhythmical, hardnosed, urban blues. Of course, there are other stylistic influences too as Wilentz describes: alongside '1940s Memphis and Chicago blues', there is 'turn-of-the-century vintage New Orleans processionals, contemporary pop, and blast-furnace rock and roll' (Wilentz, *Dylan in America*, 106).

However, if the blues predominates, it is the blues as invigoratingly transformed through this singing and music that outlandishly stretches it and infuses it with something exotic. As Marqusee puts it, the collection takes such influences as Delta blues and 'boosts them into a modernist stratosphere' (Marqusee, 208). In *Blonde on Blonde* Dylan may be insisting on his own sense of alienation rather than sardonically identifying it in others, but all the while his art is endlessly displacing abjection through his own *bravura* transfiguration of it. The mercurial play of words and the elastic intonations – characteristic both of the record itself, and the concert performances of the time – are indices of this aesthetic that takes possession of confusion and raises it to a new effervescent, lyrical power. For instance, there is the audacious sway of Dylan's singing on 'Absolutely Sweet Marie' as he sings the well-known, gnomic line 'But to live outside the law you must be honest' (*Lyrics*, 208). The expansive phrasing projects an imperative of fugitive self-reliance, wholly at odds with the song's drama of imprisonment, arrested desire, and lost romance. Beating on his trumpet, stuck in frozen traffic, or holed up in the penitentiary, the figure in the song waits interminably for Marie, unable to connect, to transform things. She has left no key to her house, and he surveys from outside the 'ruins' of her 'balcony'. The song's fade out – a frantic revving on a stuck chord – is symptomatic of this broken world.[1] Nonetheless against this, all the time the irresistible elongations and surging rhythms of the vocal conduct new fluxes of desire, elusive kinds of meaning:

> And now I standin' here lookin' at your yellow railroad
> In the ruins of your balcony

At the end of the song, this is a moment of estrangement and loss, but also of transport and inspiring potential. He is stripped of transcendence, without any yellow brick road to follow, in the wreckage of the balcony and failed love. Nonetheless, there is this 'yellow railroad'. Visions of a new route to expression open up in the imagination at the same time as the familiar arterial routes, alleys, and railroads of American music are made strange through this sweeping, poetic lyricism.

I

'Ballad of a Thin Man', the last song of the *Highway 61 Revisited* sessions, was recorded on 2 August 1965. From this time until the motorcycle accident in Woodstock on 29 July 1966, Dylan's schedule was to be a relentless round of rehearsal, writing, recording, and touring – first national, then global. With this ceaseless upheaval, the invasive pressures of mass attention, and the imminent birth of Sara's baby, Dylan made a dramatic if temporary change of location at the end of September 1965. He exchanged the sublimities and solitude of the Catskills for the huge neo-Gothic façade and bohemian provenance of the Chelsea Hotel on West 23rd Street, where Sara had lived for some time. The hotel, inhabited by long-term and transitory residents (as well as the fabled creative artists), resembled a vast rabbit warren and its decorous, low-lit glamour presumably offered a congenial, mid-town retreat for the pair. Jesse was born in January 1966.[2] Whatever Dylan's personal circumstances and motivation (or possible struggles with drug-use alluded to years later in 'Sara'), it is worth remarking the artistic imperative that he associated with the move. In a conversation with Robert Shelton in March 1966, he conveyed his urgent sense, both that what he was writing must be totally new, and that this demanded a change of milieu:

> I don't believe in writing some total other thing in the same place twice. It's just a hang-up, a voodoo kind of thing. I just can't do it. When I need is someplace to make something new, I can't go back there.[3]

From the artistic point of view, fresh inspiration demanded a change of scene, and it is indisputable that residence in the Chelsea was associated with the strange creative alchemy of these months. The first version of 'Visions of Johanna', a song of interiority and the city, was recorded on 30 November, eight days after Dylan and Sara's secretive wedding, and it marks a significant artistic departure.[4]

One can say that residence in the Chelsea Hotel marked a time between times, both domestically and in broader ways. As such, it provides a useful marker for the creative transition that led to the writing and recording of the songs on *Blonde on Blonde*, between late November 1965 and early March 1966, first in New York, then in Nashville. Marcus has written eloquently about the larger cultural expectations targeted at Dylan at this time:

> Once a singer stood at a world crossroads. For a moment he held a stage no one has mounted since – a stage that may no longer exist [...] Bob Dylan seemed less to occupy a turning point in cultural space and time than to be that turning point. As if culture would turn according to his wishes or even his whim; the fact was that for a long moment it did. (Marcus, *Invisible Republic*, ix)

Marcus's imagery – of decisive moments, crossroads, turning-points, of someone who appears to possess and embody the times – corresponds to this book's emphasis on the creative and ethical motif of becoming. But specifically, it emphasises Dylan's scarcely imaginable sense of creative opportunity, isolation, and burden of mass-expectation, amidst the furious forces of world fame and cultural change that converged upon him at the turn of 1965. In this last respect, Mike Marqusee has described the insupportable ironies of the situation for someone not yet twenty-five years old:

> All kinds of people have expectations of you. You're asked to explain and justify everything, but you can't because you're winging it, moving restlessly forward on intuition and inspiration, and as far as you're concerned it's perfectly obvious what you're doing. (Marqusee, 167–8)

What is remarkable, though, is how creatively Dylan lifted this self-uncertainty to expression on *Blonde on Blonde*. The effect of the songs is utterly transporting, yet they sweep by us, obliquely alluding to people, places, situations, events as if they were familiar and leaving us without any means genuinely to resolve what we hear or make it intelligible ('Mona tried to tell me / To stay away from the train line'; 'Somebody got lucky / But it was an accident' [*Lyrics*, 198, 192]). Experience is unstable, in motion, unframed, enigmatic, potentially overwhelming, but also thrillingly in excess of where we are and what we know, the effect as dislocating as a big dipper.

In a way comparable to the songs of *Highway 61*, the expressive self in these songs is emancipated by the voicing of confusion, though this is now unequivocally his own. In song after song on *Blonde on Blonde* the conscious self is figured as belated and internally divided. He is oppressed by pain ('I got a poison headache', 'I can hardly breathe' [*Lyrics*, 132]), or emotion ('If I just did not feel so all alone' [210]) or perplexity ('I don't know how it happened but …' [209]). He has the subordinate, reactive status of a passenger on troubled, heaving waters, so to speak, rather than the confident, navigational assurance of any 'river-boat captain' (*Lyrics*, 206). Yet the songs are liberating for the listener because they give voice to the anxious, inward realities of consciousness, and dislodge social illusions of subjectivity. The songs inhabit a mind wrestling with its own private instability, as in Marcus's own memorable nautical image for *Blonde on Blonde*: 'the sound of a man trying to stand up in a drunken boat, and, for the moment, succeeding'.[5] Hence 'Stuck Inside of Mobile' offers lucid moments, where the mind reflects on its subjugation within the inescapable, ironic circuits of experience – while all the time the voice itself refuses and flexes against constraint. 'And here I sit so patiently / Waiting to find out what price', he sings, 'You have to pay to get out of / Going through all these things twice' (*Lyrics*, 200).

If words in *Blonde on Blonde* no longer secure the stabilities of identity, narrative, reference, and objectivity, so according to Wilentz (who has had enviable access to the studio reels) they often evolved out of hastily sketched gibberish or randomness (Wilentz, *Dylan in America*, 105–28). Nonetheless, what marks out the recorded songs is the singular way in which each tends to crystallise out a singular, differentiated, artistic version of the vortical, dissolving subjectivity that they collectively voice. '4th Time Around', for example, is a song in which the inner and outer worlds won't separate and resolve. Consciousness and unconsciousness, the real and the surreal, are subject to endless, repetitive confusion. This instability, at once seductive and ominous, is replicated in the seesaw chord pattern and filigree guitar accompaniment. The song's persona inhabits a world that oscillates between resembling a dream that is weird yet pressingly familiar, and a mundane reality that appears transfigured, as if encountered for the first time: ('She threw me outside / I stood in the dirt, where ev'ryone walked.') Stray details stand out with strange eloquence (the pictured woman in the wheelchair, the drum on which he absently taps), as if obscure motifs for this alienated world where nothing stabilises or connects. Human relations appear also on the edge of disintegration. The song begins in the middle of an anti-conversation ('When she said / 'Don't waste your words, they're just lies' / I cried she was deaf'), and personal details and gestures are full of alienated, fetishistic suggestion ('And she buttoned her boot / And straightened her suit', 'I filled up my shoe', 'I looked through her drawer'). Within this estranged world the gum that passes between singer and woman amounts to the equivalent of an act of knightly gallantry:

> So I forced my hands in my pockets
> And felt with my thumbs
> And gallantly handed her
> My very last piece of gum (*Lyrics*, 207)

'4th Time Around' is a song in which the psyche is fractured – where nothing holds together, and experience endlessly seesaws undecidably between the daylight world, and hallucination, dream, and fantasy. In 'One of Us Must Know', it is the relationship between the girl and the singer that is falling apart. The distinguishing trope is misrecognition, the failure of communication. Dylan sings four times the phrase 'I couldn't see' ('what you could show me … how you could know me … when it started snowin' … where we were goin'') and voices over and again his failing desire for recognition and understanding ('I didn't realize just what I did hear / I didn't realize how young you were'… 'you said you knew me and I believed you did'). The song is a testament to desire as miscarried intention ('I never really meant to do you any harm'), and to the renewed hope of acknowledgment, that '[s]ooner or later one of us must know / That I really did try to get close to you'. In the closing lines, the song's sense of a vulnerable 'I' fighting for self-integrity amidst the violent fall out of a baffling romance precipitates in the final image of his vulnerable 'eyes', his failing capacity to see:

> And then you told me later as I apologized
> That you were just kiddin' me, you weren't really from the farm
> And I told you, as you clawed out my eyes
> That I never really meant to do you any harm (*Lyrics*, 195)

The girl who 'clawed out' his eyes, reveals that (unlike the girl in 'Motorpsycho Nitemare', from two years before), 'she wasn't really from the farm'. In 'One of Us Must Know' intention cannot be distinguished from misunderstandings, facts from illusions. In this world of missed chances, desire and love – the attempt to connect – have fateful consequences. For the singer, as for Oedipus, desire is oblivious to the facts, and eventual knowledge, seeing the truth, only entails a deeper form of suffering and separation. In this song, as throughout the album, mutual knowledge, the human face-to-face, seem bafflingly impossible, endlessly ironic and postponed. The song enacts the stand-offs of knowledge and desire through its own climactic, yearning, reiteration that 'sooner or later, one of us must know'. Equally, when Dylan sings 'I couldn't see what you could show me / Your scarf it kept your mouth well hid/ I couldn't see how you could know me…' the impossible complications of seeing, showing, knowing are condensed on the girl's mouth. Provocatively hidden, it is both a focus of physical desire as well as a tantalising, withheld, means of speech. For the singer, body and mind, significance and fact, just will not cohere. We cannot make ourselves understood to each other. Knowledge is endlessly postponed, divided between the intelligible and the material, as when he sings that he did not 'realize just what I did hear' even though 'Your voice was all that I heard.' At the close, Dylan's voice comes to figure its own mercurial beauty in the white-out of the snow-storm which expresses the disorientations of the song's scenario of longing, all the singer's failed designs for now obliterated as the song yields to its final ravishing chorus.[6]

Before 1965 there had been the sense that Dylan was no more responsible for the predicaments he found himself in than he was for the weather. The victimising, romantic, poetic staples often found in English folk song – the snow that drifts, the wind that blows, the rain that falls – had been suitable accompaniments of this. By this album, though, as in 'One of Us Must Know', these become internalised in the unstable scenarios of songs where wind, rain, snow, cold, and so on figure an urban, subjective drama of disorientation and entrapment, of vertiginous personal dissociations of the self from itself and from others. Time and again the figure in the songs inhabits cryptic dramas where he can longer tell what effect his words will have, or even what he can see or say. The songs persistently turn on, and refer to, impairments of vision, misunderstandings, deafness, intoxication, lameness, confusion, repetition and imprisonment. In this world, the self is hanging off its hinges, or stuck in unavailing cycles of confusion, desire, loss or frustration.

Suitably enough 'One of Us Must Know' was initially labelled 'Song Unknown' as Wilentz points out (Wilentz, *Dylan in America*, 113),[7] and as much as any song on the album it triumphantly registers the split between the powerless, unknowing self represented in the song, and the visceral and affective self who voices it, bobbing up and down or majestically carried away by the tides of the music and the transporting, idiolectic imagery. A similar discordance can be identified in 'Most Likely You Go Your Way, and I'll Go Mine'. This song outwardly portrays a singer lambasting his former lover for her failings. From the first splenetic drumburst, and Charlie McCoy's spikey, unresolved 7th trumpet figure, the song inhabits an aggressive whirlwind of dismissive outrage. The motif for this song is a display of score-settling that also appears self-defeating. His reasons for leaving her are mere unavailing levers against need and abjection. Within the theatre of the song, it is abasement and humiliation that prime his declamations:

> I just can't do what I've done before
> I just can't beg you anymore

or:

> You say my kisses are not like his
> But this time I'm not gonna tell you why that is

In this unbalanced world, where consciousness is a hostage to resentment, the judge in the middle-eight is a cautionary figure ('Well, the judge, he holds a grudge / He's gonna call on you' ...). Dylan fixes how precarious is his self-elevating desire for condemnation. The imagery of the stilts conveys how the desire to judge masks vengeance, inadequacy, self-aggrandisement:

> But he's badly built
> And he walks on stilts
> Watch out he don't fall on you.

At this moment, this reflexive critique of judgement threatens to rebound against the singer, so intent himself on adjudication and punishment. However, the deft and fluent intonation (such as the half-comic, assured pause before 'fall') shows someone expressively sidestepping in performance the song's entangling negativity. Again, as at the end of 'One of Us Must Know', the song comes to identify its own emancipating expressive power with its own emergent reflexive awareness.

In such ways, Dylan's art sublimes its registration of negativity within its animating, inventive, expressive excess, subjecting this vision to endless creative variation, and releasing invigorating, fugitive occasions of self-awareness. In phrasing, this corresponds to how the voice departs from itself to forge its own improvised rhythms and *outré* rules. When Dylan sings 'patiently' or 'Panamanian moon' on 'Stuck Inside of Mobile' or 'fortunately' or 'obviously' on 'Absolutely Sweet Marie', for instance, the adverbs threaten to break free from the primary responsibilities of stress and meaning and the imprisoning world of the song, to flourish like magical blooms in some cautionary fable. Perhaps nowhere is this baroque extravagance of voice and idiolect more evident than on 'Sad-Eyed Lady of the Lowlands', which takes on a quasi-symphonic grandeur. Obscurity on this song though is not a matter of confusion or self-division, but of how the images trail off into an allusive, vague out-of-field, as it induces a free-floating response flowingly adjusted to the singer's mysterious, quasi-devotion. If listening to '4th Time Around' is like a dissociated state where one does not know if one is dreaming, and where time engulfs us, then 'Sad-Eyed Lady of the Lowlands' creates an effect more like incantation, or a trance where time is suspended. The narcotic swathes of sound, and the long accumulations of the verses, make us react to the images as to a kind of mysterious procession:

> With your silhouette when the sunlight dims
> Into your eyes where the moonlight swims
> And your matchbox songs and your gypsy hymns
> Who among them would try to impress you? (*Lyrics*, 211)

Different aspects of the woman – other worldly, a *femme fatale*, a daughter, a wife – are cumulatively threaded together, as the singer transmits his captivation by the fantasy of this woman whose outsider's charm incorporates the physically seductive, the visionary, and nameless private griefs ('your streetcar visions', 'your gypsy hymns', 'your ghostlike soul').

For Coyle and Cohen, such features are the problem with 'Sad-Eyed Lady of the Lowlands'. It is too intent on sounding impressive while meaning merely free wheels, with Dylan coming fatally close to sounding merely worshipful, even sentimental (Coyle and Cohen, 149) In his Denver hotel room on 13 March 1966, Dylan refers to it as the best song he has ever written which seems just plain wrong, although it is almost certainly his most ambitious to date (though much closer to 'She Belongs To Me' or 'Love Minus Zero' than to any other song on this album). Yet still, close attention can indicate how far its hypnotically unifying effects conceal evident conflicts in the singer. He channels bewildering kinds of insecurity into majestically dismissive, yet still jealous, hostility against the men who could presume to possess her:

> Oh, who among them do you think could bury you?
>
> Who among them do you think could carry you?
>
> Who among them would try to impress you?
>
> Who among them do you think could resist you? (*Lyrics*, 211–12)

In this way, at least, the song implies a *ménage à trois* pattern noted throughout the album by Marqusee (Marqusee, 183–92). It seems to date back to the lacerating 'She's Your Lover Now' (which can be said perhaps to inaugurate the world of *Blonde on Blonde*) – a song in which the love scenario is rivalrous, riven by jealousy and abjection. In this respect at least 'Sad-Eyed Lady of the Lowlands' can appear a stable-mate of songs like 'I Want You', 'Pledging My Time', 'Leopard-Skin Pillbox Hat', 'Most Likely You Go Your Way', or 'Temporary Like Achilles'. At the other pole from 'Sad-Eyed Lady' in terms of ambition, perhaps, 'Temporary Like Achilles' is nonetheless a more authentically powerful *Blonde on Blonde* offering: an acerbic blues, yet marked by trapped, ironic-lyrical, suggestions of waltz time, in its relentless 12/4 rhythm. It is a song of powerlessness, sung by one caught 'standing ... looking ... kneeling ... helpless ...' (*Lyrics*, 205), in a situation treacherously configured both as pitiless rigour ('But is your heart made out of stone, or is it lime, / Or is it just solid rock') and by gorgeous, yet deeply ominous, promise ('your velvet door ... your scorpion / Who crawls across your circus floor' (*Lyrics*, 205).

II

Interviewed at the Hotel Flamingo in Stockholm on 28 April 1966 by local disc jockey, Klas Burling, Dylan described how he had 'been up all night', and 'taken some pills and ... eaten bad food'. He wearily complained at 'all this business' (Artur, 360). Nonetheless, in a seemingly throwaway remark he said his new single, 'Rainy Day Women ♯12 & 35' was about 'a minority of, you know, cripples and orientals and, uh, you know, and the world in which they live'.[8] 'Cripples' and 'orientals', one might say, are pretty much the only two subject positions feasible in the world of *Blonde on Blonde*, and the album places the listener, like the singer, in perpetual transit between them. Since society is crippling and disorientating, the only recourse is 'to live outside the law' to be eccentric, exotic, unknown, other. By the same token, the album is for the self-selecting 'minority' of those who are able to identify with such an image of the self as incapacitated and alienated. The iconic chorus of 'Rainy Day Women ♯12 & 35' itself, 'Everybody must get stoned', captures this double sense of the self as both constrained or targeted by others, and as discovering aversive resources of elation, escaping by refusing one's bearings – like Dylan's off-key harmonica playing. The song is an appropriate introduction to the world of *Blonde on Blonde*. Its thumping anti-music converts experience and condemnation by others into something like the carnival, an overturning of custom suggested by the band's use of tuba, tambourine, trombone and the rest. Howard Sounes describes it as recorded by musicians collectively in an altered state because of alcohol and/or marijuana (Sounes, 244).[9] The infectious hilarity or hysteria of 'Rainy Day Women ♯12 & 35' is clearly not typical of this album, but it is another variation of Dylan's ways of using sound and delivery to transform alienation into exhilarating art.

As with other songs, 'Rainy Day Women ♯12 & 35 ' offers no stable vantage point outside of the giddy displacements and fissures of subjectivity. The self in *Blonde on Blonde* appears recurrently as caught, perplexed, betrayed, and tricked. In the claustrophobic, blues-inflected world of 'Pledging My Time', for instance, he finds himself pledged to a future he cannot believe in, hoping the woman will 'come through too'. But he is haunted by the hobo, another obscure and opportunistic figure, who takes whatever there is, whether pledged or not.[10] In this song residence within the prison of time is configured as impotent detention within a malign, random world. In contrast, in 'Stuck Inside of Mobile' time confines the singer within spiralling, intensifying patterns of repetition. The 'ragman' who 'draws circles up and down the block', is the presiding figure here, suitable for the circuits of a song whose verses increasingly round on the speaker, encrypting his experience within a world where again reality borders paranoia and hallucination, and where communication is confounded: 'And I would send a message / To find out if she's talked /But the post office has been stolen /And the mail box is locked' (*Lyrics*, 198).

Rather differently, 'I Want You' is propelled by the relentless, unfulfilled projections of desire. This surfaces in the irresistible music that reiteratively plots a descending and re-ascending trajectory, suggestive of the passion that expends and renews itself through the pressing, swerving intonations of the song's voice. Consciousness is the plaything of sexuality, the song identifying those (the 'guilty undertaker', 'the lonesome organ-grinder') who set out to restrict passion, but who merely in fact embody its resentful and failed alternatives – suicidal self-denial or mechanical and solitary self-abuse. They inhabit the world of the 'cracked', the 'washed out', and the scornful. Desire needs to be protected from their possessive, constricting designs, but also from those who seek to divert it into substitutive, socialised, supposedly higher forms: politicians, mothers, saviours. Once more, the grain of autonomy in the song's scenario is the singer's awareness that he is more controlled by his desire than in control of it, and that the attempt to think otherwise results in life-poisoning illusion. It is this unillusioned reflexivity that identifies desire and creativity, and prises open again the album's fugitive sense of self-freedom, conveyed here through the song's exuberant, rushing brio.

'I Want You' betrays once more the form that the struggle for yet unattained expressivity takes on *Blonde on Blonde*, as renewed capacities of panache and vigour well up out of frustration, dislocation, vertigo or groundlessness. In *Highway 61* subjective freedom and expression were based on outfacing other people or one's society, but in *Blonde on Blonde* they are about outfacing the self, as the songs conduct inspiring powers and potentials of selfhood that automatically follow on the acknowledgment of self-loss. This emergent, provisional self is menaced by those figures in the song whose 'bad company' threatens its potentiality: all those obscure, liminal, stalking, figures – alter-egos, doppelgängers, sirens or *belle dames sans merci* – who threaten to draw him into their dissociative worlds: the hobo, little boy lost, the rainman, the dancing child, the railroad man, Achilles, the Persian drunkard, the senator, Ruthie, or Queen Mary (*Lyrics*, 206). Such figures are part and parcel of the swirling, bipolar, zone of *Blonde on Blonde* where selfhood is perpetually at stake, and where experience resembles often a kind of threshold, hypnagogic condition or lucid dream.[11] And for the listener too, the distinctions between the singer's subjectivity and our own are broken down by Dylan's surging, mannered inflections, which draw us into the dynamic irreality and exuberance, the transformable and transferable theatre of identity, of the songs' world. The elongated vowels, the dynamic figures and flights of phrasing, the abrupt changes of timbre, transport us, producing the effect of 'spellbinding excess' that Polizzotti identifies with *Blonde on Blonde* (Polizzotti, 8). The result is an estranging intimacy, similar in effect to a hypnotist taking over our physiology, as well as our consciousness, through a vocal insistence that uncouples us from the daylight world, and raises to expression our rootless, inchoate, selves.

For many listeners, 'Visions of Johanna' is the epitome of the dislocated, urban, solipsistic world of *Blonde on Blonde*. Musically, the song begins with twisting harmonic phrases and deliberate, reined-in, strumming. This creates a tension, full of subdued portent, that is then taken up by the far-off ghostly looping of the organ playing against the hostile, snapping blues figures of Robertson's guitar. From the first, those Dylan sings about are 'stranded', thwarted, caught in a desultory marking of time. Human agency has dwindled into the unthinking reflexes of a nocturnal consciousness caught between disillusion and the future repetition of error:

> Ain't it just like the night to play tricks when you're trying to be so quiet?
> We sit here stranded, though we're all doing our best to deny it
> And Louise holds a handful of rain, temptin' you to defy it (*Lyrics*, 193)

Though we might seek to 'deny' or 'defy' the truth of our confusion, the voice prises open obscure regions of the self and taps into them.[12] Aside from the spell of the music, it is worth briefly examining how the opening lines work to ensnare us through a mode of address that swiftly moves from the innocent to the mesmerising and confounding. The opening rhetorical question innocuously addresses us within the impersonal 'you', drawing us into the song's world, before the singer identifies us as one of the stranded 'we' in the second line. In line three he swiftly applies the *coup de grâce*, the words leaving us powerless and disorientated, struggling to deny or defy the disconcerting import of what is offered: words, like rain, that are now strangely transformed, so that we don't know whether they offer sustenance, or betrayal. Louise's 'handful of rain', like the image itself, is there to tempt us but the scenario of challenge disquietingly accentuates our sense of being stranded and implicated in a situation we do not control. As between Louise and her lover, so for us, there is only entwinement, but neither relation nor knowledge.

In such ways, the singer's voice and words infiltrate and assume our consciousness, an effect augmented by the restrained expressive potency of the performance. Our minds enter into the uncertain present tense of the song, caught between the automatic need for significance and the deep-seated, anxious expectation of disappointment. The performance creates its anonymous intimacy as we shuttle between loss and confusion. We have no alternative but these potentially treacherous, addictive, alluring, figurations of redemption:

> And these visions of Johanna that conquer my mind [...]
> And Madonna, she still has not showed [...] (*Lyrics*, 192–3)

Questions ramify in the listener's mind, flooding it with connective possibilities that leave us with either too much, or too little significance. Who is Louise, and why and how does she hold a 'handful of rain', and what is it? And who are those other characters – little boy lost, or Mona Lisa, or the peddlar or fiddler – who are sinking or swimming in the world of the song? In 'Visions of Johanna', everything, including the words themselves, stands out as in a dream with hallucinatory singularity, endlessly seductive yet treacherous. Nothing and no-one is ultimately definite or knowable. The contexts that would allow us to understand seem in abeyance or elided, and fact and fantasy appear endlessly interwoven.

The effectiveness of the song is in these ways of enacting and representing this subjective predicament. It offers disjointed glimpses, and oblique, telegraphic impressions of its world, leaving the listener in pursuit of illumination and a viable selfhood like the night watchman who clicks his flashlight and '[a]sks himself if it's him or them who's really insane'. The mind struggles to comprehend, inundated and destabilised by fragmentary images and elliptical musings. Alongside the confusion though, the song offers intimations of another kind, like the visions of Johanna that grip the singer. For us, this is notable in the famous stand-out lines that draw together disjoined elements into visionary flashes:

> The ghost of 'lectricity howls in the bones of her face
>
> The harmonicas play the skeleton keys in the rain[13]
>
> Oh, jewels and binoculars hang from the head of the mule (*Lyrics*, 192)

Synesthesia is one index here of a language that moves outside the laws of cognition and logic, the captive mind finding captivating, visionary, powers of its own amidst the confusion. In such ways, 'Visions of Johanna' manifests how the songs of *Blonde on Blonde* explore a self turned in on itself, yet conjuring from its plight virtual expressive potentials of a new kind.

It is a further measure of the transformable, perplexed subjectivity in the album that it intermittently interrogates, as did the music of 1965, fluidities of sexual desire and gender identity. 'Leopard-Skill Pillbox Hat' brings to mind the arbitrary conjunctions and drives of fetishistic desire, while other songs are often mordantly shot through with homosexual suggestion:

> Now your dancing child with his Chinese suit
> He spoke to me, I took his flute
> Though I wasn't that cute to him, or was I? ('I Want You', *Lyrics*, 197)
>
> Well, the hobo got too high
> He came to me natur'lly
> He stole my baby
> Then he wanted to steal me ('Pledging My Time'[14])

Again, the complex, resonating world of 'Just Like a Woman' would be impoverished without the indeterminate zone of gender identity that it seems obscurely to inhabit. Within this liminal world, one can note too how masculine figures of authority in the songs are endlessly absurd, violent, exploitative, or helpless, as with the senator or preacher in 'Stuck Inside of Mobile' or the fathers or politicians in 'I Want You', the doctor in 'Leopard Skin Pill-Box Hat', or the 'Kings of Tyrus with their convict list', 'waiting in line for their geranium kiss' (*Lyrics*, 211).

III

On 28 August 1965 at Forest Hills, Dylan backed by a band made up of Levon Helm, Al Kooper, Harvey Brooks and Robbie Robertson played the fabled concert that Marcus described as the first pitched battle in 'a cultural war': 'When Dylan came back with the band ... again and again fury coursed through the crowd like a snake; the wails of hate are beyond belief' (Marcus, *Like a Rolling Stone*, 161). Mark Jakobson gives an inimitable account:

> I was there ... booing Dylan for going electric. Nowadays there are 20 million ponytailed ex-hipsters claiming to have been at the old 15,000-seat tennis stadium heralding the zeitgeist as 'Tombstone Blues' serrated the late-summer air. But really, it was better to have booed. All the real Dylan fans booed. Booing was part of the Dylanological continuum – having expectations shattered, feeling rejected, and then realising how better, way better it was to live in this new, better world he'd thrust you into.[15]

Around the same time, Dylan was interviewed by Nora Ephron and Susan Edmiston, quipping that 'I don't call myself a poet because I don't like the word. I'm a trapeze artist' (Artur, 174). And never did Dylan appear more to be courting danger than in these performances. Indeed, D.A. Pennebaker's *Eat the Document*, like Martin Scorsese's *No Direction Home*, gives substance to the legend of a singer who seemed on stage moment by moment to be propelling himself across a void: carried away in the glamorous and disjunctive world of *Blonde on Blonde*, or the furious firestorm of the European leg of the World tour. I have been showing how the self who sings on the album is departing from himself and creating compelling, transporting effects – spectacular, unapologetic, and profuse – from the indefinite self expressively figured within the new songs. And in the drug-driven concert performances of the 1966 tour this conversion of disorientation into artistic flight became extreme, elevated to ever-new levels – of shamanistic enthralment in the acoustic sets, and of antagonistic power and intensity in the electric. What is clear is that the state of affairs could not long continue. David Hajdu wrote:

> 'He was obviously starting to lose it,' Pennebaker recalled. Backstage during an intermission one night, Bob was wondering around alone, disorientated, and his stream-of-consciousness rambling offstage was sometimes far more incoherent than usual. 'Nobody could go on like that much longer.' (Hajdu, 282)

These aspects of the tour performances can be taken to be extensions of the self-explorations inaugurated by *Blonde on Blonde*. Again, to use the image of a genie unleashed from the bottle, Dylan at this period mysteriously conjures from a state of subjection or disorientation a transfiguring art of self-in-process, an art of double-location and transit, elliptical and dynamic.[16] The famous remark about 'that thin, that wild mercury sound' of the album is suitable for the mercurial self that inhabits the songs, the wing-footed and inspirational messenger.[17] Certainly, Pennebaker's films capture much of the divided and variable quality of 1965–66 – by turns offering us farce, satire, or comedy (as Dylan confronts the hidebound obliviousness of those not attuned to the moment) or else a theatre of cruelty (as he turns to repel the misguided advances of all those who seek to confine him within clichés of who he should be). The fascinating turbulence conveyed through these films conveys why *Blonde on Blonde* should be so powerfully an album of a dissociated self: if you are in the eye of the whirlwind, then it is little surprise if the vortical pressures should drive the self in on itself, or cause its elements to spin apart centrifugally ... Hence the record wrests its powerful creative impetus from this situation, representing the inhuman, cyclonic, pressures and disintegrative demands that were bearing in on Dylan, while also displacing and escaping from them, *qua* triumphant artistic expression.[18]

What is indisputable is that this was a time whose massive cultural possibilities placed Dylan artistically on his mettle. His concert performances – often so searching or searing – are fuelled by his capacity to move in the act of performance itself outside and beyond the predicament of derangement and subjection that the songs communicate. These dynamics took on new heights of intensity and expression as the live shows evolved through 1966, with Dylan vanishing into the songs as if into a fiery cloud on a nightly basis.[19] Songs like 'Desolation Row', 'Just Like Tom Thumb's Blues', or 'Like a Rolling Stone', were never so much themselves as in the performances of this fabled tour, where they took on something of the exorbitance, spectacle, extravagance, and self-abandonment of opera. Listen to the extraordinary version of 'Positively 4th Street' which closes the show at Sydney on 4 April 1966, for instance, and the song changes from the exuberant, lancing hostility of the record into the visceral ululation of someone tearing himself up in the need to tear himself away from a dangerously interminable negativity. Dylan's voice – keening, hoarse, pressed right up to the microphone – makes each line end an extended arabesque. Hudson's whirling organ all the time encircles the agonised nuances and deriding impetus of the singer, as if to figure his inability to extricate himself from the seductive artistry, the destructive spell, of his hatred. As mentioned, to listen to the evolution of Dylan's performances during this world tour, is to be aware of how far they gain in intensity in proportion to his mounting indifference or hostility towards his audiences. As Marqusee puts it, '[t]he sense of embattlement drove Dylan to ecstatic heights as a performer' (Marqusee, 211). The sets with The Hawks were gloriously disdainful – crashing, cacophonous raids on the sensibility and expectations of the audience – so that enjoyment of the music is inseparable from relishing a performance in which Dylan was demolishing the images of self in which he and his audience had jointly invested a few years earlier. The performances of 'Like a Rolling Stone' as it became the finale of the concerts were the climactic invitation to the listener to dissociate himself from the collective, to enjoy how far the song was targeted at those in the audience who weren't – so to speak – with it.

At the same time, the nuances and dynamics of the performance differ, and create different kinds of inwardness with the listener. At the 26 May Royal Albert Hall show, for instance, Dylan introduces the song with excruciating irony and barely able to string his words together, his 'mush-mouthed voice' in Marcus's words 'suddenly a snake's tongue, focused on a single point, the venom pure sarcasm' (Marcus, *Like a Rolling Stone*, 181). He offers an endlessly faltering preamble, identifying all the band members as poets and dedicating the song to the 'Taj Mahal':

> We're gonna leave after this song, an' I wanna say goodbye to all of you people [...] you've been very nice people [...] and believe me, we've enjoyed *every... min*ute of *being* here.

The performance that follows is one whose searing abrasiveness also appears self-abrading. The sardonic delivery – Dylan whipping up intensity out of exhaustion, phrase by phrase, his voice shot – calls out for an identification with the self who seems exhaustedly at stake within it, defiantly expending and emptying himself in the singing. So the song sounds, as Marcus notes, 'ragged, furious, bitter', before at the end it 'falls apart, falls on the singer and the band, but there is enormous applause' (Marcus, *Like a Rolling Stone*, 181). Very differently, at Manchester or Newcastle the sublimities and intensities of the performance of 'Like a Rolling Stone' offer the visceral fuel of a more outwardly aggressive, energetic, voice, hell-bent on turning adversity into triumph. After the celebrated Manchester exchange where Dylan drawls 'You're a liar ... you're a *fuck*ing liar' in response to the 'Judas' cat-call,[20] The Hawks come 'sweeping in behind him' in Charles Nicholls's phrase, with this 'great rip-tide of music'.[21] Dylan's voice increasingly is borne aloft on this wave, until at the end he soars above it like some demented banshee, while Jones's drums crash and foam beneath.[22]

Although rejection of his former self and his audience have long been the watchwords for the electric sets in 1966, these things were no less evident in the solo, acoustic, sets. Dylan alone on stage is not so much hostile or disdainful to his audience as wholly unmindful to them, consumed by the ways in which the songs arrive through him. To listen to the Melbourne or Manchester versions of 'Visions of Johanna' or '4th Time Around', for instance, is to hear a captive self musing at night alone, his searching, insurgent or fading incantations transmuting solipsism and alienation into expansive theatre. Dylan's voice resembles some strange, magical accordion – now raspy and importunate, now mellifluous and delicate. It stretches and compresses lines, words, and syllables, according to that aspirated expressivity that Ginsberg observed. By turns languid, apathetic, soothing, sour, delicate, abrasive, steely, Dylan's voice unfolds a dissociative zone that is at once utterly intimate and utterly anonymous, wholly oblivious to social identity. The songs appear to hang in the air, entrancingly introducing us into the internal process of mind itself, as it momently weaves imagery, intonation, and response from the disjunctive, vivid strands of sensation, desire, reflection, feeling and pain. The effect sublimes identity for singer and audience into something collective, poetic and inspired, and making the songs themselves as infinitely capacious as lyric poetry, or exquisite as chamber music in the attention they rivetingly demand. Lee vividly described the transfixing effect of listening to 'Desolation Row' at Manchester as like watching a virtuoso tight-rope walker, who left 'leaving an audience thrilled, hypnotised, knocked out' (Lee, 129) [23]

To listen to the Manchester performance of 'Mr Tambourine Man', for instance, is to hear the rhyme scheme take on a life of its own, as rhymed words become emphatically placed within incantatory loops at odds with the purposes of ordinary speech, wheels within wheels in the song's circling motions. It is a trick used in many of these acoustic performances at the time – the line is interrupted by a pause, before the last syllable is slowly unfurled, occupying its own interval, obeying a different timbre, as if the singer were singing with a different voice, and for a different purpose than to make himself understood. He exploits the sheer sound of the syllable, stretching the moment. Tempo, meaning, and intonation are thrown into a different kind of mix as music, sound, break away to mesmerise the listener. So this last syllable is prefaced by a pause, and obeys a different tempo, and a purely impersonal, impassive, apathetic, intonation. As Dylan emphasises it, it is as if another voice were taking the song and the listener somewhere else, into some other realm. In such a way, the song's words move between sound and meaning, expressively enacting the song's promise of musical transport – from a place of sorrow to a sense of a world transfigured by new visitations of joy and harmony. Again, this is a feature in the extraordinarily beautiful and beguiling harmonica cadenzas of those concerts, and on this song in particular – by turns grooved, chugging, revisitings of melodic motifs; incidental fortissimo star bursts; then tender, yearning diminuendos, and writhing, elongated notes that open a prolonged counter-melodic space, changing in and out of themselves.[24]

In both halves of these 1966 concerts, then, Dylan takes popular music beyond itself. If the second set in these concerts is often described as some kind of guerrilla raid or air-raid on an entrenched audience, the atmosphere and dynamics of these acoustic sets involve this contrary kind of hypnotic surrender, by both singer and audience, to the unfathomable, transporting, creative sorcery that is taking place on stage. In both, creative excess or efflorescence is a marker of a huge yet ironic breakthrough brought about in these songs of subjective impoverishment, confinement, betrayal, disillusion and anger. More locally, within the songs one appears to hear the innately poetic functions of mind itself as it pursues its possibilities of response, imagery, reflection and identity within the maze of the self. Indeed, the expressive fertility and authenticity are such that one can understand how Marcus might identify Dylan's inspiration as a creative turning point for the whole decade. At the same time, though, there is the further paradox that Dylan's insouciant assumption of so much expressive beauty and potency coexists with his own physical fragility. He appears emaciated, drawn, his skin paper-thin, almost like a ghost, as if he were an avatar for the bewitching inspiration that he appears to channel, or a cautionary figure for the personal cost of making this music. In one way, these things can be linked also to the effects of the drug-taking. Listen to the first Albert Hall concert on 26 May and this appears all too evident in the spoken passages. The sound engineer, Brian Carroll observed Dylan (a 'Phoenix in April' according to the famous bootleg of the Sydney '66 concert) conversing – appropriately enough perhaps – with a fire extinguisher:

> I was backstage after helping to set up the recording equipment. Another engineer and I stared in disbelief as we saw Dylan walk up the stairs that led to the stage. This man seemed so out of it that we saw him talking to a fire extinguisher and we both thought that there was going to be a riot when he either failed to appear or stumbled around the stage. Suddenly a man in a suit led him to the bottom of the stairs and we watched in amazement as he walked up into the lights and gave one of the best performances of the tour.[25]

Certainly, by the time Dylan had reached England, the solo sets had raised this art of enthralment to a new power and spaciousness. Lee described the rapt atmosphere at the Free Trade Hall as being 'like a church service'. Indeed, listening to Dylan's harmonica solos on some of these performances, such as the famous 'Mr Tambourine Man' solo at Leicester (shown on *Eat The Document*) is a little like hearing a church organist who has gone off the rails on narcotics. Often Dylan will interrogate a musical or rhythmical figure over and over, interrupting the song by subjecting one moment of it to a potentially infinite, spiralling process of variation, until for a time the song is supplanted by the gorgeous, provisional, occasional musical structure that rises up from within it, like some Cathedral or Xanadu hallucinated in sound.

This estranging art is nowhere more evident than in the British performances of 'Just Like a Woman'. Like 'Visions of Johanna', 'Just Like a Woman' has always engendered somewhat wrong-headed and footling speculation, as to its biographical context, or the identity of the woman in the song. Clearly, though, the language of the verses is as unfathomable as it is compelling, appearing to confront the listener like a crossword in a dream, or like a set of interlocking, overlapping, cryptic puzzles that leave one not knowing where one is in relation to a line, or how to connect it with the next one. This principle is memorably set up by the opening line ('Nobody feels any pain'), which reverberates with divergent possibilities: that in fact there is or should be pain, but that it has been displaced, or numbed; or else that collectively there are forms of pain that are not disclosed, or acknowledged, and so on. Again, in the second line ('Tonight as I stand inside the rain'), the preposition 'inside' puzzles in a similar fashion, leaving us uncertain how to locate or understand what we hear. How is rain not outside?

(Unless, perhaps, the word here is metaphorical code for internal distress, or street argot for heroin, or both.)

The gathering suggestion of these words is of an estranged self, of things not being felt or experienced in their proper, natural places, and of a language adjusted not to the public world, but to incommunicable, paradoxical private pain or obscure longing. Throughout the song, questions proliferate without issue or proper context, spiralling inwards like the voice itself as it spins its coils of internal rhyme, and its elliptical phrasing. For the listener the provocative, unresolved words leave us caught between disappointment and desire, as between feast and famine, outside or inside, or rain and thirst. In the second verse, the song's principles of seduction and insecurity are personified in 'Queen Marie' (or Mary) for whom the uncertainty of selfhood can only be appeased by extravagant performance. She is 'blessed', in this secular world, when she 'sees finally that she's like all the rest / With her fog, her amphetamine and her pearls'. In the middle eight, though, blessing turns to 'curse' and the links of rain, pain, and an abyssal, alientated inner world are clearly drawn out ('It was raining from the first / And I was dying there of thirst / So I came in here'). Suffering under her 'long-time curse', the singer's awareness that 'I just don't fit', appropriately enough, over-runs into the next verse, leaving the 'I' stranded, divided:

> I can't stay in here
> Ain't it clear that –
> I
> … just can't fit … (*Lyrics*, 202)

In the 1966 acoustic performances, this increasingly to my hearing becomes the signature song of the opening set, and nowhere is it sung with more soulful, mysterious inwardness than at the Free Trade Hall or the Royal Albert Hall. Dylan's singing becomes a kind of hypnotic, ruminative fugue of circulating voices. At moments the phrasing will empathetically mimic the woman's processes of breaking, curling or falling; or he will link words into local rhythmical or rhyming arrangements like pearls on a string; or then he will make the song momentarily hesitate, or rotate on a single syllable, a vowel, a word, a phrase, a note on the harmonica, a plucked string. One second the song is a musing, bitter soliloquy; the next a rueful, veiled lyric of need; and the next a lullaby that threatens to vanish into the ether. Bewitching, forceful, tender, gentle, regretful, riven, the performance expressively enacts the values of the song's opaque, dissociative scenario – of displacement and temporary connection – of beauty embraced and, eventually, lost.

Figure 8   Dylan and The Band (Robbie Robertson, Richard Manuel, Rick Danko, Garth Hudson, Levon Helm), Woodie Guthrie Memorial Concert, Carnegie Hall, New York City, 1968. Photo © Elliott Landy, LandyVision Inc.

Figure 9 Dylan with son Jesse Dylan outside his Byrdcliffe home, Woodstock, NY, 1968. Photo © Elliott Landy, LandyVision Inc.

Figure 10 Dylan and Sara Dylan on the porch of Byrdcliffe home, Woodstock, NY, 1968. Photo © Elliott Landy, LandyVision Inc.

Figure 11   Dylan in his living room, Byrdcliffe home, Woodstock, NY, 1968. Photo © Elliott Landy, LandyVision Inc.

Figure 12   Dylan outside his Byrdcliffe home, Saturday Evening Post session, Woodstock, NY, 1968. Photo © Elliott Landy, LandyVision Inc.

Chapter 5
'Ghosts Passing Through on Their Way to Tangiers'

The Basement Tapes

On 29 July 1966 Sara Dylan was driving behind her husband to pick him up after he had ridden his motorcycle into the Garage in Woodstock for repairs. On the way, he was to tell Sam Shepard in 1987:

> I went blind for a second and I kind of panicked or something. I stomped down on the brake and the rear wheel locked up on me and I went flyin'… [Sara] picked me up. Spent a week in the hospital, then they moved me to this doctor's house in town. In his attic. Had a bed up there in the attic with a window lookin' out. Sara stayed there with me.[1]

Holed up with cracked vertebrae and concussion, and wearing a neck brace, he slowly recuperated. However, for Dylan's brother David the real casualty was Dylan's manager: 'Albert broke *his* neck' (Shelton, *No Direction Home*, 259). Grossman had scheduled sixty concerts over the next year, and is reported to have reacted to the news of the accident with unfeigned emotion: 'How could he do this to me?' (Shelton, *No Direction Home*, 259). However, if it damaged Dylan's career in the short term, this accident 'that nearly killed him', Lee says, 'probably saved his life' (Lee, *Like the Night*, xiv). Certainly it allowed him the space to 'see everything through different glasses', taking him out of the 'rat race' so that he could find his priorities in family and 'raise my children with those ideals', the American values of 'freedom and independence' (Dylan, *Chronicles*, Vol. 1, 114–15).

For The Hawks (or The Honkies or The Crackers as they considered being named, though soon to be The Band) the period was a hiatus, since they remained on the payroll. When Rick Danko and Richard Manuel arrived in Woodstock in February 1967 it was to act in a film project that Dylan 'had vaguely in mind' as a spin-off from the editing work he was carrying out on *Eat The Document* under the aegis of Howard Alk. This project was apparently to lead to large swathes of footage of the 1966 world tour being irrevocably consigned to the cutting-room floor. Once in Woodstock, Danko and Manuel had a chance conversation with a restaurateur that led to them hiring Big Pink, 'a large split-level building, painted the colour of a strawberry milk shake' (Sounes, 221). The house, a fairly featureless A-frame construction, had been built in 1952 and was situated down a dirt road in a hundred acres in West Saugerties, amidst ancient woodland beneath the red oaked slopes of Overlook Mountain. Garth Hudson moved in with Danko and Manuel, and from about March 1967 until October it was the primary location where Dylan and The Hawks would record the miscellany of jams, covers, and original songs that would become known as the Basement Tapes. The basement itself was a fairly confined space, with huge multi-paned windows that would be opened as the weather turned warmer, while Dylan's spaniel, Hamlet, lay on the floor asleep. Other songs were recorded in New York, in the Red Room at Dylan's house, Hi Lo Ha, and a few at the Ohayo Mountain home of Clarence Schmidt, an 'eccentric retired mason who ... had a long beard matted with creosote, paint and tar' and who built a large 'junkyard folly, decorated with oddments of wood, metal, and plastic, car-fenders ... broken-down kitchen appliances ... fragments of mirror, religious figures, and plastic flowers' (Sounes, 223–4).

Though he is an incidental figure, Schmidt's strange *bricolage* and eclecticism seem of a piece with the haunting recordings that began to appear. At first, the sessions were an on the hoof, recreational way of exploring a tradition and somewhat randomly recapitulating and splicing together an archive. They took place in the Red Room, subject to family curfew, and were more about straightforward music-making as Sid Griffin points out:

> What they eased into at first was the sound of young men singing like old men on old songs, since the Red Room sessions do consist primarily of covers and past favourites, with a few improvisational songs also captured on tape. (Griffin, 112)

Robbie Robertson described the initial exchanges:

> 'With the covers Bob was educating us a little', recalls Robertson. 'The whole folkie thing was still very questionable to us—it wasn't the train we came in on. ... He'd come up with something like 'Royal Canal', and you'd say, 'This is so beautiful! The expression!' ... He remembered too much, remembered too many songs too well. He'd come over to Big Pink, or wherever we were, and pull out some old song—and he'd prepped for this. He'd practised this, and then come out here, to show us.'[2]

In 1966 Dylan had described folk music of an uncanny, irresistible kind that brings to mind this music with The Hawks:

> Folk music [... has] never been simple. Its weird, man, full of legend, myth, Bible and ghosts. I've never written anything hard to understand, not in my head anyway, and nothing as far out as some of the old songs. They were out of sight ... 'Nottamun Town', that's like a herd of ghosts passing through on the way to Tangiers. (Gill, *Bob Dylan*, 159)

Sid Griffin's meticulous research shows how the sessions took a more definite shape and purpose as the months wore on. They revolved increasingly around new compositions, mostly by Dylan himself and prompted by contractual requirement for fourteen new songs. Dylan and The Hawks would often revisit these and other songs, changing arrangements, keys, harmonies, lyrics, time signatures, or tempos (for instance, the listener can hear a waltz time 'Tears of Rage'). The musicians would convene after mid-day for a few hours a day, most days a week, for the next seven to eight months. The informal creative exchanges were in part a feature of the lay-out. Robbie Robertson described how because of the unforgiving cement floor, cinder-block walls and metal furnace, the sound would leak between the few mikes that were set up, with little to mitigate for the acoustic but a large rug on the floor.[3] The musicians could not play too loud, and would have to face each other, these factors helping to contribute to what Andy Gill has called the 'warm and intimate', conversational aura of the recordings, or what Elvis Costello describes as their sounding 'like they were made in a cardboard box' (Marcus, *Invisible Republic*, xvi).[4]

According to Garth Hudson, Dylan's spontaneous methods were a revelation: 'Some were old ballads and traditional songs ... but others Bob would make up as he went along. We'd play the melody, he'd sing a few words he'd written, and then make up some more, or else just mouth sounds or even syllables as he went along. It's a pretty good way to write songs' (Griffin, 104). Hudson added, 'It amazed me, Bob's writing ability. How he would come in, sit down at the typewriter, and write a song. And what was amazing was that almost every one of those songs was funny' (Sounes, 222). Robertson's account is more deprecatory and wry: 'We went in with a sense of humour ... It was all a goof' (Marcus, *Invisible Republic*, xiv). What is clear is that the sessions were recreational in many ways beyond Dylan's post-crash recuperation: recreational as musical collaboration; as respite from the infernal demands of touring; as searching and free artistic process; as the reanimation of a musical archive; and as pure youthful high spirits.[5]

Undeniably, at the one pole there is the sheer madcap, haphazard, fun of it all. The tapes are full of scratchy, scratch performances, with the musicians working up riffs and sequences. One or another saws away at a fiddle, honks on a euphonium, thrashes an auto-harp, blows a trumpet inside-out, yodels, yawls, or preachifies. The ensemble ranges between different tones and types of material without regard to any other listener. Musicians swap and try out instruments, so one can trace through the tapes how Robbie Robertson and Richard Manuel work up their drumming in the absence of Levon Helm, who would return from the oil-rigs later in the year. Often we hear a song playfully or ominously shape itself as an improvisation, or an incidental jam or riff, and a holiday spirit gusts through many fragments. This is audible in the joyful, unmisgiving absurdity of 'See You Later, Alligator', 'Bourbon Street', 'Big Dog Won't You Please Come Home', 'Silhouettes', 'You Gotta Quit Kickin' My Dog Around', 'I Am Your Teenage Prayer', 'The Spanish Song', or on the versions of 'Even If It's a Pig'. The recordings often start or stop mid-song, and at times the impression is of a spinning radio dial, picking out strange stations, moving between all kinds of genres and styles, so that the listener is never quite sure what is coming next, or where the musicians are coming from. At one point, Garth Hudson gives an extraordinary disquisition, spinning comic gold out of a self-regarding, mannered, professorial idiom. It begins in parody, but becomes a kind of virtuoso verbal fantasia equivalent to the irresistible, timeless spirals of his organ-playing:

> Too many of us are ignorant of the vast, untamed wilderness to the north, and the *odd* graces of Canadians that have contributed to the scene, if you'll pardon the fashion. Here, is a *flower song*, a veritable prayer dance for mushroom sauce, invented by the *Sasquatches*, a great beautiful tribe of more than a dozen happy, happy, happy, souls, completely covered with hair, if you can imagine.[6]

Indeed, Hudson's remarkable organ playing is a thing of wonder everywhere on these tapes, and the purest incarnation of their spirit. One moment it offers a cathedral organ wall of sound, the next the swirls of a fairground waltzer, and the next a sound that evokes both the chugging train, and the steam that whistles, curls and rolls above it.

Perhaps the first thing a new listener to the tapes would notice, though, is that Dylan's voice has a mysterious, pared-down flatness which can alternate between a deadpan, swaggering insouciance, a drained, withdrawn monotone, or a more stricken, soulful register. Yet it maintains throughout an imperious, inaugural quality that invests the songs with the sense that meaning and value for the self are always at stake within them, however unresolved, preposterous, fragmentary, or commonplace the songs appear. In fact, Dylan's voice on these sessions always appears as if breached against itself by some metaphysical import or reckoning, his syllables inflected with spiritual vertigo or possibility. At times it seems as if he could sing the phone book or a nursery rhyme and somehow make it sound like the Book of Revelation.[7] The effect is that even the most absurdist or playful songs can appear enactments of a mind in flight from oblivion, or caught in self-deluding mental loops, or stumbling towards uncertain redemption. Again, Dylan sings many of the covers with a deadpan *sang-froid*, but this only accentuates the tension of the way a haunted sense of mortality infiltrates his words, flipping a song of heartbreak or betrayal into something altogether more resonant and unappeased. Given these things, the more tragic songs become central to the whole collection, since within them the forced confrontation with mortality or nothingness is all at once the abiding theme, undertone, and perspective. On 'This Wheel's On Fire' or 'Too Much of Nothing', for instance, the voice sounds like a final soliloquy delivered by someone whose every syllable is informed with loss and tragic knowledge. It is these songs, I believe, that ultimately take the measure of what the Basement Tapes are about.

In pursuing these things then, this chapter will draw out how Dylan's inspiration in these tapes is wrapped up with his way of being possessed by the mind's own struggle with emptiness and value. 'Sign on the Cross', for example, is an opaque song in process, its disparate, often unintelligible early verses held together by Dylan's desolate, haunted voice. It is almost impossible to imagine another version of the song, so audibly is Dylan's slow, searching vocal prompted by Hudson's billowing organ passages and Robertson's yearning, pointed guitar. Lyrically speaking, much of 'Sign on the Cross' is disparate, unformulated or opaque, and the performance turns inside-out, tailing off into extemporised pastiche and parody, with the singer ending up searching for the song itself as much as for God. Yet in the early verses Dylan's voice twists and turns unforgettably on the hook of religion, his words compounded out of an anxious sense of daily loss ('I heard that front door slam'…) and a besetting sense of spiritual uncertainty, of plummeting dread. We don't know whether he is seeking God or running from him, dreading that religion might be true or dreading that it might not be. Yet this indeterminacy is all grist to the mill, as certain lines shape themselves suddenly, unforgettably, as if emerging from the most clouded, remote, covert, anguished, and abiding depths of the self: 'Yes, but I know in my head / That we're all so misled/ And it's that old sign on the cross/ That worries (wearies?) me.'[8]

The subjective enthralment of *Blonde and Blonde* thus takes on more metaphysical resonances in these basement sessions. A sense of the pathos of the human predicament may appear to be the last thing on the singer's mind on the desolate 'One For The Road', or on a rough-cast Red room song like 'Baby, Won't You Be My Baby', yet it grips every nuance.[9] Similar things can even be said of one version of 'Apple Suckling Tree'. Dylan begins by spinning an imponderable comedy out of this song that initially rises and falls exuberantly, like the old man in the dinghy in the opening verses, between meaning and nonsense, the real and the surreal, the bucolic and the sexual. Dylan pounds the piano, stops and starts, while Hudson's virtuoso organ swells, punches, glides, whistles, or breezes. But as it goes on, Dylan fleetingly improvises a religious dimension, punctuating the raucous performance with fleeting references to howling souls and hellfire.

In this context, it is worth mentioning a recording that exemplifies directly many of these distinctive features of the basement songs and collaboration. 'I'm Not There' is a song that is often felt by Dylan's admirers to be at the mysterious heart of his output (an impression now enshrined by Todd Haynes's film), as well as these tapes. In this song, delivery and phrasing are undeflectable and compelling. Yet as every listener knows, meaning comes and goes. Significance shines forth in ephemeral flashes, 'like the rainbow that shining yesterday', in the same way as the chord changes transmit now influxes, now failings, of energy. Nothing and nobody sticks around, and even words won't be identified or settle down. Within the song, the play of obscurity and illumination is so obviously uncontrived that it makes it seem as if we are overhearing, in the engrossing, rhythmical uncoilings of the song, ruminations so intimate that they convey the most inward, preverbal motions of thought criss-crossing the frontiers of language, even of waking consciousness.[10]

And it might be that it is the view from the border territory of mind that would allow one to read the song as an investigation of the captive nature of consciousness itself. The song enacts contingency, the radically unsettled nature of the everyday.

At the same time, it suggests how the human mind seeks to compensate for its deep-down unfixity, with its vocabulary of mental yearning and projection (words like 'wish',' trust' and 'believe', recur throughout 'I'm Not There'). Within the song, mental investments – in others, or God or the future – appear idle dreams of stability, temptations of order. For instance, the line, 'the kingdom weighs so high above her' flashes with the idea that belief in transcendence, in a higher realm of the spirit, can produce a disabling burden of guilt. And so, throughout the song, human dislocation creates various passing mirages of stability and value. Human beings are driven on in search of an abiding home for the spirit. But, our emptiness, our too much of nothing, breeds compensatory traps, and lead us to latch on to metaphysical or spiritual kingdoms that bring only a commitment to subservience.

Part of the mysterious effect of the song, though, is the way it also suggests how emptiness, uncertainty and need may lead us to seek refuge in the mundane domain of the here and now. If not in the kingdom above, then, in 'my neighbourhood', which, in the American way, we imbue with greater value and stability than it can hold. Home is a dream generated by the very instability that makes it impossible for us, and that also makes us dream of escape ('I am leased on the house, but I dream about the door...').[11] In the end, we are not situated or connected – to place or to others – any more than the girl, 'lone, forsaken, beautiful', perhaps, can be. The drama of not being there, then, is one for singer, and for girl, and for the listener, who struggle between opacity, and the returnings of clarity and meaning that are all we have, but that we do not know how to trust because we over-invest in them. One apparent truth in the song is that no-one can be clear to themselves or others in the settled way we desire. One cannot, certainly, as the phrase has it, be there for someone as they would need ...

As in a play by Samuel Beckett (who was, according to Pennebaker 'a real big Dylan fan' [Corcoran, ed., 5]) then, there is only the inevitable and enigmatic movement forwards, both tragic and comic, and the abandoning of a prior state. The final line is, suitably enough, clearly enunciated, yet completely enigmatic, 'I wish I was there to help her, but I'm not there, I'm gone.' At the same time, the exposure of our need for illusion generates, as in the other songs, a sense of liberation that can recur through the replaying of the song, and the sense that any interpretive activity can appear misguided, an attempt to get to the end of the rainbow. Lastly, I take 'Santa Fe', as a kind of companion song. Interestingly, this is a song that is often overlooked (I can't remember Greil Marcus referring to it in *Invisible Republic*, and Clinton Heylin is positively disparaging.[12]) To me, it has always seemed a masterpiece of the same kind as 'I'm Not There', though irradiated by wholly different, infectious mood towards absence, and non-intelligibility. The Dylan who quipped in San Francisco that all of his songs said 'Good luck' was speaking the truth, and none clearer than 'Santa Fe', with its wonderful, extended line, that turns 'no' into 'don't'. So, negativity is transmuted, into a liberating refusal of negativity itself: 'no, no, no, no, doh, doh, doh, doh, don't feel bad'.

Part Two: The 1960s 161

I

The aura of self-forgetful spontaneity that suffuses so much of the Basement Tapes corresponds to the fact that so many of the songs were written rapidly, often jotted down *in situ*, for the sheer exploratory pleasures of music-making. Dylan's role – to begin with at least – was largely just to provide songs, or to write something to perform, and often to write or just sing out of the blue. Marqusee writes, '[t]his is music liberated by its sheer inconsequentiality', and in their communal freedom Dylan and The Hawks 'found freedom ... The freedom to plagiarise and to improvise, to say everything or to say nothing, to leave experiments incomplete, to indulge whims. The freedom to play' (Marqusee, 225). This ludic, open-ended quality is evident in both the *ad hoc*, improvisatory, occasional nature of the sessions themselves, and in the often off-the-cuff, sketchy nature of the material. The effect is compounded with the ludicrous too, in exuberant songs like 'Get Your Rocks Off', 'Odds and Ends', 'Please, Mrs Henry', or 'All You Have to Do is Dream' which deal up their disjointed vignettes of ribaldry, innuendo, nonsense and randomness. At times, the result is just sheer horsing around, on 'See You Later, Allen Ginsberg' or 'Teenage Prayer', or when The Hawks' rendition of 'Gloria in Excelsis, Deo' morphs into 'The Banana Boat Song' ('Deo-o, Deo-o, Day-O, Daylight come and me wanna go home').

Riley describes this playfulness vividly, though with a certain telling bemusement as to the discrepancy in effect between the exuberant, seemingly random nature of the words and their powerful, quasi-proverbial, aura of meaning:

> ... you get the feeling that [the lyrics] were largely words that just happened to pass through Dylan's mind as the verse kept coming around. *The Basement Tapes* is like an open spigot to Dylan's thought process, and it lets you know how much of a feel he has for twisting shopworn homilies into non sequiturs that sound as though they should make sense ('The louder they come, the harder they crack' in 'Million Dollar Bash'... [Riley, 161]).

Riley valuably observes how these lines from 'Million Dollar Bash' traffic in nonsense, as if Dylan were merely exuberantly taking words out for a spin. Nonetheless, for all their air of abandonment and the aleatory, and the fact that the songs compound meaning and absurdity, my conviction is that the effect depends on Dylan rarely abandoning meaning. Rather, the songs characteristically occupy an unfolding interval where meaning comes and goes, and where words oscillate between the banal and profound. In this respect, for all their seeming tomfoolery, banality, skittishness and randomness, they remain dynamically in transit towards intelligibility. And as they do so Dylan's vigilant verbal sensibility, as singer and writer, resembles a gyroscope, always in motion yet self-regulating, on its mettle and intuitively summoning unforeseen trajectories of meaning, and incidental self-reflective possibilities, out of its own disequilibrium.[13]

Appropriately enough, the songs recurrently adopt tropes of travel to represent consciousness in its unavailing pursuit of stability and coherence. In 'Lo and Behold!', the self-deluding persona ('I never felt so good') circles back in the final verse to his initial scene of departure. It is a song of coaches, trucks, trains – of pullin' out for San Anton, comin' into Pittsburgh, goin' down to Tennessee, and back to Pittsburgh again. The Ferris wheel on which the singer rides into town is a surreal and comic dream-image. However, it also has a residual symbolism, reflecting experience as some crazy dislocated, unstable, travelogue of hopeful-disappointed, pleasure. As with Spinoza's image of someone in a downhill cart, the image suggests that we mistakenly imagine we are steering the desires or forces or words that transport us. In this way, the song's scenario of journeying and ferris wheel can be taken as a reflexive, allegorical figuration of the mind's cyclical and comically futile pursuit of redeeming significance:

> Well the comic book and me, just us, we caught the bus
> The poor little chauffeur, though, she was back in bed
> On the very next day, with a nose full of pus (*Lyrics*, 289)

For all the playful spell of a song like 'Lo and Behold!', I am suggesting, Dylan's poetic gift exerts a torque of its own. Abetted by its vigorous intonations, words apparently thrown off return towards significance like boomerangs. So, returning to the lines above, we might hear them as vivid nonsense, or we might choose to parse them as suggesting a moral that bears out this sense that we need to be carried along by the songs towards meaning but should not seek to impose it. Hence this moral would be: if we seek mere distraction and pleasure from the song, we will be its passengers, reading a comic book; however, if we believe that we can take the song somewhere, then we are more likely to get a bloody nose, like the chauffeur. (It is probably worth emphasising that my point is not that such an interpretation fixes the song, but that it accommodates such resonances).

The impression of the troubled journey towards meaning as something enacted, represented, and produced in the songs, is intensified by Dylan's delivery which is matter-of-fact, deadpan – as if utterly insistent on what he says, however nonsensical it seems. Like the grandstanding Tiny Montgomery, the voice brooks no argument but leaves us listeners hanging on, feeling at stake and waiting for something important yet to arrive. We are left ultimately like the 'everyone' in 'The Mighty Quinn', waiting for Quinn to fulfil our thirst for revelation and deliver us from our self-escaping distractions (making monuments, building ships, jotting notes, making haste, feeding pigeons, reciting animal noises). While the songs resist the authoritative finalities and destinations to which they signal, so also they often appear to have begun without us, addressing us *in media res*, 'Well, I stand in the hall and I shake my face' ('Odds and Ends' [*Lyrics*, 277),[14] or presenting a speaker who is already *en route*: 'I'm going down to Rose Marie's' ... ('Goin' to Acapulco' [*Lyrics*, 280]); 'I pulled out for San Anton / I never felt so good' ('Yea! Heavy and a Bottle of Bread' [*Lyrics*, 289]). And as they journey through horseplay, arbitrariness and obscurity, they still resonate with unsecured reflexive possibilities, describing as well as enacting their endless search for communication, fulfilment and expression:

> Long Distance Operator
> I believe I'm stranglin' on this telephone wire' (*Lyrics*, 298)
> Tomorrow's the day
> My bride's gonna come (*Lyrics*, 293)

This split between absurdity and reflexive intimation is replicated in the songs' surreal deadbeat personae who are dogged by the split between the mind's desire for self-extinguishing, oblivious pleasure, and a certain incipient consciousness of their predicament. Emptiness and profundity interchange endlessly for them. In the irrepressible 'Million Dollar Bash', for instance, the hapless figure's bouncy invocation of the great bash can appear a displacement, a profligate fantasy that covers the wastefulness, pain, self-destruction, nothingness, and uncertainty that leak out everywhere in his tones and his words. His words resemble nonsense verse, as when he sings 'I looked at my watch / I looked at my wrist, / I punched myself in the face / With my fist' (*Lyrics*, 279). However, the words might also be taken as signalling Dylan's refusal or unfitness any longer to fashion in song a subjectivity fit to read the signs of the times. From this angle, Dylan is ripping up any sense of mission, seeking out a good time, though all the time a disquieting undertow of punitive-comic self-mutilation stirs beneath his words: 'I took my potatoes down to be mashed.' In a comparable way, one can ponder the significances that provisionally expand in the listener's mind in 'Open the Door, Homer' as the singer refers to his friend 'Mouse / That fella who never blushes'. Mouse sounds a little like a cut-down, furry, grey Moses. So we can perhaps imagine him as in part a prophet for these secular times, a modest, creaturely figure whose obscure commandments suggest a reduction of spiritual issues of redemption, guilt and shame to the physical, even the lavatorial: 'one / Must always flush out his house, / If he don't expect to be housing flushes'.[15] Such a mingling of the sacred with the profane would bear out Marcus's original liner comments that the tapes move 'easily from the confessional to the bawdy house', a feature evident in the scatological, and sexual references that circulate and abound in songs such as 'Get Your Rocks Off!', 'Please, Mrs Henry', 'Yea! Heavy and a Bottle of Bread', and 'Odds and Ends'.

The impression that even the most extemporary, comic, or nonsensical songs from the Basement Tapes can throw long – if unresolved – philosophical shadows is nowhere more evident than in 'Clothes Line Saga', one of the masterpieces of the sessions. Dylan's tone in the song appears to drain all significance and value from its quotidian world. The song, about putting out the clothes one day then taking them in the next, certainly does not sound like any saga. In place of epic narrative, it offers mere unmeaning succession: 'After a while ... It was January the thirtieth ... The next day ...' No-one in the song can make themselves understood to others or themselves, and words and ideas tail off, leaving only the zone of the unexpressed and the obscure, and language estranged from itself ('Someone else asked, "What do you care?"' / Papa said, "Well, just because"' [*Lyrics*, 283]). And yet the song divides us between feeling that its flatness is the point, and feeling that it reverberates with far-reaching resources of meaning. Craziness is identified with the Vice-President who has gone mad, but it also appears indistinguishable from the featureless normality which the speakers inhabit, and which appears to cloak something far more desperate, and fragmented. The conventions of time, narrative, family, and social living, the song appears to say, are our boundaries, our garden fences, our saving routines against death, oblivion, forgetting, social paranoia, madness, and the mysterious destructive-generative, presenting, power of time. In this respect at least, the song is indeed like a saga, ritually celebrating the known world in its fight against monstrosity and death. And yet, the song closes by uneasily implying how terrified and terrifying is the boy's self-limitation, his seemingly Oedipal refusal of new possibilities. Papa yells to the son that Mama wants him to come inside with the clothes, to which he replies:

> Well, I just do what I'm told
> So, I did it, of course
> I went back in the house and Mama met me
> And then I shut all the doors (*Lyrics*, 283)

II

Dylan's motorcycle accident immediately took on the status of a myth, generating rumours in the ensuing months, as Barbara Kerr noted, of 'paralysis, disfigurement, insanity and drug addiction', even of his being 'cryogenically frozen' as reported on the *Biograph* liner notes (Artur, 608, 859). Although Dylan's own account to Shepard is more prosaic, it suggests the cautionary fable of Icarus. The young artificer overreaches himself, reckless in pursuit of illumination: 'I was blinded by the sun ... I was drivin' right straight into the sun, and I looked up into it even though I remember someone telling me a long time ago when I was a kid never to look straight at the sun' (Griffin, 53). Certainly, the accident can be taken as an obvious motif for the songs themselves, given that they divide us between a beguiling sense of transport and possibility on the one hand, and a coming to earth, a falling flat on the other. If Woodstock was a place associated with happiness and fulfilment for Dylan, it was also the place where he confronted his mortality. He commented to Shelton how the everyday was daily breached there with a sense of emptiness:

> Although the three years in Woodstock after the accident may have looked idyllic, Bob told me afterward: 'Woodstock was a daily excursion to nothingness.' (Shelton, *No Direction Home*, 262)

Certainly, in many ways the basement tapes are inseparable from the perception that the post-crash period allowed Dylan to take stock, offering him the opportunity of a necessary retreat and a re-alignment that was about more than his back wheel.[16] Marcus's liner notes recognised that the *esprit de corps* and creativity of the musicians in the basement were of a piece with their growing inwardness with the past:

> there are two elements the three sessions do share; a feeling of age, a kind of classicism; and an absolute commitment by the singers and musicians to their material. Beneath the easy rolling surface of The Basement Tapes, there is some serious business going on. What was taking shape, as Dylan and The Band fiddled with the tunes, was less a style than a spirit – a spirit that had to do with a delight in friendship and invention.

Certainly too, the 'spirit' is also a matter of opportunity, of the occasional, informal, day-to-day, nature of the sessions. These men are young enough to enjoy the juvenile silliness of 'I Am Your Teenage Prayer' and the hard-won pleasures of leisure, booze, reefers, time-off. They are also musically seasoned, gifted, and intuitive enough to be able to take the measure of the music they play. The chemistry of the sessions is importantly a function of the mutually inspiring, transformative relations between Dylan and The Hawks. Together they were creating music that was of its moment, yet which was to prove so influential because it sounded timeless. By 1969 both Dylan and The Band (in no small part because of the techniques Elliott Landy evolved) often appeared as if they belonged on some mid-nineteenth century photographic plate, Dylan resembling a reclusive, bespectacled writer, The Band cultivating the imagery of backwoodsmen or saloon owners. But by the same year The Band had become the group that made Eric Clapton disband Cream, that inspired Fairport Convention, and that drove even The Beatles and The Rolling Stones to emulation.[17]

In covering traditional songs or songs by other artists Dylan in the basement was often revisiting songs that he would have sung in his early youth, written by or strongly associated with artists like Johnny Cash, John Lee Hooker, Bo Diddley, Ian Tyson, Woody Guthrie and Hank Williams.[18] What counts in these performances is that fundamental subtractive gift mentioned earlier, for disappearing into a song. For Paul Williams, the effect of Dylan's self-erasure on the cover performances on the Basement Tapes can be surprising, 'startling, and a little scary' (Williams, *Performing Artist*, 226). Nonetheless, many of the versions of traditional songs on the Basement Tapes are often more or less speculative. Some can be designated merely as run-throughs, even throw-away versions, such as 'Ol' Roison The Beau', 'Comin' round The Mountain', '(They) Gotta Quit Kickin' My Dog Around'. Others are works-in-progress, such as 'Down on Me', or 'Come All You Fair and Tender Ladies'. Yet others are clearly just thrown off, such as 'Johnny Todd' and 'Po' Lazarus'.

The casual, understated nature of a performance, though, does not prevent it being absorbing. 'Young But Daily Growing' was a song sung by Dylan on the Minnesota party tape and the Carnegie Chapter Hall in 1961. It is a variant of an age-old British folk song of true love, mostly narrated by a young girl who loves the one her father has arranged for her to marry, only for him to die and leave her with their son to raise. Dylan's spare performance intuits a point of balance in the song, expressible as the paradox that while death shadows life, it is the passing of time that makes joy possible, that brings renewal:

> Oh, the springtime is leavin' now, and summer's comin' on
> With ornaments and fans the ladies all pass on
> Oh yes, once I had a true love, but now I have none.
> But I'll watch his bonnie son, while he's growin'.

Dylan's magnetic performance is dispassionate, suitably slow, elongated, and understated. Williams identified an effect of 'impenetrable mystery' in such songs, and specifically with 'The Bonnie Ship the Diamond'. A whaling song, it is sung for Williams in a 'unique, spine-tingling' way (Williams, *Bob Dylan: Performing Artist,* 231). It begins uncertainly, with Dylan's voice wavering or faltering, as if he is girding himself for departure. The song is swiftly full of dark portent, as this seafarer looks back over voyages of storm and hardship, while calling out in the choruses for cheer, courage and comradeship. For Marcus, the song is pervaded by an ominous sense of death and disappearance: 'it is impossible to imagine the ship returning' and '[t]he melody weights every word of the chorus with fatal prophecy: "So its rise up, my lads / Let your hearts / Never fail / ... the Bonnie Ship the Diamond goes / Fishing for the whale"' (Marcus, *Invisible Republic*, 241). Dylan's enunciations are often obscure, and it is likely he is uncertain of the words, and seeking just to put the essence of the song across. But again, he does this according to that strange, characteristic algorithm by which he makes a song live by disappearing into it, by becoming its medium. Whether or not the ship returns, what matters to us is that the song departs again through this performance, testimony to the uncanny power of art to survive and overcome time.

In a related way, many of the most powerful, addictive interpretations on the Basement Tapes appear as songs of destitution, sung by displaced voices inhabiting the margins of their existence and caught in their residual desires, as if the song were their testament, and their life a kind of after-life. 'That Old Triangle' (or 'The Banks of the Royal Canal') is Dominic Behan's song about the nineteenth-century Mountjoy prison where he had been himself imprisoned. Dylan's voice, drained of affect, is a bleak register of the prisoner's life. Yet it is not prison that haunts him, but the 'hungry feeling' that steals over him, the human susceptibility to pleasure and expression. Dylan's phrasing and tones brilliantly bring out how the prisoner's mind is inadvertently invaded by its impossible longings:

> In the female prison
> There are seventy women
> And it's with all of them
> That I'd li----ke to dw---ell ...

He stretches syllables and injects small melodic flourishes or effects of rhythmical impetus into his flat, dragging, singing, creating tiny disjunctive intervals where the voice begins to swing or soar. Within the prison the old jingle-jangle triangle plays routinely over and again, but what really imprisons him are the unpredictable, invigorating, insurgent refrains of nature, beauty, and freedom:

> On a fine spring evening
> The lag lay dreaming
> The sea-gulls beaming
> High ab---ove the wa---ll ...

Other songs deal with the politically betrayed ('Joshua Gone Barbados', 'The Bells of Rhymney') or those suffering lost love (like 'You Win Again', 'I Forgot to Remember to Forget', 'Four Strong Winds', 'Still in Town', 'Rock, Salt and Nails', 'The French Girl', 'Waltzin' with Sin' 'I Can't Come in With a Broken Heart', 'I'm a Fool For You' and 'I Don't Hurt Anymore'). From their opening words, these songs sound a note of utter abandonment, and send a plumb-line down into a consuming loneliness. They are voiced by castaways, by men wrecked by life and unable to find remission from the desert-island circuitry of memory, rejection, exploitation, or regret. Within the familiar precincts of form and genre, the singer keeps coming to the same dark, obsessive, places – the edge of town, the prison (in 'Folsom Prison Blues'), and the borders of reminiscence, reproach, and desperation. And within them, as in 'That Old Triangle' Dylan's voice is shot through with yearning while Robertson's guitar, usually up in the mix, intensively hits and bends notes out of the scale.

In Marcus's influential account in *Invisible Republic*, the aura of mystery, gravity, and timelessness on the Basement Tapes is in large part a matter of Dylan's imagination turning at this time towards one of its deepest influences: the often oblique, unfathomable, tragic, absurd, or bawdy voices caught on the *Harry Smith Anthology*. Marcus hears the sessions as an experiment in researching or recreating cultural origins, with the *Anthology* as its deepest template:

> Heard as something like a whole – as a story, despite or even because of its jumble of missing pieces, half-finished recordings, garbled chronologies of composition or performance – the Basement Tapes can begin to sound like a map; but if they are a map, what country, what lost mine is it that they center and fix? They can begin to sound like an instinctive experiment, or a laboratory: a laboratory where, for a few months, certain bedrock strains of American cultural language were retrieved and reinvented. (Marcus, *Invisible Republic*, xiii)

Though categorised in seemingly unexceptional and diverse ways – in terms of ballads and narratives; songs of social occasions; religious and gospel songs, and songs of everyday life – Smith's collection functions for the Basement Tapes, on Marcus's view in *Invisible Republic*, as something like an Old Testament or Apocropha. It is a repository of texts and secret knowledge that provides them with esoteric references. Dave Van Ronk wrote of Smith's collection in a comparable, typically generous, way:

> That set became our bible. It was how most of us first heard Blind Willie Johnson, Mississippi John Hurt, and even Blind Lemon Jefferson. And it was not just blues people, by any means. It had ballad singers, square-dance fiddling, gospel congregations. It was an incredible compendium of American traditional musics, all performed in traditional styles. That was very important for my generation … because we were trying not only to sing traditional songs but also to assimilate the styles of the rural players. Without the Harry Smith *Anthology* we could not have existed. (Van Ronk, 46-47)

For Marcus, it was this tradition that Dylan was sharing with The Hawks in the basement, as if he were the medium in a séance, seeking its reanimation. Marcus hears in Smith's collection something like the underlying truth of another outlawed America. The self-inaugurating American imagination cannot separate its figures of authority from their opportunist simulacra because those who lie or commit violence in order to take possession of the territory cannot but replicate, in the arbitrariness of their claim to power and legitimacy, the natives, drifters and outlaws they displace. The weird, transgressive, murderous America of Harry Smith is both there and not there, a kind of perpetually hallucinated or ghostly other-America. Ford refers to 'John Winthrop's vision of the first Puritan settlement as a "City upon a Hill"' (Ford, 'Trust Yourself', 131), but Smith for Marcus identifies America with the places such as the fatal flower garden, the places on the outskirts, or the banks of the river where unspeakable deeds are committed. The American mind finds itself intimately populated not only by its founding self-mythologists, but also by their troubling alter-egos: hoaxers, whores, robbers, witches, killers, false lovers, demons, snake oil salesmen, absurdist comics, blues men.

One can respect the deep imaginative resonances of Marcus's book, while also acknowledging Dylan's part-dismissive response to this line of discussion in a 2001 interview: 'Well, he makes way too much of that … He intellectualises it too much.' Dylan cites the facts that in the early 1960s '[y]ou could hear Clarence Ashley, Doc Watson, Dock Boggs, The Memphis Jug Band, Furry Lewis'. Also, musical influence was a much broader affair, and there was a myriad of other labels and urban scenes where music of many diverse kinds could be heard: 'It wasn't like someone discovered this pot of gold somewhere … It wasn't the only thing that people had – that *Anthology of American Folk Music*' (Artur, 1329).[19] One needs to remember too, as Marqusee and Giffin oddly seem to forget, the non-American nature of the much of the Basement collection. Both claim that 'the sole non-American song recorded ... is Rimsky-Korsakov's 'Flight of the Bumble Bee' (Giffin, 80).[20] To this, one can reply that 'Young But Daily Growin'' is a British Broadside ballad; that 'The Bells of Rhymney' derives from Welshman Idris Davies' poem; that 'That Auld Triangle' was written by Irishman Dominic Behan; that Canadians Ian And Sylvia wrote 'Big River' and 'Four Strong Winds'; and that 'Johnny Todd' comes from Liverpool. For Heylin, such range and eclectism are in fact the watchwords:

> The diversity of popular songs they recorded is quite remarkable: everything from Johnny Cash to the Stanley Brothers, from Ian Tyson to Eric Von Schmidt, from sea shanties to country tearjerkers, from pure gospel to morality tales, culling their material from the English and Irish dales, the Appalachian Mountains, the Mississippi Delta, Nashville's Music Row, and even Tin Pan Alley. (Heylin, *Behind the Shades*, 274)

For Marqusee, though, the main difficulty with Marcus's view is that it is itself both too programmatic and too mythologising:

> In the end Marcus commits the very sin with which he charges Lomax and the popular front: he homogenizes a variegated tradition in pursuit of a political vision. That vision may be darker, more fatalistic than anything Lomax (or Harry Smith) would have endorsed, but it is, no less than theirs, the product of ideology and historical experience. (Marqusee, 228)

Against this, Marqusee would like to fold the sessions back into late sixties America:

> In the Basement Tapes, Dylan is once again writing against the times, though also very much from within them. The songs might even be interpreted as a running critique of the ephemeral delusions of the summer of love. (Marqusee, 227).

What is indisputable, though, and useful for my purposes, is that Marqusee and Marcus agree, like almost everyone else, about the mysterious dialogue of tradition and timelessness of the Basement Tapes. Both see Dylan and The Hawks as attempting to 're-establish a relation to a tradition from which they felt they had been severed' (Marqusee, 228). As Riley put it, 'they created an imaginary past ... while everyone else was chasing an empty psychedelic future' (Riley, 158). But more than that, too, Marcus's approach brings out how potent is Dylan's self-eclipsing art on the Basement Tapes as it channels the songs of the past from within its transitional moments.[21]

III

In discussing 'I'm Not There' I linked the song's mysterious lure with the singer's all-embracing expression of contingency. He is cut off from everything: from his past, from the woman in the song, and from his words which seem themselves always unstable, perpetually in the process of departing or arriving, of taking and losing form. I suggested that the song is so gripping because Dylan commands this liminal zone to register expressively how, at the margin of daily awareness, we are unfixed, unknown to ourselves. As the sessions developed into the summer of 1967 and as Dylan concentrated on his fourteen demo songs, it can seem that contingency became ever more the abiding, conscious, theme in the writing at the same time as the fourteen songs tended towards the twin poles of the comic-absurd and the tragic-reflective. On the one hand, there is the comic, freewheeling world of 'Lo and Behold!', where one can self-admiringly catch a ferris-wheel into town and where the world is open, as in a fable, laid before us as if a promised land, where one has 'never felt so good' (*Lyrics*, 281). On the other hand, there is the world of lost hope – informed by fatality. Here the figure in the song is bound, like Lear, to a wheel of fire, and annihilation appears the agonising outcome of any plan, any relation, any attempt to remember or connect.

These cryptic songs of tragic dissociation are at the heart of the Basement Tapes, songs like 'Too Much of Nothing', 'Nothing Was Delivered', 'Tears of Rage', 'I Shall Be Released', 'This Wheel's On Fire', and even 'One Man's Loss'. They give voice to someone taking stock of some radical experience of abandonment, captivity, loss, or emptiness. Further, in each case the singer appears as if forced by his situation to acknowledge a more profound reality: that time is a void that ultimately fractures, divides, and undoes all human designs. Again, it is Dylan's singing – matter-of-fact, neutral, lacking in histrionics – that creates the compelling spell, as of someone who has moved to a place of reckoning where he acknowledges that all his plans were scratched in sand, that nothing was delivered, that nothingness makes us lose control, that human consciousness is endlessly yearning for release, or in flight from 'false instruction'. Within the destitute, riven theatre of consciousness unfolded in the songs' often oblique *mise-en-scènes* the mind confronts itself as a structure of illusion and avoidance, an unstable locus of failing significance. 'I'm Not There' is clearly a kind of paradigm of this, its circulation of unmoored intimation, unformulated words, and unresolved relations revealing the self as struggling with and acknowledging the whirlpool of time and obscurity out of which it passingly emerges.

One might take 'I Shall Be Released' as an illustration of how the songs generate this variety and depth of meaning. Consider, to begin with, how many criss-crossing interpretive trails might be pursued in the song. Most obviously, firstly, it can be taken vaguely as an all-purpose complaint against injustice. Clearly also, though and secondly, one can hear in it a social myth: within the 'lonely crowd' of social subjugation we are all imprisoned. We need to be released from the walls of our secrecy or self-estrangement or socialised guilt, while over them we glimpse intimations – possibly illusory – of some unknown redemption. Equally, thirdly, we might read the song as an allegory of spiritual yearning and deliverance. Here someone might say that it is impossible to listen to the words without feeling that this 'light' may be absolution, and that the reflected self, 'so high above the wall' might represent spiritual transcendence. Fourthly, we might even read this release as something like the Freudian death-drive, the secret condition of human striving, the underlying need to be released from desire itself (perhaps identified here as an annihilating light from the west that has shone from the beginning). However, as suggested, my point is that such multiplication is inward with the further, underlying, sense that the song can be taken as about the ultimately treacherous processes of identity and interpretation themselves. It is the need to make meaning that holds us captive, that frames and fixes us, dividing us from the world and making us dream of transcendence. Consciousness finds itself the lifelong prisoner of intelligibility, and Dylan has found in the song an expressive idiom that takes the measure of this, his dissociative intonations scoring his words with an abyssal sense of powerlessness and longing so that every syllable seems etched into our hearing like the repetitive, fragmentary markings of time on a prison wall.

This commerce between the scenarios of these songs, and their subjective, transcendental condition, their concern with ultimate human realities, is everywhere evident. To listen to 'Tears of Rage' or 'This Wheel's On Fire', is to hear a voice tormented by ironic experiences that break up the self. In 'Tears of Rage', the surface situation is apparently of a parent's grief at a child's unfeeling betrayal, ingratitude, or greed. Family love goes from bad to worse. The heart corrupts itself with illusory treasures:

> And now the heart is filled with gold
> As if it was a purse
> But, oh, what kind of love is this
> Which goes from bad to worse? (*Lyrics*, 287)

Again, though, the song sounds a deeper, inescapable sense of instability wound into its apparent situation. If there is 'no-one true', the suggestion is that this is because language and culture offer us impossible images of truth and trust, of self and other. Rhyming 'sand' and 'stand', the singer's vision, projected through its unconsoled tones, is of the inevitably treacherous nature of relationships given the weight we place on them. We are left mired in the need to overcome solitude, yet incapable of either lasting connection or independence: 'We're so alone / And life is brief' (*Lyrics*, 287). '[F]alse instruction' can thus be taken as a motto for these songs that reveal tragic disappointment as the inevitable outcome and fate of the human pursuit of happiness (*Lyrics*, 299). And as in 'I'm Not There', the songs effectively wrap up meaning and expression with their disappearance, making a song's confounding emotional situation inward with the opaque, elliptical, and disjointed features of its own language, as the voice struggles to take stock of his inevitably vanishing contexts of hope, love, relation, release, significance, and connection.

On 'This Wheel's On Fire' the image of being stretched out on a wheel of fire is a motif for imminent destruction. Dylan's words move back and forth between what makes for human connection – memory, meeting, speech, tales, lace, family, kin, wheels, planning, telling – and what unmakes everything: the time that obliterates memory; the death that severs us from our next of kin; the impulses to punishment, confiscation, and secrecy that divide us from others and ourselves; the besetting sense of loss, forgetting, pointlessness, mutability, or failure that hover over our schemes ... Like 'I'm Not There', or 'I Shall Be Released', 'Too Much of Nothing', or 'Tears of Rage' the song's own cryptic scenario is indissociable from its reflexive, tragic sense of the dissociative nature of our existence. As with those songs, too, it expressively draws the listener into its tormenting, vortical mental space. The complex time signature places it somewhere between a slow shuffle and a blues, and this, along with the chromatic effects of the music, helps give it a slow, restless tension, an uncoiling sense of foreboding and despair. This climaxes in the final stretched syllables of each chorus that enacts the destructive explosion to which they refer. Within this disintegrative world, all the elements of dialogue or narrative, like all projects and schemes, appear to have become torn away from their context, persisting like unremembered fragments reconstituted in a dream. Again, Dylan's voice appears at some obscure border zone between life and nothingness, his words sounding as if they are being torn apart, crushed or dismembered into accented, anguished syllables. Rationality persists outwardly in the almost syllogistic structure of the song ('If ... So ... But ... If ... If. But. But. If ... If ...'), but the voice struggles to overcome his sense of lost connections and to unpack the truth of his life, of 'all my things'.

In 'This Wheel's On Fire', then, the singer is consumed by the gathering sense that truth and significance now are irrevocably lost or illusory, that 'ev'ry plan had failed', that the supports and contexts that would supply meaning are no longer firmly in place, that logic is unavailing, and that memory fails to serve us well enough (*Lyrics*, 299). Finally, 'Too Much of Nothing' is perhaps the song on the collection that most directly and implacably addresses these themes. Dylan's voice has the flat, unillusioned intensity of someone returning from the fiery furnace, purged of desire and full of unconsoled vision. The images in the song condense its awareness of the human mind as an unstable system sunk in insubstantial fictions. Tormented, ill at ease, we seek to mask the void at the heart of our desire: 'And too much of nothing can make a man a liar / It can cause some man to sleep on nails / An' another man to eat fire.' In its series of thumbnail sketches the song unfolds how we fill our exorbitant nothingness with masochism, confessions, boasts, mockery, books, lies, dreams, envy, self-destruction, idols and meanness. In desperate flight from the oblivion that threatens to engulf us, we pursue a 'Valerie' or 'Vivian' and lose ourselves to salary and materialism (*Lyrics*, 288).

Figure 13   Dylan outside Elliott Landy's home, Nashville Skyline photo sessions, Woodstock, NY, 1969. Photo by © Elliott Landy, LandyVision Inc.

Figure 14 Dylan at his Byrdcliffe home, Nashville Skyline photo sessions, Woodstock, NY, 1969. Photo by © Elliott Landy, LandyVision Inc

Chapter 6
'Not Too Far But Just Far Enough So's We Can Say That We've Been There'

John Wesley Harding and *Nashville Skyline*

Woody Guthrie, a patient at Creedmore Psychiatric Hospital for the last year of his life, died of Huntington's chorea on 3 October 1967. It was two weeks before the first recording session for *John Wesley Harding* (eventually released on 27 December). At the Guthrie memorial benefit three weeks or so later, at Carnegie Hall on 20 January 1968, Dylan backed by The Hawks (or The Crackers as they were announced) played a brief set, singing rockabilly, drum-driven interpretations of 'Grand Coulee Dam', 'Dear Mrs Rooseveldt', and 'I Ain't Got No Home in This World Anymore'. Shelton described Dylan entering from the side of the stage wearing a blue shirt and grey suit. Landy's photographs show him carrying a small acoustic guitar fixed to his neck by a strap so thin it resembled a cord or rope. His hair was short, clear of his forehead, his face framed by a sparse, curly beard. He looked of an indeterminate age, blending in with his band who collectively resembled a group of civil war survivors. Unsurprisingly, he was unrecognised at first by most of the audience. Where the Dylan of 1966 could appear to have arrived from another planet, here his aspect is more timeless, almost biblical, like he might have stepped onto the stage from the Book of Daniel (Shelton, *No Direction Home*, 270).

The performances themselves have a spontaneous looseness, with rolling piano and rough-edged harmonies. Shelton reported Dylan appearing 'serene' on stage, possibly as if paying tribute to Guthrie were liberating him from the gathering pressures of his own myth. He would raise his guitar one moment and conduct the group through chopping motions at another, while his 'voice soared over the ensemble' (Shelton, *No Direction Home*, 271). Certainly the fervour of the performances is unmistakeable. The opening song, 'I Ain't Got No Home', is visited by rollicking exchanges between Dylan's catapulting vocals and Robertson's butting or yowling guitar. Throughout the set, the drive of the performance converts what risks being ragged, ramshackle, or extemporary into something ardent and unfettered. The raucous harmonies on 'Grand Coulee Dam' or the agile phrasing on 'Dear Mrs Rooseveldt' commute what is bleak in the songs and situation into something electrifyingly true to Guthrie's spirit, so that the whole ensemble can sound to the enthusiast like it has been thrown together within some sublime box-car.

The regenerative effect of the performance is certainly bound up with the opportunity it grants Dylan both to reject his immediate past and to revive an older one, reprising Guthrie's work and sharing the stage with Odetta, Pete Seeger and Arlo Guthrie. More broadly, there were other events of the time (aside even from the basement sessions, and the birth of two children) that would have made for a similar kind of revaluation. At the Guthrie concert, according to Levon Helm, 'we noticed that Bob and Albert [Grossman] were not speaking to each other', and Clive Davis reported categorically that the 'pair had stopped working together' (Heylin, *Behind the Shades*, 290, 291).[1] Despite Dylan's later denials to Weberman there have been few who have not considered 'Dear Landlord' as in some way a *cri-de-coeur* addressed against Grossman at this time of contractual wrangles. More significantly, Dylan's father, Abe, would die on 5 June 1968, just shortly before the birth of Samuel Abram Isaac. In May 1969, Toby Thompson interviewed Dylan's mother Beatty in a diner where she alternated between chiding him for his pursuit of her son ('Why can't you journalists stop torturing this boy!') and for not eating his dessert. But she also gave out nuggets indicative of Dylan's shifting sensibility, such as the famous remark that the bible stood open and often consulted on a stand in his study in his Woodstock home.[2]

It is a striking index of these changes that one might plausibly say that Dylan's most vibrant live performances of 1968 and 1969 were of songs associated with Guthrie, such as these and the singing of 'East Virginia Blues' with Earl Scraggs and Family for American TV in 1969. This turning back to Woody gives a nice ironic twist to the fact that it would be the Dylan of *Highway 61 Revisited* or *Blonde on Blonde* who would remain the prince across the water for his late 1960s audience. Thus it is obvious that *John Wesley Harding* and *Nashville Skyline* are as driven by refusal as any earlier album. Indeed even *Self Portrait* in 1970, as Dylan himself acknowledged, constituted not so much a refusal to fulfil his audience's claims as something like a desire to rip them up in full view. Retreat at Woodstock in the late 1960s was becoming less and less viable. In an interview with Kurt Loder for *Rolling Stone* in 1984 he forcibly expressed his growing realisation that he had been 'workin' for these *leeches*', and that while people mistakenly demanded leadership from him, he 'just wanted to see' his 'kids'. Meanwhile there were people 'comin' through the woods, at all hours of the day and night' and knocking on his door:

> It was really dark and depressing. And there was no way to *respond* to all this, you know? It was as if they were suckin' your very *blood* out. I said, 'Now wait, these people can't be my fans. They just *can't* be.' And they kept comin'. We *had* to get out of there … . This was just about the time of that Woodstock festival, which was the sum total of all this bullshit. And it seemed to have something to do with *me*, this Woodstock Nation, and everything it represented. So we couldn't *breathe*. I couldn't get any space for myself and my family, and there was no help, nowhere. I got very resentful about the whole thing, and we got outta there.[3]

By 1969 or 1970 Dylan's need to repel the fantasies and investments of his audience were all too comprehensible.

I

John Wesley Harding has often been known as an album that renewed its times by rejecting them, and its influence remains massive to this day.[4] For Dylan's audience in 1968 the effect was startling, as the world of *Blonde on Blonde* – all vertiginous interiority, lyrical flamboyance, whirlwind musical profusion, and luxuriant elaboration – was succeeded by this album of cryptic, inscrutable ballads populated by mysterious, archetypal figures traversing an historically indeterminate world. '[W]as that really Dylan singing of saints and sinners with gunfighter ballad candour and canonical sincerity?' asked Toby Thompson, responding to the pared-down unfathomable songs as 'a new testament to construe', its 'fresh parables' luring him and his friends into endlessly fruitless exegesis (Thompson, *Positively Main Street*, 9). Determined to outflank the excesses of this 'season of hype', of this most extravagant of years, Dylan had *John Wesley Harding* released with no publicity.[5] Jon Landau picked up on the album's attitude of insouciant self-reliance in *Crawdaddy*: 'For an album of this kind to be released amidst *Sgt. Pepper*, *Their Satanic Majesties Request*, *After Bathing at Baxter's*, somebody must have had a lot of confidence in what he was doing.'[6]

This air of withdrawn self-possession asserts itself right from the opening, with the first track's cowboy ballad mode and loping evocation of hooves and spurs. The cover also captures the intriguing mixture of the available, the sidelong and the incomprehensible that marks out *John Wesley Harding* and that led Riley to refer to the songs as 'riddles posing as revelation' (Riley, 172). On the inset black-and-white photo, Dylan is smiling in an unusually unguarded way. In broad sunlight, he looks directly at the camera. His expression is familiar, inviting, and he appears naturalised within this rural world. He is lightly bearded, and wears a large broad-brimmed hat and the same double-breasted suede coat as on the *Blonde on Blonde* cover. However, he is also looking sideways and squinting slightly. His hands are in his pockets, and he is puzzlingly flanked by two genial figures in ethnic garb. Though they resemble native Americans, in fact they were Bengali brothers, musicians with The Bauls of Bengal, championed by Grossman and The Band and staying in Woodstock:

> They were real gypsies and real players, happy to get high and sing all night about rivers and goddesses and play their tablas, harmonium, and fiddles. (Helm, 157–8)

Behind Dylan looms the head and shoulders of a local stonemason, an incongruous yet indisputable figure, his face utterly obdurate and inexpressive.[7] On the reverse side, too, the liner notes invite yet resist meaning, while comically unfolding what appears as a zany, mazy, dream-like parable about the interpretive illusions of seekers after truth. Three kings come looking for the key to the new songs and are told that the key is Frank. When Frank asks them how far they want him to open up the record, they answer 'Not too far but just far enough so's we can say that we've been there.' Frank obliges by ripping off his shirt, stamping on a lightbulb, and punching 'his fist through the plate glass window'. He asks, 'Far enough?' to which the second king answers 'Yeah, sure, Frank.' When they leave, they are seemingly healed and enriched, as if the real truth of Frank's work were his liberating rejections of the role of the saviour, and of gospels offering illumination and transparency. Finally, Frank's wife upbraids him as if after all he had gone too far, 'Why didn't you just tell them you were a moderate man and leave it at that instead of goosing yourself all over the room?'

Bizarre as they are, the photo and notes link to the way the songs draw us in, producing a search for significance and value, yet leaving us uncertain where the singer is coming from, where the songs are going, and how far to go in pursuit of meaning. Within a song, the foreground is often diverting, matter-of-fact (frank even). However, nothing quite coheres or resolves, while the background remains enigmatic and obscure. In form, the oblique, fragmentary narratives resemble timeless folk tales, ballads, myths, or parables. Like remnants of some oral or folk tradition, or mysterious palimpsests, they are imbued with uncanny dream-like consistency and immemorial significance. Musically, each song travels light, summoning its expansive effects out of its reduced means. The songs have a single-minded rhythmical impetus, the session musicians locking on to the initial strumming of Dylan's guitar, their meagre accompaniment urgently driven by vivid bass figures and simple changes. The musicians seem fellow-travellers, living hand to mouth, and bent on conveying the songs' propulsive effects. Wisely on hearing the tapes, Robbie Robertson counselled Dylan against overdubbing himself and Garth Hudson as had been originally planned (Heylin, *Behind the Shades*, 288).

The bracing indeterminacy of the songs on *John Wesley Harding* means that in his or her own uncertain and adaptive way the listener resembles the autonomous, if obscure figures and seekers who people the album: outlaws, walkers, saints, hobos, apocalyptic horsemen, pilgrims, jokers, refugees, prisoners, siren women, passing strangers, prostitutes, gamblers, tenants, immigrants, lonesome hobos, drifters, messengers, new lovers, assistants, little neighbour boys, cynical judges and troubled philosophers.. These figures are characteristically fighting to emancipate themselves from the past, in pursuit of uncertain redemption. Often, they are fugitives from the law, from a former identity, or from the accusations of others, their narratives generated by their need to elude judgement in this world where judgement appears violent and questionable. Under this aspect, is as if the only certain moral of the songs was: don't judge nothing at all except judgement. Like the drifter, we not only seek to escape the courthouse in which we unaccountably find ourselves, but long for the miracle of its destruction.

In this respect, the continuing cultural force of *John Wesley Harding* is clearly linked to the new twist that Dylan gives to the complexities of self-estrangement and expressivity – as of a self divided between social fate and ethical opportunity – that have governed the shifting modalities of his work through the 1960s. The need to keep ahead of the confining designs of others is a dominant motif of *John Wesley Harding*, and a key source of the listener's inwardness with these songs that consistently stage selfhood (for listener, singer or character in the song), as a resistance to definition and interpretation, as a function of mobility and search. Hence I take the songs ultimately less as narratives than as allegories of an ethical renewal based on embracing the uncertainty of a quest that eludes social identification. One might feel that the ultimate revelation in 'I Dreamed I Saw St Augustine', for example, is of how society necessarily employs the mechanics of scapegoating and condemnation to identify its subjects, and exact their conformity. Augustine himself, like Tom Paine in 'As I Went Out One Morning', might be taken as a troubled visionary or prophet, returning to accuse or overturn a contaminated world. Within the world of *John Wesley Harding*, for these figures as for the Wicked Messenger these two positions are often in circulation: the desire to escape the world that accuses me, and the often failing desire to transform its judgements, to bring or find good news.

The limitations and temptations of judgement are directly sounded in the closing lines of 'Dear Landlord': 'And if you don't underestimate me / I won't underestimate you' (*Lyrics*, 229). Similarly, in 'Drifter's Escape' the voracious, 'cursed jury' is left crying 'for more' as the drifter is carried away from the courtroom, not knowing what he has done wrong. In 'Drifter's Escape' socialisation appears inseparable from processes of adjudication that mask prejudice, paranoia, and hostility. However, even here the crowd is itself tellingly ambiguous, perhaps divided. We hear it is 'stirring', though whether in incipient, sympathetic, revolt (demanding proper justice), or in collective bloodlust (impatient for the judicial theatre of cruelty) we do not know. In either case, as in the polarised politics of 1968, the response is a mass one, and as such is too volatile and hysterical to be trusted by the drifter who makes his escape while 'everybody' kneels to pray. In 'I Am a Lonesome Hobo', the hobo is a similarly liminal figure, but a cautionary one. He is cut off from friends, family and his former wealth, wandering now in 'fatal doom and shame'. In his earlier life he had pursued prosperity through blaming his brother, and twisting truth into 'bribery, blackmail and deceit'. At the end of the song he counsels us to:

> Stay free from petty jealousies
> Live by no man's code
> And hold your judgment for yourself
> Lest you wind up on this road (*Lyrics*, 230)

The 'poor immigrant' in the succeeding song is similar to this mystery hobo, but he lacks the latter's cursed self-awareness. Unlike the hobo who wanders self-accusingly outside society, the immigrant is committed utterly to the self-betraying pursuit of worldly advancement. He is one for whom leaving home has meant turning 'his back' on those close to him. If immigration is a trope for the kinds of uncertainty that other characters like Harding or the drifter savingly embrace, the immigrant's problem is that such uncertainty is intolerable for him. He possesses a violent drive for self-fixing status and assimilation that leads him to lie and cheat.[8] Like the hobo's former self, his projects of self-enrichment, his 'visions' and 'towns', are built on fatal betrayals. In love with wealth, he has a hunger he cannot fill, regrets he cannot escape, and a blindness to others fatally born of his self-avoidance:

> Who eats but is not satisfied
> Who hears but does not see
> Who falls in love with wealth itself
> And turns his back on me

The immigrant is left unable to escape the hidden self-hatred that drives him, and which all the time shadows him with the possibility that his self-image and world will 'shatter like the glass'. Unlike the hobo, he has not been forced to face his life, and the voice in the song ends with the chilling, ambiguous lines that signal to the time when he will ultimately have to confront his illusions and emptiness: 'I pity the poor immigrant / When his gladness comes to pass' (*Lyrics*, 231).

Contrastingly, John Wesley Harding himself seems to seek to escape the contaminating effects of judgement , and to keep one step ahead of society. The art of the title song is to surround Harding with the snares of definitive statements that he manages still to elude, so that everything recedes into a hazy background of contingency, ambiguity, and myth. In the song's opening verse, he is identified as 'a friend to the poor' like Dylan's boyhood hero, Robin Hood, or many a romantic highwayman of folk ballads.[9] He is one who 'opened many a door' on his travels, and he is iteratively placed within a familiar, recognisable world: 'this country-side', 'the time they talk about', 'Chaynee County', 'the situation there', 'the telegraph'. However, the song plunges such fixities and definite articles into question, following the statement that he 'opened many a door' with the line: 'But he was never known to hurt an honest man.' The word 'But' makes questions ricochet around our minds like pinging gun-shots: How did he open doors? Did he threaten and rob honest men even if he did not hurt them? Did he hurt even if it never became known?[10] Such cross-hatching enigmas shadow our portrait of Harding with obscure depths (as Gray has discussed at some length). In the second verse we hear that, backed into a corner, he 'took a stand' with 'his lady by his side':

> Within the cowboy ethic, the hero should neither have needed his lady by his side to give him courage nor have placed her inside the danger zone. (Gray, *Song and Dance Man III*, 35)

Gray takes the song's clouding and darkening of the image of Harding as amounting to a 'keen critique' of cowboy mythology, an explosion of 'clichés of thought' that still grip the American cultural imagination (Gray, *Song and Dance Man III*, 35). However, we can suspect that Gray's judgement is itself too definitive, if it is true that ethical and creative value on this record are identified with mobility and indeterminacy. Perhaps more to the point, I would argue that freedom on *John Wesley Harding* is essentially identified with questioning, so that our fascination with Harding can be traced to Dylan's cultivation of his mysterious elusiveness. In such a way the album steps away from the world of *Blonde on Blonde* by externalising self-obscurity, the search for expression, within small epic narratives or parables that reveal identity as something like an enforced social lie, and that stage uncertainty as aesthetic pleasure, ethical opportunity and interpretative resource. Dylan does not demythologise Harding or cowboy music so much as create an interval of saving indeterminacy, of onward pressing and animating openness – semantic, subjective, verbal – that binds us to Harding, and to Dylan himself as artist and singer here (though evidently also to Dylan as an actual figure of fact, myth, rumour at the time). If Harding is exemplary, it is because he too is a survivor, a fugitive from the confining contexts of society and words, someone who aspires to autonomy until, backed into a corner, he must take his stand. Vigilance and the avoidance of foolish moves are the key values for Harding, and for Dylan on this album, and for the listener who must respond to the words, be carried along with them perhaps, while needing to remain aware that, like Harding, they will defeat single-minded attempts to track or chain them down.

II

Cultivating the effect of the timeless and universal, the songs on *John Wesley Harding* variously employ obscurity as the means of eluding their time and confronting their society with forgotten fundamentals. Narratively, the songs identify self-possibility with opacity, ambivalence, and escape, while musically and spiritually Dylan returns to idioms that revive obscured traditions. The songs' bare, enigmatic scenarios, immediate, stripped-down arrangements, and urgent vocals appear indices of this consuming concern with human essentials. Shorn of choruses, their elliptical composition makes them appear not only timeless, but like strange testaments to their own powers of survival. Their anonymous qualities evoke previous times and lost origins. The songs appear quasi-mythical, as if they are also not only historical but historicising, the resource of cultural and spiritual imagination, parables for times to come. Dylan himself described *John Wesley Harding* as 'the first biblical rock album',[11] and in interviews with John Cohen and Happy Traum identified his interest in parables and the bible.[12] In January 1968, he told Herbert Saal that 'a song is a moral just by being a song' (Heylin, *Stolen Moments*, 112). So, for Michael Gray, the album seems 'not a part of the 1960s world at all'. It constitutes 'a most serious, darkly visionary exploration of the myths and extinct strengths of America'. Its 'eerie power' is in 'mixing the severely biblical with a surreal nineteenth-century American pioneer ethos' (Michael Gray, *Song & Dance Man III*, 6). In such unforeseen ways, *John Wesley Harding* rings the changes on the logic of revisiting and bringing it all back home that had underpinned Dylan's renewals of rock and roll in the mid-60s.

If sure-footedness in uncertainty is the supreme virtue in *John Wesley Harding*, it is again evident in Dylan's singing throughout. Robert Christgau's commented in his review how 'the directness of attack is so uncharacteristic that it undercuts itself, becoming a source of mystery and surprise'.[13] Dylan's singing preserves an unswerving casual conviction that is all the more intriguing because of the obliquity of the narratives he unfolds. The effect is often of someone passing through a song rather than presiding over it, with no responsibility for the questions triggered by his words. Often this means that the songs ultimately resist our desires to understand or decode them, while also appearing on a deeper level to stage the complex search for meaning. 'The Wicked Messenger' is an obvious example of this, a song often persuasively taken as about Dylan's own feet of clay, and his inability or unwillingness to be cast any longer in the role of a prophet or exemplar, the fleet-footed bringer of messages. Yet still, in its actual narrative and verbal texture, its content, it remains perhaps the most confounding song on the album. Within it, questions proliferate: Why the echoes from the bible? Why are the soles of his feet burning? Why does he answer with his thumb? In what ways does his tongue only flatter? What does seem eventually clear, though, is that the burden of meaning, of multiplying the smallest matter for his audience, is one from which the messenger is delivered at the end of the song. The crowd come to the seemingly outraged recognition that he is one, like Frank with the Three Kings, who cannot gratify their thirst for gospel:

> And the people that confronted him were many
> And he was told with these few words
> Which opened up his heart
> 'If ye cannot bring good news, then don't bring any' (*Lyrics*, 232)

The Messenger has feet of clay, and the song's explicit pay-off is that we should avoid false promises, and conflations of the carnal and the transcendent. The same is true for Frankie Lee, who mistakes a whorehouse for Paradise and who is betrayed by a Priest named Judas. Safer perhaps to adopt the sharp little neighbour boy's dictum that '"Nothing is Revealed"' (*Lyrics*, 227). The songs counsel that we must learn from experience, and avoid filling emptiness and uncertainty with destructive illusion and fantasy. By such means we can keep a step ahead, and maintain a certain sharp-eyed renunciation of what is self-confounding in our desire to possess and know.

This identification of freedom with uncertainty brings us to an important crux. I have argued the songs solicit and resist us. Like dreams, visions, uncertain reports down the telegraph, prophetic messages (or perhaps even the women in the house with 'four and twenty windows' [*Lyrics*, 226]), they invite us in, but not far enough to satisfy our desire for possession. Of course, there is much in the textures and construction of the songs themselves that contributes to this resistance too – much that is truncated, opaque, undirected, unexpressed, haphazard, ragged and unresolved. However, my conviction is that issues of interpretation, and the need to acknowledge its failings, are resonantly at the heart of these songs, as with the songs on the Basement Tapes, and in ways that bring out crucial aspects of Dylan's work. After all, this book may not claim that Dylan is a poet in the narrow sense, but it does argue that he is possessed of poetic, imaginative, and vocal gifts that centrally precipitate around the conversion of obscurity and inexpression into subjective meaning and inspiration. My argument has been that the very groundlessness of subjectivity in Dylan's art – the sense that it is constantly, inventively at stake, caught up with its enactments – means that his work is all the time inevitably concerned with its own shifting conditions of meaning and expression. Hence, my concern throughout this book has been with how Dylan's career in the 1960s turned on its various scenarios of self-genesis. Further, though, in the quasi-mythical world of *John Wesley Harding* this has also come to lead to songs that can be taken more overtly, like parables, to be readable as scenarios of interpretation, as hermeneutic fables about the mind's endlessly renewed, fallible, encounters with meaning, value, and identity.

Insofar as they can be taken as reflexive allegories of unstable self-constitution, then, the songs on *John Wesley Harding* both produce and represent the thirst for meaning. In producing it, as we have seen, these songs of pilgrims and outlaws clearly revisit Dylan abiding creative impulse in the 1960s, his expressive need to step free of fixed roles, relations and simple messages, and make a virtue of indeterminacy. But how do they represent it, and offer themselves as cautionary fables about the dangers of interpretive desire? 'As I Went Out Morning' can be taken as an example of these things, a song that both incites multiple interpretations and that can be taken as an effective parable about the need to resist simple, appropriative readings of experience. So, in the first place, Gibbens plausibly enough takes the song as a fable of Dylan's early years, and his eventual 'finding his muse in bondage to good causes' (Gibbens, 261). Others have seen the song as being more specifically about the folk community and the political left, linking it to Dylan's notorious address to the Emergency Civil Liberties Committee on receipt of the Tom Paine award in December 1963, the night he met Allen Ginsberg. Again, others have taken the song as a personal allegory about the seductive promise, yet imprisoning chains, of drug use. But why stop there, since one can imagine further interpretations? Maybe the song is about the chains of family life or fame? Or about the complexities of female emancipation – at this time of white-hot feminist protest in the USA – where girls remain in chains, and trap men as a function of their own entrapment within available images of themselves? Or again, maybe it is about Dylan's felt difficulties at the time in ever having any kind of equal relationship with *anyone at all*, where every seemingly pleasant encounter quickly appears fraught with distorting, possessive, need, and impossible enchaining fantasy?

So, part of my point is to emphasise the strange effect of these straitened songs that they can nonetheless proliferate and accommodate such interpretive riches. At the same time, I am claiming that sanity in the world of *John Wesley Harding*, involves a certain withdrawn autonomy, a renunciation of fixity, a saving awareness of the violent possibilities of final meanings. Thus a fatal mistake for any listener (think A.J. Weberman) would clearly be to take the songs as any kind of gospel or code. But beyond this too, as I am suggesting, the songs can be taken as more far reaching in the ways they figure, narrate, and counsel the uses of a vigilant, vagrant uncertainty. Returning to 'As I Went Out One Morning' for illustration, one might then suggest that the ultimate desire which the songs produces and performs is the desire to step free, to move away from the invasive temptation of interpretation itself, from the desire to catch hold of the song, to take it by the arm (not the hand, as it were), and to make it mean as (and what) we want it to mean. My suggestion is that its air of profundity and mystery might ultimately derive from the extent to which it can become further viewable as a mysterious parable of interpretation itself. Tom Paine's rescuing of the singer from the captivating blandishments of a young damsel would thus figure our need to resist merely transporting and seductive possibilities of significance that will reveal themselves to be, in truth, confining and enchaining. In such a way the song can be taken, like the others, as an enactment of recreation inseparable from a free interrogation of the conditions of meaning, a further instance of Dylan's art of becoming, of Emerson's search for what is yet unattained, for what eludes fantasy or social prescriptions.

Marcus made a comparable point about this song, offering a brilliant unravelling of verbal knots within it, only to dismiss his own ingenious reading as too single-minded and false to its spirit. So, the lyric could be taken, he says, as a second-order myth about how America has perverted its own founding myths, so that Tom Paine has – with bitter irony – to police and restrain a girl who 'runs for freedom' to the South. However, what counts, Marcus says, is that we ultimately reject such interpretations as distorting the casual generative (and generous) openness of the song: 'Dylan's music is about possibilities rather than facts, like a statue that is not an expenditure of city funds but a gateway to a vision' (Marcus, *Writings*, 26). Hence, one might say positively that the song resembles a morning walk, in which Dylan revisits time-honoured terrain – of folk song, love, and the American political imagination – as if to encounter them anew and rehearse his own sense of expressive freedom. Marcus's image of the 'gateway' confirms this positive view: that this inviting mystery and openness is not only fundamental, but also ultimately heartening rather than dispiriting. Hence one might emphasise that the songs' own openings are wide and inviting ('John Wesley Harding was a friend to the poor'... 'Well, Frankie Lee and Judas Priest, they were the best of friends' ... '"Oh, help me in my weakness"/ I heard the drifter say' ... [*Lyrics*, 221, 225, 228]). With their strange ratios of directness and insolubility, the songs take us like the three kings, just far enough into meaning.... But what would be the point if they abandon us in uncertainty? At this point I take Marcus to suggest importantly that the songs provoke us to question, affirming that thereby we can rediscover ourselves as questers, as seekers after truth, as in flight from false certainties. The singer's blithe, definite delivery itself would appear an expression of this way in which the songs seek to instil in the listener this attitude of self-reliance, the sense that we are on our mettle, that spiritual renewal and value are up to us to find. By reeling us in, then leaving us in uncertainty – within songs that dramatise the shortfall and betrayals of the desire for fixity – the songs inspiritingly leave us to fend and take responsibility for ourselves. As surely as in the songs of 1963 or 1965 they force us into autonomy.

To illustrate these points again, one might begin by multiplying readings for 'The Drifter's Escape'. A first person might take it as a sort of condensed Kafkaesque parable of the kind that John Cohen was pressing Dylan to read at the time.[14] Society on this view is a strange theatre of punishment, and we are either held accountable, or seduced into judging others. Secondly, though, the song might be taken as a sort of Freudian parable, as if the mobile id were on trial within the courtroom of the ego. On another level, the judge as superego is robed, seemingly superior, judicious and sympathetic. However, stepping down and fatalistic, he reveals himself ultimately to be a reactive function of the social herd stirring outside ... Thirdly, in more philosophical terms, we might take the final bolt of lightening in many different ways: as pure random chance, as the force of a higher justice, as divine retribution, as the instrument of nature, as desire, or as unmeaning temporality. Lastly, in more political terms, we might say that the crowd in the song is brought to prey but stays to pray as it were, substituting one socialised form of blindness for another, representative of a nation where religion, utopia and enslavement have always co-existed. And so on ...

Again though, my aim in proliferating these diverse, often complicated, interpretations, is to show how the song both invites and yet ultimately dislocates such framing convictions. And as it does so, it expressively enacts a link with the drifter. At the end, still unable to understand, he escapes from the judge, the out of shape courthouse, and society, and embraces again his transporting, indefinite, sense of experience ('My trip has been a pleasant one...'). In such ways, 'Drifter's Escape' reiterates this threefold focus. Firstly, the songs support divergent interpretations. Secondly, in refusing single interpretations, they keep a step ahead of the desire to appropriate, embracing provisionality and exemplifying the values of Dylan's creative imagination. Thirdly, they take on further resonances insofar as they resound with the possibility of being read themselves as allegories of the search for expression itself, reflexively staged in the songs as inimical to a socially conditioned or violently self-assertive pursuit of identification. In all these resonating ways, then, they allow us to inhabit the open time of becoming as a time of quest, escape, and search.[15] Most important, again, the encounter with obscurity is ultimately uplifting, not because of what the songs might be taken to say, but because of what they *do*: they revive, like parables, our spiritual capacities. The singer's assurance in contingency forges in the listener an answering attitude of resourcefulness, and the sense that a desire for truth is predicated on seeing through seductive illusions, on heightening our consciousness of our situation, and confronting the world anew.

By the same token, of course, it is always possible to take the songs more pessimistically, perhaps as secular parables voided of God and leaving us to pursue an impossible, non-existent salvation. Michael Gray's vocabulary earlier of the 'serious', the 'dark', and the 'severe' implies a more apocalyptic view, reiterated in Court Carney's grave comment that 'Dylan uses biblical parables not as messengers of truth but as damning examples of unresolvable mystery.'.[16] Here one might emphasise how what seems definite and declarative in the songs can also swiftly appear troubling, and opaque, so that the listener can feel he has left the broad way to vision, and is in a position that has become uncertain, transitional, with paths dividing in every direction. Suddenly he is more like Dante in the inaugural scene of the *Inferno*, in the middle of a dark wood, the true way lost. For example, one might take the singer's dark epiphany at the end of 'I Dreamed I Saw St Augustine' as one of utterly mortifying isolation. For Pichaske, certainly the meaning is conclusively negative: that human beings will 'always martyr the prophet, kill the Christ' (Pichaske, 270). In the martyrdom the singer dreams for the saint, he 'was amongst the ones / who put him out to death', and awakens to an awful sense of fear and desperation:

> Oh, I awoke in anger
> So alone and terrified
> I put my fingers against the glass
> And bowed my head and cried (*Lyrics*, 223)

Certainly the possibilities all seem dark: Perhaps the glass reveals or reflects human depravity and violence? Perhaps it signifies the absence of any revelation that can meet our spiritual needs for transparency, meaning, and truth? Perhaps it signifies a terrifying nothingness, the absence of transcendence? The glass might appear, whichever way we look at it, like a nightmare version of the glass of faith through which St Paul strives to see darkly in *1 Corinthians*. Without wanting to dispute that Carney, Pichaske or Gray might justifiably argue otherwise, my view is that because the song is incapable of resolving the significances it variously appears to reflect, its particular kind of indetermination inspiringly stimulates and confirms our status as spiritual seekers. However bleak the alternatives, it empowers us to try and wake, to escape and recreate ourselves, returning us to a moral world where our powers are confirmed, where significance, value and renewal are the fundamental assumptions, and where we press on, still *en route* to expression, however much final meanings elude us.

All the same, finally, one must acknowledge that 'All Along the Watchtower' remains a much more insistently apocalyptic song. The music begins as if from nowhere – with a single note, then a strum, a wailing harmonica, bass and drums – and it ends with a single twisting harmonica phrase. At the beginning, the joker and thief seem exemplary, liminal, resistant figures of the kind encountered elsewhere. They complain of exploitation by businessmen and farmers, and desire a way 'out of here', from this desacralised, corrupted world ... Yet as the song presses on, its ominousness tips towards a growing sense of menace and annihilation. Now it seems as if human existence itself is in the balance, and we are in the end times. The community of the watchtower is swiftly unfolded (as in an external tracking shot), and human beings appear movingly vulnerable, dignified by their predicament. We see watchful, protective princes, ladies and servants, as well as the thief and joker. Meanwhile in the far distance, there is the sense of obscure forces and approaching cataclysm – signalled by horsemen riding in the howling wind. The extreme uncertainties that circulate in the song condense on this closing scene, leaving us not knowing if the horsemen are riding towards or back, or if they are visitors from outside of time like the horsemen in *Revelations*. What seems certain is that they are associated with destruction, but whether this cosmic fate is natural violence or supernatural retribution and final judgement is uncertain. To this, the wild cat beginning to growl adds a further unsettling note of animal savagery, anticipating the imminent erasure of human desire, meanings, and settlements. In contrast, 'Down Along the Cove', and 'I'll Be Your Baby Tonight' are songs that anticipate *Nashville Skyline*. Here love offers some saving respite from conflicts and uncertainty, and from the need or desire to move away.

III

Barely twenty-eight minutes long, *Nashville Skyline* was recorded fifteen months or so after *John Wesley Harding*, between 13 and 18 February 1969. Dylan appears to have arrived in Nashville on the 13th without a clear sense of the album that would result, or even a firm intention that he would cut a whole album. Later he would say that 'The first time I went into the studio I had, I think, four songs' (Heylin, *Behind the Shades*, 195). What happened in those five days? Heylin plausibly suggests that Dylan might have had half a mind to see how the collaboration with Johnny Cash that took place on 18 February would turn out, while in the meantime the album that we know incrementally shaped itself in the studio as he wrote and cut songs to fill it out. 'Lay, Lady, Lay', 'To Be Alone With You', 'I Threw it All Away', and 'One More Night' were clearly written before the 13th, when they were recorded. However, on the next day, Dylan recorded songs that Heylin argues were largely written over night or on the day for the evening session of the 14th: 'Peggy Day', 'Country Pie', and 'Tell Me That It Isn't True'.

If Heylin is right that Dylan was partly waiting on a possible collaboration with Cash, in the event it proved something of a distraction. It has some wonderful moments – notably a lyrical, plaintive version of 'I Still Miss Someone' and a dynamic 'Ring of Fire' – but the sound overall is too sketchy, with both singers sounding too guarded, too defensively grooved in showcasing their own contrasting manners of delivery. What is unquestionable is that Dylan is now singing in the voice of *Nashville Skyline*, a mode that can still surprise, even dismay. He is still unrecognisable, still inaccessible, but the essential dynamics of his self-projection appear to have radically shifted. For the urban hipster of the mid-60s, or the mythic outlaw of the previous year, selfhood was a matter of fighting free in some way, and of the drive to futurity. Differently, the self of *Nashville Skyline* is one who consciously inhabits a precarious present. Outwardly, he comes across as determinedly familiar, neighbourly even. He is no longer the figure of the basement who is 'not there'. Instead he is available, upfront, determinedly 'standing in front of you' (*Lyrics*, 242). Taking stock of his losses and mindful of what he might yet lose, he is driven to make the most of this moment, this night, this place, this person, this need to connect. In the earlier albums the present continuous of the singing was a means of escape, releasing a transitional, unknown self. However, in *Nashville Skyline* the singer's all-engrossing desire is to stay here, to prolong the moment, to accept, even celebrate his surroundings, and to make himself known. This appears all the more the case because this present moment is shadowed by an encroaching past and future.

Accordingly, these are songs about holding off time or holding onto it, about expansively valuing, making the most of what life brings. The album projects a voice that both takes refuge in melody, rhythm, intonation, sonority, and seeks renewal through them. Musicality, the swing and sway of phrasing, take on a kind of priority over the words in a way that is new for Dylan. The way he glidingly sings a line, or inhabits a pause are microcosms of someone intent on grasping in his hands the threads of his past, present, and future, and savouring immediate pleasures. The singing exemplifies the album's sense of both the precariousness and value of these intervals of resolution and equanimity, of having and holding. The smooth singing extends and sustains syllables, phrases, lines or verses. The voice glides, soars, or executes a swallow-dive, as if fashioning a plaintive beauty against the background of silence and time, as the voice narrates its songs of lost or threatened love. Happiness is perpetually at stake for the figure in the songs, as he strives to wrest pleasure from the present amidst haunting echoes or fears of loss. Similarly, passing effects of dissonance or melancholy contribute an expressive tension musically, in the bluesy twang of the guitar work, the plangent sounds of the pedal steel, or the pensive swirls of the organ. Such accompaniment provides a suitable backdrop for Dylan's voice – determined, susceptible, poignant and self-possessed – as it seeks a haven in its sonorous, modulating intonations and vowel music.

Nonetheless, despite this expressive complexity, it needs saying that individual songs on *Nashville Skyline* can still come across as drastically uneven, with about half the songs resembling homework exercises, even parodies, in the country idiom. This can make one feel that much of the album is itself a sketch of a more developed album. There is an almost provocative vapidity, for instance, about 'To Be Alone With You', 'Country Pie', or 'Peggy Day'. Even the ebullient 'Nashville Skyline Rag', for instance, can too easily sound as if hastily put together for purpose, like a standard warm-up sequence redeemed by stellar session players.

From this viewpoint, as much as any other album, *Nashville Skyline* can be said to turn its back on its world and audience. As Sid Griffin put it:

> In a way the man on the *Nashville Skyline* jacket began to reject everything: rock'n'roll music, the demands of the world around him, the adulation of the students gathered in Berkeley and on the other 400 or more American college campuses that protested the escalation of the Vietnam war. (Griffin, 288)

In Robbie Robertson's words, the instinct that united Dylan and The Hawks came to be that '[w]e were rebelling against the rebellion' (Griffin, 289).[17] On *John Wesley Harding*, the elusiveness of the self had been fundamental to the searching, emancipating impetus of the songs, as they used their opaque scenarios to reject constricting frameworks of identity, judgement, genre, language, and representation. On *Nashville Skyline*, Dylan's fugitive self functions with this fundamental difference: that it is his own instincts for rebellion and disappearance that the songs appear bent on leaving behind. Well might Toby Thompson have asked: 'What *was* Bob doing with his new countrified album?', unable to comprehend not the country aspect but his trafficking in 'will-you-still-love-me-tomorrow? schlock', in endless 'well-wrought clichés' (Thompson, *Positively Main Street*, 99).

One might begin in an approximate way by responding that *Nashville Skyline* is Dylan's pastoral album, following on from the satires of the mid-decade, or the comic and tragic world of the basement. On this view, it is an album of romance that confronts the denaturing world of the city with the affirmative simplicities and continuities of country life. On *Blonde on Blonde* the magical, eccentric phrasing appeared a musical analogue of an intoxicating art of urban estrangement. On *Nashville Skyline*, by comparison, the singing celebrates Dylan's immersion within the country idiom, and its identification of desire with location. The former abrasiveness of timbre, the confrontational, slingshot intonation, the borderline yawp, sneer, or caterwaul, are all but discarded by someone whose 'tonsils' are now 'drenched in peachy syrup', in James Wolcott's phrase.[18] Jim Miller records how mystifying was this change to the 'trumped-up smoothie' of *Nashville Skyline* (Miller, 'North Country Blues', 31). This voice is self-delighting, and the audacity of Dylan's art now lies in its projecting, at this time of political ferment, the seductive values of settling, of throwing troubles out the door, and of finding harmony, if only temporarily. Elliott Landy, a Woodstock resident and friend from this time, wrote that the therapeutic context of Woodstock, a retreat for Dylan as artist as well as family man, was crucial:

> 'He was learning to love and express it and experience it in the family way. That's what *Nashville Skyline* was about – very introspective, very country-like, very haven-like music.' (Heylin, *Behind the Shades*, 282)

Leave-taking for the Dylan of *Nashville Skyline* now can seem to take the form of a benign reclusiveness, of a troubled desire fenced against the possibility or memories of heartbreak, conflict and exploitation. Much of this is caught in Landy's cover photo. Dylan's cordial face is back-lit by a seeming fading winter woodland sun. His light beard, hat, and genteel hat-tipping gesture intimate settledness and leisure, while the high tree and beautiful Gibson acoustic suggest a rapport between nature and art. *Nashville Skyline* might be said to affirm the human through a certain wistful turning away from society to nature, towards an America conceived not in terms of alienation, but the inalienable.

IV

What does seem clear is that *Nashville Skyline* was designed to exacerbate the listener's initial bewilderment at the lack of anything like irony or self-division in many of the songs. The listener waits three songs until 'I Threw It All Away' for anything that appears to draw on Dylan's inspiration. The album opens with Dylan and Cash covering an old song ('Girl From the North Country'), an instrumental ('Nashville Skyline Rag'), and then a non-song ('To Be Alone With You'). A first hearing of 'Nashville Skyline Rag', an instrumental in which guitars, pedal steel, and piano trade solos in corny, good-natured emulation, for instance, can leave the listener bemused and irritated by Dylan's non-appearance. In a comparable way to 'All the Tired Horses' on *Self Portrait* one feels that Dylan's rejection of his audience is here less an imaginative instinct than a deliberate, even covertly hostile, gesture. On 'Peggy Day', 'Country Pie', and 'To Be Alone With You', Dylan's celebration of the rural idyll is so bracingly lacking in irony that the listener can similarly feel repelled, angered, or deflated. Certainly it is difficult to take it all at face value. Unsurprisingly, Ralph Gleason concluded at the time that Dylan's mouthing of down-home country clichés was all a 'conscious manipulation of a stereotype' (Scaduto, 261), while Marqusee describes *Nashville Skyline* as 'a charade: the restless one pretending to be at rest' (Marqusee, 285).

However one puts it, it is hard not to feel that there is something forced or wilful in the album's affirmations of pastoral harmony, and something inherently unstable and temporary in its valorisation of the present. If Dylan's art had always turned on evacuating the present, on propelling itself out of a cancelled past into an indeterminate future, on *Nashville Skyline* the present can seem all too evident, with Dylan's selfhood coming across as bewilderingly vacant and complacently bland. Having said this though, closer acquaintance with the songs reveals saving complexities and subtleties that give both the album a more complex dynamic, and individual songs a certain subjective drama and depth. The persona that clings to happiness in some songs is himself shadowed by a more elided, troubled, bereft, and fleeting self on others. The two measure and stalk each other through the album, and sometimes within the same song. In this respect a significant number of the songs can be linked to the tradition of country music that meant most to Dylan growing up, where singers like Jimmie Rodgers, Johnny Cash, or Hank Williams, straddled a mysterious division between what is stricken, lonely, or defiant in the songs, and the impersonal, stabilising artifice and clichés of the country genre itself.[19] Pichaske touches on this when he writes that '[s]everal of the country comfortable songs of *Nashville Skyline* are actually songs of lost, discarded, or threatened love figured by gray skies or "dark and rolling sky"' (Pickaske, 134).

So, on four songs at least the singer has been ejected from his earthly paradise, and is lost, in exile: 'Girl From the North Country', 'Tell Me That It Isn't True', 'One More Night', and 'I Threw It All Away'. In these songs the country genre itself offers an imaginative locus, like the Nashville Skyline itself perhaps, that contains and transcends heartbreak. On 'One More Night' and 'Tell Me That It Isn't True', for example, images of loss and disconnection expressively play against the recreational values and idiom of the songs. In the first, the singer is outside at night, unable to find any sense of joy or illumination in the light of the moon and the stars. He exists in a darkness that seems spiritual as much as romantic, as if his inability to 'be what she wanted me to be' is bound up with a more profound sense that his world, his destiny, has vanished from him. His life is the mere enumeration of 'One more night'. He cannot respond to the world around him, or be inspired by it, '[f]or tonight no light will shine on me'. Against this sense of a devalued, withdrawn world though, the bouncy musical idiom lifts up his voice, which comes mysteriously and beautifully to soar in the repetition of the line, 'the wind blows high above the trees', the word 'high' reprised now an octave higher. At this moment, it is as if the song, with its jaunty, importunate pedal-steel and irrepressible, rolling bass, transmits a power of transport and regeneration, an expressiveness and sense of joy, that the singer is powerless to command in life.

A similarly effective tension between the outward stabilities of the country idiom and our inwardness with a voice that sings of loss is evident in 'Tell Me That It Isn't True', where Dylan is surely paying homage to Hank Williams and his way of inflecting country music with wrenching, unappeased emotion. In *Chronicles* Dylan described his admiration for Williams's grasp of the 'archetypal rules of poetic song writing ... architectural forms ... like marble pillars' (Dylan, *Chronicles*, Vol. 1, 96). If Williams's songs are archetypal, though, it is not simply because they use the most recurrent, formulaic kinds of structure, imagery, and verse form, but because they create a powerful expressive tension between form and the singular predicament of isolation unfolded within the songs. The effect of Williams's music essentially is of a reluctant, anguished voice inhabiting a world suddenly thrown off kilter, reaching for rules that don't apply any more. The formulaic and the familiar are together dislocated by some new emotional reality: something incursive and aching, or unsettlingly effusive and euphoric. In 'Tell Me That It Isn't True', this kind of tension surfaces in a voice that sings against itself, wishing he could deny what he knows, and everyone else too: that his lover has found another man, and 'They say ... [t]hat he's tall, dark and handsome, and you're holding his hand' (*Lyrics*, 244). He cleaves to cliché, but at this moment even cliché becomes ironically the vehicle of the irresistible truth that is breaking into his mind, leaving him bereft, shattering his familiar world. Like the torn voice in Williams's 'You Win Again' (surely the song in Dylan's mind) he is disjoined from himself and his lover by something that he can't accept and that drives him restlessly to patrol the familiar precincts of his town, his vanishing past, and the song itself.

In such aspects, the country idiom at its best has always dealt in bitter-sweet effects, as where the formulaic returns of cliché and genre circulate with the involuntary, moving sense of someone holding to a disintegrating reality. The versions of 'Girl From The North Country' with Cash (on the album and 'The Johnny Cash Show') are interesting in this respect. In the song's situation the singer finds his present dislocated by the past that revisits him. In the *Freewheelin'* version, the quiet poignant tension of the song came from the sense that he was divided against himself by the invasive images and feelings that he can't shake off, and which interrupt his future. In the versions with Cash these temporal divisions are still evident, but regret and sadness are now absorbed within performances that strive after an attitude of mature recollection, as the singing itself strives after harmony, recreation, self-possession. The values of Dylan's voice – smooth, resolute, mellifluous, judicious – are knowingly those of one who has come through, who is projecting a poised assimilative sensibility in which past pain is acknowledged and consciously redeemed in art. For the first time in his career, self-projection and self-difference for Dylan do not appear to mean rejecting the past in the name of a somewhat dissonant art that bears urgently on the future. Instead, the shadows of loss appear acknowledged as effects within an art that muses sonorously at the borderline of past and present. Singing with Cash, Dylan consciously accommodates his own past, and earlier performances of the song, within this performance, as if like nested Chinese boxes.

As this suggests, then, the best songs on *Nashville Skyline* still express the tensions of a temporally divided self, but now as consciously contemplated by the mellifluous voice that presides over the songs, valuing continuity even as he acknowledges the incursions and dangers of loss. Happiness in these songs is poignantly susceptible to vanishing, and the future has become a threatening rather than animating dimension. Dylan's voice is one that expresses this more or less explicitly vulnerable, defensive evaluation of the present, opposing rather than seeking the future. For such a reason Wilfred Mellers wrote that the voice on *Nashville Skyline* is both 'more affirmative and more aware', as if the songs were voicing a singer consciously surveying and reflecting on time, and resisting its divisive power. Within the conservative theatre of these songs longing and loss, future and past, are destabilising forces that the singer now consciously confronts, rather than being any longer the mutually oblivious, temporally disjunctive, conditions of his subjectivity. Beauty and sensuality are what this voice desires to hold on to against the disintegrative powers of loss and time, and Mellers points out how Dylan's own singing displays how 'passionately committed' he is to their values, as on 'Girl From The North Country' where Dylan artfully employs a 'delayed rhythm on "one who lives there"', or uses the 'quavery melismata' on the phrase 'counting on you' in 'Tell Me That It Isn't True' (Mellers, 162). The effect of this phrasing is of a fugitive present whose affirmations and beauties are shadowed by the inevitability of passing time.

Strangely enough, one can feel that the values of continuity in the songs are part of the larger way in which this is a personal album in a new way. Dylan the man and Dylan the artist are much more continuous, and the persona projected in the songs is himself more visible and knowable. In conversation with Scaduto, Dylan cut through the queries about why or how he could have come to write these songs by commenting rather defensively: 'There's no attempt there to reach anybody but me' (Scaduto, 261). The commitment to reclusive pleasure is evident in the way the singer erects the present time as a barrier against transience in 'Tonight I'll Be Staying Here With You' and 'Lay Lady Lay'. In both, he addresses a woman in the hope that he can overcome past sadness. In the first song, she is used to draw him away from his former restless, itinerant life ('Throw my ticket out the window / Throw my suitcase out there, too'), and his former self ('If there's a poor boy on the street / Then let him have my seat'). However, the middle-eight suggests his struggle, torn as he still is between the 'whistle blowin'' outside, and the woman whose 'love comes on so strong' (*Lyrics*, 246). Dylan's voice is itself expressively poised between a residual yearning for his former, restless, life as a 'stranger', and a self-delighting pleasure in the seductions of the moment, a dissonance comparable to the way the captivating pedal steel plays against the more acerbic, twangy, country-blues figures on the guitar. The song unfolds the conflicts of a self who seeks to give up his ticket, his suitcase, his troubles, in embracing the here and now. Yet everything suggests that this night is itself all too transitional.

In 'Lay Lady Lay', it is love and passion that offer the promise of renewal ('His clothes are dirty but his hands are clean'). Emancipation, vision, and inspiration are here emotional and physical, functions of sexual connection ('Whatever colours you have in your mind / I'll show them to you and you'll see them shine').[20] The song expresses desire and outwardly confident seduction ('I long to see you in the morning light'). However, a more unguarded, tentative self is also evident, as in the line 'When he's standing in front of you'. The pause after 'standing' communicates delay and longing, but also uncertainty, because it is followed by the different kind of intonation – languishing, crooning, tender, yearning – that visits the phrase 'in front of you'. The singing is once more an index of a consciousness shadowed by the knowledge of how unsettled are its affirmations, and how difficult it is for two people to make themselves present to each other. It is such uncertainty that expressively accompanies the singer's ambition to hold to the present and to embrace the world again through physical desire. When he sings 'Why wait any longer for the world to begin' (*Lyrics*, 242), he is also singing about himself and his own need to begin again.

Finally, in the album's finest song, 'I Threw It All Away', the desire for possession, for holding manifests itself as a fundamental problem that inhabits love. In a fascinating essay about cliché in Dylan's work, Ricks wrote of how the elements of the formulaic are often regenerated by small twists that make all the difference:

> So if you find someone who gives you all of her love,
> Take it to your heart, don't let it stray…[21]

Ricks brilliantly shows how much is gained by the substitution of 'it' (her love) for the expected 'her' (her person), so that cliché is turned over by a more intriguing, mysterious, private need. The substitution reveals subtle depths in the song because it betrays a strange, familiar human perversity – that we can throw away another person's love, even if we reciprocate it, out of a deep need to treat it as a fixture, a possession. Why? Human beings, the song suggests, would rather throw love away than be subject to its unsettling claims and unpredictability. Identifying the lover with her love, as if it were a treasure, expresses a reifying fantasy of power, but one that sets itself defensively against the reciprocal fear: that in loving one makes oneself disposable, an object for the other person similarly to treasure or discard as they see fit. The more one ponders this, the more the song reveals new nuances. His imagery is of holding her in his arms, of having mountains in the palm of his hand. Beautiful and romantic though the lines are, they suggest still this unconscious pattern of possession, and the refusal of genuine self-presentation and mutuality in love. Even in his most heart-broken expressions of love and self-awareness, a certain reductive, objectifying language returns: 'I must have been mad / I never knew *what I had.*' In such ways, the song reverberates with query about the complex human tendency to discard love itself. The suggestion is ultimately that this is preferable to disowning the fantasy that love is ownership, that love, indeed, is a *thing* that it is within our power to *throw* away. By such means, the song stages the album's issues of holding to the present within the song's scenario of love as having and holding.

In the world of *Nashville Skyline*, then, the fluctuating intensities of the personal subsist movingly within the generic universe of the songs, a little like some solitary figure against a landscape, or a river amidst mountains, and Dylan uses the country idiom to stage issues of location and personal instability. It is ironic how massively influential Dylan's country phase would prove to be, given that *Nashville Skyline* was also so determinedly a way of turning his back on the claims of his audience. It is ironic too, how hugely successful it was at the time, but even in 1969 the listener must surely have felt that it would be impossible that Dylan would settle in this mode, with its use of the present as a kind of bulwark against the divisive forces of past and future, and its restricted themes of love lost and love found. Eric Andersen, visiting Dylan in Woodstock around the time of the album's release, movingly told Scaduto of Dylan's restlessness: 'he wanted to get back to the streets. He told me he didn't have anything to write about, he felt sort of lost being in the woods all the time' (Scaduto, 264). Soon, of course, Dylan and his family were to turn their back on Woodstock for the last time. In the early part of 1969, around the time of the recording of *Nashville Skyline*, they moved house within Woodstock, but by September they would have left it altogether, returning to New York.

Notes

Preface

¹ Except where stated, citations from all interviews are from Artur's edited collection, *Every Mind Polluting Word* (Dont Ya Tell Henry Publications, 2006). Hereafter this is shortened to 'Artur'. The KQED interview is available in audio on the CD: *Bob Dylan: The Classic Interviews, 1965–1966* (New Malden: Chrome Dreams, 2003), and reproduced in Artur, 234–46. An article about the San Francisco Conference and the personnel involved can be found by Blair Miller, 'San Francisco Press Conference 1965: A Closer Look', *The Bridge*, 23 (Winter 2005), 91–6; and on line: http://kripes.proboards.com/index.cgi?board=general&action=display&thread=1 (accessed April 30, 2012).

² This notorious cryptographer-cum-homicidal psychopath would terrorise the city in the following years.

³ *Studio A: The Bob Dylan Reader*, ed. Benjamin Hedin (London: Norton, 2004), 97.

⁴ When pressed on his message by Les Crane on 17 February Dylan had replied in terms that suggest the ideas of movement and temporal self-division that run through this book. His message was: 'Swing. Swing. Love. Be. Is. Was. Were. Double.' ('The Les Crane Show', in Artur, 99) At London Airport on 26 April his words offered a more obvious trope for artistic illumination. He said that his 'real message' was 'Keep a good head and always carry a light bulb' ('London Airport Press Conference', in Artur, 123).

⁵ *Sunday Telegraph*, 26 September 2004, in Artur, 1347.

⁶ Anthony Scaduto, *Bob Dylan: An Intimate Biography* (New York: Grosset & Dunlap, 1971), 18.

⁷ Ashbery continues 'just as religions are beautiful because of the strong possibility they are founded on nothing'. John Ashbery, 'The Invisible Avante Garde', in *Reported Sightings*, ed. David Bergman (New York: Knopf, 1989), 391.

⁸ Interview with Mikal Gilmore, *Rolling Stone*, July 17/31, in Artur, 965, 986.

⁹ Transcribed from *Bob Dylan: The Classic Interviews*.

¹⁰ It is hard to pin down whether Marcus attended the concert of the 3rd or 4th of December or both. In 'Free Speech and False Speech' (reprinted in *Bob Dylan*) he refers to the 3rd (187), but in *Invisible Republic* (32) he refers to hearing 'a still unfinished version of "Visions of Johanna"', which would make it the 4th.

¹¹ Neil Corcoran was struck at Newcastle City Hall on 6 May 1965 by the eloquent ambivalence of withdrawal and invitation in Dylan's body language, and distinctive way of moving: 'It was alluring, don't-give-a-damn, a little come-on that was also a put-off'. See his Preface to *'Do You, Mr Jones?': Dylan among the Poets and Professors* (London: Pimlico, 2003), 1–6. In a comparable way, C.P. Lee gives a fascinating account of the detail and atmosphere of Dylan's concert at the Free Trade Hall, Manchester, 17 May 1966 in *Like*

the Night (Revisited): Bob Dylan and the Road to the Manchester Free Trade Hall (London: Helter Skelter, 2004).

12 Toby Thompson reports Dylan's ex-babysitter Don McKenzie remembering that Bob was 'kind of *slinky* the whole time he was growing up' (Toby Thompson, *Positively Main Street*, new edition [Minneapolis: University of Minnesota Press, 2008], 18).

13 Anthony Scaduto cited Dylan's need also to escape himself:

> During one of our talks, Dylan conceded that I was 'right on target' in discussing the inner Self that he could not repress, that brought him so much pain he had to make himself invisible, and provided him with the strength to reach for higher levels of consciousness. (Scaduto, 18)

14 Mark Polizzotti makes a similar point: 'So powerful is the emotional response it can evoke, at least in a certain kind of listener, that it demands a certain kind of outpouring in return' (Mark Polizzotti, *Highway 61 Revisited* [London: Continuum, 2006], 9).

15 All future references to this film are to the DVD as cited here: *No Direction Home*. Directed by Martin Scorsese (Hollywood: Paramount Home Entertainment, 2005).

16 Perhaps as something like 'authenticity', in Lionel Trilling's famous formulation in *Sincerity and Authenticity* (Cambridge, MA.: Harvard University Press, 1972).

17 These links between Dylan's fabled elusiveness or recalcitrance and the subjective freedom he projects were suggested in a 1974 *New Yorker* piece by Hendrik Hertzberg and George Trow, who described his attractive cultivation of 'mythic distance'. This served an attitude of self-reliance, the ethical resource of one who always seemed 'some distance ahead', living 'by his wits' (Hertzberg and George Trow, 'Dylan', in Hedin, 97).

18 Gilles Deleuze and Claire Parnet, *Dialogues II*, trans. Hugh Tomlinson and Barbara Habberjam (London: Continuum, 2006), 6–7. For Deleuze, creativity was the resource of forces of becoming and self-change that would overturn reactive, imprisoning forms of social subjectivity, themes that return over and again in the following pages.

19 Ralph J. Gleason, 'In Berkeley They Dig Bob Dylan', in Hedin, 61.

20 Sam Shepard, *The Rolling Thunder Logbook* (London: Penguin, 1978), 32.

21 When I talk about the attitude that Dylan transmits, I am not talking about any kind of positive content, or ideology (his Christian phase possibly excepted). Dylan's attitude is rather essentially subtractive, and his influence is a matter of his strengthening our capacity to refuse the attitudes of others, as well as to take on selfhood as a matter of self-refusal, of no longer identifying as they might see us. Even his protest songs, like his Christian songs, after all, are distinguished by twists of perspective, a recalcitrant rejection of the obvious that resist their easy assimilation. Rather, his work involves perpetually the surprising recognition of our own self-opacity, that we do and can experience ourselves in ways that outflank whatever version of the self we have internalised.

22 See, for instance, the following works by Clinton Heylin: *Bob Dylan: The Recording Sessions, 1960–1994* (New York: St Martin's, 1996); *Bob Dylan: A Life in Stolen Moments, Day By Day, 1941–1995* (London: Schirmer, 1996); *Revolution In The Air: The Songs of Bob Dylan*, Vol. 1 (1957–73) (London: Constable, 2009); and *Behind the Shades: The 20th Anniversary Edition* (London: Faber & Faber, 2011).

23 See also Gray's *The Bob Dylan Encyclopedia* (London: Continuum, 2006).

²⁴ Mike Marqusee, *The Wicked Messenger: Bob Dylan and the 1960s* (New York: Seven Stories, 2005).

²⁵ Stephen Scobie, *Alias: Bob Dylan Revisited* (Calgary: Red Deer Press, 2003) and Christopher Ricks, *Dylan's Visions of Sin* (London: Harper Collins, 2003).

²⁶ Daniel Mark Epstein, *The Ballad of Bob Dylan: A Portrait* (London: Souvenir Press, 2011).

²⁷ Robert Shelton, *No Direction Home: The Life and Music of Bob Dylan*, Revised and Updated Edition, edited by Elizabeth Thomson and Patrick Humphries (London: Omnibus, 2011).

²⁸ Paul Williams, *Bob Dylan: Performing Artist 1960–1973, The Early Years* (London: Omnibus, 1991), and *Bob Dylan, Watching The River Flow, 1966–1995* (London: Omnibus, 1966).

²⁹ David Hajdu, *Positively 4th Street* (London: Bloomsbury, 2001), Sean Wilentz, *Bob Dylan in America* (London: The Bodley Head, 2010), and David Pichaske, *Song of the North Country* (London: Continuum, 2010).

³⁰ C.P. Lee, *Like the Night (Revisited): Bob Dylan and the Road to the Manchester Free Trade Hall* (London: Helter Skelter, 2004) and Toby Thompson, *Positively Main Street* (new edition. Minneapolis: University of Minnesota Press, 2008).

³¹ Greil Marcus: *Like a Rolling Stone: Bob Dylan at the Crossroads* (London: Faber & Faber, 2005), and *Bob Dylan: Writings 1968–2010* (New York: Public Affairs, 2010). His *Invisible Republic: Bob Dylan's Basement Tapes* (London: Picador, 1997) was updated as *The Old, Weird America: The World of Bob Dylan's Basement Tapes* (New York: Random House, 2007).

³² Perry Meisel, 'Dylan and the Critics', http://perrymeisel.blogpot.com/2011/03/dylan-and-critics.html (accessed 24 April 2012).

³³ Perry Meisel, *The Myth of Popular Culture* (Oxford: Wiley-Blackwell, 2010), 153.

³⁴ John Hughes, '"It's not British Music, It's American Music": Bob Dylan and Britain', in *Transatlantic Roots Music: Folk, Blues and National Identities*, ed. Neil Wynn and Jill Terry (Jackson: University of Mississippi Press, 2012), 111–37; 'Invisible Now', *The Bridge* 35 (Winter 2009): 83–103; '"Through the Looking Glass": Photographic Images of Bob Dylan in the 1960s', *The Bridge*, 41 (Winter 2011): 27–43; and '"There Was No In-Between": Dylan's Voice in the 1960s', *The Bridge*, 43 (Summer 2012): 54-71.

Part I

I

¹ Richard Williams, *Dylan: A Man Called Alias* (London: Bloomsbury, 1992), 19.

² Greil Marcus, *The Old, Weird America: The World of Bob Dylan's Basement Tapes* (New York: Random House, 2007), xviii.

³ Michael J. Gilmour, *The Gospel According to Bob Dylan* (Louisville: WJK, 2011), 124.

⁴ Nicholas Roe, 'Playing Time', in Corcoran, 86–7.

⁵ Roe's discussion is more subtle and searching than to buy into this view wholesale, but it does leave open-ended the question of how self-process might mean something different than imitation or modelling the self on someone else.

⁶ Marcus, *Invisible Republic*, 87.

⁷ Bob Dylan, *Lyrics 1962–2001* (London: Simon & Schuster, 2004), 168. Hereafter cited within text as *Lyrics*. Where I do not cite the *Lyrics* it is because the Lyrics transcribe the audio incorrectly, or because the song is not included there. The context will make this clear.

⁸ In April 1963, Dylan discussed with Studs Terkel the book he was writing about his 'first week in New York', saying it was about 'someone who's come to the end of one road, y'now, and actually know it's the end of one road and, er, know there's another road there but doesn't exactly know where it is' (Artur, 59).

⁹ In the notes to 'Up To Me': Bob Dylan, *Biograph*, 3 CD set (New York: Columbia, 1998).

¹⁰ Hamlet, a figure similarly burdened by people's intrusions and expectations, has always haunted my perceptions of Dylan since I first saw the pictures of Dylan at Elsinore castle taken on 1 May 1966. In 2002, 8mm home movie footage of Dylan goofing around in suitably antic manner in Elsinore was turned up, after thirty five years in Mickey Jones's garage (*Bob Dylan – 1966 World Tour, the Home Movies*, DVD. Directed by Mickey Jones and Joel Gilbert [Stanmore: Wienerworld, 2004]).

II

¹ Interview with Nat Hentoff, *Playboy*, March 1966, in Artur, 319. He confided to Hentoff in June 1964 that 'I disappear a lot. I go to places where I'm not going to be noticed' (*New Yorker*, 24 October 1964, in Artur, 89).

² In order to register redundancies and hesitancies, I have chosen to transcribe all references from this Press conference from the Chrome Dreams CD mentioned in footnote 1 above.

³ Dave Van Ronk (with Elijah Wald), *The Mayor of MacDougal Street* (Cambridge MA.: Da Capo, 2005), 161.

⁴ Billy James Interview, October 1961, in Artur, 17.

⁵ *The Bootleg Series Vol. 6: Bob Dylan Live 1964, Concert At Philharmonic Hall*, CD (New York: Columbia, 2004).

⁶ Nat Hentoff Interview, *Playboy* March 1966 interview, in Artur, 312.

III

¹ Edna Gundersen Interview, August 31, 1990, in Artur, 1085.

² Kramer's memoir describes Dylan's reluctance in front of the camera and recalls '[a]nother time, at Woodstock, [when] he borrowed one of my cameras and photographed

me. It was a Western shoot-out, with each of us trying to "catch" the other' ... (Daniel Kramer, *Bob Dylan: A Portrait of the Artist's Early Years* [London: Plexus], 2001, 110).

3   For this image by Feinstein (and all others by him), see *Real Moments: Bob Dylan by Barry Feinstein* (London: Vision On/Omnibus, 2009).

4   *The Bootleg Series: Vol. 9: The Witmark Demos: 1962–1964*, CD (New York: Columbia, 2010).

5   *Live At The Gaslight 1962,* CD (New York: Columbia, 2005).

6   Full footage of this embarrassing superstar bout is available on outtakes from *Eat the Document*.

7   The Woodstock shoot was in Summer of 1968, and the *Nashville Skyline* one in March 1969.

8   Elliot Landy, *Landy Vision Photo Gallery*, http://www.landyvision.com/photos/Bob_Dylan/index.html (accessed 24 April 2012).

9   Henry David Thoreau, *Walden* (Oxford: Oxford World's Classics, 1997), 17. And the words that immediately follow are worth citing since they could almost be a motto for this account of Dylan. Thoreau's narrator introduces his work by hoping that:

> You will pardon some obscurities, for there are more secrets in my trade than in most men's, and yet not voluntarily kept, but inseparable from its very nature.

IV

1   Bono's list of Dylan's vocal aspects is worth citing: 'howling, seducing, raging, indignant, jeering, imploring, begging, hectoring, confessing, keening, wailing, soothing, conversational, crooning' ... (Bono, '100 Greatest Singers of All Time', *Rolling Stone*, http://www.rollingstone.com/music/lists/100-greatest-singers-of-all-time-19691231/bob-dylan-19691231#ixzz1dDoXqxyS (accessed 24 April 2012).

2   Robert Shelton, 'Bob Dylan: A Distinctive Stylist', *New York Times*, 29 September 1961. Reprinted in Hedin, 12.

3   Meredith Deliso, 'Holy Greil! Marcus in Brooklyn to discuss Dylan!', *Brooklyn Daily*, 31 October 2010. Reproduced online: http://www.brooklyndaily.com/stories/2010/43/courier-yn_bay_news-24_greilmarcusondylan_-2010_10_29_bk.html (accessed 24 April 24, 2012).

4   Joyce Carol Oates, 'Dylan at 60', in Hedin, 259.

5   Betsy Bowden, *Performed Literature: Words and Music by Bob Dylan* (Maryland: University Press of America, 2001), 3.

6   Tim Riley, *Hard Rain: A Dylan Commentary*, updated edition (New York: Da Capo, 1999), 4.

7   NWC News Desk, 'Mike Masterson talks about Bob Dylan's voice Tuesday, Feb. 12', http://www.northwestcollege.edu/news/detail.dot?inode=180726 (accessed 24 April 2012).

8   Bono might say (with something of a connoisseur's air) in the *Rolling Stone* piece cited above that he can hear the 'iron ore in there, and the bitter cold of Hibbing', but this

might prompt the sceptic to reply that Dylan sounds to him like a castrated coyote, someone who is being strangled, or a poor man's Dock Boggs..

[9] Aidan Day, *Jokerman* (Oxford: Blackwell, 1988), 2.

[10] David Yaffe, *Bob Dylan: Like a Complete Unknown* (New Haven: Yale University Press, 2011), 5.

[11] Daniel Kramer described the paradox of hearing Dylan for the first time on the TV singing 'Hattie Carroll': 'On the screen I saw a young man with a sensitive, poetic face, yet the voice I heard was that of an older, more seasoned man ... This slight young man was doing what many of us feel we should be doing – speaking out' (Kramer, 9).

[12] Bob Dylan, 'Rambler, Gambler', http://www.bobdylan.com/songs/rambler-gambler (accessed 24 April 2012).

[13] Alex Ross, *Listen to This* (London: Fourth Estate, 2011), 289.

[14] Levon Helm and Stephen Davis, *This Wheel's On Fire* (Chicago: Chicago Review Press, 2000), 130.

[15] Cited by Peter James, *Nashville Skyline*, http://warehouseeyes.netfirms.com/nashville.html (accessed 24 April 2012).

[16] As John Wraith, editor of *The Bridge*, put it in an email to me, the voice comes 'full circle' in the 1960s.

V

[1] Larry Sloman, *On the Road With Bob Dylan* (London: Helter Skelter, 2002), 288–89.

[2] In conversation with Epstein (whose book is exceptionally good on this facet of Dylan's career), Pennebaker pithily remarked that 'Normally people ... aren't called upon to take up the lance' (Epstein, 144).

[3] Epstein: There was not a riot among the peaceable folk of Newport the night of 25 July, but there were a lot of very upset and angry folk music fans. They found themselves arguing with more open-minded spectators, younger ones mostly, who thought Dylan's new sound was just fine. The old guard felt betrayed – politically and aesthetically' (Epstein, 160).

[4] Writes Marcus:

> Dylan's performance now seemed to mean that he had never truly been where he had appeared to be only a year before, reaching for that democratic oasis of the heart – and that if he had never been there, those who had felt themselves there with him had not been there. If his heart was not pure, one had to doubt one's own. It was as if it had all been a trick – a trick he had played on them and that they had played on themselves. That was the source of the betrayal felt when Bob Dylan turned to his band, and he along with Danko and Robertson turned to face the drummer, who raised his drumstick, the three guitarists now leaping into the air and twisting to face the crowd as the drummer brought the stick down for the first beat. That was the source of the rage. (Marcus, *Invisible Republic*, 31)

[5] Long-time Bootleg videos of this and other press conferences have recently surfaced on You Tube, but as mentioned above, Chrome Dreams have packaged the San Francisco

conference, along with the Los Angeles 1965 conference, and a 1966 Montreal interview on the CD, *Bob Dylan: The Classic Interviews*.

[6] Of course the dust of rumour circulates around this story too, and in an earlier book, Richard Williams has the janitor as the one cutting the cable, and the event taking place in 1956, *The Golden Chords* apparently having already disbanded (Williams, *Dylan: A Man Called Alias*, 18).

[7] Clearly, so much of the early conflicts about Dylan's political purposes came from misunderstanding on this point. The lyrics of 'To Ramona' counsel the girl in the song against the draining moralism and conformity of identifying simply with political schemes and causes, and Dylan evidenced this time and again, as in 'Positively 4th Street', or the liner notes of *Highway 61 Revisited*: 'Lifelessness said when introducing everybody "go save the world" & "involvement! that's the issue".'At Newport, as Gibbens wrote: 'there was something about that tribal gathering that brought out the young folksinger's antagonism. At the 1963 festival, he'd adopted the bullwhip as a fashion accessory, strolling the grounds with it coiled around his shoulder; while in '64 his protection was a be-shaded minder, just like a presidential secret serviceman' (Gibbens, 124).

[8] Cited by Robert Hilburn, 'Abroad the never-ending tour bus', in *The Dylan Companion*, ed. Elizabeth Thomson and David Gutman (London: Da Capo, 2001), 302.

[9] Ed Bradley, '60 Minutes Interview with Bob Dylan', http://videosift.com/video/60-Minutes-Interview-with-Bob-Dylan (accessed 25 April 2012).

[10] Ralph Waldo Emerson, *The Portable Emerson*, ed. Carl Bode, in collaboration with Malcom Cowley (London: Penguin, 1981), 259.

[11] Mark Ford, "Trust Yourself": Emerson and Dylan', in Corcoran, 127–42.

[12] Ralph Waldo Emerson, 'The Over-Soul', in *The Portable Emerson*, 214.

[13] Pichaske identifies indeed (among a less conscious nostalgia and a sometime 'journey into slippery post-modern relativism)', 'five types of conscious Dylan Journey':

> ... the journey as escape, the allegorical Christian journey from sin to redemption, the journey into memory, the journey which abandons goals and hope and even journey itself, the journey through culture in a universal time present. (Pichaske, 192)

A slightly separate point, the Old Testament, and Dylan's Jewish inheritance remains an oddly neglected strain in Pichaske's discussion, though somewhat at odds with its regional emphasis.

VI

[1] Stanley Cavell, 'Aversive Thinking: Emersonian Representations in Heidegger and Nietzsche', in *Emerson's Transcendental Etudes* (Stanford: Stanford University Press, 2003), 141–70.

[2] Cavell adds immediately the laconic observation that 'I guess this is not realism exactly; but it is not solipsism either.'

[3] There are clear correspondences as well as divergences between this discussion and Scobie's account of 'identity as doubled, divided, or deferred' in his highly nuanced

(though admittedly Derridean) account of the metaphysics of subjectivity in Dylan's work (Scobie, 35).

⁴ Stanley Cavell, *'Cities of Words': Pedagogical Letters on a Register of the Moral Life* (Cambridge MA.: Cambridge, 2004), 2.

⁵ The well-known phrases, from Emerson's 'New England Reformers', and Chapter 1 of Thoreau's *Walden* are discussed by Cavell, *Transcendental Etudes*, 253.

⁶ Gamble, 'The Drifter's Escape', *The Political Art of Bob Dylan*, ed. David Boucher and Gary Browning [Exeter: Imprint-Academic, 2009], 23.

⁷ Sally Bayley, *Home on the Horizon: America's Search for Space, from Emily Dickinson to Bob Dylan* (Oxford: Peter Lang, 2101), 21.

⁸ John Gibbens, *The Nightingale's Code: A Poetic Study of Bob Dylan* (London: Touched Press, 2001), 4.

⁹ Epstein cites Ginsberg's great admiration, as a Buddhist, of the fact that Dylan was always in the moment (Epstein, 268).

¹⁰ Suze Rotolo, *A Freewheelin' Time: A Memoir of Greenwich Village in The Sixties* (London: Aurum, 2008), 105.

¹¹ Both interviews have recently become available on CD: *Bob Dylan: Folksingers' Choice* (Leftfield Media, 2010); and *Bob Dylan: Studs Terkel's Wax Museum* (Leftfield Media 2011).

¹² Shelton, 'Bob Dylan: A Distinctive Stylist', in Hedin, 13.

¹³ Caspar Llewellyn Smith, 'Flash-back', Music Monthly supplement, *The Observer* (Sunday 18 September 2005), 54.

¹⁴ Interview with Paul J. Robbins, LA Free Press, March 1965, in Artur, 115.

¹⁵ 1976 Interview with Neil Hickey, in Artur, 522.

¹⁶ Contrarily, Andrew Gamble identifies Dylan's allegiance at this time might be said to be to 'what the Japanese call the floating world':

> the world which is outside straight society and peopled by jugglers, clowns, vagabonds, criminals, misfits of all kinds, beats, bohemians, hippies, the world of Desolation Row and the St James Hotel, where people apply different standards and higher levels of honesty (Gamble, 45).

¹⁷ Geoff Dyer, *But Beautiful* (London: Abacus, 2009), 201.

VII

¹ 'Dylan's Garbage's Greatest Hits', in *Twenty Minute Fandangos and Forever Changes*, ed. Jonathan Eisen (New York: Random House, 1971), 179.

² Riverrun, 'A. J. Weberman', *Everything 2*, http://everything2.com/title/A.+J.+Weberman (accessed April 24, 2012).

³ Jofre, 'A.J. Weberman vs. Bob Dylan', *Expecting Rain*, http://expectingrain.com/discussions/-viewtopic.php?f=6&t=1619 (accessed April 24, 2012).

⁴ Hence Meisel's mischievous reference to Michael Gray as 'Weberman's upscale counterpart' (Meisel, *Myth of Popular Culture*, 157). But perhaps the truth of Weberman's decodings is even more ironic, since one can say that his drugged up, freak's reductions

replicate not so much literary interpretation as the social impulse to fixity, the nailing down of meaning and 'painting the passports brown', that Dylan's work and subjectivity set out to side-step (*Lyrics*, 181).

⁵ Bob Dylan, *Tarantula* (London: Harper, 2005), 45.

⁶ A film version of one version of the song from *Eat the Document* is available on Scorsese's *No Direction Home*. Other versions can be heard on the collection, *Jewels and Binoculars* which is a compilation of all available press, concert, rehearsal, and studio recordings of 1966 (26 CDs, New Orleans: Vigotone, 2000). Aside from references to *Blonde and Blonde* and the Columbia release of the Free Trade Hall CDs, all references to 1966 recordings in my text are to this collection. By the same token, the collection *1965 Revisited* (14 CDs, Italy: Great Dane Records, 1998) is my source for recordings from 1965 aside from those clearly mentioned in the text.

⁷ *Renaldo and Clara* was initially distributed by Circuit Films in 1978, but later withdrawn by Dylan.

⁸ Though my workings out of the obscure lyrics of this great version differ from those of Daniel Martin's website, he offers a wonderful resource for tracing the variants of this and other songs: http://homepage.mac.com/danielmartin/-Dylan/html/songs/A/AintGonnaGoToHell.html (accessed 24 April 2012).

⁹ Bob Dylan et al., *Don't Look Back – 65 Tour*, DVD. Directed by D. A. Pennebaker (New York: Sony BMG, 2007).

¹⁰ Stephen Scobie, *Alias Bob Dylan Revisited* (Calgary: Red Deer, 2004), 21.

Part II

Chapter 1

¹ In 1966 he has described how as a somewhat disaffected youth he would paint, sing, or write, and 'dissolve myself into situations where I was invisible' (Jules Siegel Interview, March 1966, in Artur, 325).

² John Keats, extract from Letter to George and Tom Keats, 21 December 1817, in *Romanticism: An Anthology*, ed. Duncan Wu (Oxford: Blackwell, 2006), 1351.

³ Indeed, one might describe Dylan's transitional subjectivity in terms of a movement between an inexpressive self, left behind, and an unexpressed self, still pursued.

⁴ The verse from which this line is taken is missing from the transcription in *Lyrics*, but clearly audible on the CBS 3 CD set: *The Bootleg Series Volumes 1–3 (Rare & Unreleased) 1961–1991* (New York: Columbia, 2010).

⁵ Wilfred Mellers, *A Darker Shade of Pale: A Backdrop to Bob Dylan* (London: Faber & Faber, 1984), 118.

⁶ As Marqusee has also noted, this latter collection was clearly rooted in the music, times, places and performers of the late 1920s and 30s: 'these were "race" and "hillbilly" records, released on commercial labels, and recorded between 1927, when new technology boosted the quality of musical reproduction, and 1932, when the depression finished off the

regional markets. The performers were anonymous members of a folk tribe: they included a host of distinctive stylists – Clarence Ashley, Buell Kazee, Blind Lemon Jefferson, Charlie Patton (disguised as the Masked Marvel), the Carter Family, Mississippi John Hurt, Dock Boggs, Blind Willie Johnston' (Marqusee, 34).

[7] According to Hajdu and Heylin (see following references).

[8] Hajdu has Underhill as the driver of the car, where Heylin has Dylan and Underhill being driven by one Dave Berger, who silenced Dylan's singing by telling him to 'Shut the fuck up' (Heylin, *A Life in Stolen Moments*, 12).

[9] See Heylin, *A Life in Stolen Moments*, 12.

[10] Howard Sounes, *Down The Highway: The Life of Bob Dylan* (London: Doubleday, 2001), 79–80.

[11] 'Handsome Molly', *Dylan Chords*, transcribed Eyolf Østrem, http://dylanchords.info/00_misc/-handsome_molly.htm (accessed 24 April 2012).

[12] Marcus, *Bob Dylan*, 152.

[13] Lines transcribed from the recording.

[14] One can see Dylan's lifelong inwardness with death as topic and trope as a feature of the kind of division between past and future that I am identifying in this book with his creative subjectivity.

[15] Scaduto has Kevin Krown remembering Dylan singing 'Song For Woody' in Chicago before Christmas 1961, and speculates that Dylan may have written the song out for Guthrie (rather than composed it), in the copy signed 'Written by Bob Dylan in Mills Bar on Bleeker Street in New York City on the 14th day of February for Woody Guthrie.' It seems likely that Dylan had already sung the song to Guthrie before this date, and possible that he had later conspired with the myth that he wrote it after meeting him (Scaduto, 57).

[16] Clive James, 'Bob Dylan – Bringing Some of It All Back Home', http://www.peteatkin.com/cjcream3.htm 9 (accessed 24 April 2012).

[17] And as the song unfolds, it does something similar, as Ricks brings out in his reading, in seeking a balance between the risks and chances of presumption and excessive modesty (Ricks, *Dylan's Visions of Sin*, 52–5).

[18] Dylan was also to sing, and rework two American folk songs, 'Hang Me, O Hang Me' and 'Cuckoo Bird' and to alter, in performance apparently, the lyrics furnished by Jones for another song, 'Ballad of the Gliding Swan'. Caspar Llewellyn Smith's highly readable and informative *Observer* article, 'Flash-Back' from 18 September 2005, and available on-line, is my source for the Auden connection: http://guardian.co.uk/music/2005/sep/18/folk.popandrock (accessed 24 April 2012).

[19] Hajdu describes Dylan's nightly performances in the different folk clubs, and his often marijuana-driven interactions with Martin Carthy, Eric von Schmidt and Richard Fariña, while Clinton Heylin describes the nuances of the reception that Dylan was afforded by a folk scene that greeted his burgeoning celebrity, performances, and self-regard, with varieties of rapture, dismissal, or outright antagonism (Hajdu, 125–42, and Heylin, *Dylan: Behind the Shades*, 60–65).

[20] Richard William, *Dylan: A Man Called Alias* (London: Bloomsbury, 1992), 46; Tim Cumming, 'Talking Bob Dylan's Blues', *Independent*, 28 September 2005.

²¹ The link is to the Met Office web site: http:www:metoffice.gov.uk/corporate/pressoffice/anniversary/winter1962–63 html (accessed 20 October 2010).

²² Caspar Llewellyn Smith's article cited above follows the alternative tradition, identical in other respects, that the axe was, in fact, a samurai sword. Martin Carthy corroborated this version in a newspaper piece for Dylan's 70th birthday: Various, *Observer*, May 22, 2011, http://www.guardian.co.uk/music/2011/may/22/bob-dylan-70-birthday-present (accessed 24 April 2012).

²³ In an interview with Dave Brazier for the Dylan magazine, *The Telegraph* on 26 September 1991, Carthy spoke of how while Dylan sat

> 'in all those folk clubs in '62, he was just *soaking stuff up all the time*. He heard Louis Killen, he heard Nigel Denver, he heard Bob Davenport, he heard me, he heard The Thameside Four, dozens of people. Anybody who came into The Troubadour, or came into The King & Queen, or The Singers' Club, and he listened and he *just gobbled stuff up*. Huge, huge, huge difference. His coming to England had an enormous impact on his music, and yet nobody's ever said it properly. He came and he learned.' (Dave Brazier, 'A Conversation with … Martin Carthy', *The Telegraph*, 42 [Summer 1992]: 96).

Selections from the interview, and interviews with other prominent figures, are available on: *Bob Dylan Roots*, 'Martin Carthy', http://www.bobdylanroots.com/carthy.html (accessed 25 April 2012).

²⁴ A multi-talented and exuberant figure, Von Schmidt had been a friend since the two of them had attempted a game of croquet in Cambridge, Mass. under the influence of red wine and cannabis. My source for this anecdote is Von Schmidt's fascinating 1996 interview with Elijah Wald: 'Eric Von Schmidt: Adventures of a Folk Buccaneer', http://www.elijahwald.com/vonschmidt.html (accessed 25 April 2012).

²⁵ According to Eric Von Schmidt and Jim Rooney, Dylan had pestered Jackie Washington over and again to perform his minor key version of this extraordinary, surreal, old English folk song. See their book, *Baby Let Me Follow You Down: The Illustrated History of the Cambridge Folk Years* (Amherst: University of Massachusetts, 1979), 219. 'Nottamun Town' was also somewhat bizarrely branded as family property by Jean Ritchie who became litigious with Dylan over his appropriation of her version of the song. Ritchie referred to it as 'the Ritchie Family [Kentucky version]': Roger McGuinn, 'Fair Nottamun Town', http://www.ibiblio.org/jimmy/folkden-wp/?p=6932 (accessed 25 April 2012). An out of court settlement of $5000 dollars was even reached according to Howard Sounes in his *Down The Highway* (132). Finally, Hajdu has Carthy's friend Bob Davenport as the person from whom Dylan learned 'Nottamun Town' and 'The Miner's Lament' on this first visit (Hajdu, 126). This is less persuasive perhaps since Washington's version had made it onto his first LP, *Jackie Washington* for Vanguard Records in December 1962.

²⁶ Though there is the obvious inconsistency between this and Dylan's following remarks that he wrote the song, apparently over several days, during his stay in England in response to the daily papers covering of the missile crisis.

²⁷ Heylin, *Behind the Shades*, 64.

²⁸ Carthy, *The Telegraph*, 1992, 96.

²⁹ An expanded version of Zuckerman's article, '"If There's An Original Thought Out There, I Could Use It Right Now": The Folk Roots of Bob Dylan' is available at http://expectingrain.com/dok/div/influences (accessed 25 April 2012).

30   Bob Dylan, *Chronicles*, Vol. 1 (New York: Simon & Shuster, 2004), 239–41. In Robert Shelton's *No Direction Home* (56), Webber (or Weber as he is there) figures as a 'PhD candidate in Latin literature and a ballad scholar', until Dylan promotes him in *Chronicles* to full tenure, and (seemingly) Anglicises him too.

31   This has long been recognised, though Clinton Heylin usefully cites the lyric with the original spelling (Heylin, *Revolution in the Air*, 87):

> O westron wynde when wyll thow blow
> The small rayne downe can rayne
> Cryst yf my love wer in my armys
> And I yn my bed agayne.

32   Heylin, *A Life in Stolen Moments*, 32.

33   Epstein, 19.

34   Dylan made this connection in the liner notes to *Biograph* This was presumably a version of 'The Water is Wide' that he would revisit so memorably in 1975 with Joan Baez with the Rolling Thunder Revue. A version is available on the CBS anthology from the tour, *The Bootleg Series Vol.5: Bob Dylan Live 1975* (New York: Columbia, 2010).

35   Christopher Ricks, 'Clichés and American English', in Thomson and Gutman, 165.

36   The phrase is from the 1965 song, 'Tombstone Blues' (*Lyrics*, 170).

37   The *Biograph* booklet has no pagination. It is part transcribed in Artur, *Every Mind Polluting Word*, and I will reference that version where possible and except where stated.

38   These are the lines Dylan sings, as opposed to those in the Lyrics.

39   Phil Ochs, 'The Art of Bob Dylan's Hattie Carroll', *Broadside* 48, 20 July, 1964, 2; http://web.cecs.pdx.edu/~trent/ochs/hattie-carroll.html (accessed 25 April 2012).

40   Mike Marqusee, Christopher Ricks and Richard Brown have offered far-reaching accounts of this important song that are worth briefly considering. Ricks brilliantly analyses the song's intrinsic verbal and formal enactments, showing how they contribute to what he takes as its song's informing perspective wherein 'everything in it is seen under the aspect of politics', and under the aspect, too, of our deep need for social and legal justice. It follows from this 'the anger is there all right, but to be contained, to be held in check in contrast' to the analytical restraint that controls the words (Ricks, *Dylan's Visions of Sin*, 222). Marqusee's discussion places verbal analysis in the service of returning the song to its external contexts and origins (Marqusee, 87–8), whereas Brown (Boucher and Browning, eds, 56–61) is concerned with seeing the song's dominant context as the aesthetic, in the Kantian sense that places the political under the rubric of a play of reflective judgement which signals through feeling teleologically, indefinitely, to progress as in his essay 'Idea For a Universal History From a Cosmopolitan Point of View' in Immanuel Kant, *On History*, ed. Lewis White Beck (New York: Macmillan, 1989), 11–26.

41   Marqusee's book offers a highly nuanced and detailed account of the complex and intolerable position Dylan found himself in the 1960s, writing 'both within the historical tide and against it', seeking to protect his autonomy and privacy amidst the ever-shifting configurations and imbrications of the personal and political (Marqusee, 120). Marqusee's account of Dylan's reactions to these shifting currents parallels that given here in many ways, insofar as Dylan's desire to opt out becomes the increasingly personal reaction against those who attempted to co-opt him, whether for commercial, ideological, or radical purposes.

Chapter 2

¹ *The Other Side of the Mirror: Bob Dylan Live at Newport Folk Festival 1963–65.* Directed by Murray Lerner (New York: Sony BMG, 2007).

² Lawrence Wilde, 'Dylan's Expressionist Period' in Boucher and Gary Browning, 106. His argument, more broadly, is that 'Chimes of Freedom' inaugurates a movement from protest to a 'social expressionist' mode for these songs, constituting a visionary mode of social critique and subversive evocation that provides one powerful strand until the end of *Highway 61 Revisited* at least: 'The emphasis switches to a biting critique of the everyday social practices and attitudes which sustain a society in thrall to the pursuit of wealth and the preservation of relations of domination and subordination', songs which evoke an 'imaginary counter-culture' (133).

³ Epstein is particularly good at bringing out the grotesque and eviscerating viciousness practised by Dylan, Neuwirth, Grossman et al., as well as the circumstances that brought it about. The pages in which he describes encounters with Phil Ochs, Brian Jones, and (even, alas) Dave Van Ronk are vivid, to say the least (Epstein, 129–38).

⁴ Epstein writes that '[t]he crowd at the Newport Folk Festival in 1964 was dismayed that he played songs like 'It Ain't Me, Babe' and 'Mr Tambourine Man' instead of the Brechtian dramas of social protest (Epstein, 145).

⁵ Irwin Silber, 'An Open Letter to Bob Dylan', *Sing Out* (November, 1964), http://www.edlis.org/twice/threads/open_letter_to_bob_dylan.html (accessed 25 April 2012).

⁶ Wilentz, *Bob Dylan in America* (London: Bodley Head, 2010), 80.

⁷ Heylin identifies a decisive creative nexus at this time in influences that open the mind by way of the body – pointing to the combined influence of hallucinogenic drugs and Rimbaud's aesthetic of 'dérèglement de tous les sens', whereby the artist surrenders rationality to possibly incomprehensible visions (Heylin, *Behind the Shades*, 151.

⁸ Shelton's *No Direction Home* offers a very full account of this trip (171–8).

⁹ Heylin, *Stolen Moments*, 54.

¹⁰ The word 'much' isn't transcribed in *Lyrics*.

¹¹ Heylin writes of the early days of the *Bringing It All Back Home* session:

> It may have taken Dylan several months and much soul-searching, but the path laid out by Hammond [Jr] and The Animals proved irresistible, even though when he turned up at Columbia Studio A for the first time since the *Another Side* session, it was to record solo, with piano and guitar [...] In fact for his fifth album, Dylan clearly conceived of some kind of mix of acoustic and electric, as with the original *Freewheelin'*. (Heylin, *Behind the Shades*, 174–5)

¹² See Heylin for Neville Kellett's account to C.P. Lee of an encounter in England in 1964 which suggests that Grossman was handling drugs of a stronger kind for Dylan. Kellett narrates a furtive minute or two before Dylan went on stage. Continues Heylin: 'the fact is that Dylan was stoned to Betsy and back in a matter of minutes ... Dylan's description, that he was "very strung out"' after Suze and him split up, begins to acquire a degree of credence' (Heylin, *Behind the Shades*, 154). Of course, more recently Dylan's confession of a heroin habit in the early 1960s has surfaced, with revelations of comments made to Robert Shelton in March 1966. The fact that the comments were both made to

Shelton, in this most intimate interview, on a night-flight, and then edited out, gives them a high measure of credence: Rebecca Jones, 'Dylan Tapes Reveal Heroin Addiction', *Today*, Radio 4, 23 May 2011, http://news.bbc.co.uk/today/hi/today/newsid_9492000/9492886.stm (accessed 25 April 2012).

[13] Hajdu writes of early 1964 that, '[f]or months, Dylan's poetry, prose-poems, and other literary experiments had been drawing him into personal creative territory [...] When he started writing songs in earnest again, he picked up where his work for the page had taken him, eschewing topical and political themes to write songs in a new style – introspective, ruminative work about his own life, with dense, symbolic lyrics and music drawing upon folk, blues, rhythm, and pop influences. Whether or not he thought he had found what he had been seeking on that cross-country road trip, the music Dylan wrote afterward was like a dream memory of his stops, a mixture of Carl Sandburg, New Orleans, Woody Guthrie, and The Beatles, filtered through his increasingly distinctive voice' (Hajdu, 202).

[14] Nat Hentoff Interview, *New Yorker*, October 24, 1964, in Artur, 84.

[15] The issue also raises confounding questions about those very distinguishing gifts of taste and intuition so evident in his work. Many questions have become clichés, bearing on what appears a strange perversity, indifference or lack of discrimination: Why did he pull the first version of *Blood on The Tracks*? Why was he reluctant to release 'Blind Willie MacTell', 'Ain't Gonna Go to Hell for Anybody', 'Dignity', 'Caribbean Wind'? Why no official live album of the wonderful Earls Court concert of 30 June 1981, or of the many covers of folk songs from the late 80s and early 90s? Sean Egan opines (like many others) that the 'long tradition of leaving great songs in the vaults ... in ways' even suggests at times 'deliberate self-sabotage' (Sean Egan, *The Mammoth Book of Bob Dylan* [London: Robinson, 2011], 8).

[16] Though the Dali-meets-Disney imagery on 'Farewell, Angelina' is perhaps overly experimental.

[17] The image is supposedly suggestive of a turning LP, with Dylan at the centre of the musical world.

[18] Jean Tamarin, 'Bringing It All Back Home', *The Cambridge Companion to Bob Dylan*, ed. Kevin J.H. Dettmar (Cambridge: Cambridge University Press, 2009), 132.

[19] Heylin, *Revolution in the Air*, 208; Wilentz, *Dylan in America*, 100.

[20] David Pichaske's neat summation is close to my view: 'Whereas the rat-race of 'It's Alright, Ma' is inescapable and the 'Gates of Eden' remain closed and inaccessible, the tambourine-music-machine-ship transports Dylan into a rebirth in music and art' (Pichaske, 130).

[21] Mark Polizzotti writes that the song 'with its triumphant put-downs and sadly mocking tone, points the way in everything but arrangement to 'Like a Rolling Stone', Dylan's next release' (Polizzotti, 18).

[22] Mark Ford, 'Bob Dylan and the Vignette', unpublished lecture delivered at 'The Seven Ages of Dylan', a conference at the University of Bristol, 24 May 2011, 5.

Chapter 3

[1] James Brewer, *Beyond the Roots of American Popular Music: The Legacy of Alan Lomax* (13 June 2003) World Socialist Web Site: http://www.wsws.org/articles/2003/jun2003/lom-j13.shtml.

[2] Phillip Larkin, *All What Jazz* (London: Faber & Faber, 1985), 151.

[3] Gray, *Bob Dylan Encyclopaedia*, 313–14.

[4] Perhaps there is an echo between this and Dylan's boyhood heroes, 'Robin Hood and St. George the Dragon Slayer', as he confided to Archibald McLeish (Bob Dylan, *Chronicles*, Vol. 1, 113).

[5] Polizzotti, 22.

[6] Stanley Cavell, 'Aversive Thinking: Emersonian Representations', *Emerson's Transcendental Etudes*, ed. David Justin Hodge (Stanford: Stanford University Press, 2003), 141–70. He suggests as well (ironically enough) that Emerson's thought underpins the Nietzschean vision that predominates in what is usually seen as the alternative tradition of contemporary continental thought.

[7] Bruce Springsteen, 'Speech at the Rock-and-Roll Hall of Fame', in Thomson and Gutman, 286–7. Also, 'Bruce Springsteen inducts Bob Dylan into Rock and Roll Hall of Fame 1988', http://www.youtube.com/-watch?v=SRu66l3QI_U (accessed April 25, 2012).

[8] Marcus, *Invisible Republic*, 37.

[9] Polizzotti, 128–31.

[10] Jim Miller, 'Bob Dylan', in Thomson and Gutman, 31.

[11] Ricks, *Dylan's Visions of Sin*, 186. The song as a whole is discussed on pages 179–92.

[12] Robert Polito, *Highway 61 Revisited*, in Dettmar, 138–9.

[13] Heylin surmises that the song was written in the meantime, as a reaction perhaps, and maybe incorporating off-cuts from epic drafts of 'Like a Rolling Stone' (Heylin, *Revolution in the Air*, 255–6). While these suggestions appear very plausible, his suggestion that the song might be addressed to a woman, as part of the fall-out of a relationship, appears less likely, particularly given the fact that Dylan had lived on 4th Street when in Greenwich Village. I find myself in agreement on this one with Christopher Ricks who outlines many of the textual cruxes of this issue (Ricks, *Visions of Sin*, 65–8).

[14] Collectively, one might say, these songs could have been entitled 'Don't Love Nothing at all, except Hatred'.

[15] Dylan is like no-one in that song so much as the youthful Cassius Clay/Mohammed Ali, that other unmisgiving, sublimely gifted, hero of the mid-60s, and another great mover inhabiting the eye of cultural as well as personal change ...

[16] Perhaps one might even take this as a way of saying that rationalist philosophy is an illusion, that philosophy is merely a reflective component embodied within art.

[17] I have always taken Dylan to be singing 'To the old folks home *in* the college' rather than '*and* the college' as it is always transcribed.

[18] Hunter S. Thompson, 'Excerpt from Owl-Farm – Winter of '68', in Hedin, 70.

[19] In the televised KQED San Francisco conference, when asked which 'commercial interest' he might choose if he had to 'sell out' to one, Dylan replies 'Ladies garments'. In a May 1965 *New Musical Express* questionnaire, he indicates his personal and professional

ambitions as respectively: 'To be a waitress', and 'To be a stewardess'. On the autumn 1965 Les Crane show he says that he will be playing his mother in the horror Cowboy movie he and Ginsberg were planning. In the *Playboy* interview of March 1966, he says that 'I guess I've always wanted to be Brigitte Bardot, too [as well as Anthony Quinn]; but I don't really want to think about that too much' (Artur, 237,142, 193, 100).

Chapter 4

1   In Epstein's terms, it is a song about failed promises, and the 'penitentiary' of a life where 'we are all stuck if we are not honest enough to envision a greater or more compelling reality or form of penitence' (Epstein, 291).

2   For a discussion of the Village's bohemian provenance, see Hajdu, 33–4.

3   Heylin, *Revolution in the Air*, 274.

4   Howard Sounes recounts the anecdotes where Dylan denied to Rambling Jack Elliott, in front of Sara, the marriage of a few days earlier, or the time on tour when he diverted her into a closet when two disc jockeys came back stage (Sounes, 193, 207).

5   Greil Marcus, 'Epilogue: Treasure Island', in *Stranded: Rock and Roll for a Desert Island*, ed. Greil Marcus (New York: Capo, 1996), 267.

6   In a related way, Michael Coyle and Debra Rae Cohen have talked of the 'destabilizing impulse' of the songs, their way of resisting exegesis by an endless displacement of positions of knowledge, such as in Dylan's surreal treatment of names, numbers, definite articles, or self-undermining use of the word 'obviously in the line 'anybody can be just like me obviously' (Michael Coyle and Debra Rae Cohen, *Blonde on Blonde*, in Dettmar, 143). At the same time, though, this destabilising impulse is inseparable from the counter-balancing artistic conjuration of open-ended effects of transport and grace. The songs are sure only about their aesthetic power to express a mind unresolved between the real and the surreal, a mind that fashions something inexhaustible and eloquent out of what seems exhausted and inexpressive.

7   Wilentz brings a historian's forensic eye, as well as a critic ears to Columbia's files and recording reels, which allows him to offer a fascinating account of the evolution of the songs.

8   See also Sean Wilentz, *Oxford American Magazine*, 58, 2007, *http://theband.hiof. no/articles/mystic_nights-_tmobob.html* (accessed 25 April 2012).

9   The mythology of the session requires of course, that others assert the diametric opposite, as in Wilentz's account:

> After a couple of quick phone calls, the trombonist Wayne Butler showed up, the only extra musician (with McCoy playing trumpet) whom Johnston thought was needed. But at this point in the story recollections clash once again. Legend has it – and more than one of the Nashville musicians have affirmed – that at someone's insistence, possibly Dylan's, potent marijuana got passed around, along with a batch of demonic drink ordered in from a local bar. But not everybody was interested. And Charlie McCoy, who by all accounts did not partake, denies categorically that *anybody* was intoxicated. 'It just didn't happen', he asserts, either at this session or (with isolated exceptions) at any of the many thousands of others on which he has performed in Nashville. Al Kooper, who had given

up alcohol years earlier, agrees that the *Blonde on Blonde* sessions were sober, and says that the hyper-professionals, Dylan and Albert Grossman, would never have permitted pot or drink inside the studio. (Wilentz, *Oxford American Magazine* (see reference above). An almost identical discussion can be found in Wilentz's *Bob Dylan in America*, 123.

[10] The hobo is a Blakean figure, reminiscent of the fluent 'traveller' in the fragment 'Never seek to tell thy love' (William Blake, *The Complete Poems*, ed. Alicia Ostriker (London: Penguin, 1977), 134.

[11] In a suggestive passage, Gibbens identifies as a dominant trope in *Blonde on Blonde* the image of '[t]he room which someone can't get out of or can't get into' [Gibbens, 239]).

[12] In this way, Dylan again is the heir to Emerson or Whitman, as one who expresses, and figures, the common, repressed, fitful truth of the inner life, secreted beneath social fictions of identity.

[13] I hear the line as 'the skeleton keys in the rain' rather than the 'skeleton keys and the rain' (*Lyrics*, 194).

[14] Again, my hearing of these songs differs from *Lyrics* which has 'No, I wasn't very cute to him' (197) and 'Well, the hobo jumped up / He came down natur'lly /After he stole my baby / Then he wanted to steal me' (192).

[15] Mark Jakobson, 'Tangled Up in Bob', in *Da Capo Best Music Writing 2002*, ed. Jonathan Lethem (Cambridge, MA.: Da Capo, 2002), 105.

[16] Marqusee makes this point when he says that Dylan creates an art of liberation out of experiences of strandedness in *Blonde and Blonde*.

[17] Interview with Ron Rosenbaum, *Playboy*, March 1978, in *Artur*, 539.

[18] Lee memorably asks:

> Have you ever been on the road? Have you ever covered the crazy miles of endless highways gazing through a bus window at nothing? You become psychically dislocated, your spirit can't settle. You're stuck in the loop with the Beast and the Beast is always hungry. It demands things, things you wouldn't dream of back in the safety of your home, but you don't have a home anymore. Just an endless chain of hotel rooms, all blurring into one another. Rooms that the Beast claims as his territory, stalking through your chamber with two of his Daemons, Sleep, and Nosleep. (Lee, *Like the Night*, 45)

[19] The French philosopher Gilles Deleuze identified Dylan as someone whose creativity was coterminous with the charmed operations of a form of becoming that eludes the given and conventional forms of personality, and that affirms its condition as a charmed negotiation of self-renewal in pure contingency, chance:

> In life there is a sort of awkwardness, a delicacy of health, a frailty of constitution, a vital stammering which is someone's charm. Charm is the source of life just as style is the source of writing. Life is not your history – those who have no charm have no life, it is as though they are dead. But the charm is not the person. It is what makes people be grasped as so many combinations and so many unique chances from which such a combination has been drawn. It is a throw of the dice which necessarily wins, since it affirms chance sufficiently instead of detaching or mutilating chance or reducing it to probabilities. Thus through each fragile combination a power of life is affirmed with a strength, an obstinacy, an unequalled persistence in the being [...] They are not people, but the figure of their own combination [...] Their only aim of writing is life, through the combinations which it draws. (Deleuze and Parnet, *Dialogues*, 4)

[20] Almost universally transcribed as 'Play fucking loud', I have never been able to hear it that way.

[21] Charles Nicholl, 'Just Like the Night', in *The Bob Dylan Companion*, ed. Thomson and Gutman (New York: Da Capo, 2000), 122.

[22] In a memorable passage in *Mystery Train*, Marcus writes of how 'the UK performances explode in all directions and reverse themselves in an instant, a dance of will and chance, risk and pleasure, a physical liberation based in the inner control of perfect timing' (*Mystery Train: Images of America in Rock'n'Roll Music* [New York: Penguin/Plume, 2008], 257).

[23] Johnny Black, 'Dylan in 1966', in *The Mammoth Book of Bob Dylan*, edited by Sean Egan (London: Running Press, 2011), 116.

[24] The most famous harmonica solo is probably the one at De Montfort Hall in Leicester, featured on *Eat The Document*.

[25] Johnny Black, 'Dylan in 1966', 122–3.

Chapter 5

[1] Sid Griffin, *Million Dollar Bash: Bob Dylan, The Band, and the Basement Tapes* (London: Jawbone, 2007), 53.

[2] Marcus, *Invisible Republic*, 240.

[3] 'Robbie Robertson Talks About Bob Dylan and the Basement Tapes', http://www.youtube.com/watch?v=1lD-64YsRg0&feature=related (accessed April 26, 2012).

[4] Andy Gill, *Bob Dylan: The Stories Behind the Songs, 1962-1968* (London: Carlton, 2011), 158–9.

[5] All of this raises, though, an important crux. Writing on the basement tapes, Alex Abramovich finds himself drawn – somewhat reluctantly it seems – to making qualifying, moderating, even faintly dismissive, statements about their quality and importance, in the light of their circumstances, and perhaps the often deprecatory remarks of the performers themselves:

> Which is to say that the charm of *The Basement Tapes* might have less to do with the quality of the songs themselves than with the informal, experiential qualities of the recordings: the false starts, botched verses, buried vocals, and muttered obscenities which mark any given set of home recordings, as well as the no-fidelity which gives home recordings an aura of low-rent, audio-verité authenticity. Alex Abramovich, 'The Basement Tapes', *The Cambridge Companion to Bob Dylan* (Cambridge: Cambridge University Press, 2009), 153.

> And yet, to my ears, this music is perhaps the most remarkable, and sustained evidence of Dylan's spontaneous, unpremeditated form of inspiration, call it genius. To put it another way: how could one make the case for Dylan's talents while dismissing this material, for all its occasional unevenness? For my purposes the need, clearly is to make the case for them as central to his achievement and our understanding of his gifts, notwithstanding even Dylan's own remark that 'I never really liked *The Basement Tapes*. I mean they were just songs we had done for the publishing company, as I remember […] I wouldn't have put 'em out' (Artur, 771).

⁶   Marcus's description of the tapes for these nights is marvellous (*Invisible Republic*, 72–86), and I have transcribed the Hudson quotation from pages 80–81.

⁷   So, in a related vein, Marcus noted on the original liner notes, the songs often deal with final things, with death, with 'pointed themes': 'put up or shut up, obligation, escape, homecoming, owning up, the settling of accounts past due'.

⁸   All references to the *Basement Tapes* songs are transcribed by me from the 4 CD *Tree With Roots* collection (New York: Scorpio, 2001) where the lyrics are not available in *Lyrics*.

⁹   Indeed, even the ephemeral and chance nature of many of the recordings contributes to their aura of eloquent contingency, as with fragments like '900 Miles', or 'Po' Lazarus'. The latter, a ballad of death-by-cop sung by Dylan in Bonnie Beecher's apartment in 1961 is here given a leisurely bluesy rendition before being untimely chopped.

¹⁰   Writing of 'I'm Not There' Sid Griffin: '[Garth] Hudson has commented that Dylan would become inspired or The Hawks would have a riff going, and some chord changes, and that was all that was needed, that Dylan would come down into the basement and start singing along through nonsense lyrics, scat singing, or even la-la las. What is heard here is only a step or two forward from that kind of thing, and yet the performance is masterful … on paper the words are incomplete. When heard performed, when heard sung by Dylan, they seem monumental … The effect is like an out-of-focus photo slowly coming into focus or like a blurred photograph of something you recognize as familiar but cannot place' (Sid Griffin, *Million Dollar Bash* [London: Jawbone, 2007], 194).

¹¹   Clinton Heylin trusts in the authenticity of a typescript that would have the word 'height' in place of 'house' here. See *Revolution in the Air* (London: Constable, 2009), 341.

¹²   'Just another discarded ditty, it relies on the usual wordplay and slurred diction to obscure any pretence to a deeper meaning' (Heylin, *Revolution in the Air*, 336).

¹³   Clearly Dylan himself is not consciously intending, controlling or processing the kinds of meaning I illustratively tease out in these songs, but his consciousness is possessed by such possibilities.

¹⁴   The *Lyrics* has 'I plan it all and I take my place' (*Lyrics*, 277).

¹⁵   The *Lyrics* has 'ev'ryone / Must always flush out his house / If he don't expect to be / Goin' round housing flushes' (*Lyrics*, 297).

¹⁶   In November 1977, interviewed by Ron Rosenbaum for *Playboy*, Dylan was pressed on what he had meant by saying that the accident meant that 'Something had to be evened up'. His joking reply was that 'I meant that the wheel had to be aligned' (Artur, 554).

¹⁷   In image and process, the *Basement Tapes* sessions became massively influential, and The Stones and The Beatles would seek to imitate the companionable looseness and creativity on *Exile on Main Street* and *Let it Be*.

¹⁸   Johnny Cash ('Belshazar', 'Big River', 'Folsom Prison Blues', 'Still in Town'), Bobby Bare ('All American Boy'), The Carter Family ('Wildwood Flower'), Charles Badger Clark ('Spanish is the Loving Tongue'), John Lee Hooker ('Tupelo', 'I'm in the Mood for Love'), The Rays ('Silhouettes'), Bo Diddley ('Bring it On Home'), Gene Pitney ('Baby, Ain't That Fine'), Bob Nolan ('Cool Water'), Eric Von Schmidt ('Joshua Gone Barbados'), Elvis Presley ('I Forgot to Remember to Forget'), Hank Snow ('I Don't Hurt Anymore', 'A Fool Such as I'), Derinda Morgan ('Confidential'), Pete Seeger ('The Bells

of Rhymney'), Ian Tyson ('Four Strong Winds', 'One Single River', 'The French Girl'), Flat and Scruggs ('Rock, Salt and Nails'), Blind Lemon Jefferson ('See That My Grave is Kept Clean'), Curtis Mayfield ('People Get Ready'), Woody Guthrie ('Nine Hundred Miles'), and Hank Williams ('You Win Again', 'The Stones That You Throw').

[19] Raymond Foye writes of how Harry Smith had been staying with Allan Ginsberg in his East 12th Street apartment in the summer of 1985 when Dylan came round to play the poet a tape of 'Empire Burlesque'. Smith, who had just gone to bed, disappointed and impressed Dylan by refusing to get up and meet him as he sat with Foye and Ginsberg. 'Turn down that music! Don't you know I am trying to sleep!' he shouted from his bed (Raymond Foye, 'The Night Bob Came Round', *Wanted Man: In Search of Bob Dylan*, ed. John Bauldie [London: Penguin, 1992], 157).

[20] 'It's a rich and idiosyncratic selection of American people's music (the sole non-American number is Rimsky-Korsakov's "Flight of the Bumble Bee"' (Marqusee, 225).

[21] The kinds of reanimation and depersonalisation involved can bring to mind T.S. Eliot's rather necromantic account of literary influence in 'Tradition and the Individual Talent'.

Chapter 6

[1] Shelton suggests that relations were more cordial at the concert (Shelton, *No Direction Home*, 271).

[2] Toby Thompson, interview with Terry Kelly for *The Bridge*, http://www.two-riders.co.uk/toby.html (accessed 26 April 2012).

[3] John Howells, 'The Story Behind *Self Portrait*', http://www.punkhart.com/dylan/reviews/self_portrait.html (accessed 26 April 2012).

[4] Set in a mythological landscape of outlaws and pilgrims, the songs clearly bore on the roots of American music and cultural consciousness and their influence is clear on so much of The Band's self-fashioning, and the various strains of the Americana movement from this time. The album, together with *Nashville Skyline*, could be taken also as one of the first alt-country albums, as well as a galvanising influence on British equivalents like Fairport Convention from around this time.

[5] *John Wesley Harding*, Wikipedia, http://en.wikipedia.org/wiki/John_Wesley_Harding (accessed 26 April 26, 2012).

[6] Cited by Tim Riley, *Hard Rain: A Dylan Commentary* (New York: Da Capo Press, 1997), 177.

[7] It is scarcely surprising perhaps that rumours would persist that the faces of The Beatles were detectable in the tree behind Dylan.

[8] Dylan's sequencing of songs on an album is a study in itself, and it is certainly possible to hear these songs as a continuation of the dialogue of 'Dear Landlord', perhaps stimulated by Dylan's deteriorating relationship with Grossman and musical executives.

[9] In *Chronicles*, Archibald MacLeish reportedly replied, astutely, to Dylan's statement that Hood and 'St George the Dragon Slayer' were his childhood heroes by saying that 'You wouldn't want to get on their bad side' (Dylan, *Chronicles*, Vol. 1, 113). One thinks here too of songs like 'A Roving Blade' (sung by Dylan in the late 1990s).

10   Similarly, in the second verse the account of the gunfight ends mystifyingly with the lines about the 'situation there' being 'all but straightened out' and the statement, 'For he was always known / To lend a helping hand' (*Lyrics,* 221).

11   Robert Shelton, *No Direction Home* (London: Omnibus, 2011), 266.

12   In interviews with John Cohen and Happy Traum for *Sing Out* that took place in June and July Dylan is typically contrarian about the war, about reading Gideon's bibles in a hotel room, and about his interest in parables: Biblical ones in particular, though also those of Khalil Gibran and Franz Kafka (Artur, 407–9).

13   Robert Christgau, *John Wesley Harding,* in *Hedin,* 67.

14   David Pichaske makes the connection to Kafka on page 272 of *Song of the North Country.*

15   As a further example, consider again 'I Dreamed I Saw St Augustine'. This is a song that can be taken as a religious parable, about a saint killed by those who resist his message. However, even within this, Augustine's fate and message can be taken in radically different ways. Firstly, for instance, one might take Augustine straightforwardly as a martyr confronting the worldliness of those who kill him. Secondly, though, wearing a 'coat of solid gold', and addressing 'ye gifted kings and queens' he could be taken as someone who comes to suffer because he has too much embraced the world. Thirdly, he might be take to be ironically counselling us against searching for martyrs, to be preaching that we must embrace spiritual values as immanent, within the world seen *sub specie aeternitas.* From this last viewpoint, his 'sad complaint' is that there is only this world, redeemed though it is by the eternal values that inhere within it. We need to understand that we have our gifts, we rule our own worlds, and must go on our own ways. Further, though, as a song about the need to resist interpretation we can take the singer's final despair as produced by the terrifying ironic revelation of how human beings can void the world of value, while perpetrating horrific collective acts of punishment in pursuit of transcendent illusions, elevating significances.

16   Court Carney, "'A Lamp is Burning in All Our Dark': Bob Dylan and Johnny Cash', *Highway 61 Revisited: Bob Dylan's Journey from Minnesota to the World,* ed. Colleen J. Sheehy and Thomas Swiss (Minneapolis: University of Minnesota Press, 2009), 40.

17   Paul Williams makes the same point: 'In *Nashville Skyline* he gives his fans as little of the "old Dylan" as possible (his refusal to rebel itself an act of characteristic rebelliousness' (*Bob Dylan: Performing Artist,* 251).

18   James Wolcott, 'Bob Dylan Beyond Thunderdome', in Thomson and Gutman, 277.

19   So perhaps one needs to revise one's own clichés and acknowledge perhaps that such a tension is the internal dynamic of much, even all, country music.

20   Ricks makes the comparison with Donne's 'To His Mistress Going to Bed': 'this love's hallow'd temple, this soft bed' (Ricks, *Dylan's Visions of Sin,* 157).

21   Christopher Ricks, 'Clichés and American English', in Thomson and Gutman, 165.

Select Bibliography

Abramovich, Alex. 'The Basement Tapes'. In *The Cambridge Companion to Bob Dylan*, edited by Kevin Duttmar, 150–54. Cambridge: Cambridge University Press, 2009.

Ashbery, John. 'The Invisible Avante-Garde'. In *Reported Sightings*, edited by David Bergman, 389–95. New York: Knopf, 1989.

Artur (editor). *'Every Mind Polluting Word': A Collection of Speeches, Interviews, Press Conferences, etc,* 2nd edition. Dont Ya Tell Henry publications, 2011. http://content.yudu.com/-Library/A1plqd/BobDylanEveryMindPol/resources/637.htm (accessed 30 June 2012).

Bauldie, John (editor). *'Wanted Man': In Search of Bob Dylan*. London: Penguin, 1992.

Bauldie, John. 'Bob Dylan in New York – January to April 1961'. In *Wanted Man: In Search of Bob Dylan*, edited by John Bauldie, 28–45. London: Penguin, 1992.

Bauldie, John. 'A Meeting with A.J. Weberman, Summer of '82'. In *The Mammoth Book of Bob Dylan*, edited by Sean Egan, 330–4. London: Running Press, 2011.

Bayley, Sally *Home on the Horizon: America's Search for Space, from Emily Dickinson to Bob Dylan*. Oxford: Peter Lang, 2011.

Black, Johnny. 'Dylan in 1966'. In *The Mammoth Book of Bob Dylan*, edited by Sean Egan, 108–25. London: Running Press, 2011.

Bono. 'Dylan at 60'. In *Studio A: The Bob Dylan Reader*, edited by Benjamin Hedin, 254–5. New York: Norton, 2004.

Boucher, David and Gary Browning (editors). *The Political Art of Bob Dylan*. Exeter: Imprint-Academic, 2009.

Bowden, Betsy. *Performed Literature: Words and Music of Bob Dylan*. Maryland: University Press of America, 2001.

Boyd, Joe. 'Newport '65'. In *Wanted Man: In Search of Bob Dylan*, edited by John Bauldie, 65–74. London: Penguin, 1992.

Brown, Richard. 'Highway 61 and Other American States of Mind'. In *'Do You, Mr Jones?': Bob Dylan with the Poets and Professors*, edited by Neil Corcoran, 193–220. London: Pimlico, 2003

Brown, Richard. 'Bob Dylan's Critique of Judgement: "Thinkin' about the Law".' In *The Political Art of Bob Dylan*, edited by David Boucher and Gary Browning, 50–57. Exeter: Imprint-Academic, 2009.

Bulson, Eric. *'The Freewheelin' Bob Dylan'*. In *The Cambridge Companion to Bob Dylan*, edited by Kevin Duttmar, 125–30. Cambridge: Cambridge University Press, 2009.

Cavell, Stanley. *'Cities of Words': Pedagogical Letters on a Register of the Moral Life*. Cambridge MA.: Harvard University Press, 2004.

Cavell, Stanley. *Philosophy The Day After Tomorrow*. Cambridge MA.: Harvard University Press, 2005.

Cavell, Stanley. *Emerson's Transcendental Etudes*, edited by David Justin Hodge. Stanford: Stanford University Press, 2003.

Christgau, Robert. 'John Wesley Harding'. In *Studio A: The Bob Dylan Reader*, edited by Benjamin Hedin, 84–7. New York: Norton, 2004.

Cohen, John. *Young Bob: John Cohen's Early Photographs of Bob Dylan* (New York: Powerhouse Books, 2003.

Cott, Jonathan (editor). *Dylan on Dylan: The Essential Interviews*. London: Hodder & Stoughton, 2006.

Corcoran, Neil. 'Introduction: Writing Aloud'. In *'Do You, Mr Jones?': Bob Dylan with the Poets and Professors*, edited by Neil Corcoran, 7–24. London: Pimlico, 2003.

Corcoran, Neil. 'Death's Honesty'. In *'Do You, Mr Jones?': Bob Dylan with the Poets and Professors*, edited by Neil Corcoran, 143–74. London: Pimlico, 2003.

Court, Carney. '"A Lamp is Burning in All Our Dark": Bob Dylan and Johnny Cash'. In *Highway 61 Revisited: Bob Dylan's Journey from Minnesota to the World*, edited by Colleen J. Sheehy and Thomas Swiss, 39–43. Minneapolis: University of Minnesota Press, 2009.

Coyle, Michael and Cohen, Debra Rae. 'Blonde on Blonde'. In *The Cambridge Companion to Bob Dylan*, edited by Kevin J. H. Dettmar, 143–9. Cambridge: Cambridge University Press, 2009.

Crowe, Cameron. Interview (August–September 1985) and liner notes for *Biograph*. In *'Every Mind Polluting Word': A Collection of Speeches, Interviews, Press Conferences, etc,'* 2nd edition by Artur, 851–69. Don't Ya Tell Henry publications, 2011.

Day, Aidan. *'Jokerman': Reading the Lyrics of Bob Dylan*. Oxford: Blackwell, 1988.

Day, Aidan. 'Looking for Nothing: Dylan Now'. In *'Do You, Mr Jones?': Bob Dylan with the Poets and Professors*, edited by Neil Corcoran, 275–94. London: Pimlico, 2003.

Deleuze, Gilles. *Nietzsche and Philosophy*, translated by Hugh Tomlinson. London: Athlone, 1983.

Deleuze, Gilles and Parnet, Claire. *Dialogues II*, translated by Hugh Tomlinson and Barbara Habberjam. London: Continuum, 2006.

Dettmar, Kevin J.H., editor. *The Cambridge Companion to Bob Dylan*, Cambridge: Cambridge University Press, 2009.

Dylan, Bob. 'My Life in a Stolen Moment'. In *Studio A: The Bob Dylan Reader*, edited by Benjamin Hedin, 3–7. New York: Norton, 2004.

Dylan, Bob. *Lyrics 1962–2001*. London: Simon & Schuster, 2004.

Dylan, Bob. *Tarantula*. London: Harper, 2005.

Dylan, Bob. *Chronicles*, Volume 1. Simon & Schuster, New York, 2004.

Dyer, Geoff. 'Figured I'd Lost You Anyway'. In *The Bob Dylan Companion*, edited by Elizabeth Thomson and David Gutman, 279–81. Cambridge, MA.: Da Capo, 2001.

Dyer, Geoff. *But Beautiful*. London: Abacus, 2009.

Egan, Sean (editor). *The Mammoth Book of Bob Dylan*. London: Robinson, 2011.

Emerson, Ralph Waldo. *The Portable Emerson*, edited by Carl Bode with Malcom Cowley. London: Penguin, 1981.

Epstein, Daniel Mark. *The Ballad of Bob Dylan: A Portrait*. London: Souvenir Press, 2011.

Fariña, Richard. 'Baez and Dylan: A Generation Singing Out'. In *The Bob Dylan Companion*, edited by Elizabeth Thomson and David Gutman, 81–7. Cambridge, MA.: Da Capo, 2001.

Feinstein Barry. *'Real Moments': Bob Dylan by Barry Feinstein*. London: Vision On/Omnibus, 2009.

Ford, Mark. '"Trust Yourself": Emerson and Dylan'. In *'Do You, Mr Jones?': Bob Dylan with the Poets and Professors*, edited by Neil Corcoran, 127–42. London: Pimlico, 2003.

Ford, Mark. 'Bob Dylan and the Vignette'. Unpublished lecture delivered at 'The Seven Ages of Dylan', a conference at the University of Bristol, 24 May 2011.

Freud, Sigmund. 'Beyond the Pleasure Principle'. In *'Beyond the Pleasure Principle', 'Group Psychology' and Other Works*, translated James Strachey with Anna Freud, 7–66. Volume XVIII of *The Standard Edition of Complete Psychological Works of Sigmund Freud*. London: Vintage, 2001.

Gamble, Andrew. 'The Drifter's Escape'. In *The Political Art of Bob Dylan*, edited by David Boucher and Gary Browning, 22–49. Exeter: Imprint-Academic, 2009.

Gibbens, John. *The Nightingale's Code: A Poetic Study of Bob Dylan*, London: Touched Press, 2001.

Gilbert, Douglas R. *Forever Young: Photographs of Bob Dylan*, with text by David Marsh and introductory note by John Sebastian. Cambridge, MA.: Da Capo, 2005.

Gill, Andy. *Bob Dylan: Stories Behind the Songs 1962-69*. London: Carlton, 2011.

Gilmour, Michael J. *The Gospel According to Bob Dylan*. Louisville: WJK, 2011.

Gleason, Ralph J. 'In Berkeley They Dig Bob Dylan'. In *Studio A: The Bob Dylan Reader*, edited by Benjamin Hedin, 58–61. New York: Norton, 2004.

Gray, Michael. *The Bob Dylan Encyclopedia*. London: Continuum, 2006.

Griffin, Sid. *Million Dollar Bash: Bob Dylan, The Band, and the Basement Tapes*. London: Jawbone, 2007.

Gross, Michael. *Bob Dylan: An Illustrated History*. London: Elm Tree Books, 1978.

Guthrie, Woody. *Bound for Glory*. New York: Plume, 1983.

Hajdu, David. *'Positively 4th Street': The Lives and Times of Bob Dylan, Joan Baez, Mimi Baez Farina & Richard Farina*. London: Bloomsbury, 2001.

Hedin, Benjamin, editor. *Studio A: The Bob Dylan Reader*, New York: Norton, 2004.

Helm, Levon and Davis, Stephen. *This Wheel's On Fire*. Chicago: Chicago Review Press, 2000.

Hendrik, Hertzberg and Trow, George. 'Dylan'. In *Studio A: The Bob Dylan Reader*, edited by Benjamin Hedin, 94–7. London: Norton, 2004.

Hentoff, Nat. 'The Crackin', Shakin', Breakin' Sounds'. In *Studio A: The Bob Dylan Reader*, edited by Benjamin Hedin, 32–9. London: Norton, 2004.

Heylin, Clinton. *Bob Dylan: The Recording Sessions, 1960–1994*. New York: St Martin's, 1996.

Heylin, Clinton. *Bob Dylan: A Life in Stolen Moments, Day By Day, 1941–1995*. London: Music Sales/Schirmer, 1996.

Heylin, Clinton. *Revolution In The Air: The Songs of Bob Dylan*, Volume 1 *(1957–73)*. London: Constable, 2009.

Heylin, Clinton. *Behind the Shades: The 20th Anniversary Edition*. London: Faber & Faber, 2011.

Hilburn, Robert. 'Abroad the never-ending tour bus'. In *The Dylan Companion*, edited by Elizabeth Thomson and David Gutman, 301–5. Cambridge, MA.: Da Capo, 2001.

Hinchey, John. *Like A Complete Unknown: The Poetry of Bob Dylan's Songs 1961–69* Ann Arbor: Stealing Home Press, 2002.

Hughes, Charles. 'Allowed to Be Free: Bob Dylan and the Civil Rights Movement'. In *Highway 61 Revisited: Bob Dylan's Journey from Minnesota to the World*, edited by Colleen J. Sheehy and Thomas Swiss, 44–59. Minneapolis: University of Minnesota Press, 2009.

Hughes, John. *Lines of Flight*. Sheffield: Sheffield Academic Press, 1996.

Hughes, John. '"It's not British Music, It's American Music": Bob Dylan and Britain'. In *Transatlantic Roots Music: Folk, Blues and National Identities*, edited by Neil Wynn and Jill Terry, 111–37. Jackson: University of Mississippi Press, 2012.

Hughes, John. 'Invisible Now'. *The Bridge* 35 (Winter 2009): 83–103.

Hughes, John. '"Through the Looking Glass": Photographic Images of Bob Dylan in the 1960s'. *The Bridge* 41 (Winter 2011): 27–43.

Hughes, John. '"There Was No In–Between": Dylan's Voice in the 1960s'. *The Bridge* 43 (Summer 2012): 54-71.

Jacobson, Mark. 'Tangled Up in Bob'. In *Da Capo Best Music Writing 2002*, 89–110. Cambridge, MA.: Da Capo, 2002.

James, Clive. 'Bringing Some of It All Back Home'. In *Studio A: The Bob Dylan Reader*, edited by Benjamin Hedin, 98–108. New York: Norton, 2004.

Kant, Immanuel. 'Idea For a Universal History From a Cosmopolitan Point of View'. In *On History*, edited by Lewis White Beck, 11–26. New York: Macmillan, 1989.

Kermode, Frank and Stephen Spender. 'The Metaphor at the End of the Funnel'. In *The Bob Dylan Companion*, edited by Elizabeth Thomson and David Gutman, 155–62. Cambridge, MA.: Da Capo, 2001.

Kramer, Daniel. *Bob Dylan: A Portrait of the Artist's Early Years*. London: Plexus, 2001.

Landy, Elliott. 'Elliott Land's Landy Vision,' http://www.landyvision.com/photos/Bob_Dylan/-index.htm.

Larkin, Phillip. *All What Jazz*. London: Faber & Faber, 1985.

Lee, C.P. *Like the Night (Revisited): Bob Dylan and the Road to the Manchester Free Trade Hall*. London: Helter Skelter, 2004.

Lee, C.P. 'Like the Night: Reception and Reaction Dylan UK 1966' In *Highway 61 Revisited: Bob Dylan's Journey from Minnesota to the World*, edited by Colleen J. Sheehy and Thomas Swiss, 78–83. Minneapolis: University of Minnesota Press, 2009.

Marchbank, Pearce (editor). *Bob Dylan In His Own Words*. London: Omnibus, 1987.

Marcus, Greil. *Invisible Republic: Bob Dylan's Basement Tapes*. London: Picador, 1997.

Marcus, Greil. *Like a Rolling Stone: Bob Dylan at the Crossroads*. London: Faber & Faber, 2005.

Marcus, Greil and Christgau, Robert. *Stranded: Rock and Roll For a Desert Island*. Cambridge, MA.: Da Capo, 2007.

Marcus, Greil. *The Old, Weird America: The World of Bob Dylan's Basement Tapes* New York: Random House, 2007.

Marcus, Greil. *Mystery Train: Images of America in Rock'n'Roll Music*. 5th Revised Edition. New York: Penguin/Plume, 2008.

Marcus. Greil. 'Hibbing High School and the "Mystery of Democracy"'. In *Highway 61 Revisited: Bob Dylan's Journey from Minnesota to the World*, edited by Colleen J. Sheehy and Thomas Swiss, 3–14. Minneapolis: University of Minnesota Press, 2009.

Marcus, Greil. *Bob Dylan: Writings 1968–2010*. New York: Public Affairs, 2010.

Marqusee, Mike. *'The Wicked Messenger': Bob Dylan and the 1960s*. New York: Seven Stories, 2005.

Marshall, Lee. *Bob Dylan: The Never Ending Star*. Cambridge: Polity, 2007.

McGregor, Craig. 'Two Encounters with Bob Dylan'. In *The Mammoth Book of Bob Dylan*, edited by Sean Egan, 255–96. London: Running Press, 2011.

Meisel, Perry. 'Dylan and the Critics,' http://perrymeisel.blogpot.com/2011/03/dylan–and–critics.html.

Meisel, Perry. *The Myth of Popular Culture*. Oxford: Wiley-Blackwell, 2010.

Mellers, Wilfred. *'A Darker Shade of Pale': A Backdrop to Bob Dylan*. London: Faber & Faber, 1984.

Miller, Jim. 'Bob Dylan'. In *The Bob Dylan Companion*, edited by Elizabeth Thomson and David Gutman, 18–32. Cambridge, MA.: Da Capo, 2001.

Nelson, Paul and John Pankake. 'Flat Tire'. In *Studio A: The Bob Dylan Reader*, edited by Benjamin Hedin, 16–19. New York: Norton, 2004.

Nelson, Paul. 'What's Happening'. In *Studio A: The Bob Dylan Reader*, edited by Benjamin Hedin, 47–50. New York: Norton, 2004.

Nietzsche, Friedrich. *The Genealogy of Morals: An Attack*, translated by R.J. Hollingdale. Cambridge: Cambridge University Press, 1983.

Oates, Joyce Carol. 'Dylan at 60'. In *Studio A: The Bob Dylan Reader*, edited by Benjamin Hedin, 258–61. New York: Norton, 2004.

Ochs, Phil. 'The Art of Bob Dylan's Hattie Carroll'. *Broadside* 48 (July 20 1964): 2; http://web.cecs.pdx.edu/~trent/ochs/hattie-carroll.html.

Paglia, Camille. 'Dylan at 60'. In *Studio A: The Bob Dylan Reader*, edited by Benjamin Hedin, 261–2. New York: Norton, 2004.

Pichaske, David. *Song of the North Country*. London: Continuum, 2010.

Polito, Robert. *'Highway 61 Revisited'*. In *The Cambridge Companion to Bob Dylan*, edited by Keven J.H. Dettmar, 137–42. Cambridge: Cambridge University Press, 2009.

Polizzotti, Mark. *Highway 61 Revisited*. London: Continuum, 2006.

Ricks, Christopher. 'Clichés'. In *The Force of Poetry*, 356–368. Oxford: Oxford University Press, 1987.

Ricks, Christopher. *Dylan's Visions of Sin*. London: Harper Collins, 2003.

Riley, Tim. *Hard Rain: A Dylan Commentary*. Cambridge, MA.: Da Capo Press, 1997.

Roe, Nicholas. 'Playing Time'. In *'Do You, Mr Jones?': Bob Dylan with the Poets and Professors*, edited Neil Corcoran, 127–42. London: Pimlico, 2003.

Ross, Alex. *Listen to This*. London: Fourth Estate, 2011.

Rotolo, Suze. 'Bob Dylan'. In *The Bob Dylan Companion*, edited by Elizabeth Thomson and David Gutman, 71–80. Cambridge, MA.: Da Capo, 2001.

Rotolo, Suze. *'A Freewheelin' Time': A Memoir of Greenwich Village in The Sixties*. London: Aurum, 2008.

Scaduto, Anthony. *Bob Dylan: An Intimate Biography*. New York: Grosset & Dunlap, 1971.

Scobie, Stephen. *Alias: Bob Dylan Revisited*. Calgary: Red Deer Press, 2003.

Sheehy, Colleen J. and Smith, Thomas (editors). *'Highway 61 Revisited': Bob Dylan's Journey from Minnesota to the World*. Minneapolis: University of Minnesota Press, 2009.

Shepard, Sam. *The Rolling Thunder Logbook*. London: Penguin, 1978.

Shepard, Sam. 'A Short Life of Trouble'. In *Studio A: The Bob Dylan Reader*, edited by Benjamin Hedin, 182–9. New York: Norton, 2004.

Shelton, Robert. *No Direction Home: The Life and Music of Bob Dylan*. Revised and Updated Edition, edited by Elizabeth Thomson and Patrick Humphries. London: Omnibus, 2011.

Shelton, Robert. 'Bob Dylan: A Distinctive Stylist,' *New York Times*, 29 September 1961. http://beatpatrol.wordpress.com/2010/03/15/robert-shelton-bob-dylan-a-distinctive-stylist-1961-2/. And *Studio A: The Bob Dylan Reader*, edited by Benjamin Hedin, 8–13. New York: W.W. Norton & Co., 2004.

Silber, Irwin. 'An Open Letter to Bob Dylan,' *Sing Out*, November, 1964. http://www.edlis.org/twice/threads/open_letter_to_bob_dylan.html (accessed 25 April 2012).

Sloman, Larry. *On the Road With Bob Dylan*. London: Helter Skelter, 2002.

Smith, Caspar Llewellyn. 'Flash-back,' *The Observer*, 54, 18 September 2005, Music supplement.

Springsteen, Bruce. 'Speech at the Rock-and-Roll Hall of Fame'. In *The Bob Dylan Companion*, edited by Elizabeth Thomson and David Gutman, 286–7. Cambridge, MA.: Da Capo, 2001. Also, 'Bruce Springsteen inducts Bob Dylan into Rock and Roll Hall of Fame 1988'. http://www.youtube.com/watch?v=SRu66l3QI_U.

Spitz, Bob. *Dylan: A Biography*. New York: McGraw-Hill, 1989.

Sounes, Howard. *'Down The Highway': The Life of Bob Dylan*. London: Doubleday, 2001.

Tamarin, Jean. *'Bringing It All Back Home'*. In *The Cambridge Companion to Bob Dylan*, edited by Kevin J.H. Dettmar, 131–6. Cambridge: Cambridge University Press, 2009.

Thompson, Toby. *Positively Main Street*. New edition. Minneapolis: University of Minnesota Press, 2008.

Toby Thompson. Interview with Terry Kelly for *The Bridge*. http://www.two-riders.co.uk/toby.html.

Thomson, Elizabeth and David Gutman, *The Bob Dylan Companion*. Cambridge, MA.: Da Capo, 2001.

Thoreau, David Henry. *Walden*. Oxford: Oxford University Press, 2008.

Toynbee, Polly. 'Pop Festival Blast-Off'. In *The Bob Dylan Companion*, edited by Elizabeth Thomson and David Gutman, 127–8. Cambridge, MA.: Da Capo, 2001.

Trilling, Lionel. *Sincerity and Authenticity*. Cambridge, MA.: Harvard University Press, 1972.

Van Ronk, Dave (with Elijah Wald), *The Mayor of MacDougal Street*. Cambridge MA.: Da Capo, 2005.

Von Schmidt, Eric and Rooney, Jim. *'Baby Let Me Follow You Down': The Illustrated History of the Cambridge Folk Years*. Amherst: University of Massachusetts, 1979.

Vulliamy, Ed. *'Highway 61 Revisited'*. In *The Bob Dylan Companion*, edited by Elizabeth Thomson and David Gutman, 98–101. Cambridge, MA.: Da Capo, 2001.

Walden, Henry David. *Walden*. Oxford: Oxford World's Classics, 1997.

Weberman, A.J. 'Dylan's Garbage's Greatest Hits'. In *Twenty Minute Fandangos and Forever Changes: A Rock Bazaar*, edited by Jonathan Eisen, 174-9. New York: Random House, 1971.

Wolcott, James. 'Bob Dylan Beyond Thunderdome'. In *The Dylan Companion*, edited by Thomson and Gutman, 269–74. Cambridge MA.: Da Capo, 2001.

Wilde, Lawrence. 'Dylan's Expressionist Period'. In *The Political Art of Bob Dylan*, 2nd enlarged edition, edited by David Boucher and Gary Browning, 104–35. Exeter: Imprint Academic, 2009.

Wilentz, Sean. "'Mystic Nights': The Making of *Blonde on Blonde* in Nashville'. *Oxford American Magazine*, 58, 2007. http://theband.hiof.no/articles/mystic_nights_tmobob.html.

Wilentz, Sean. *Bob Dylan in America*. London: The Bodley Head, 2010.

Williams, Paul. *Bob Dylan: Performing Artist 1960–1973, The Early Years*. London: Omnibus, 1991.

Williams, Paul. *Bob Dylan, Watching The River Flow*, 1966–1995. London: Omnibus, 1966.

Williams, Richard. *Dylan: A Man Called Alias*. London: Bloomsbury, 1992.

Wolcott, James. 'Bob Dylan Beyond Thunderdome'. In *The Bob Dylan Companion*, edited by Elizabeth Thomson and David Gutman, 275–8. Cambridge, MA.: Da Capo, 2001.

Yaffe, David, 'Bob Dylan and the Anglo-American Tradition'. In *The Cambridge Companion to Bob Dylan*, edited by Kevin Duttmar, 15–27. Cambridge: Cambridge University Press, 2009.

Yaffe, David. *Bob Dylan: Like a Complete Unknown*. New Haven: Yale University Press, 2011.

Zuckerman, Matthew. '"If There's An Original Thought Out There, I Could Use It Right Now": The Folk Roots of Bob Dylan'. http://expecting rain.com/dok/div/influences.

Select 1960s Bob Dylan Discography (By Year of Release)

Bob Dylan. New York: Columbia, 1962.
The Freewheelin' Bob Dylan. New York: Columbia, 1963.
The Times They Are A-Changin'. New York: Columbia, 1964.
Another Side of Bob Dylan. New York: Columbia, 1964.
Bringing It All Back Home. New York: Columbia, 1964.
Highway 61 Revisited. New York: Columbia, 1965.
Blonde on Blonde. New York: Columbia, 1966.
(with The Band). *The Basement Tapes*. New York: Columbia, 1975.
John Wesley Harding. New York: Columbia, 1968.
Nashville Skyline. New York: Columbia, 1969.
Biograph. New York: Columbia, 1965.
The Bootleg Series: Volumes 1–3. Rare & Unreleased 1961–91. New York: Columbia, 1991.
Freewheelin' Bob Dylan Outtakes. New Orleans: Vigatone, 1994.
The Dylan/Cash Sessions. Italy: Spank Records, 1994.
The Bootleg Series: Volume 4. Live 1966 (The Royal Albert Hall Concert). New York: Columbia, 1995.

1965 Revisited. Italy: Great Dane Records, 1998.
Jewels and Binoculars. New Orleans: Vigotone, 2000.
Tree With Roots. New York: Scorpio, 2001.
Bob Dylan: The Classic Interviews, 1965–1966. New Malden: Chrome Dreams, 2003.
The Bootleg Series: Volume 6. Live 1964, Concert At Philharmonic Hall. New York: Columbia, 2004.
Bob Dylan – 1966 World Tour, the Home Movies. DVD. Directed by Mickey Jones and Joel Gilbert. Stanmore: Wienerworld, 2004.
No Direction Home. DVD. Directed by Martin Scorsese. Hollywood: Paramount Home Entertainment, 2005.
Live At The Gaslight 1962. New York: Columbia, 2005.
The Other Side of the Mirror: Bob Dylan Live at Newport Folk Festival 1963–1965. DVD. Directed by Murray Lerner. New York: Sony BMG, 2007.
Don't Look Back – 65 Tour. DVD. Directed by D. A. Pennebaker. New York: Sony BMG, 2007.
The Bootleg Series: Vol. 9. The Witmark Demos: 1962–1964. New York: Columbia, 2010.
Bob Dylan: Folksingers' Choice. Leftfield Media, 2010.
Bob Dylan: Studs Terkel's Wax Museum. Leftfield Media 2011.
Bob Dylan: The Minneapolis Party Tape. Firefly 2011.
Bob Dylan: Live in Minneapolis, Bonnie Beecher's Apartment December 22 1961. Firefly 2012.

Select Web Sites

Andersen, Karl. 'Expecting Rain', http://www.expectingrain.com.
Bjorner, Olof. 'About Bob', http://www.bjorner.com/bob.htm.
Dylan, Bob. 'Bob Dylan', http://bobdylan.com.
Gray Michael. 'Michael Gray', http://www.michaelgray.net.
Kelly, Terry and John Wraith (editors). *The Bridge*, http://www.two–riders.co.uk/menu.html.
Pagel, Bill. 'Bob Links', http://www.boblinks.com.
Østrem, Eyolf. 'Dylan Chords', http://www.dylanchords.com.

Index

'1913 Massacre', murdered victims 59
4th Time Around 139

'Absolutely Sweet Marie' 139
   estrangement and loss 134
absurdity of Dylan, subversive 94
   and exaggeration 13
accusatory songs of 1965 133
Achilles, (*Lyrics*) 142
acoustic performances 1966
   soulful mysterious inwardness 150
After Bathing at Baxter's 177
AIDS sufferer 52
'Ain't Gonna Go to Hell for Anybody' 55
'Aladdin and his lamp' 101
alcoholism 65–6
alienation into art 98, 141
'All Along the Watchtower' 186–7
'All I Really Want to Do', film 87, 91
'All the Tired Horses' 190
'All You Have to Do is Dream' 161
alter-egos 142
American
   capitalism 100
   counter-culture, 1960s 48
   cultural imagination
      Dylan's engagements with 41
   folk culture 61, 75
   God's Chosen People 45
   Left 48
   perfectibility 78
   philosophy 44
   Protestantism 45
   traditional music 119
Animals, Rock and Roll, The 92
   traditional music 74
Another Side of Bob Dylan, 1964 84, 89, 93, 96
antagonism of Dylan 36
Anthology of American Folk Music 168

anti-interviews 9–10
anti-love song 92
'Apple Suckling Tree' 159
artistic vision 105
'As I Went Out One Morning' 179, 184
assassinations 48
Auden, W. H., poet 73
aversiveness 43–9

'Baby, Won't You Be My Baby' 159
Baez, Joan 11, 128
   relationship with 91
'Ballad in Plain D' 35, 93, 94
'Ballad of a Thin Man' 86, 135
   Mr Jones 127
'Ballad of Donald White' 70–71
'Ballad of Hollie Brown' 70, 74, 76, 80
'Ballad of the Glidin' Swan' 73
Ballads and Blues Club, The
'Banana Boat Song' The 161
Band, The 40
'Banks of the Royal Canal', The 166–7
'Barbara Allen' 65
'Barbed Wire Fence' 31
Basement Tapes 55, 92, 158, 161, 163–9
Bauls of Bengal 177
Bay of Pigs 48
Beatles 165
   reaction of Dylan 90
   rock and roll 92
Beats 88
Beckett, Samuel, playwright 160
becoming, idea of xv
Behan, Dominic
   song of Mountjoy prison 166–7
belle dames sans merci 142
'Bells of Rhymney' The
   from Idris Davies' poem 169
   politically betrayed 167
betrayal by our silence 72

'Big Dog Won't You Please Come Home' 157
Big Pink, house hiring, West Saugerties 155–6
Biograph interview, 1985
   Cameron Crowe 100–101
biography, Dylan's evasion of 45
Birds, The, rock and roll 92
birth of Jesse 135
'Black Crow Blues' 91–2
Black Panthers 48
Black Power 48
Blake, William 87, 98, 100
Blind Lemon Jefferson 168
Blind Willie Johnson, 168
'Blind Willie McTell' 55
Blonde on Blonde, 21, 26, 30, 32, 92, 117, 133–53
   culmination of Dylan's achievement in 1960s 133
   disorientation 126
   hydraulic metaphors 31
   inward space 27
   sense of self 43
Blowin' in the Wind 52, 71–3, 124
   feeling about destiny 36
Bob Dylan and the Hawks
   Marlon Brando on 121
'Bob Dylan's 115th Dream' 73, 96, 104
Bob Dylan's Views 78
bomb threat 48
'Bonnie Ship the Diamond', The 166
Bono, singer with group U2 25
booing Dylan for going electric 145
Book of Revelation 158
'Boots of Spanish Leather' 35, 73, 75, 81
'Bourbon Street' 157
Brewer, James 112
Bringing It All Back Home 18, 88, 102, 105
   album cover 96
British and Irish models 76
British folk music 61
'Brownsville Girl', Bob Dylan and Sam Shepard 55
Bruce, Lenny 9
'Buffalo Skinners' 65
Bunyan, John 41

Cain and Abel 126
'California' 95
camera, wariness of 15
'Can You Please Crawl Out Your Window' 93
   song of resentment 120
'Caribbean Wind' 55
Carnaby Street motley and drainpipes 37
Carnegie Hall concert, *Behind the Shades*
   Dylan's embarrassment about past 46
Carthy, Martin 74, 84
   'Scarborough Fair' 73
   'The Franklin' 73
Casanova 126
Cash, Johnny 192
Cavalier interviews 12
Cavell, Stanley
   Cities of Words, world as cursed 44
   Emerson's Transcendental Etudes 43
'Changing of the Guards' 55
Chaplin, Charlie, Dylan's idol 11
charisma of Bob Dylan 59, 63
Chaucer, Geoffrey, *Canterbury Tales* 41
Chelsea Hotel, West 23rd Street 135
Chicago blues 121
Child, Francis James, nineteenth-century ballads 61
Chimes of Freedom 84–9, 92, 99
Christ, American mythology of the road 41
Cinderella 126
Civil Rights Movement 48, 95, 128
Civil Rights Struggle 61–2
Clancy Brothers, Irish singers 76
Clapton, Eric 165
'Clothes Line Saga', Basement Tapes 163
'Cocaine, Cocaine' 29
cocaine addict, self-hood of 59
Cold War paranoia 48
Coltrane, John, saxophonist
   music as test of soul 48
'Come All You Fair and Tender Ladies' 165
Comin' Round the Mountain 165
concerts of 1966
   popular music beyond itself 148
confessions 172
conflict in live performances 38
conformity, rejection of 43

contempt for camera 20–21
Cooper, Fenimore 41
corpsing when singing 86
'Corrina, Corrina' 65
counter-culture 38, 44, 89
country blues 113
'Country Pie' 187, 188, 190
cowboy music 181
'creative commerce with the unseen'
    Dylan's's art xii
creativity of Dylan xiii
'Cross The Green Mountain' 55
Cuba outlawing of boxing 83
Cuckoo', 'The 73
cultural unconscious 133
curiosity of Bob Dylan 51

dancing child, (*Lyrics*) 142
Dante Alighieri 41
    Inferno 186
'Dear Landlord' 176, 179
'Dear Mrs Rooseveldt' 175
death, Dylan's fixation with 66
Death of Emmett Till','The 71
defence against effects of fame 37
Deleuze, Gilles, French thinker, on Dylan's
    work xiv
'Denise' 95
'Deo-o, Deo-o, Day-O, Daylight come and
    me wanna go home' 161
desire as psychic wild zone 93
'Desolation Row' 11, 38, 86, 102, 125, 146
    Manchester 148
Dignity 55
'Dink's Song', abandoned woman 59
disorientation, *Highway 61 Revisited* 126
disregard of audience 39
Don't Look Back 10, 55, 86
'Don't Think Twice, It's Alright' 35, 81
'Doors of Perception' opening 89
'Down Along the Cove' 187
'Down on Me' 165
drama of identity 4
'Drifter's Escape' 179, 185
drug dependence of Dylan
    for imaginative freedom 90, 149
'Dusty Old Fairgrounds' 95
Dyer, Geoff, *But Beautiful*
    jazz and human toll, 49
Dylan, Bob
    Aidan Day 26
    backlit on stage, Forest Hills Stadium
        110
    Band 1968 **151**
    Betsy Bowden 25
    Bringing It All Back Home, session
        108
    Britain and xvi–xvii
    Byrdcliffe home **153, 174**
    changing qualities of 28–9
    children, Liverpool **131**
    Chronicles 25, 63
    'missing person inside of
        myself' 19
    conversing with fire extinguisher
        Albert Hall concert 149
    in Dark Glasses **107**
    descriptions of voice 26
    Greil Marcus, Andrea Svedburg 25
    guitar work 30
    hammer rather than nail 26
    Hawks 165, 168, 189
    identification as No-One from nowhere
        45
    image 22
    inspiration 51
    intense put-downs of humans 36
    Kevin Buttery 27
    in living room, Byrdcliffe home,
        Woodstock, 1968 **153**
    Midwest 43
    nervous energy 51–2
    outside Elliott Landy's home **173**
    outside his Byrdcliffe home,
        Woodstock, 152
    pop figure 21
    recreation of self 46
    refusal of demands on identity 48
    relation to camera 18
    Sara Dylan, porch of Byrdcliffe home,
        Woodstock, 1968 **152**
    self-division 44
    self-presentation 51
    as self-reliance, self-reality 45
        singing as demonic, Jim Miller 31
    song writing 54–5, 157

on stage, England, 1966 **130**
theatre of cruelty 36–7
Tim Riley 25
trapeze artist 145
voice, 25–33, 158
    changing qualities of, by David Yaffe 28–9
    description by Mark Polizzotti 28
    description by Robert Shelton 25
    in Manchester or Melbourne 147–8
    with son Jesse Dylan **152**
    with Victor Maymude in Tree, Woodstock 106
    world gone wrong, American idea 45
    youthful courage and self-trust 36

East Village Other
    advertisement for Dylan's urine 52
'East Virginia Blues' 176
Eat the Document (film)
    representation of Dylan 21, 53–4
electric music 119
Eliot, T.S., poet 126
Emergency Civil Liberties Committee
    Dylan's address to 183
emergent counter-culture 48
Emerson, Ralph Waldo 45, 78, 114, 118, 122
    European metaphysical disjunction 44
    Experience 43, 44
    on growths of genius 40–41
    metaphors of 28, 56
    New England 23
    on the poet 115
    secret melancholy 44
    sense of recoil 44
    The Poet 41, 43
    what makes a poem 28
English folk songs 113
English musical models 75
ephemerality 43
Epstein, Daniel Mark, *The Ballad of Bob Dylan* xvi
Epstein, Jacob 86
    Dylan as becoming a poet 95
escapist bolt-holes 90
escapology of Dylan 48
'Eternal Circle' 95

'Even If It's a Pig' 157

facial expressions 17
Fairport Convention 165
Fall, from innocence to sin 12
'Farewell' 35
'Farewell Angelina' 95
Fariña, Richard 21
Feinstein, Barry 23
    photos of Bob Dylan **130, 131**
    poet-photographer 22
    sense of alienation in photograph 19
Ferlinghetti, Lawrence xi
fictiveness of Dylan 47
Fielding, Henry 41
Fields, W.C. xi
films of Dylan 53–4
Finn, Huckleberry, 63
'Fixin' to Die' 66–7
folk-revival audience 89
folk scene in New York 29, 62–3
'Folsom Prison Blues' 167
Forest Hills Stadium sound check **109**
'Four Strong Winds'
    fracturing of psyche 137
    suffering lost love 167
Free Trade Hall concert, England
    'like a church service' 149
The Freewheelin' Bob Dylan 60, 78, 90, 98
'Freeze Out' xii
French Girl', 'The
    suffering lost love 167

Gaslight performance of 'Handsome Molly' 64–5
Gaslight recording 30
'Gates of Eden' 11, 86, 89, 98, 101–2
    biblical protest song 100
    drug song 99
gender identity 144
gestures when singing, Dylan 51
'Get Your Rocks Off' 161, 163
Ginsberg, Allen xi, 56, 87, 88, 100
Ginsberg, Ellis 98
Girl From the North Country 54, 73, 81, 190, 192
Gleason, Ralph J. xi, xiv
    country genre 191

'Gloria in Excelsis, Deo' 161
'Goin to Acapulco' 162
   secular to spiritual 32
Golden Chords, The 37, 114
Good Samaritan 126
'Gospel Plow' 66
'Grand Coulee Dam' 175
Gray, Michael
   Song and Dance Man III xv, 181–2
Greenwich Village 62
Grossman, Albert 112, 155
'Guess I'm Doin' Fine' 95
Guthrie, Arlo 176
Guthrie memorial benefit, Carnegie Hall 175
Guthrie, Woody 60–61, 65, 67, 76–7, 176
   Bound for Glory 62
   death of Huntington's chorea 175
'Gypsy Davey' 76
'Gypsy Lou' 95

habits of avoidance 72
Hajdu, David xvi, 62
   'Dylan starting to lose it' 145
   Dylan writing songs 96–7
   influence of Guthrie on Dylan 67–9
Hamlet 8, 9
Hammond, John 17
'Handsome Molly' 65
'Hang Me, O Hang Me' 73
'Hard Rain's A-Gonna Fall' 71, 86
   Dave Van Ronk's experience 29–30
   'The Gaslight' 75
'Hard Times in New York Town' 60
Harrison, George, The Beatles 47
Harry Smith Anthology 167
Hawks (The Crackers) xii, 175
'He Was A Friend of Mine' 29
   a grieving friend 59
Hedin, Benjamin xi
Helmstrom, Echo, ex-girl-friend 111
heroin addiction 52
Heylin, Clinton
   Behind the Shades xv, 88, 89
'Hezekiah Jones/Black Cross'
   murdered victims 59
Hibbing childhood
   sense of dislocation 38

Hibbing High School performance, 1958 37–8
'Highlands' 35
Highway 61 Revisited 11, 21, 31, 92, 105, 111–29
   calling society down 27
   cover photo, by Daniel Kramer 39
   'going electric' 121–2
   graveyard of our illusions 129
hobo (*Lyrics*) 141
holocaust denier 52
homosexual allusion 128
hostility against interviewers 9–10
hostility of 1966 tour 37
'House of the Rising Sun', 59
Hudson, Garth 157
   organ playing 158, 159
human dignity 60
humour of Dylan 7, 10–12, 86–7
Hunchback of Notre Dame 126

'I Ain't Got No Home in This World / Anymore', a vagrant 59, 175
I Am a Lonesome Hobo' 179
'I Am Your Teenage Prayer' 157, 165
'I Can't Come in With a Broken Heart'
   suffering lost love 167
'I Can't Leave Her Behind' 55
'I Don't Believe You' 35, 92
'I Don't Hurt Anymore'
   suffering lost love 167
'I Dreamed I Saw St Augustine' 179, 186
'I Forgot to Remember to Forge' suffering lost love 167
'I Shall Be Free' 78, 94, 104
'I Shall Be Released' 170, 172
'I Still Miss Someone' 187
'I Threw it All Away' 40, 54, 187, 190
   country genre, 191
'I Wanna Be Your Partner' 30
'I Want You' 140, 142
   desire, controlled by 142
'I Was Young When I Left Home' 35
   singer's home 29
Icarus, fable of 164
iconic photograph images of Dylan 15–16
iconoclasm of Dylan 36, 123
iconographic style of Dylan 21

'If You Gotta Go, Go Now' 11, 95
'If You See Her Say, Hello' 35
'I'll Be Your Baby Tonight' 187
'I'll Keep it with Mine' 95
'I'll Remember You' 35
'I'm a Fool for You'
    suffering lost love 167
'I'm Not There' 159–60, 170, 172
'In My Time of Dying' 66
incest 129
indefiniteness 4
inhumanity of humans 60
inspiration xiv, 51
interview with Nat Hentoff, for *Playboy* 12–13
interviews 9–10
invisibility of former self 16
Invisible Republic, by Greil Marcus 167–8
Isaac, Samual Abram 176
'It Ain't Me Babe' 35, 91
'It Takes a Lot to Laugh (It Takes a Train to Cry)' 30, 126
'It's a Hard Rain' 89
'It's All Over Now, Baby Blue' 35, 56, 96, 102–3, 111
'It's Alright, Ma (I'm Only Bleeding)' 35, 86, 98
    non-intelligibility 101, 102
'It's Hard to Be Blind', a blind man, 59

Jagger, Mick, career narcissism 22
James, Clive, on Dylan's admirers 69
jazz, self-destruction of major creators 49
Jesse James 105
'Jet Pilot' 30
'John Brown 71, 75
John the Baptist 124
John Wesley Harding 92, 175, 176–7
    figures who people the album 178–84
    'first biblical rock album' 181
    fugitive selves 43
    lyricism of songs 27–8
Johnny Cash show, June 1969 54
'Johnny Todd 165
    Liverpool 169
Jokers, The 114
Jones, Evan, *The Madhouse on Castle Street,*
    BBC play, Dylan to act in 73
'Joshua Gone Barbados'
    politically betrayed 167
Joseph Campbell, 41
'Journey Through Dark Heat' 55
'Judas' cat-call, Manchester, 147
'Just Like a Woman' 144
    British performance 149
'Just Like Tom Thumb's Blues' 115–17, 146

Kerouac, Jack, 41
Kettle of Fish, The 36
'Kingdoms of Experience' 100
'Kings of Tyrus with their convict list' 145
Kramer, Daniel, 96, **106**, **107**, **108**, **109**, **110**
    photographic memoir of Dylan 18
    poet-photographer 22
Kretchmer, Arthur, on Dylan 64

Landy, Elliott 189
    Nashville Skyline 22
    photo of Dylan and son Jesse **152**
    photo of Dylan and wife, Sara **153**
    photo of Dylan in Byrdcliffe etc **153**
    photo of Dylan outside his home **153**
    photos of Dylan in Woodstock 22
    poet-photographer 22
    Woodstock world 23
Landy, Elliott, photo 173, 174
Larkin, Philip, poet
    review of *Highway 61 Revisited* 113
'Lakes of Pontchartrain' 76
'Lay, Lady, Lay' 187
    love and passion for renewal 193–4
'Lay Down Your Weary Tune' 95
    source, Scottish Ballad 76
leave taking, 35–42
Leaving of Liverpool','The
    'Farewell' 76
Lee, C.P. *Just Like the Night* xvi, 54
Lennon, John 21
'Leopard-Skill Pillbox Hat'
    homosexual suggestions 140, 144
Lerner, Murray
    The Other Side of the Mirror (film) 85
'Let Me Die In My Footsteps' 59–60
liberation within society 31

'Like a Rolling Stone' 31, 39, 40, 103, 112–20, 127, 146–7
'little boy lost' 143
   (*Lyrics*), 142
'Liverpool Gal' 35
'Living the Blues' 54
'Lo and Behold' 162, 170
Lonesome Death of Hattie Carroll', 'The 70, 76
   murder of young servant 81–4
'Long Time Gone' 35
'Lord Randall' 75
Los Angeles press conference, December 1965 7–8
loss of contact with people, Newport 87
love in Dylan's songs 35, 91
'Love is Just a Four Letter Word' 95
'Love Minus Zero' 96, 140
'Love Minus Zero/No Limit' 105
'Lunatic Princess Revisited' 30, 119
lyricism of songs, 27

McClure, Michael xi
MacColl, Ewan
   The Singers' Club, London 74
'Maggie's Farm' 96, 104, 112
magic of Dylan xv
Malcolm X 48
'Mama, You've Been On My Mind' 81, 95
'Man of Constant Sorrows' 65, 67
Man on the Street, nameless vagrant 59
Manuel, Richard, drummer 157
Marcus, Greil xii–xiii, xvi, 112, 145, 169
   on Dylan 64–5
   The Old Weird America 3
Marqusee, Mike xvi, 79–80, 134, 169
Marxist determinism, none
'Mary Hamilton'
   'The Lonesome Death of Hattie Carroll' 76
masks of Dylan 3
masochism 172
'Masters of War' 77
   Cuban crisis 74, 75
Masterson, Mike
   description of Dylan's voice 25
Max's Kansas City 36
meaning of life xiii

'Medicine Sunday' 30, 93
Meisel, Perry, *The Myth of Popular Culture* xvi
melancholy and loss 81
Melville, Herman 41, 45
Mighty Quinn', 'The 162
militarism 133
   of United States, uncontrolled 126
'Million Dollar Bash' 161, 163
'Minstrel Boy' 40
'Mississippi' 36, 55
Mississippi John Hurt 168
Mixed Up Confusion 103
Mona Lisa 143
'Moonshiner' 16
   Appalachian ballad 65
moral revolution 45
'Most Likely You Go Your Way and I'll Go Mine' 35, 138, 140
motorcycle accident in Woodstock, 1966 135, 155, 164–5
'Motorpsycho Nitemare' 77, 94, 137
'Mozart' 123
'Mr Tambourine Man' 92, 101, 102, 111
   drug song 99
   London, Royal Festival Hall 84
   Manchester 148
   meaning of 98
'Mrs McGrath' 75
'Muddy Waters' 114
musicality, priority over words 188
'My Back Pages' 94

Nashville Skyline, pastoral album 22, 52, 54, 176, 187, 189, 190
   beguiling modulation 32
   calling on country tradition 28
   Dylan's self-projection 188
   Echo Helstrom on 32–3
   'trumped-up smoothie' 189
'Nashville Skyline Rag' 190
National Emergency Civil Liberties Committee 83
necessity not to be known, Dylan's 45
'Never Ending Tour' 38
Newport electric set 37
Newport Folk Festival, 1963–5 85–6, 88, 105, 111, 114

confrontation with audience 37–8, 112
Nietzsche, Friedrich Wilhelm 26, 122
   Genealogy of Morals 100
   nightmare world 125
Nissenson, Jack, on Dylan 64
No Direction Home (Martin Scorsese) 4, 15, 42, 56
'North Country Blues' 11, 81
'Nothing Was Delivered' 170
nothingness 172
'Nottamun Town', Jackie Washington 73
nuclear destruction 72

Oates, Joyce Carol
   description of Dylan's voice 25
obscurity 4
oceanic sound, Michael Gray 32
'Odds and Ends' 161, 162, 163
Odetta 176
Odysseus 41
Oedipus 138
Ohayo mountain home of Clarence Schmidt 156
Okie hobo troubadour 60
'Ol Roison The Beau' 165
'Omie Wise', murdered victims 59
ominous atmosphere in music 30–31
'On a Rainy Afternoon' 55
'On the Road Again' 104
'One Man's Loss' 170
'One More Night' 187
   country genre 191
'One of Us Must Know' 32, 137–9
'One Too Mornings' 54
'Only a Hobo' 95
'Only a Pawn In Their Game' 83
'Open the Door, Homer' 163
Oswald, Lee Harvey 83
'Outlaw Blues' 96, 104

'Panamanian Moon' 139
Parting Glass', 'The, into 'Restless Farewell' 76, 84
'Pastures of Plenty' (Woody Guthrie) 60
'Paths of Victory' 60
Patriot Game','The
   'With God On Our Side' 76
'Pattie's Gone to Laredo' 55

Patton, Charley 114
Pawn in their Game 76
'Peggy Day' 187, 188, 190
Pennebaker, D.A.
   Bob Dylan 21, 47
   Eat the Document (film) 145, 146
'Percy's Song' 95
Persian drunkard, (*Lyrics*) 142
'Phantom Engineer' 31, 112
'Phoenix in April' 149
photogenic power over camera 15
photograph scenes of Bob Dylan 18
photographic style, inimitability of 22
photographs 15–24
Pichaske, David, *Song of the North Country* xvi
Playboy interview March 1966 7, 11
'Playboys and Playboys' 95
playfulness in songs 161
'Please, Mrs Henry' 161, 163
'Pledging My Time' 140, 141, 142

poetic gift of Dylan 162
poetic technique and social criticism 86
political
   alienation 31
   change 87
   critique 75
   indignation in ballad modes 61
   moralising 94–5
   subjugation 72
   sympathy, art of 86
politics of race, gender, sexuality 48
Polizzotti, Mark
   Highway 61 Revisited xvi
   on Mexico 115–16
   on 'Tombstone Blues' 124
'Poor' Lazarus', murdered victims 59, 165
Pope, Alexander, poet 103
popular songs
   recording from other countries, areas 169
'Positively 4th Street' xvi, 31, 86, 113, 117–18
   ejection of hatred 119
   show at Sydney, April, 1966 146
Positively Main Street, Toby Thompson, xvi, 177

possession by a song 15
Pound, Ezra 126
pounding rhythms of guitar 29
poverty and the outsider 68
Presley, Elvis 114
privacy, walled 98
'protean', 'chameleon' figure, 3
protest movement 38
protest songs and singers 7, 9, 89, 119
    Dylan 41
    refugee from 90
provocation of Dylan 36
Puritan settlement, first
    'Citty Upon a Hill' 168

quavery melismata 192
'Queen Jane Approximately'
'Queen Jane is a man' 128
'Queen Marie'
    uncertainty of selfhood 150
Queen Mary, (*Lyrics*) 142
'Quinn the Eskimo' 40
'Quit Your Low Down Ways' 66

racial discrimination 133
'Railroad Boy'
    murdered victims 59
railroad man, (*Lyrics*) 142
rainman, (*Lyrics*) 142
'Rainy Day Women' #12 & 35' 141
'Rambler Gambler' 29
'Ramblin' Down Thru the World' 95
rambling and gambling, motifs
    'Gypsy Lou' 70
    'Rambling, Gambling Willie' 69
'Red River Shore' 55
reincarnation of Paul Revere's horse 124
relations with public and press, Bob Dylan 7
'Remember Me' 65
Renaldo and Clara 55
repartee with interviewers 8–9
'Restless Farewell' 35, 95
retrospection and youthful persistence 29
revelation by pictures, none 20
revolutionary songs 30
Ricks, Christopher
    cliché 77

Dylan's Visions of Sin xvi, 68, 76
Rimbaud, Arthur xi, 4, 22, 87, 98
    Dylan's attachment to 88
Rimsky-Korsakov, Nikolai
    'Flight of the Bumble Bee' 169
'Ring of Fire' 187
road maps for the soul 77
Road and Miles to Dundee', 'The
    'Walls of Red Wing' 76
Robertson, Robbie 157, 159
'Rock, Salt and Nails'
    suffering lost love 167
rock and roll, 90 114
    rhythms 85
    structures 97
Rolling Stone
    on Dylan in, Country Joe McDonald 32
Rolling Stones 165
Romeo 126
Rotolo, Suze 89, 96
    'Tomorrow is a Long Time' 91
Royal Albert Hall concert, Dylan 21
Royal Albert Hall, Free Trade Hall, England 150

sacred and profane 163
'Sad-Eyed Lady of the Lowlands' 139–40
    Dylan's sanity fear, 27
sado-masochism 101
'Sally Gal' 66
Scaduto, Anthony, *Bob Dylan* xvi
Scobie, Stephen, *Alias Bob Dylan Revisited* xvi
Scorsese, Martin
    No Direction Home xiii, 3, 62, 145
'See that My Grave is Kept Clean' 66
'See You Later, Allen Ginsberg' 161
'See You Later, Alligator' 157
Seeger, Pete 38, 176
segregationism, confrontation 90
self-abandonment 99
self-cancellation 20
self-deletion 33
self-destruction 116, 172
self-dissimulation 3
self-emancipation 60
self-estrangement 179
self-exploration

Blonde on Blonde 146
self-genesis of Dylan 183
selfhood of Dylan 15, 118
   at stake 142
   voice as image of 26
self-loss 65
self-mythologizing of Dylan 66, 97
self-mythologists of American mind 168
self-mythology of rootlessness 45–6
Self Portrait 22, 32
   John Cohen's cover on 32
self-presentation 20, 97
self-renewal 4
self-transformation 3
sense of dislocation, Dylan on stage 19–20
sense of self in changing times
   'One Too Many Mornings' 81
'Series of Dreams' 55
'Seven Curses' 95
   Measure for Measure, Shakespeare 76
sexuality, repressed 123
Sgt Pepper 177
Shadow Blasters, The 114
shamanistic presence of Dylan 56
'She Belongs to Me '56, 96, 105, 140
Shelley, Percy Bysshe, poet 88
Shelton, Robert 85
   Dylan's vagueness about antecedents 47
   No Direction Home xvi
Shepard, Sam, *Rolling Thunder Logbook,* xv
'She's Your Lover Now' 140
'Sign on the Cross' 158–9
Silhouettes 157
Simon, Paul, 26
sincerity as conformity xiii
sirens 142
slapstick 12
Smith, Harry
   Anthology of American Folk Music 61, 73
social alienation 104
social change, absence of 83
social conformity or escape xii
social consciousness 114
social estrangement 31
social subjugation 170

society as a freak-show 105
society scourging 31
'solidarity with powerless and oppressed'
   Lawrence Wilde, 86
song about women
   'Love Minus Zero/ No Limit' 96
   'She Belongs to Me', 96
'song and dance man' xi
'Song for Woody' 71
Song of the North Country
   David Pichaske xvi, 41
song on a knife-edge 69
'Song to Bonny' 35
'Song to Woody' 1961, 67, 68
songs
   of artistic vision 98
   of city angst 98
   of mysterious romance 98
   of surrealism 98
   unreleased 95
song-writing of Dylan 55–6
Spinoza, Baruch 162
'Spanish Harlem Incident' 92
'The Spanish Song' 157
spiritual seekers 186
Springsteen, Bruce, on Dylan 115
St Paul *I Corinthians* 186
state of society 28
Steinbeck, John 41
'Still in Town', suffering lost love, 167
Stockholm interview 141
'Stuck Inside of Mobile' 136, 139, 141
   desire, controlled by 142
student unrest in America 48
subjectivity, dynamics of, in Dylan's work xiii
'Subterranean Homesick Blues' 96

'Taj Mahal' 147
'Talkin' Bear Mountain Picnic Massacre', 64
'Talkin' New York', 60, 69
'Talkin' World War III Blues' 78
'Tangled Up in Blue' 35
Tarantula 12
'Tears of Rage' 156, 172
   parent's grief 170, 171
'Teenage Prayer' 161

telegraphic impressions of world
'Visions of Johanna' 144
'Tell Me That It Isn't True' 187, 192
tension in song 191
Temporary Like Achilles 140–41
tension 65
'That Auld Triangle'
by Dominic Behan 166–7, 169
Times They Are A-Changin', The 76, 87, 90, 98–9, 127
influence of Irish and Scottish ballads 79
Titanic sails at dawn', 'The 113, 125
Troubadour, The 73, 74
Twa Sisters', 'The
'Percy's Song' 76
Twilight Zone', 'The 121
Their Satanic Majesties Request 177
'(They) Gotta Quit Kickin' My Dog Around' 165
'This Land is Your Land' 29
'This Wheel's On Fire' 158, 170–72
Thomas, Dylan 98
Thompson, Toby, *Positively Main Street* xvi
Thoreau, David Henry 45, 120
New England 23
'quiet desperation' 44
'Times They Are A-Changin' 95
'To Be Alone With You' 187, 188, 190
'To Ramona' 40, 93
Tom Paine award, 1963 183
'Tombstone Blues' 123, 124
'Tonight I'll be Staying Here With You' 193
'Too Much of Nothing' 158, 170, 172
traditional British and Irish influence on Dylan 61, 74–5
'Trapeze Artist' 133–55
trial of Abbie Hoffman 48
'truth attacks' on hapless victims 36
Twain, Mark 41

understatement of Dylan's singing 29
urban blues 134
urban self-reliance 96
'Utopian hermit monks' 101

Van Ronk, Dave 63
on Dylan 64

on invention of characters 46–7
Smith's collection 168
verbal sensibility of Dylan 161
Vietnam war 48, 124, 126, 189
vignette, Dylan's use of 103–4
Village Voice
interviews, March 1965 12
'vision music' 120
visionary transcendence 30
'Visions of Johanna' xii, 32, 135, 143
voice of Dylan
calling for political change 27
full of nervous energy, defiant 31
qualities of 28–33
voices of traditional songs 59
Von Schmidt, Eric
illustrator and singer xii, 73
vulnerability with girl 92–3

'Walls of Red Wing' 95
'Waltzin' With Sin'
suffering lost love 167
war 72
'We Shall Overcome' 112
Webber, Harry, English literary professor 75
Weberman, A.J.
Dylan Liberation Front 52
Dylan to English Dictionary 52
wedding of Dylan, with Sara 135
'When the Ship Comes In' 80
'Where Are You Tonight' 35
'Which Side Are You On', 38
Whitman, Walt 41, 45
Whitmark Tapes booklet (CBS) 16, 17
picture in the Singer's Club, London, 1962 17
'Who Killed Cock Robin'
'Who Killed Davey Moore' 70, 76, 83, 95
Wicked Messenger','The
Dylan's feet of clay 182
'Wild Mountain Thyme' 40
Wilentz, Sean
Bob Dylan in America xvi, 100
Williams, Hank
'You Win Again' 191–2
Williams, Paul 11
Bob Dylan: Performing Artist xvi

Watching the River Flow xvi
Winthrop, John 168
'With God On Our Side' 83
woman, aspects of 140
Woodstock
    leaving it 176
    meaning for Dylan 164
    woods 23
world left behind 44
world tour
    evolution of Dylan's performances 146
'Worried Blues' 29, 65
Wraith, John xvii

Yaffe, David

changing qualities of Dylan's voice 28–33
'Yea! Heavy and a Bottle of Bread' 162, 163
'Years of Creation' for Dylan, 1960s, 56
'You Gotta Quit Kickin' My Dog Around' 157
'You Win Again'
    suffering lost love 167
'Young But Daily Growing'
    British Broadside ballad 169
    British folk song variant 166
'You're a Big Girl Now' 35

Zimmerman, Bob (Bob Dylan) 3
Zodiac killer, San Francisco xi

For Product Safety Concerns and Information please contact our EU representative GPSR@taylorandfrancis.com
Taylor & Francis Verlag GmbH, Kaufingerstraße 24, 80331 München, Germany

www.ingramcontent.com/pod-product-compliance
Lightning Source LLC
Chambersburg PA
CBHW062135300426
44115CB00012BA/1932